BITTER FAME

A Life of Sylvia Plath

If you can't give me love and peace,
Then give me bitter fame.
— Anna Akhmatova

BITTER FAME

A LIFE OF
SYLVIA PLATH

ANNE STEVENSON

WITH ADDITIONAL MATERIAL BY
Lucas Myers, Dido Merwin, and Richard Murphy

A PETER DAVISON BOOK

A Mariner Book
Houghton Mifflin Company
Boston   New York

FIRST MARINER BOOKS EDITION 1998

Preface copyright © 1998 by Anne Stevenson
Copyright © 1989 by Anne Stevenson
Appendix I © 1989 by Lucas Myers
Appendix II copyright © 1989 by Dido Merwin
Appendix III copyright © 1989 by Richard Murphy
All unpublished material by Sylvia Plath and
Ted Hughes copyright © 1989 by Ted Hughes

For information about permission to reproduce selections from
this book, write to Permissions, Houghton Mifflin Company,
215 Park Avenue South, New York, New York 10003

Library of Congress Cataloging-in-Publication Data

Stevenson, Anne, date.
Bitter fame : a life of Sylvia Plath / by Anne Stevenson ; with
additional material by Lucas Myers, Dido Merwin, and Richard Murphy.
p. cm.
"A Peter Davison book."
Bibliography : p.
Includes index.
1. Plath, Sylvia—Biography.   2. Poets, American—20th
century—Biography.   I. Title.
PS3566.L27Z9134   1989   811'.54—dc20
[B]   89-7530   CIP

ISBN 0-395-45374-7
ISBN 0-395-93760-4 (pbk.)

Printed in the United States of America

QUM 10 9 8 7 6 5 4 3 2 1

Acknowledgment of permission to quote from published and
unpublished sources appears on pp. 387–388.

Book design by Anne Chalmers

There was a tremendous power in the burning look of her dark eyes; she came "conquering and to conquer." She seemed proud and occasionally even arrogant; I don't know if she ever succeeded in being kind, but I do know that she badly wanted to and that she went through agonies to force herself to be a little kind. There were, of course, many fine impulses and a most commendable initiative in her nature; but everything in her seemed to be perpetually seeking its equilibrium and not finding it; everything was in chaos, in a state of agitation and restlessness. Perhaps the demands she made upon herself were too severe and she was unable to find in herself the necessary strength to satisfy them.

— Dostoevsky, *The Devils*

Oh, only left to myself, what a poet I will flay myself into.

— Sylvia Plath,
Journals, May 11, 1958

AUTHOR'S NOTE

In writing this biography, I have received a great deal of help from Olwyn Hughes, literary agent to the Estate of Sylvia Plath. Ms. Hughes's contributions to the text have made it almost a work of dual authorship. I am particularly grateful for the work she did on the last four chapters and on the Ariel poems of the autumn of 1962.*

*Olwyn Hughes provided the following texts on poems in this book: the last paragraphs on "The Disquieting Muses" (concept only); "Blackberrying"; "Little Fugue"; "The Rabbit Catcher"; "Berck-Plage"; the introductory material to the Ariel poems in the first pages of Chapter 12; "Stings"; "The Applicant"; "Daddy"; "Fever 103°"; "Lady Lazarus"; "Purdah"; "The Munich Mannequins"; "Gigolo"; and "Kindness."

CONTENTS

Illustrations follow p. 174

PREFACE
TO THE MARINER EDITION

WHEN I FIRST began piecing *Bitter Fame* together in the late 1980s, it was evident that Sylvia Plath's suicide had projected her into a public legend catastrophically at odds with the personal myth that almost certainly determined her fate. For some time I hoped I could simply let Plath tell her own story. Since almost everything she wrote had its place in the "great, stark bloody play" that she believed was "acting itself out behind the sunny façade of our daily rituals" (*Bitter Fame*, page 148), it seemed feasible to select passages from her journals, letters, poems, novel and short stories, and then demonstrate with linked examples how they do indeed form the "chapters in a mythology" that Judith Kroll, in her ground-breaking study of Plath's imagery, identified as long ago as 1976.

Unfortunately, it proved not possible to base a biography wholly on the written evidence of its subject. The life story of any artist has, too, to be the story of others who knew and formed opinions about a living person. So although every scrap of Plath's accessible writing had been made available to me, and though I had been granted permission to quote as much as I wished, I was still to a great extent dependent upon the testimony of her contemporaries.

As every Plath scholar knows, there is no dearth of written material in the libraries. A great many people who had met Plath, roomed with her, loved her, hated her, were puzzled by or pitied her, rushed their opinions into print in the years following her death. When I began my researches, the posthumous reportage that had accumulated around Plath's name (some of it written by people who hardly knew her) had reached impressive proportions, and yet firsthand evidence from those who had been closest to her was oddly scarce. Richard Sassoon, for example, the boyfriend Plath pursued to Paris in the spring of 1956 soon after she met Ted Hughes, had effectively disappeared (at least at the time), and Warren Plath, Sylvia's brother, consistently refused interviews. More serious was the absence of testimony from Hughes himself and from the friends who had kept silent over the years out of respect for his proud and prolonged reticence. When Olwyn Hughes suggested that a biography might help to redress the balance, I was excited to receive fresh material from, among others, Dido Merwin, Lucas Myers and Richard Murphy, who contributed their memoirs to the appendices.

Ted Hughes, of course, was aware that *Bitter Fame* was being written, and I was pretty sure at the time that he viewed the venture with ambivalence. After sending me one long, characteristically persuasive letter, he made it clear he would supply and check facts for accuracy; otherwise he preferred to let his friends express their views without involving him. No doubt he anticipated that *Bitter Fame*'s publication would create trouble—for me, perhaps; for himself and his sister, almost certainly. As it turned out, his instincts were proved correct.

However silent about his personal feelings over the years, by the late 1980s Ted Hughes had brought out and edited one volume after another of Sylvia Plath's poetry and prose, contributing introductions in which he explored, each time with more insight, the phenomenon of her terrified genius and her immolation in a deathly psychodrama quite beyond her (or his) power to control. Anyone who has read with an open mind Hughes's essays on Plath reprinted in *Winter Pollen* (1994) or followed over the years the development of his ideas relating to Plath's predicament must find his prose representations of her plight moving.

Still, *Bitter Fame* was a biography written around a gap. As a study of Sylvia Plath's palingenetic obsession and the two or three personal traumas constantly recapitulated in her work, it owes much to Hughes's readings of her poems. As a love story and the story of a life, it lacks the counterpoise of her husband's presence. Here is Juliet's tale without Romeo's, Eloise's without Abelard's. The skirted-around incompleteness was something I regretted but could do nothing to remedy when *Bitter Fame* first appeared. Only Hughes could supply the missing pieces, and no one then anticipated that, nearly ten years on, he would astound us all by releasing the eighty-eight poems of *Birthday Letters*. In January of 1998, almost overnight, the literary world woke up to find the balance between the two poets restored. Plath's late, plangent outpourings had at last been answered in a sequence of poems that, far from merely filling a gap in a biography, confronted them with stinging personal challenges equal in force to her own.

Yet while these *Birthday Letters* remain a sensation, we must be careful to distinguish them from the main body of Hughes's poetry. Plath's *Collected Poems* are multidimensional and complex. Rooted in her life's experience, her poems reach out far beyond it, to touch us as only the best art can. Plath is a poet for her time and all time; her voice, as she might have put it, still echoes among the archetypes. *Birthday*

Letters, in contrast, is one book of poems among many. Personal, even "confessional" as Hughes has never been before, they give his version of his wife's myth, showing themselves to be an important element in a healing process that never took place after her death. As a sequence of personal messages to the dead, then, *Birthday Letters* is devoted to the single purpose of getting things "right" about Hughes's past. Reviewers, with good reason, have called it a book of love poems, though it claims to be no more than a collection of recollections, musings and monologues written for and dedicated to both poets' grown children. We outsiders who have been invited to read these private letters over Hughes's shoulder still have to adjust our minds to the fact of our utter exclusion from them.

This means that a fair number of the *Birthday Letters* may seem at the least opaque, at the most meaningless to readers who are unfamiliar with the particulars of the poets' life together. To help their understanding, they could do worse than set side by side on the desk before them Plath's *Collected Poems* and *Journals,* Hughes's *Birthday Letters,* together with *Bitter Fame* as a commentary. It is possible—for I have done it—to "match up" almost every one of his letters with a poem or journal entry of hers and then, through the pages of *Bitter Fame,* to place them both in context. For example, on page 41 of *Birthday Letters,* a poem called "Moonwalk," set in Spain, is hurled out in the choked words of a man just freed from an evil spell. The lines become more fascinating, more spell-like, once they are paired with a passage from Sylvia Plath's journal of August 1956, quoted on page 93 of *Bitter Fame.* "Alone, deepening. Feeling the perceptions deepen with the tang of geranium and the full moon and the mellowing of hurt; the deep ingrowing of hurt, too, far from the bitching fussing surface tempests. The hurt going in, clean as a razor, and the dark blood welling. Just the sick knowing that the wrongness was growing in the full moon. . . ." Then, further on, "The light is cold, cruel and still. All could happen: the willful drowning, the murder, the killing words." It's not that Hughes adds to our knowledge of "what happened" on that nightmare night in Spain; it's more that he gives it a new dimension, a different and validating focus.

Bitter Fame also provides a context for the desperately cheerful tone Plath adopted when she wrote to her mother at the worst of times. A letter, for instance, written in June of 1962 (*Bitter Fame,* page 247) when the idyll of her Devon life was disintegrating around her, describes Plath and her husband setting up as beekeepers: "We placed the hive in a sheltered out-of-the-way spot in the orchard—the bees were furious from being in a box. Ted had only put a handkerchief over his head where the hat should go in the bee-mask, and the bees crawled into his hair, and he flew off with half-a-dozen stings." Compare this jaunty, rather breathless reportage with the bitter vindictiveness of her poem "Stings," in the bee sequence (*Collected Poems,* page 215): "The bees found him out, / moulding onto his lips like lies, / complicating his features." Then look at the end of Hughes's "Bee God" (*Birthday Letters,* page 150):

> A lone bee, like a blind arrow,
> Soared over the housetop and down
> and locked into my brow, calling for helpers.

Hughes's sequence makes it pretty clear that this lone attacking bee was Otto Plath, Sylvia's enraged father, arriving in the guise of a Bee God to carry his daughter off to the underworld. *Bitter Fame* had to leave Hughes's reaction to these myth-laden stings to the reader's imagination; now the biography helps to place it in the context of an epiphanic clash between the poets.

Bitter Fame, then, can be used as a guide to *Birthday Letters* as well as to Plath's *Collected Poems.* Readers, make what they will of the myth, will find it fascinating to follow both poets through their ordeal of enactment. Of course, any biography is a species of history, an attempt by an outsider to explain the lives of people in the light of what we know about them. No one's account can be proved perfectly true. If we are to be fair to their story, neither Hughes nor Plath can be simplified into a goody or a baddy. But a taste for authenticity and real evidence can at least prevent rumor from gaining the ascendancy and fixing itself as a permanent version of what happened. Plath's poetry, of course, is her apotheosis, the life after death that she demanded for herself and, at the cost of her reason and happiness, did achieve. Like any other biography, *Bitter Fame* is not a work of art but the story of a life. The unforeseen irruption of *Birthday Letters* into its "plot," however, shows it to be a credible one.

Ten years ago, while writing about Sylvia Plath's happy years at Cambridge and the lectures by Dorothea Krook she followed with rapt attention, I thought of borrowing for my epigraph the quotation from Henry James's preface to *The Wings of the Dove* which Krook herself used as an epigraph to the book that grew out of those lectures, *The Ordeal of Consciousness in Henry James.* The epigraph may perhaps serve also as an epitaph to the unmitigated tragedy of Sylvia Plath.

> The case prescribed for its central figure a sick young woman, at the whole course of whose disintegration and the whole ordeal of whose consciousness one would have quite honestly to assist.

—ANNE STEVENSON
"Pwllymarch," Llanbedt,
Greywedd, North Wales
February 1998

PREFACE

Dying
Is an art, like everything else.
I do it exceptionally well.

I do it so it feels like hell.
I do it so it feels real.
I guess you could say I've a call.

— "Lady Lazarus"

ON FEBRUARY 11, 1963, the American poet Sylvia Plath, living in London with her two small children, put an end to her life at the age of thirty. Her suicide gave rise to a vast popular mythology. After her death, with the publication of *Ariel* in 1965, many people, especially women, discovered in her work a shocking revelation of extremist elements in their own psyches. Plath became a spokeswoman for the angry, the disillusioned, the bewildered generations of the 1960s and 1970s. The tragedy of her suicide and the power of her last poems seemed to sweep the polarities of life and art (carefully separated by T. S. Eliot and the New Critics) into one unanswerably dramatic gesture of female defiance: "The blood jet is poetry, / There is no stopping it."

This biography of Sylvia Plath has been written with a view to confronting some of the misunderstandings generated by her meteoric rise to fame, replacing them, as far as possible, with an objective account of how this exceptionally gifted girl was hurled into poetry by a combination of biographical accident and inflexible ideals and ambitions. People who knew Sylvia Plath are divided in their response to her intense, volatile character, but they invariably find her poetry compelling. Many of them remember her as a vivacious and stimulating girl whose brilliance, like her "harsh wit," was uniquely exciting. Some of her friends speak warmly of her charm, her humor, her great gifts and huge capacity for affection. Others recall a complex, completely self-absorbed, stubbornly ambitious American whose outer shell of bright capability contained a seething core of inexplicable fury. Any biography of Sylvia Plath written during the lifetimes of her family and friends must take their vulnerability into consideration, even if completeness suffers from it. Until now a whole side of her story — that of her marriage — has been inadequately or erroneously presented. This was due primarily to Ted Hughes's understandable insistence on the privacy of his life and the lives of his children, but also to the reluctance of many who knew Plath and Hughes well during this time to make their memories public until the children were grown up.

Important among new witnesses who have generously contributed to this book are Lucas Myers, who first met Sylvia at Cambridge; Dido Merwin, then the wife of W. S. Merwin, who knew Sylvia in Boston, London, and France; and Richard Murphy, Sylvia's host when she visited Ireland toward the end of her life. I never met Sylvia Plath, and since all three presented me with written firsthand accounts, invaluable for the light they throw on Sylvia Plath's mature years, I have included them in full as appendices to the book while drawing on them directly and indirectly in the text. Much of the new material will surprise those who have accepted the current view of Sylvia Plath. W. S. Merwin wrote, when applied to for his impressions, of his dismay at the image "— nurtured in great part by people who did not know her — of Sylvia as the pathetic victim of [Ted Hughes's] heartless mistreatment." What Merwin, like so many others, had seen was "first the bright and smiling mask that she presented to everyone, and then, through that, the determined, insistent, obsessive, impatient person who snapped if things did not go her way, and flew into sudden rages . . . I came to feel that there was something in Sylvia of a cat suspended over water, but it was not Ted who had put her there or kept her there."

That Sylvia Plath was conditioned by her German-American background and by the social and cultural climate of her time, that she was an ambitious woman and mother in the decade just preceding the feminist revolution of the late 1960s, that her identity until the last years of her life always remained to be proved, that she was at the age of eight psychologically injured by the death of her father — all these facts naturally have to be taken into account when we consider how her life affected her poetry. But finally, it is as a writer that she matters and would have wished to be remembered. This book tries to comprehend Plath's valiant, lifelong struggle with herself by reconciling the contradictory testimonies of her writings as well as the different views of those who knew her. What I have tried to do is to approach this extraordinary artist as I believe she herself would have asked to be approached — as a poet.

After the publication of *Ariel*, Sylvia's mother, Aurelia Schober Plath, sought to counter the violence of her daughter's poetry with the bubbling optimism of *Letters Home*, published in 1975. However understandable as a gesture of protest — essentially saying, "Whatever she said in her art, *this* is what she wrote to me" — the publication of *Letters Home* served only to confuse the public. How could the author of *The Bell Jar* and *Ariel* possibly have written the effusive, gossipy, transparently naive outpourings of the letters on display? The confusion was exacerbated by the publication in America in 1982 of selections from her journals. These reveal a Sylvia Plath even further removed from the newsy letter-writer, yet at first they can hardly be reconciled with the sure artistry of the poems.

In many ways the extreme contradictions in Sylvia Plath's character were the tensions that gave rise to her genius. Before everything, she was a possessed, a driven artist. To attempt to reconstruct her life as an exceptionally talented but otherwise ordinary woman, or to assess her contribution to the feminist movement as being politically of the same order as that, say, of Adrienne Rich, is to misunderstand Plath with a degree of perversity equal to her own. For most of her life Plath wanted above everything to be accepted as "ordinary," while at the same time conceiving of the ordinary in terms of unattainable perfection. Brought up in a privileged society, protected by a tightly knit family that closed in about her (as families will) after her father's death, cosseted by her teachers, laden with scholarships and honors, she rebelled in some deep part of herself against the very image she labored to create.

At some time early in her life, possibly even before Otto Plath's death, she learned how to win attention and praise from adults by producing works for them. Her competitiveness and extreme intolerance of rivals seems to have been rooted in a tremendous hunger for love, which she construed as the *exclusive* approval mainly of her mother. In a fine prose piece about her early childhood written for radio shortly before her death (at a time when she was in defiant good spirits), she describes her insulted feelings upon learning of the imminent arrival of a sibling:

A baby.
I hated babies. I who for two and a half years had been the center

of a tender universe felt the axis wrench and a polar chill immobilize my bones. I would be a bystander, a museum mammoth. Babies!

Having refused offers from her grandfather to play on the verandah, she makes her way in a huff along the beach.

Hugging my grudge, ugly and prickly, a sad sea urchin, I trudged off . . . As from a star I saw, coldly and soberly, the *separateness* of everything. I felt the wall of my skin: I am I. That stone is a stone. My beautiful fusion with the things of this world was over.

Plath is telling us here that her discovery of separateness was associated from the first with jealousy and fear. Indeed, separateness or isolation was ever a source of her inner torture — the more so because being "different," another favorite word, also meant that she was set apart as an artist and therefore not really "forever to be cast out" but, as the finding of a "Sacred Baboon" on the beach in the story seemed to prove, elect and special. Long after Sylvia's death, her mother wrote that Sylvia had, in fact, not found that wooden baboon; a friend's father had found it. Is it not likely that Sylvia's metaphysical confrontation with separateness at the age of two was also a fabrication too fine to leave out of the story? Whatever "facts" she invented, however, Sylvia's fictive isolation was quite true. So although she never listened to the pounding of S.S. boots outside her place of hiding, never experienced prison, hunger, homelessness, or physical deprivation of any sort, she was confined as defiantly and agonizingly within her skin as any victim of political oppression, her heart beating "I am I" from the hour of her self-discovery.

The hell Sylvia Plath experienced was an inner hell (she also, of course, had a personal heaven), but it was a real one, and as such it resembled all the hells human beings have contrived for themselves throughout the ages; hence its universal appeal and its terrible danger. It may be that the psychic wound from which Sylvia never recovered had its origin in no particular childhood event but grew out of repeated realizations of her powerlessness to re-create the world in her image. Her creative urges were very strong, so strong that in the ordinary run of things mere reality scarcely stood a chance. Sylvia needed to impress and oddly possess those upon whom she depended for love, endowing her friends and lovers with dazzling perfections until — sometimes because they insisted on living their own lives and sometimes because they looked shrewdly at hers — they proved unworthy and, in her word, "betrayed" her. When she could not control her hurt vulnerability (and she was terribly vulnerable), her raging vindictiveness would burst out like a shocking and violent bloom. Yet she herself seemed unaware — or so the journals and poems tell us — of its startling disproportion. "The last thing we learn about ourselves," Carolyn Kizer has written, "is our effect."

For a long time Sylvia Plath did not know why she *had* to be a writer or what it was she had to express. Only toward the end of 1959, when she all but stumbled into writing "Poem for a Birthday," did she see how to be true to her own "weirdness." There was something, evidently, she had to beat out of herself: "Oh, only left to myself, what a poet I will flay myself into," she wrote in her notebook on May 11, 1958. Apparently it was only after such flayings, after her great rage had spent itself in writing, that she was able to approach what at the end appeared to be the real world — a projection in large, alas, of the deathly cycle she had enacted repeatedly in her life and poems.

> The world is blood-hot and personal
>
> Dawn says, with its blood-flush.
> There is no terminus, only suitcases
>
> Out of which the same self unfolds like a suit
> Bald and shiny, with pockets of wishes,
>
> Notions and tickets, short circuits and folding mirrors.
> I am mad, calls the spider, waving its many arms.
>
> And in truth it is terrible,
> Multiplied in the eyes of the flies.
>
> They buzz like blue children
> In nets of the infinite,
>
> Roped in at the end by the one
> Death with its many sticks.

◄ ◄ ◄

In searching for the author of *Ariel* and *Winter Trees,* I have been assisted by many people who knew Sylvia Plath in America and in England. I have avoided repetitious interviews with writers of published memoirs and with her American family. Mrs. Plath, in a final essay in Paul Alexander's collection, *Ariel Ascending,* indicates politely that she has said in writing all she wishes to say about her daughter. So I have left her in peace, as I have Sylvia's brother, Warren Plath, and his family.

Ted Hughes was good enough to supply me with an outline of the trip around the United States and the Cape Cod holiday he and Sylvia took together. Beyond this, as he writes, "I have read through the text simply to check, and if necessary correct, the limited number of facts about which I feel I can be reasonably certain. That leaves the main bulk of the book to other people's reports, opinions, and interpretations, for which I take no responsibility." Through Olwyn Hughes I was able to make contact with many who had hitherto kept silent and who have made valuable contributions to this book: W. S. Merwin in Hawaii, Lucas Myers in California, Dido Merwin in France, Richard Murphy in Ireland, and, in London, Jillian Becker, Nest Cleverdon, Doris Lessing, Suzette Macedo, and Nicola Tyrer. I am also indebted to Ruth Fainlight, Dr. John Horder, Michael Horovitz, Daniel and Helga Huws, Gordon Lameyer for his unpublished memoir, James Michie, Clarissa Roche, Elizabeth Sigmund, Marcia Brown Stern, May Swenson, David Wevill, and others. I have also made use of some excellent previously published portraits, among them those by A. Alvarez, Elizabeth Compton, Jane Davison, Peter Davison, Jane Baltzell Kopp, Dorothea Krook, Gordon Lameyer, Clarissa Roche, and Nancy Hunter Steiner. Every effort has been made to reach Richard Sassoon, whose letters in the Lilly Library at Indiana University have had to be referred to without his permission.

Without the assistance and patience of my editors, this book, originally commissioned by Emma Tennant for her Penguin Lives of Women series, would not exist. Peter Davison at Houghton Mifflin not only contributed his own memories of Plath, thus enlarging my understanding of her character and completing my information about literary Boston in the 1950s, but went over three drafts of the manuscript, making invaluable suggestions. At Viking, Judith Flanders worked day and night on an earlier version; I am grateful to Tony Lacey for his part in completing this book.

Finally, I wish to thank Ruth Mortimer and her colleagues in the Rare Book Room at Smith College's Neilson Library and the librarians of the Lilly Library at Indiana University for friendly, cooperative assistance in locating manuscripts and other source material. I extend warm thanks, too, to Cynthia Lewis and Dorothy Winstanley, who helped type a chameleon manuscript, and to Katarina Rice, who meticulously checked and edited the final draft. To Peter Lucas, who traveled with me, suffered with me, and married me while contributing tactfully to the exposition and style, I give all such thanks as can be expressed in language — and out of it.

A.S.
David Hume Tower
University of Edinburgh
February 1989

THE GIRL WHO
WANTED TO BE GOD
1932-1949

As soon as my children were old enough to comprehend it, I
shared with them the belief my husband and I had held concerning
the importance of aiming and directing one's life toward an ideal-
istic goal in order to build a strong inner life.

— Aurelia Schober Plath,
in *Letters Home*

When mother goes away from me
I miss her as much, as much can be.
And when I go away from mother
She misses me, and so does brother.

— Sylvia Plath, age seven

WHEN SHE WAS not yet fifteen, the young Sylvia Plath astonished
her high school English teacher, Wilbury Crockett, with a group of
poems, some of which he read aloud to his tenth-grade class in Wellesley, Massachusetts. Sylvia recorded the incident in her diary: "Today
I brought a group of original poems to Mr. Crockett . . . In class he
read aloud four of them, commenting mainly favorably. He liked 'I
Thought That I Could Not Be Hurt' above the rest and encouraged
me greatly by remarking that I had a lyric gift beyond the ordinary."
Mr. Crockett showed this favorite poem to a colleague, who remarked
that it was "incredible that one so young could have experienced
anything so devastating." But the poem was occasioned by a very

minor mishap: the poet's grandmother had accidentally smudged a
pastel drawing of which Sylvia was particularly proud.

> I thought that I could not be hurt;
> I thought that I must surely be
> impervious to suffering —
> immune to mental pain
> or agony.
>
> My world was warm with April sun
> my thoughts were spangled green and gold;
> my soul filled up with joy, yet felt
> the sharp, sweet pain that only joy
> can hold . . .
>
> Then, suddenly my world turned gray,
> and darkness wiped aside my joy.
> A dull and aching void was left
> where careless hands had reached out to
> destroy
>
> my silver web of happiness . . .

Even then, writing was a need, living a complicated necessity that
writing had to manage. "I was overjoyed," Sylvia wrote in the light
of Mr. Crockett's praise, ". . . although I am doubtful about poetry's
effect on the little strategy of 'popularity' that I have been slowly
building up." Praise at home and prizes at school were threads she
was already adeptly weaving into a "web of happiness" she instinctively knew to be threatened. From within, the high school girl felt
menaced by inklings of duality and fragility: "How frail the human
heart must be — / a mirrored pool of thought," she wrote, already
reaching for the images of pool, mirror, and beating heart that would
later haunt her mature poems. She sensed that the world could hurt
her badly if she was not careful to conceal her true feelings and earn
its admiration by meticulous conformity to its requirements.

Sylvia's strategy was always to do *better* than was required. Because
she was "different," it was essential to appear more than usually
"normal." As late as January 1963 she was remembering the strain
of adapting to high school conventions and, in her brusque, mocking
style, scornfully resurrecting them:

The girls' guidance counselor diagnosed my problem straight off. I
was just too dangerously brainy. My high, pure string of straight
A's might, without proper extracurricular tempering, snap me into
the void. More and more, the colleges wanted All-Round Stu-

dents. I had, by that time, studied Machiavelli in Current Events Class . . . "Usage is Truth, Truth, Usage," I might have muttered, leveling my bobbysocks to match those of my schoolmates.

The tone is contemptuous but intense. What every fierce, snapping sentence conveys is just how much hard work she put into chalking up A's, getting her pageboy hairdo "squeaky clean" and the skirt-sweater-loafer uniform of the time exactly right.

In Sylvia's day the Gamaliel Bradford Senior High School, now Wellesley High School, boasted two sororities. Girls who aspired to popularity had to be invited to belong. Sylvia got herself elected to Sub-Debs and, before she was admitted, endured a humiliating initiation week during which she was forbidden to wash, comb her hair, change her clothes, or smile. Slavish obedience to a Big Sister bore a curious resemblance to sadism. Was the Okay Image worth having at the price? Maybe she was "just too weird to begin with." In the same late essay she commented sourly: "What did these picked buds of American womanhood do at their sorority meetings? They ate cake; ate cake and catted about the Saturday night date." It is not surprising that Sylvia Plath despised these girls; what is surprising, but characteristic of her, is that she *cared* so much.

In her writing Sylvia made the most of every scrap of personal experience she thought she could use for literary material. That high school initiation (significantly altered; her heroine finally refuses to join the sorority) later went into a short story called "Initiation," which won her a $200 prize and publication in *Seventeen* magazine in January 1953, when she was a junior in college. Was it a just reward for misery? Or a way of coming to terms with an existence she sometimes found almost impossible to sustain? By the time Sylvia was a senior in high school she was already dependent on writing and success in publishing for social survival. She was afflicted, not with too much sense of her own value, but with too little. Wherever she was, that little pronoun "I" which traveled around with her had to be bolstered, propped up by social approval, or she became, in her extreme words, a "zero," a "hollow nothing." Haunted by a fear of her own disintegration, she kept herself together by defining herself, writing constantly about herself, so that everyone could see her there, fighting and conquering an outside world that forever threatened her frail being.

◄　◄　◄

It is not clear how much of Sylvia Plath's existential anxiety can be traced to her social isolation as a girl and how much to her father's death, which occurred when she was eight. As a family, the Plaths were culturally aspiring and ambitious, staunchly liberal in outlook, steeped in Emersonian ideals of loyalty, hard work, self-reliance, and puritan optimism. Yet they were in fact classic American immigrants.

Otto Plath, Sylvia's father, had emigrated in 1901 at the age of sixteen from Grabow, a Prussian town in the Polish Corridor. Grandparents in Wisconsin paid for his passage. His father, who with the rest of the family emigrated much later to Oregon, was a mechanic or engineer; in Germany he had worked as a blacksmith. Otto, considered clever (his interest in bumblebees began well before he came to America), landed in New York, where he worked for a year in an uncle's delicatessen and liquor store. Mrs. Plath records in her introduction to *Letters Home* that during that year he patiently sat at the back of successive classrooms in the local elementary school until he had sufficient mastery of the language to "graduate" from the eighth grade as a proficient English speaker. His grandparents offered to put him through Northwestern College in Wisconsin on condition that after graduating in classical languages he would train for the ministry in a Lutheran seminary. By 1910, however, a liberal education at Northwestern had converted him to Darwinism. On entering the seminary he discovered that all Darwin's books were proscribed reading. There being no way to reconcile his conscience as a scientist with a career in Lutheran theology, Otto proposed that he become a teacher. His German family, horrified at this betrayal of faith, disapproved so fiercely that, on Otto's persisting in his rebellion, they struck his name from the family Bible. For the rest of his life, Otto Plath was on his own.

The American tradition of the enterprising male European immigrant who makes good by pulling himself up by his bootstraps might have been made in the image of Sylvia's father. First he worked his way through an advanced program at the University of Washington, in Seattle, from which he took a Master of Arts degree in 1912. Then he found work teaching languages (he knew five) at the University of California, where apparently he studied biology between 1912 and 1914, and again, after studying at Columbia and teaching at the Massachusetts Institute of Technology, from 1918 to 1920. He began work in zoology at Johns Hopkins University in 1920 and in entomology at Harvard in 1925. It was not until 1928, eighteen years after his first degree at Northwestern, that he received his doctorate from Harvard. He was rewriting his thesis for publication while teaching an advanced course in German at Boston University when he met his future wife, Aurelia Schober, in 1929. He was forty-three; she, his student-admirer, twenty-two.

Aurelia, too, was of Germanic extraction. Significantly, however, she was a second-generation Austrian brought up to speak German at home until persecution in grade school (patriotic Americans were frequently vicious to German-speaking immigrants during the First World War) convinced her parents that they must conform to American social patterns if they wished their children to find places in the superior ranks of the egalitarian society. In her introduction to *Letters Home* Aurelia Plath draws touching vignettes of her childhood in Winthrop, just outside Boston. Tales of her isolation at school, of punishment incurred when she greeted her father with "Shut up!" (the only English she had picked up on the school playground), and of her subsequent withdrawal from the rough-and-tumble of Winthrop school life into a dream world of poetry and novels, became, when passed on to her children, important myths.

Aurelia's father, Sylvia's "Grampy," had come to America from Vienna intending to make a fortune on the stock market. Like most, he was unlucky. After financial disaster struck him in the early 1920s, he more or less turned his family — Aurelia, her younger sister, Dorothy (Sylvia's "Aunt Dot"), and a much younger brother, Frank — over to the management of his capable wife, contenting his conscience with a humble cost-accounting job in Boston. Aurelia, sensitive, efficient, and clever, left high school desiring nothing so much as a liberal arts education in a small college. Her father, however, was too poor to think of a nonvocational education for his daughter, so in 1924 he sent her instead to the Boston University College of Practical Arts and Letters.

After two years Aurelia prevailed upon her parents to allow her to study English and German with a view to becoming a high school teacher, a profession that seemed ideal for someone of her temperament. In pursuit of this career she found part-time jobs to offset a perennial, soul-eroding shortage of money: she worked in a public library and spent one summer typing dreary letters for an insurance company. During the summer of her junior year in college she found work as a secretarial assistant to a cultured professor of German descent at the Massachusetts Institute of Technology. She returned home from late working suppers with her employer, notebooks bulging with exciting suggestions for reading Greek drama, Russian literature, the world's great philosophers, and, in German, the poetry of Rilke and Hesse. Yet at an age when her daughter would be setting off to a fine women's college with three scholarships and high hopes for a dazzling career, Aurelia was battling to achieve an education that would enlarge her view of the world. Her dream was to realize her ideal of self-education as a "lifelong adventure"; her respect for learning was the only legacy she would be able to hand down to her children.

When Aurelia Schober enrolled in Professor Plath's course in Middle High German in 1929, she had already taught for a year at Melrose High School in Massachusetts. Dr. Otto Plath was handsome, learned, and authoritative. She was honored to be among his chosen students, and even more honored when, to her surprise, he asked her to become first his confidante and then his wife.

On January 4, 1932, after a year and a half of teaching German and English at Brookline High School, Aurelia Frances Schober married Dr. Otto Emil Plath in Carson City, Nevada (Otto had first to obtain a divorce in Reno from an estranged wife whom he had not seen for fifteen years). At her husband's request, Aurelia gave up teaching to become a full-time housewife and, shortly afterward, a mother. Soon after the couple had settled into an apartment on Prince Street in Jamaica Plain, near Boston, Aurelia became pregnant and plunged herself into a study of books on childrearing, about which she and her husband had liberal — for those days, radical — ideas. Both of the Plath children would be cuddled, fed on demand, rocked, sung to, brought up in the natural way that in the 1930s was considered unorthodox but is widely approved by psychologists and pediatricians today. Sylvia was born in Robinson Memorial Hospital on October 27, 1932, "a healthy eight-and-a-half-pound baby." Otto, boasting to his colleagues at lunch that day, admitted that he hoped for one more child — "a son, two and a half years from now." Warren appeared right on schedule, on April 27, 1935.

Aurelia Plath's introduction to *Letters Home* takes the view that the Plath marriage was viable principally because Aurelia accepted a secondary, wifely role. If she wanted peace, she realized, she would have to submit to her husband's rule, although, as she confesses, she was not naturally submissive. She and Otto shared a veneration for work, to which almost every self-indulgence had to be sacrificed. They had few outside pleasures and no social life. Aurelia's dreams of throwing her house open to students faded under the necessity of preparing the manuscript of Otto's *Bumblebees and Their Ways* for publication during 1933. After that she became Otto's assistant in the preparation of a chapter on insect societies for *A Handbook of*

Social Psychology, which came out in 1935. During these years pregnancy and motherhood were diversions from her duties as secretary-typist to her husband.

Although the marriage appears to have been strong, life for Aurelia cannot have been much fun. Otto soon conceived a dislike for his study and requisitioned the dining room for his files. No paper or book could be moved, unless by stealth while Otto was away teaching, to make room for guests. Aurelia's parents, indeed, were welcome, and her mother, Sylvia's "Grammy," willingly helped with the babies. Otto, however, was the absolute *paterfamilias,* supervising household economies, shopping at the cheapest markets, assuming dominance as his natural right.

In early childhood, Sylvia was the center of her father's attention, while Warren, a sickly baby afflicted with asthma and bronchitis, absorbed most of his mother's time.* Sylvia evidently gloried in being the family darling, a special favorite with Grammy and Grampy and with Uncle Frank, Aurelia's brother, who was only thirteen years older than his niece. A number of files containing Sylvia's early writings and keepsakes are to be found in the Lilly Library at Indiana University; here are Sylvia's first letters, diaries, school papers, juvenile poems (one of which was published in the *Boston Herald* when she was eight), cards, drawings, paper dolls, locks of hair, and reams of letters written to her mother from summer Girl Scout camps. All are confirmations — if we need them after the fulsome outpourings of *Letters Home* — that the relationship between Sylvia and her mother was abnormally claustrophobic, even for Germanic Americans with a strong sense of family.

Almost all Sylvia's childhood writings reflect the Horatio Alger ethic of the era: happiness is the right of everyone, to be achieved through hard work; success is the reward for work; and fame and money are the measure of success. It was a philosophy Sylvia would have imbibed at school as well as at home. A few weeks before her death in London in 1963, she wittily lampooned the conformist ideology of her up-

---

*In her introduction to *Letters Home* Mrs. Plath describes her scheme to distract Sylvia, who always wanted most attention when her mother was tending to Warren. Sylvia, apparently, had already learned to read capital letters from advertisements. Whenever Mrs. Plath sat down with Warren, Sylvia was encouraged to "read" the letters from a newspaper on the floor beside her. Soon she was "reading" the STOP sign at a nearby crossroad as POTS. What Mrs. Plath does not say — a fact surely relevant to Sylvia's recourse to language in times of difficulty — is that even at two and a half her daughter was being urged to treat negative emotion (jealousy of her brother) with words.

bringing in a piece for *Punch,* "America! America!," but her childhood letters suggest not the slightest irony. They are unrelievedly pious, occasionally touching but more often smug, with a prudery that intimates that happiness for Sylvia may have been a hard-won valuable among her "rowdy" peers in Winthrop, to which the Plaths moved in the autumn of 1936. In one letter from Scout camp she comments that certain ill-bred children say "ain't" and "youse." "It just hurts my ears," she complains. "I long for my family's soft sweet talk."

The Plaths' old-fashioned frame house on Johnson Avenue in Winthrop was near the town center, on the bay side of the peninsula jutting into Boston Harbor. Three miles away was the Schobers' home at Point Shirley, near Deer Island Prison on the sea-bitten coast. Each house became a focus of the poet's imagination. Letters from daughter to mother in 1939, the year of her father's illness, show that Sylvia lived for long periods with her grandparents. A plaintive verse, "Missing Mother" (quoted at the beginning of this chapter), appears, neatly written, on a little card decorated with a carefully coy illustration with the caption "HOME SWEET HOME." From 92 Johnson Avenue, Aurelia wrote (April 8) congratulating her daughter for again achieving an all-A report card; she would give her a big hug when she next saw her. In all Mrs. Plath's letters the teacher anxiously supplements the mother — for example, she introduces to her clever daughter the concept of curves, induces her to extend her vocabulary, urges her to practice the piano. Sylvia, who must really have missed her mother, soon deduced that good performances produced hugs and praise. Eating well was also hug-worthy; descriptions of large meals abound in her summer correspondence, as well as meticulous accounts of pocket money spent on minor indulgences such as sweets and stationery. At an early age, evidently, Sylvia Plath learned how to gain adult approval by performing perfectly whatever she was asked to do and behaving — or at least seeming to behave — exactly as she intuited would please her mother most.

The year after the Plaths settled into their comfortable if unfashionable house in Winthrop, a family named Freeman also moved into the neighborhood. The children, David, six months older than Sylvia, and Ruth, a year younger, became daily playmates, Warren struggling to keep up with the three older children. With Marion Freeman Aurelia struck up a lifelong friendship — and by now she needed a friend, for Otto's health had begun to deteriorate soon after the Plaths were settled in Winthrop.

To get to lectures and seminars at Boston University, Dr. Plath commuted from Winthrop by rail, ferry, and subway. He began to lose weight and suffer from insomnia. Irritable, imperious, increasingly exhausted, he refused to consult a doctor. Later it emerged that he suspected cancer, which seemed to him a weakness, practically a character flaw, to admit. At home he lurked in his study; at work he struggled through his classes, barely retaining strength enough to travel back to Winthrop in the evenings.

His wife, too, grew thin and strained with worry. To protect her husband from his boisterous offspring, and them from him, she devised what she called an "upstairs-downstairs" existence, making over the largest bedroom into a playroom where she gave the children their supper and read to them or told them homemade stories. " 'The Adventures of Mixie Blackshort,' " she says, "ran into nightly installments for several years." Aurelia also introduced Sylvia and Warren to poetry. Later Sylvia would write that she remembered the gooseflesh rising on her skin when she first listened to Matthew Arnold's "The Forsaken Merman." Here was "a new way of being happy." Downstairs, Mrs. Plath tended to her husband, permitting the children a half hour of play with him after an attempt at an adult dinner. Sylvia would dance or play the piano for her father, and both children showed him their poems and drawings.

Although Mrs. Plath was perpetually exhausted, her decision to drain off all the family's troubles into herself succeeded for a while. It seems she never complained. During the winter of 1938–39, when Sylvia was in second grade, Warren, always prone to allergies, developed bronchial pneumonia; Sylvia suffered from sinusitis. This was the time when Aurelia Plath sent Sylvia to live with Grammy and Grampy on the shore. With father and baby brother absorbing all her mother's attention, it would have been surprising if Sylvia had *not* had a classic reaction of sibling jealousy, outmaneuvering Warren when they were apart and outtalking and outspelling him when they were in competition for parental attention. Sylvia's stories and journals give evidence that as a child she often made her brother miserable. (From about 1950, however, a transformation would take place in their relationship, and during Sylvia's years at Smith and Warren's at Exeter and Harvard, the two would become loyal allies and equals.)

By the summer of 1940 both children were well enough to spend long days on the beach with David and Ruth Freeman. Dr. Plath, on the other hand, grew steadily worse. In August, dressing to go in to Boston to teach, he stubbed his little toe on a chest of drawers. By evening his foot had turned black, and streaks of unhealthy vermilion discolored his leg. This time when Aurelia called the doctor Otto did not protest. He submitted to an examination. The doctor was incredulous. Otto Plath did not have cancer; but he was suffering from *diabetes mellitus,* which, diagnosed in time, could have been contained. Now it might be too late.

The summer dragged on, but Otto showed no sign of improvement. Sylvia, in a cut-down nurse's uniform, ran back and forth with fruit juice. One day, when Aurelia was on the beach with Sylvia, Otto, seeming to believe he could overcome his illness by will power, got out of bed and started down the stairs. On her return, Aurelia found him collapsed on the staircase and somehow dragged him back to bed. All night he sweated with alternating fever and chills. The next day a specialist arrived and advised that the leg should be amputated. Leaving the house, the doctor murmured to Mrs. Plath, "How could such a brilliant man be so stupid?"

The operation was performed in the New England Deaconess Hospital on October 12, 1940, two weeks before Sylvia's eighth birthday. At first it seemed the invalid might recover. Students and colleagues at the university deluged him with offers of help. The president wrote, "We'd rather have you back at your desk with one leg than any other man with two." Yet perhaps there was something in Otto Plath's psychological makeup that caused him to resist cure. He did not, as some of Sylvia's poems intimate, commit suicide, but neither did he struggle to live. He made no effort to try the prosthesis the hospital provided, nor would he talk to his wife about leaving to come home. On the evening of November 5, shortly after she had returned home from a visit to the hospital, Aurelia Plath received a telephone call from the surgeon. Otto Plath had died of an embolism that struck his lung as he slept.

Aurelia was stunned, of course, but not unprepared. She decided to wait until morning to tell the children. Calling upon all the resources of that stoic inner life in which she and Otto had invested so much faith, she suppressed her tears as she went in, first to Warren, who was only five and a half, and then to Sylvia, who was sitting up reading in bed. Sylvia's reaction was at first silence. Then, characteristically, she made an extreme declaration, "I'll never speak to God again," and dived furiously under the bedcovers. All her life Sylvia was given to using the phrase "never again" in circumstances she considered intolerable.

The day after her father's death, Sylvia returned from school troubled by something else. Insinuating remarks had been dropped by schoolmates regarding the awful possibility of a stepfather. Sylvia held out a shakily printed paper for her mother to sign: "I PROMISE NEVER TO MARRY AGAIN." Aurelia signed it, relieving Sylvia, who immediately went out to play. Most likely, Mrs. Plath had no intention of remarrying. She would have to go back to teaching, in any case, to support her family.

Plans had already been made to rent out the Schobers' house on Point Shirley and move Aurelia's parents into the Plath household on Johnson Avenue should her husband fail to recover. Soon after the funeral, which Mrs. Plath conscientiously spared both children, the family closed in around itself. It was important to demonstrate to the world at large that all would be well. But at first nothing did go well. Two weeks after Otto Plath was buried, both children came down with measles. Warren's case was complicated by a return of bronchial pneumonia, and Sylvia suffered once again from sinusitis. There was worse to come. After Christmas 1940, Grampy lost his job when his Boston company changed management. Discouraged, he, like his daughter, began to look for work — humiliating for an elderly man with deteriorating eyesight. Most distressing of all was lack of money. Dr. Plath's life insurance provided not much more than enough to meet medical and funeral expenses. No pension from Boston University was forthcoming to his widow.

In January 1941 Aurelia Plath found temporary work teaching German and Spanish in a high school near her former home in Jamaica Plain. That meant leaving Winthrop at five-thirty every morning. In addition, three afternoons a week she went to private lessons in Spanish. By late spring a more convenient job had turned up for September in a junior high school near her home, but Aurelia herself was ill: not surprisingly, the tensions of the past year had brought on a duodenal ulcer. Piecing her life together despite intense pain, she managed to complete a year of teaching in Winthrop.

During the summer of 1942 the war's bonus of civilian jobs finally came to the rescue. Grampy Schober found unexpected work as a maitre d'hôtel at the Brookline Country Club in a wealthy suburb of Boston, and Aurelia Plath was offered a job that enabled her to move away from Winthrop, whose climate she judged to be detrimental to her children's health. The dean of the Boston University College of Practical Arts and Letters, where Aurelia had earned her first diploma years before, needed someone to develop a course for medical secretaries. Mrs. Plath, with her business qualifications and the understanding of scientific method she had picked up working with Otto, seemed the ideal person. She was to be given a free hand in creating the course; to make the teaching of stenographic skills interesting would be a challenge to her imagination. Although the starting salary was small, she thought it adequate. It made possible a move to a middle-class neighborhood with better schools and a drier climate. By autumn she had sold the house in Winthrop — at a loss — and moved herself, her two children, and Grammy Schober (during the week Grampy lived at the country club) to a tidy white frame house in a modest but pleasant section of Wellesley, a dozen miles west of Boston.

◂　◂　◂

Sylvia celebrated her tenth birthday, October 27, 1942, the day after her family moved inland, away from the ocean and its teeming beaches and the big, shabby frame house in that "rowdy seaside town" across the bay from Logan Airport where at night she had watched the incoming and outgoing planes from her bedroom window. She was moving away, too, from the reality of her dead father, who over the years was to become an absence far more potent than any presence, apart from her mother's, in her personal mythology.

Although Otto Plath had died two years earlier, the family's move away from the sea dramatically sealed him in a moonstruck, glassed-in compartment of Sylvia's imagination, where he evolved into his godlike/devillike manifestations, stripped of reality — the frightening ghost of a father she had scarcely known as a healthy man. Eventually she came to associate her father with a block of time she had sealed into a never-never land of childhood. The poet in Sylvia reduced that time to a figure in a delicately constructed work of art — a ship in a bottle, described at the end of her radio script "Ocean 1212-W" in 1962: "beautiful, inaccessible, obsolete, a fine, white flying myth."

Yet in her dreams and in her peculiarly hallucinatory imagination, it was not so easy to bury Otto under glass. Inexorably he would emerge from the shadow side of Sylvia's stories and poems as the Proteus of her Herculean effort to free herself of his image. Menacingly, irresistibly, he would reappear in her work as a Colossus, a seagod-muse, a drowned suicide, an archetypal Greek king, a bee-keeper (brave master of a dangerous colony), even, as in the famous poem "Daddy," a fictitiously brutal combination of husband and Luftwaffe Nazi. This tangle of imagery — illogical, surreal, untrue as to the fact but inseparable from Sylvia's psychic reality — has its origin, at least partly, in the two years that fell between Otto Plath's death and his daughter's physical removal from Winthrop and the sea.

Otto Plath had been a pacifist. In December 1941 America entered the Second World War, and the world became a pacifist's nightmare. The American population had a relatively easy war. All the same, there were aid-raid drills, blackouts, food shortages, and, ominously for families with young sons and brothers, the selective service. German-Americans were often given a hard time. Although it seems unlikely that at school Sylvia had to endure nastiness on the scale the Schobers had weathered during the First World War, it is evident from the stories Sylvia set in Winthrop ("Superman and Paula Brown's New Snowsuit," "The Shadow," "The Green Rock," "Among the Bumblebees") that her fragile sense of belonging had been seriously shaken. Years later, in her unpublished journals, she would write of a "complicated guilt system whereby Germans in a Jewish and Catholic community are made to feel, in a scapegoat fashion, the pain, psychically, the Jews are made to feel [by] Germans without religion."

"Superman and Paula Brown's New Snowsuit," written when Sylvia was in her final year at Smith College, is a war story. Its themes are fear, power, suspicion, envy, persecution, and disillusion. A narrator, standing for Sylvia, begins as an imaginative child, organizer of Superman games in her neighborhood, winner of Civil Defense prizes. Her sensitivity, or perhaps her acutely defensive self-consciousness, breeds resentment among her classmates, whom secretly she envies and despises. Everything the narrator has to say about Paula Brown, for instance, smacks of the bitterness of the socially rejected. Paula's "pale skin," "long red pigtails," and "watery blue eyes" are physical manifestations of unmerited social privilege. The story bears the same message as the fourteen-year-old's poems: her silver web of happiness is destroyed when reality conflicts with imagination. Growing up makes the "difference" (the word is pivotal) between playing make-believe and realizing that people really do *make beliefs*. When the entire neighborhood comes to believe that the narrator pushed Paula Brown into an oil slick, nothing she can say convinces anyone, even her family, that she is innocent.

If "Superman and Paula Brown's New Snowsuit" is the most convincing of the pieces of fiction inspired by Sylvia's childhood, her most persuasive piece of nonfictional prose is the autobiographical "Ocean 1212-W," written for the BBC toward the end of her life. Here she creates a lively, sea-fostered image of herself out of several inventive interpretations: "When I was learning to creep, my mother set me down on the beach to see what I thought of it. I crawled straight for the coming wave and was just through the wall of green when she caught my heels."

Sylvia's recall of everything that happened to her was an asset to her writing, but it also entrapped her. Working invariably from life, she tended to mow over the same ground of her past again and again, harvesting similar crops of self-justifying interpretation. According to Aurelia Plath, it was not Sylvia but Warren who, as an infant, crawled into the waves, just as it was not Sylvia but a family friend who found the Sacred Baboon on the beach that Sylvia, later in the piece, interprets as "a sign of election." Sylvia's memory, in other words, served the purposes of her art-myth; she revised her life constantly to suit her art. In "Ocean 1212-W" she needed action on the part of the sea; in a paternal fashion nature itself had to demonstrate that Sylvia was of the ocean's godlike lineage, a chosen daughter of the Colossus and therefore "not forever to be cast out."

◀   ◀   ◀

Sylvia's strangeness may have been a source of worry to her mother when the family moved from Winthrop to genteel Wellesley. Sylvia left the Annie F. Warren Grammar School in Winthrop with a straight-A average, and yet Mrs. Plath thought it wise to put her back a grade when she entered the Marshall Livingston Perrin School in Wellesley. Sylvia would have been younger than most of the children in the sixth grade, but she was also taller, and scholastically she could have swept ahead with the older group. Mrs. Plath may have sensed that Sylvia was having difficulties making friends. The more relaxed program of the fifth grade would reduce her competitive vigilance. She could rise easily to the top of the class and have time to broaden her interests, to become the "all-rounder" that the universities insisted they wanted.

Evidently her mother's scheme worked, and Sylvia, who had grown to her full height of five feet nine inches by the age of fifteen, soon gave every appearance of American teenage normality. Membership in the Girl Scouts, basketball teams, the school orchestra (in which she played the viola), the United World Federalists, and Unitarian Church groups piled up to her credit, first at Perrin Grammar School and later at Philips Junior High, where English and art became her best subjects. For six summers running she went for two weeks to Girl Scout camps. She had a best friend, Betsy Powley, with whom she shared confidences and camping trips. She wrote rhymes, illustrating them as surprise presents for Grampy when he returned to Wellesley for weekends from the country club. She left little squibs in verse under her mother's table napkin at dinner. All this time she kept diaries in her clear, round, schoolgirl's handwriting. Writing soon became as natural to her as eating. In junior high school she published continually in the school magazine while considering various careers. Should she become a dress designer (she cut out exquisite clothes for her paper dolls) or an illustrator? Or should she become a writer and win fame and money writing for the *Ladies' Home Journal* or the *Saturday Evening Post*?

By 1949, when Sylvia was seventeen and a senior in high school, she had mastered the art of achievement so well that she herself was deceived into believing she was super-normal. Her mother, of course, was delighted with Sylvia's social and literary successes. In her introduction to *Letters Home* she exclaims wistfully:

> The high school years were such fun. The sharing meant so much, for Warren had gone to Exeter and I missed him terribly. When Sylvia would come home from a dance, I could tell by the way she ascended the stairs how the evening had gone. If she came up slowly and started to get ready for bed, the event had not been "special," but if her step was a running one and she'd hurry into my bedroom, whispering excitedly, "Mummy, are you awake?" ah, then she'd picture the evening for me, and I'd taste her enjoyment as if it had been my own.

Deprived of most ordinary pleasures in her own hardworking youth, Aurelia Plath did indeed identify with Sylvia, unwittingly laying upon her daughter the heavy responsibility of keeping them both happy. Sylvia had a rare, infectious capacity for exultation — as great a gift for rapture as she had for misery. She "ricocheted," a favorite word, between extremes with alarming rapidity, recording her moods along with careful details of every "big moment" in the proliferating pages of her scrapbooks and journals. In *Letters Home* Mrs. Plath quotes a longish passage from a diary supplement dated November 13, 1949, with the purpose, one suspects, of demonstrating to the world that Sylvia was not by nature a potential suicide. The seventeen-year-old's confessions are romantic, as one would expect, but they also reveal an extraordinary understanding. Her self-analysis is profound and so detached that in fact one *can* see in her writing a blueprint for what would occur:

> I feel infinitely sad at the thought of all this time melting farther and farther away from me as I grow older. *Now, now* is the perfect time of my life . . .
> Sometimes I try to put myself in another's place, and I am frightened when I find I am almost succeeding. How awful to be anyone but I. I have a terrible egotism. I love my flesh, my face, my limbs

with overwhelming devotion. I know that I am "too tall" and have a fat nose, and yet I pose and prink before the mirror, seeing more and more how lovely I am . . .

Was not believing in herself really a matter of believing in an ideal version of herself? And was not this ideal her *real* self? Was she wrong, then, to idealize herself even when the merciless mirror showed her the ordinary truth? Sylvia had absorbed her mother's idealism together with her aphoristic tendencies and Emersonian faith. At seventeen she was already caught up in the hapless dualisms of the Romantics; already she apprehended that she "never, never, never" would attain the perfection she longed for in "my paintings, my poems, my stories." They were all poor reflections.

I want, I think, to be omniscient . . . I think I would like to call myself "The girl who wanted to be God." Yet if I were not in this body, where *would* I be? . . . But, oh, I cry out against it. I am I — I am powerful, but to what extent? I am I.

A SMITH GIRL

1950-1952

We had our college assembly this morning. I never came so close to crying since I've been here when I saw the professors, resplendent with colors, medals, and emblems, march across the stage and heard adorable Mr. Wright's stimulating address. I still can't believe I'm a SMITH GIRL!

> — *Letters Home,*
> September 28, 1950

God, who am I? I sit in the library tonight, the lights glaring overhead, the fan whirring loudly. Girls, girls everywhere, reading books. Intent faces, flesh pink, white, yellow. And I sit here without identity: faceless. My head aches . . . I'm lost . . .

> — *Journals,* September 1950

SYLVIA GRADUATED from Bradford Senior High School in Wellesley with a reputation for creativity, but not at all for artistic oddity. It seems that in her last two years of high school she had carefully cultivated the "all-round" image the colleges wanted and the boys in her class admired. During her senior year, 1949–50, she was co-editor of the high school newspaper, *The Bradford,* to which she contributed unsigned poems and articles, and was on the "art and activities" staff of *The Wellesleyan,* the high school yearbook. Her years as a "Crocketeer," one of a select group of students chosen by Wilbury Crockett for a special three-year course in English (and, apparently, in life philosophy, too), gave her an overview of American literature in the tenth grade, English literature in the eleventh, and world literature in the twelfth. She took the part of Lady Agatha in a class production of *The Admirable Crichton* and painted enlarged cartoons of Li'l

Abner and Daisy Mae for her sorority prom. Her notebooks show her keeping careful count of the boys who asked her for dates (nineteen), as well as of those whom she asked herself (four), though she seems to have been serious about only two, a freshman at Williams College named John Hall and Bob Riedeman, a sophomore at the University of New Hampshire. All this time Sylvia was writing stories and poems, attempting nearly fifty times to break into the "It's All Yours" section of *Seventeen* magazine before she finally gained acceptance for a story, "And Summer Will Not Come Again." It was published in August 1950, the summer before she entered Smith College.

During her senior year of high school Sylvia had been offered a full scholarship to Wellesley College, the noted women's institution in her own town. Her mother would have preferred her to accept; it would have kept Sylvia within bicycling distance even if she had elected (or could have afforded) to live at the college. Yet Sylvia opted emphatically for three partial scholarships to Smith, and Aurelia acquiesced. The relationship between mother and teenage daughter — now sometimes an uneasy one — could be sustained better through correspondence. Although at this time Sylvia never outwardly rebelled, at seventeen she clearly felt smothered in the atmosphere of 26 Elmwood Road. Her mother's aura of anxious self-sacrifice was easier to write to than live with. And Sylvia was beginning to take a predictable interest in sex.

In the summer of 1950, after Sylvia had graduated from Bradford and Warren had come home from his first year at Phillips Exeter Academy (where, to her delight — according to Mrs. Plath — he had grown taller than Sylvia), brother and sister took summer jobs working together on a market farm in Dover, Massachusetts, not far from Wellesley. It was a time Sylvia was to seal up, like her seaside childhood, in that glass bottle in which she preserved idealized memories of wholeness. One evening after work at the farm, an Estonian boy named Ilo lured her into his studio-bedroom in the barn and passionately kissed her; with another boy, the erotic Emile, she indulged in enough sexual experiment to convince her that physical sensuality was something she actively enjoyed, just as she enjoyed eating good food, digging in the earth, drawing, or immersing herself in books and ideas. Every experience, she believed, was grist for the writer's mill. Yet while relishing her incipient lust, she also recoiled. What later became an established pattern of sexual behavior was even then an embryonic dilemma. Hitherto Sylvia had been content to act the part of a "normal" teenager while keeping her exceptional talents to herself. Now it became evident that there were aspects of life she could not control. Senior proms, yes; "unreasoning, bestial purity," no.

Middle-class teenage Americans in the 1950s subscribed to an amazing code of sexual frustration. Everything was permissible to girls in the way of intimacy except the one thing such intimacies were intended to bring about. Both partners in the ritual of experimental sex conceded that "dating" went something like this: preliminary talking and polite mutual inspection led to dancing, which often shifted into "necking," which — assuming continuous progress — concluded in the quasi-masturbation of "petting" on the family sofa, or, in more affluent circumstances, in the back seat of a car. Very occasionally intercourse might, inadvertently, take place; but as a rule, if the partners went to the same school or considered themselves subject to the same moral pressures, they stopped just short of it. There was always the alternative of drinking — almost as wicked and sometimes itself the ally of sexual deliverance.

Whatever the extremes of amorousness, "pure" boys were not supposed to take "nice" girls to bed, although it was assumed that boys had to sow their wild oats somewhere, so what they did outside their class or neighborhood tended to be overlooked. A different standard, of course, applied to girls. The specter of pregnancy reared up in such articles as the *Reader's Digest*'s "In Defense of Chastity," mailed to Esther Greenwood by her mother in Plath's novel *The Bell Jar*. In real life, the young Sylvia was as conformist as she was scared. She was horrified when, in the course of a blind date with an ex-Marine during her freshman year at college, her partner made an improper advance. Afterward, she wrote about it in some detail to her mother and in much greater detail to herself in her journal, hovering between fascination and recoil.

A good deal of what happened in the summer of 1950 also got itself into Sylvia's journal. She recorded Ilo's kiss — "I stood there, flooded with longing, electric, shivering" — and a first real taste of literary fame. The editor of the *Christian Science Monitor* — a paper in which Sylvia published all her life — accepted a sharp political poem, "Bitter Strawberries," in August, and, in September, a nostalgic essay, "Rewards of a New England Summer," about Lookout Farm:

> When you see me pause and stare a bit wistfully at nothing in particular, you'll know that I am deep at the roots of memory, back on the Farm, hearing once more the languid, sleepy drone of bees in the orange squash blossoms, feeling the hot, golden fingers of

sun on my skin, and smelling the unforgettable spicy tang of apples which is, to me, forever New England.

Clearly Sylvia was addicted already to the sugary adjectives of advertising, where calendar-pad prose was a prerequisite for success. She was prepared to suffer any number of rejections, slave any number of hours over a story or poem, if only she could place it in one of the national "slicks," magazines that she regarded as arbiters of fashion. When *Seventeen* published her sentimental story "And Summer Will Not Come Again," about a girl who falls in love with her tennis instructor, Sylvia was ecstatic. Study your market, the editor had advised. Sylvia had studied it, drawing on her gift for pastiche to produce a problem story with a touch of pathos exactly calculated to impress the comfortable conscience of *Seventeen*'s middle-class readership.

"And Summer Will Not Come Again" brought Sylvia — besides fifteen dollars — the epistolary attention of an intelligent, older English major at Roosevelt College in Chicago who signed his name Eddie Cohen. Cohen's first letter, of August 3, 1950, explained that, having picked up by accident a copy of his sister's *Seventeen*, he had read a story which, to his surprise, had expressed emotions "rather more subtly than the usual *Seventeen* hit-'em-with-a-brick technique." Turning to the back pages to read about the author, he was even more surprised. Was she only seventeen? Perhaps, under the "chaperonage" of over a thousand miles between them, she would find a correspondence with him rewarding?

Delighted to receive her first fan letter, Sylvia replied on August 6, rather archly accepting his challenge, telling him about her farming job while rather wistfully confessing that she could never quite fit into her high school society; she was too individual. After this, both correspondents dropped their affectations. Over several years Eddie Cohen developed into Sylvia's pen-friend and conscience, a trustworthy male alter ego to whom she confessed the nightmares of her inner life while, to her mother, she was parading the joys of her Smith-girl apotheosis. Sylvia had other male friends who were not boyfriends; her Wellesley neighbor Philip McCurdy (the tennis-coach hero of her published story), for instance, was someone with whom she talked openly while in college. Cohen, however, represented not only another sex but a different, freer, wilder world. Sylvia could appeal to his experience without having to pretend she was sophisticated.

On August 11 she told him, "I'm sarcastic, skeptical and sometimes callous because I'm still afraid, deep down, of letting myself be hurt.

There's a vulnerable core in me which every egotist has ... Fellows look at me and think that no serious thought has ever troubled my little head." Cohen took up the issues both of Sylvia's egotism and of her vulnerability, quickly responding to the strengths and weaknesses of her character. By December he was accusing her of taking too light an attitude to her male admirers, particularly where sex was concerned. Compared to himself and his friends, she had "had it pretty easy ... No parental conflicts of a really important nature." (He was wrong about this, but Sylvia herself, at that time, would have agreed with him.) Cohen also criticized Sylvia's tendency to hero-worship boys she went out with. Admiration, he told her, is not the best basis for friendship or love, certainly no substitute for sharing interests and ideals.

On her side, Sylvia idealized Cohen's nonconformity and made much of his presumed sexual expertise. Twenty-one and acquainted with the rougher sides of Chicago nightlife, he had hung around the same bars as Nelson Algren and other underworld intellectuals, and he was newly embarked on an affair with a girl whose sexuality he freely discussed. Indeed, Cohen was just the person to explain to Sylvia the nature of orgasm and the use of contraceptives. He was also someone to whom she could pour out her romantic longings, her intense moods of expectation and despair, the urgency of her physical desire, her worry that animal sensuality would prove her undoing as a writer.

For Sylvia worried and worried, about her gender, about her terrible urge to survive and her craving to live every moment of now, now, now, before it was too late. She worried about the evils of human suffering, about nuclear war and the survival of the world. But she worried most of all about the nature of being — chiefly, of being a Sylvia absolutely different from everything else in the world and at the same time absolutely undifferentiated from it:

> I can't deceive myself out of the bare stark realization that no matter how enthusiastic you are, no matter how sure that character is fate, nothing is real, past or future, when you are alone in your room with the clock ticking loudly into the false cheerful brilliance of the electric light. And if you have no past or future, which, after all, is all that the present is made of, why then you may as well dispose of the empty shell of present and commit suicide.

Sylvia's mention of suicide here is in the nature, merely, of philosophical deduction, but nonetheless her journals and her letters to Eddie Cohen point to a perplexity at the root of her terror, a paradox of being in time that might have led her to study philosophy had she not been hell-bent on becoming a successful writer. Sylvia was interested not in theory but in her own private salvation. Around her troubled psyche she carefully constructed an impeccable public carapace. The Sylvia Plath she offered her friends was a girl of buoyant ambition whose affections were extreme, whose enthusiasms were contagious, whose talents cried out for recognition. Having little confidence in being and "I" at all, her ego all the more craved reinforcement. She performed not so much to the world as to her reflection, a silvery, gleaming image in which perfect grades and a collection of literary prizes assured her of safety from the dark reality of her nonbeing.

Mainly it was her mother who furnished the mirror for Sylvia's image. Yet by 1950 Sylvia had already become aware that their relationship was stifling. "But with your father dead," she wrote in one of many essays in self-analysis, "you leaned abnormally to the 'humanities' personality of your mother. And you were frightened when you heard yourself stop talking and felt the echo of her voice, as if she had spoken in you, . . . as if her expressions were growing and emanating from your face."

The letters Sylvia wrote to her mother from Smith (and indeed throughout her life) — the hundreds of letters that opened with "Dear Mum" or "Dearest Progenitor" or "Dearest darling beautiful saintly mother!" and ended with "Your happy Sivvy" or occasionally "Your hollow girl, Sivvy"— were cries for self-confirmation from an anxious daughter to a mother who would always find time to write back (*that* was the point) in bracing paragraphs full of firm moral advice. It would be a mistake to conclude with facile depreciation that Sylvia Plath did not mean what she said in her letters home. At least at the outset she meant every word of them; they were a life line. Sylvia idealized Smith, for instance, but she often found it hard to like. Uncomfortable among intelligent or rich girls of her age, she found it painful to have to attach herself to any group; hence, perhaps, her instinctive attraction to men like Eddie Cohen, Richard Sassoon, and Ted Hughes, all individualists with none of Sylvia's need constantly to conform. Sylvia longed to defy convention herself, but at the same time she needed a mother to help her believe she was perfectly adjusted, worthy of the attention she attracted, and capable of "paying back" her kindly sponsors, most of whom were older women, by achieving spectacular success.

Sylvia's letters from Smith paint her life, then, as it ought to have been: "After supper, we gathered around the piano and sang for a good hour . . . No home life could make up for the camaraderie of living with a group of girls. I like them all." Against these sunshine letters we have to set the moon side of Sylvia's character, the side that went into her journals:

> Now I know what loneliness is, I think . . . It comes from a vague core of the self — like a disease of the blood, dispersed throughout the body so that one cannot locate the matrix, the spot of contagion . . . Homesick is the name they give to that sick feeling which dominates me now. I am alone in my room, between two worlds . . . There is no living being on earth at this moment except myself. I could walk down the halls, and empty rooms would yawn mockingly at me from every side. God, but life is loneliness, despite all the opiates, despite the shrill tinsel gaiety of "parties" with no purpose, despite the false grinning faces we all wear.

It is easy to see why the sun and its reflector, the moon, became presiding symbols for Sylvia. Mirroring reflections in pools of glass and the veiling of vital but inaccessible truths enter her poetry again and again. Indeed, the bright, optimistic persona she so often displayed seemed a willed stance to disguise her inner self — that troubled, vital, inaccessible part of her, touched on in her best poems and darkly expressed in her journals. Plath's true subject was this inner self, not her outer experiences and achievements. Eventually she would yearn to kill her false self so that her real one might burn free of it. That seems to be the logic that lay behind her lifelong obsession with suicide.

At seventeen Sylvia found symbols for longing before she understood what she was longing for. The following little parable of escape, for instance, expresses her psychic imprisonment. Trapped within the safety of her mother's house in that crucial precollege summer of 1950, the scrubbed, becurled potential Smith girl is challenged by the moon. The night sky is an immensity visible only through the tiny pane of glass that shuts her in — and the moon out:

> Tonight I wanted to step outside for a few moments before going to bed; it was so snug and stale-aired in the house. I was in my pajamas, my freshly washed hair up on curlers. So I tried to open the front door. The lock snapped as I turned it; I tried the handle. The door wouldn't open. Annoyed, I turned the handle the other way. No response. I twisted the lock; there were only four possible combinations of handle and lock positions, and still the door stuck, white, blank, and enigmatic. I glanced up. Through the glass square, high in the door, I saw a block of sky, pierced by the sharp black points of the pines across the street. And there was the moon, almost

full, luminous and yellow, behind the trees. I felt suddenly breathless, stifled. I was trapped, with the tantalizing little square of night above me, and the warm, feminine atmosphere of the house enveloping me in its thick, feathery smothering embrace.

◂ ◂ ◂

Sylvia was trapped not only in her mother's house but by the very nature of the society she was to labor for years to impress, the society represented by Smith College. Founded in 1871 by a philanthropic lady on the advice of her parson, Smith was dedicated to fulfilling a moral but unrevolutionary social obligation to American womanhood. Sophia Smith, with her legacy of four hundred thousand dollars, had wished "to furnish for my own sex means and facilities for education equal to those which are now afforded in our colleges to young men." The college was conceived on liberal, ladylike principles at a time when women were coming into their own as citizens but were not yet expected to take an unwomanly role in affairs of government, business, or the arts and sciences. Not until a century after its dedication did it appoint a woman president, when Jill Ker Conway took office in 1975. During Sylvia's undergraduate years, most of Smith's faculty members were men. Smith girls, educated for careers but prepared for marriage, were unquestionably valuable on the nuptial market, trained to elevate their husbands with precisely the kind of perfect service Aurelia Plath had provided for her spouse after their marriage in 1932. The alternative to marriage was to become a teacher or a member of a profession in which Smith women would conspicuously serve the community. The formidable and influential faculty members Mary Ellen Chase and Elizabeth Drew embodied for Sylvia the heights to which distinguished women with educational advantages could aspire.

Years after their graduation, Sylvia's roommate from her senior year, Nancy Hunter Steiner, recalled the commencement address delivered by Governor Adlai Stevenson in May 1955:

Our unanimous vocation, as Governor Stevenson saw it, was to be wives and mothers — thoughtful, discriminating wives and mothers who would use what we had learned in government and history and sociology courses to influence our husbands and children in the direction of rationality. Men, he claimed, are under tremendous pressure to adopt the narrow view; we would help them to resist it and we would raise children who were reasonable, independent, and courageous.

Mrs. Steiner adds, "The speech was eloquent and impressive and we loved it even if it seemed to hurl us back to the satellite role we had escaped for four years — second-class citizens in a man's world where our only possible achievement was a vicarious one."

Mrs. Steiner's memoir, *A Closer Look at Ariel,* was published in America in 1973, a time of revolutionary feminism Sylvia never lived to see. Sylvia herself, from 1950 to 1953 and then, after her breakdown, from January 1954 to her graduation under the patronizing eye of Governor Stevenson in 1955, outwardly pursued what her roommate even then saw as a course of paralyzing conformity.

Sylvia set off for Smith in September 1950 in a smart suit and hat, with a spanking new set of luggage and an $850 scholarship from Olive Higgins Prouty, romantic novelist and creator of the radio serial *Stella Dallas.* In her first week away from home Sylvia wrote to her mother, "Never have I felt so happy." Halfway through her first term, enrolled in courses in English, art, botany, history, and French, she philosophized to Olive Higgins Prouty in a thank-you letter: "There is so much here, and it is up to me to find myself and make the person I will be . . . I don't think I've ever been so conscious of the dignity and capacity of women. Why, even in my house there is a startling collection of intelligent, perceptive girls — each one fascinating in her own way. I enjoy knowing people well and learning about their thoughts and backgrounds." She could have been writing to Sophia Smith. Mrs. Prouty liked Sylvia's letter so well that she sent it to the *Smith Alumnae Quarterly,* where it was published in February 1951.

Yet Sylvia did not easily make friends at Smith. After a lonely first term during which she suffered through a series of dismal blind dates or withdrew inwardly under the pointed sarcasm of girls who disapproved of her staying in to work on weekends, she began at last to make a reputation as a published writer. For friendship she came to rely on two girls in Haven House, where she lived. Ann Davidow, who was unhappy at Smith, found that its academic demands unnerved her, and to Sylvia's intense distress she transferred to the University of Chicago in January of their first year. Marcia Brown was a down-to-earth, sympathetic student of sociology with whom Sylvia would room, very happily, in her sophomore (second) year. Both girls remained close friends and correspondents of Sylvia's until the time of her death.

During Christmas vacation of her freshman year Sylvia was surprised when a former high school friend, several years older than she, dropped by in the middle of a training run with an invitation to a weekend dance at Yale, where he was a senior preparing for medical school. Dick Norton, his brother Perry, who was Sylvia's age, and a younger brother, David, were more or less the legendary boys-next-door. Their mother, Mildred Norton, was a friend of Aurelia's, their father a history professor at Boston University. Since the Norton boys called Mrs. Plath "Aunt Aurelia," Sylvia regarded them as cousins, rather preferring Perry to Dick.

Now Dick's flattering attentions threw her into a quandary. After several weekend visits to Yale in the spring term, supplemented by a little jealousy over a rival graduate from Dana Hall, Jane Anderson (a year ahead of her at Smith), Sylvia began considering Dick as a possible future "mate." It was after a "lush" visit to Dick at Yale that she wrote in her diary, "Dissect your sentences, oh professor! point out verb and noun and participial phrase. Dry, dry, the words; creaking dry, hissing dry and imperfectly low"— and went on to write a mocking analysis of a kiss.

In her journal or, as often, in letters to Eddie Cohen, Sylvia wrote long essays, arguing for and against marriage, questioning the advisability of attempting to be at once a writer and a wife. What awful tragedy had made her a woman, and a lustful woman at that? Yet wasn't her lust for Dick (in her letters to Eddie Cohen she renamed him Allan) only a form of refined hedonism that could as well run its course in a series of promiscuous relationships? (Cohen, looking up "hedonism" in his dictionary and applying the word to Sylvia, concluded, "No way!"; as for promiscuity, he was vehemently against it.) But then why, asked Sylvia, did men have freedom in sexual matters that women did not? Finally, assuming that there was no way for a woman to fulfill her sexual needs without marriage, Sylvia deduced that eventually she would have to marry. But Dick?

Responding to this barrage of letters after a traumatic breakup with his girl, Eddie Cohen decided on action. In March, during spring vacation, he borrowed his family's car on a pretext of visiting relatives in Detroit. After a perfunctory detour to Michigan, he headed straight for Massachusetts, driving one thousand miles in thirty hours through horrendous weather, arriving in Northampton just as Sylvia was about to set off with another friend for Wellesley. Sylvia was amazed but not amused. She was thrown off balance by this unexpected visit; apparently the Eddie Cohen of her imagination did not resemble the sleepless, unshaven, travel-worn Eddie Cohen who presented himself in the flesh. In strained silence they drove to 26 Elmwood Road in Wellesley. There Sylvia curtly introduced him to her mother and then just as abruptly dismissed him. Incredulous as well as furious, Cohen blundered through the Boston traffic until he could drive no more, slept for twelve hours in a motel, and then set off for New York, where he met a girl more hospitable than Sylvia and spent the night in her apartment. Driving back to Chicago the next day, his wound still rankling, he was involved in a head-on collision in Ohio.

Mrs. Plath, meanwhile, was horrified when she learned that the young man turned away so brusquely had been *"that* Eddie." Why hadn't Sylvia asked him in, offered him food and a bed? The boy was obviously exhausted. Sylvia made no comment. It was her right to distinguish the men she fancied from those to whom she talked or wrote. Eddie belonged to the second category and should have known his place.

Surprisingly, after writing in a state of shock on April 4 and again in anger on April 11, Cohen resumed the correspondence, writing critically of Sylvia's snobbishness and bad manners but perceptively noting (as would many of her boyfriends) that something in Sylvia was not quite "right." Cohen soon announced that he was going into psychoanalysis. His own eccentric behavior, sexual and emotional, was beginning to worry him. Sylvia wrote back long letters, but she seems not to have heeded the suggestion that she consider analysis for herself.

At the end of her freshman year Sylvia did well on her exams, although she fell short of her usual all-A performance. A persistent B in physical education merely annoyed her, but a high B in English, of all things, made her rethink her future career. Should she perhaps major in art or art history, in which she had done very well? She decided definitely to "honor" in her junior and senior years. Working toward an honors degree would mean taking fewer courses under a more directed plan of study, and this might do away with some of the conflicts she had disliked as a freshman.

In June she and Marcia Brown took jobs as mother's helpers with neighboring wealthy families in Swampscott, Massachusetts. For most of the summer both girls were thoroughly miserable. Sylvia's duties caring for the three Mayo children were not so much arduous as constant. She was treated as less than adult herself. How she envied those cocktail parties from which she was cruelly excluded on the clipped lawn overlooking the sea!

Sylvia was by now accepted in the Norton family as Dick's girl, and during that summer (Dick was working in Brewster, Massachusetts, where his parents had a vacation cottage) they met as often as they could to swim and talk. On one occasion it emerged that although

Dick set himself up as a "pure" boy, he had become involved with a waitress in the hotel where he worked as a bus boy, and he was no longer a virgin. Sylvia, half jealous of the other woman, half furious because Dick had bested her in their competition for sexual supremacy, meditated her revenge. She did not write it fully until 1961, when she transformed Dick Norton into Buddy Willard in *The Bell Jar,* bringing to the surface the enormous hostility she had carefully suppressed for so many years.

A long entry in her Swampscott journal shows her undergoing a process of self-purification after hearing about Dick, as if she had to rise above considerations of mortal weakness by becoming the poet-heroine of her own myth. The sacrificial imagery is pure Plath:

> Stretching out on the rock, body taut, then relaxed, on the altar, I felt that I was being raped deliciously by the sun, filled full of heat from the impersonal and colossal god of nature. Warm and perverse was the body of my love under me, and the feeling of his carved flesh was like no other — not soft, not malleable, not wet with sweat, but dry, hard, smooth, clean and pure.

Sylvia rose from her "orgiastic sacrifice on the altar of rock and sun . . . shining from the centuries of love, clean and satiated from the consuming fire of his casual and timeless desire," but she returned to Smith in September determined to exploit her attractiveness to men other than Dick Norton.

Within weeks she was writing to her mother in ecstasy. Together with all the other girls in Haven House she had been invited to Maureen Buckley's coming-out party in Sharon, Connecticut. The Buckleys were among the richest and grandest of New England Catholic families. Maureen's brother, William F. Buckley, Jr., had written a book, soon to be notorious, called *God and Man at Yale.* The house in Sharon was a palace. "Picture me then," Sylvia wrote, "in my navy-blue bolero suit and versatile brown coat, snuggled in the back seat of an open car, whizzing for two sun-colored hours through the hilly Connecticut valley! . . . At about 5 p.m. we rolled up the long drive to 'The Elms.' God! . . . Great lawns and huge trees on a hill, with a view of the valley . . . A caterer's truck was unloading champagne at the back."

Always impressed by displays of wealth, Sylvia knew, too, that such surroundings would particularly appeal to her mother, to whom she wrote a full description of the whole magical evening. The black Cadillacs, the Filipino houseboy, the chauffeurs, the white colonial columns, the girls in their beautiful gowns clustered by the curved stair — it was a fairy tale come true, complete with a Sylvia-Cinderella who created the story all over again in her letter: "I stood open-mouthed, giddy, bubbling, wanting so much to show you. I am sure you would have been supremely happy if you had seen me. I know I looked beautiful. Even daughters of millionaires complimented my dress."

On an evening so charmed, several Prince Charmings presented themselves, among them a Caucasian Russian at Princeton named Constantine — Sylvia would borrow his name for the glamorous simultaneous interpreter of *The Bell Jar*. Yet when Constantine asked Sylvia to Princeton for the weekend of November 3, she refused him, after arduous heart-searching. She had examinations in English on the sixth and in her government course on the seventh. To make Junior Phi Beta Kappa, an honor she greatly coveted, she would need A's in both. As usual, she sacrificed present joys for future goals, and indeed got her A's. Fully preoccupied with establishing a successful academic record, she was, she told herself, unready to fall in love. As she had chillingly confessed in her journal at the beginning of the semester, "I do not love; I do not love anybody except myself."

It was during her second year that Dick Norton, now in his first year at Harvard Medical School, smuggled Sylvia into the Boston Lying-in Hospital, where he was training. He was, it seems, putting Sylvia on trial as a possible doctor's wife. Disguised as a student nurse, she attended a film-lecture on sickle cell anemia, observed some anatomical dissection, and witnessed the birth of a baby. Sylvia survived the ordeal by adopting a pose of cool bravado, but in truth the experience proved traumatic. The scene in the hospital, remembered with nightmarish accuracy, is central to the Buddy Willard episodes of *The Bell Jar,* just as images of fetuses in bottles and the "doom mark" on the smiling face of a girl in the medical film haunt Sylvia's poems.

Although punctuated with ups and downs, crises, triumphs, catharses, and confessions, Sylvia's sophomore year at Smith was in many respects her happiest. Comfortable with her roommate, Marcia, feted as a writer, and popular as a weekend date, she did well in her courses, accumulating honors and prizes to justify her hard work. One of two in her class elected to Alpha Phi Kappa Psi (an honors society for the arts), she was appointed to the editorial board of the *Smith Review* and served on Smith's Press Board, writing articles on the college for the local newspapers. She was also selected for Honor Board, a student judiciary body. Busyness was the measure of allroundness at Smith, and so Sylvia was perpetually busy. Still, she found time to write and publish her stories. In her freshman year she had won third prize for "Den of Lions" from *Seventeen*. Now she wrote up her summer experiences for the *Christian Science Monitor* ("As a Baby-Sitter Sees It" was published, with three of Sylvia's own drawings, in November 1951) and found time to write a sixteen-page story, "Sunday at the Mintons'," for a contest sponsored by *Mademoiselle*. Marcia Brown remembers her painstakingly making flash cards from her thesaurus, building poems word by word, like novel, intricate structures.

Smith life was also full of outside lecturers. In April Sylvia applauded Robert Frost's poems one night and hissed a speech by Senator McCarthy the next. On learning that W. H. Auden was to be at Smith the following year, she wrote to her mother, "Imagine saying, 'Oh, yes, I studied writing under Auden!'. . . Honestly, Mum, I could just cry with happiness. I love this place so, and there is so much to do creatively . . . The world is splitting open at my feet like a ripe, juicy watermelon. If only I can work, work, work to justify all my opportunities."

After her final exams in 1952, Sylvia took a summer job at The Belmont, a hotel on Cape Cod. Dick Norton was pleased since he would be working again on the Cape, in Brewster. At first Sylvia disliked waiting on tables; she was relegated to the "side hall" reserved for the hotel staff, tantamount to exile. But her disappointment, together with her usual qualms about not being able to excel, was dispelled when a telegram arrived from her mother announcing that "Sunday at the Mintons' " had won one of two first prizes in the *Mademoiselle* competition and would be published in August. Overjoyed, Sylvia wrapped her arms around the neck of the astonished head waitress and then wrote home in a splatter of exclamation marks. Even more than the fame, the money was welcome. Now she need not worry about getting extra tips. "The first thing I thought of was: Mother can keep her intersession money and buy some pretty clothes and a special trip or something! At least I get a winter coat and extra special suit out of the Mintons. I *think* the prize is $500!!!!!!!!!"

Ironically, the chief character in "Sunday at the Mintons' " was intended to be a caricature, a stuffy, dictatorial Dick Norton in middle age; that was Sylvia's way of "fixing" Dick without having to break with him. Her journal registers the names of six or seven "cute" boys with whom she flirted that summer, all the time worrying because she could not quite "pal" up with the other waitresses, most of them "really wise, drinking flirts," as she prudishly told her mother.

In truth, summer hotels for jobbing teenagers were hardly more than temporary mating bureaus, and Sylvia soon wearied of the life. In mid-July she came down with feverish sinusitis. Taking advantage of a lift from her old friend Phil McCurdy, who when not at Princeton still lived in Wellesley, Sylvia returned home to recuperate and decided not to go back. Twenty-four hours later she was inundated with friendly letters from The Belmont and began to regret her decision. A letter arrived from Harold Strauss, the editor-in-chief at Alfred A. Knopf; he had read advance proofs of "Sunday at the Mintons' " with admiration and would be glad to consider any novel Sylvia might write in the future. Such encouragement spurred her to work again. Why had she run away from what she now saw as "the magnetic whirlpool of slender, lovely young devils" at the hotel? She began again to puzzle over the mystery of her character. It was somehow life and vitality against deadly depression all the time with her. Living was like running madly about in a squirrel cage of activity, "working, living, dancing, dreaming, talking, kissing, singing, laughing, learning." Yet she could not live without an externally imposed routine. The responsibility of using her "hot amorphic leisure" to write drained her energy and plunged her into melancholy. The analysis she wrote of her dilemma was more profound than she realized:

> It is like lifting a bell jar off a securely clockworklike functioning community, and seeing all the little busy people stop, gasp, blow up, and float in the inrush (or rather outrush) of the rarified scheduled atmosphere — poor little frightened people, flailing impotent arms in the aimless air. That's what it feels like: getting shed of a routine. Even though one has rebelled terribly against it, even then, one feels uncomfortable when jounced out of the repetitive rut. And so with me. What to do? Where to turn? What ties, what roots? As I hang suspended in the strange thin air of back-home?

Finally, in that summer of 1952, Sylvia took another job on Cape Cod, helping with the children of a Christian Scientist family vacationing in Chatham. Mrs. Cantor, who treated Sylvia like a daughter, was impressed by her writing and one day drove her out to visit the eccentric manager of the local bookmobile, a writer of popular fiction. Sylvia was enthralled with Val Gendron and her bohemian way of life. The " 'shack,' red half-house" with dirty washing in a basin and dirty dishes on the floor went into Sylvia's increasingly voluminous notebook, together with Val's cats, cigarettes, wallpaper, coffee, and conversation.

And what did Val Gendron have to teach Sylvia Plath? Chiefly the discipline of putting down on paper a thousand words every day.

Writing had little to do with inspiration, Val told her, but everything with hard work. She showed Sylvia her latest Western novel and a sheaf of impressive letters from other writers, agents, and publishers. After Val had driven her back to the Cantors' in her "old jalopy," Sylvia glimpsed yet another exciting future flickering before her.

Back in Wellesley, before setting off for her junior year at Smith, Sylvia considered the various courses her life might take. Like Esther Greenwood in *The Bell Jar,* she imagined her future branching out before her like a mythical fig tree: "From the tip of every branch, like a fat purple fig, a wonderful future beckoned and winked. One fig was a husband and a happy home and children, and another fig was a famous poet and another fig was a brilliant professor . . .." Sylvia's high school English teacher, Mr. Crockett, had suggested that she apply for scholarships to study abroad after graduating from Smith. That was an especially alluring fig. Then there were glamorous figs associated with houses like the Buckleys' in Sharon, or with men with romantic foreign names like Constantine and Attila. Finally there was the fig of professional bohemian, represented by Val Gendron in her shack. What was Sylvia going to make of her life, her one life, so short and precious? Like Esther, Sylvia could see herself sitting in the crotch of this fig tree, starving because she could not make up her mind which fig to choose.

As she listened to her thudding heartbeat, "I am, I am, I am," she feared, too, that all the figs were illusions. The exaggerating imagination that presented her with so many conflicting roles caused her to suspect herself. An entry in her journal for the previous summer reveals an overwhelming greed, an obsession for escape from herself by "eating" other people. Walking through the streets of Wellesley one evening, she observes the lighted windows of the houses. In each, she thinks with horror, there is a life. If only she could crawl into those lives instead of being condemned to her own. Returning home to her I-ness was hardly a consolation: "So I press thumb-down-on-latch and step up into the light, into tomorrow, into people I know by sight, by sound, by touch, by smell, by flavor . . . and the door closes behind me, and I turn the lock with a click that shuts out the disturbing wasteland of sleeping streets and fenceless acres of night."

The intensity of this egoistic fantasizing could only be that of a certain kind of poet. Her gift was for romantic self-aggrandizing, and although she resisted it in much of her prose and even in some of her poetry, the Gothic nature of her genius had to find its way out. Like Coleridge's Ancient Mariner, Sylvia was trapped in her story, condemned to telling it again and again to whoever would listen. She was indeed cursed. Desperately she struggled in the bonds of selfhood; through her writing there must be a way out! Yet every time she put pen to paper she began to analyze her strange predicament, sealing herself more securely into her frustration. Perhaps only in death, she thought, was there a way out. The idea of suicide formed in her mind like the ultimate and irrevocable fig, a green promise hanging at the tip of the highest branch of the tree.

► 3 ◄

THE CITY OF
SPARE PARTS

1952-1955

The storerooms are full of hearts.
This is the city of spare parts.
— "The Stones," 1959

WHEN SYLVIA WENT BACK to Smith for her junior year in the autumn of 1952, it was to Lawrence House, a cooperative residence for scholarship girls where everyone had to work for good marks to stay in college. There were a few nonconformists — of whom Sylvia disapproved — but no one would snub her for spending "date time" studying (although by this time Sylvia was spending most of her date time dating). Like other Lawrence House girls, she had duties at the house: waiting on tables at lunchtime and taking on various supervisory responsibilities — nothing arduous enough to interfere with her academic work. Her greatest regret was the enforced separation from Marcia Brown, whose divorced, sometimes difficult mother had moved to Northampton and persuaded her daughter to live with her off-campus.

Having elected to do honors English, Sylvia was taking fewer courses in greater depth, preparing to write a senior thesis. There was, however, the requirement that a science course had to be passed before an honors student could devote all her time to her "major." Sylvia enrolled in physics with misgiving, also electing a demanding unit in medieval literature with "dear stern lovable brilliant Mr. Patch," creative writing with an adored Robert Gorham Davis, and an art course that she almost immediately dropped to reduce her workload.

At first all went well. She found time to concentrate on writing and Chaucer as well as taking part in time-consuming Smith activities such as Press Board and the *Smith Review*. Early in October *Seventeen* awarded Sylvia second prize in a short story contest for "Initiation"— $200 with publication promised for January. But the physical science course worried her, and as winter closed in Sylvia began to feel that her work would be too much for her. Old doubts about her "worth" revived, along with an increasing terror of failure.

Another discouragement was Eisenhower's victory over Democrat Adlai Stevenson in the presidential election. Sylvia, politically a passionate Democrat, once more began to agonize over the world's probable doom. Anxieties paralyzed her even as she lashed herself up the ladder of success. *Mademoiselle* was choosing its annual team of college girls to edit the August 1953 issue of the magazine. Competition was going to be fierce, so Sylvia, determined to win a place on the board, took time off from physics and Chaucer for the *Mademoiselle* assignments and then lost hours of sleep catching up. Her lack of scientific aptitude greatly disturbed her. Warren was an able scientist, as was Dick Norton. Dick especially had urged her to acquaint herself with the impersonal laws of the universe, in which she said she believed "as in a god of sorts."

Then Dick himself was a source of worry. In his second year of medical school he was found to be suffering from tuberculosis and sent, at Harvard's expense, to a famous sanatorium at Saranac Lake in the Adirondack Mountains. Sylvia, left behind to commiserate, was increasingly doubtful about her feelings for him. With the dreadful physics course still threatening to pull down her A average, her journal for November 1952 hit a new low:

God, if ever I have come close to wanting to commit suicide, it is now, with the groggy sleepless blood dragging through my veins, and the air thick and gray with rain and the damn little men across the street pounding on the roof with picks and axes and chisels, and the acrid hellish stench of tar. I fell into bed again this morning, begging for sleep, withdrawing into the dark, warm, fetid escape from action, from responsibility . . . I thought of the myriad of physical duties I had to perform: write Prouty; *Life* back to Cal; write-up Press Board; call Marcia. The list mounted obstacle after fiendish obstacle; they jarred, they leered, they fell apart in chaos . . .

Sylvia's depression, precipitating extreme self-deprecation, was made worse by her habit of rushing her mood — whatever it was — immediately into words, pinning it down forever. Only a born writer would have inserted those "damn little men across the street pounding on the roof with picks and axes and chisels." The needling particulars helped the hellishness to be real.

Sylvia's journals record a memory of wishing, at the age of eight, that she could write what it felt like to be eight; by the time she knew how to write, she thought, she would no longer remember how it felt. Now writing about "how it felt" became an obsession with her. She tended to put her miseries into her diary while she was suffering. Only when she looked back could suffering be transmuted in cynicism, as would happen in *The Bell Jar*. In her diary that autumn of 1952, Sylvia lectured herself continually, urging rationalization. But rationalization rarely helped. She needed human support and a physical catharsis of tearful self-abasement. Shortly before Thanksgiving, loving support was immediately forthcoming from her ex-roommate Marcia Brown. And then, during the Thanksgiving break, Sylvia met a man at the Nortons' house in Wellesley to whom she was instantly attracted.

Myron Lotz, Perry Norton's roommate at Yale, was at first sight a Smith girl's dream — over six feet tall, solid, handsome, athletic, superior in all those fields in which Sylvia liked to feel, in a womanly way, inferior. For although she was exceedingly jealous of versatile women, she was drawn to powerful, all-American men. Back at Smith she sat down and whooshed off a letter to Warren at Exeter:

> Guess what [Myron] does in the summer! He pitches for the Detroit Tigers,* and last summer he earned $10,000! Isn't that amazing? Not only that, he comes from Austro-Hungarian immigrant parents who work in the steel mines and can hardly speak English. And he is going through Yale in three years, starting Yale Med School next fall. Did you ever hear of such a phenomenal character?

Before Sylvia returned home for Christmas, she had "ricocheted" up again to self-approval, planning weekends with Myron Lotz at Yale while Dick languished at Saranac. But after Christmas, when the Nortons assumed she would want to visit Dick, she felt a guilty reluctance that threatened her once more with a severe slump. Dick had been thinking sentimentally of Sylvia during his long enforced

---

*It seems Myron Lotz played semiprofessional baseball only.

rest. Sylvia had been thinking of Dick, too, deciding she preferred Myron Lotz.

One version of the trip to Ray Brook (at Saranac Lake) is told in her short story "In the Mountains," another version in *The Bell Jar*. In reality, on meeting Dick in the "liver-colored" reception rooms of the sanatorium, Sylvia like Esther Greenwood recoiled in disgust; his athlete's muscles had gone to fat and his glamour was obliterated. Like Esther, too, her revulsion led to profound feelings of guilt, worse because Dick, with a sort of patronizing humility, was treating her as a prospective wife.

On the ski slopes the next day, Sylvia hurled herself straight down Mount Pisgah on her borrowed skis and broke her leg, just as Esther does in the novel. Whenever life began to go wrong for Sylvia, as with her relationship with Dick that winter, she felt compelled to purge herself as from a sin. The purging usually took the form of a serious risk. Once the risk was taken and overcome, balance was restored and guilt banished, its occasion no longer of importance.* In *The Bell Jar,* Esther's state of mind as she hesitates on the verge of the ski run, the thought of suicide forming in her mind "coolly as a tree or a flower," was in fact Sylvia's:

> I aimed straight down.
>
> A keen wind that had been hiding itself struck me full in the mouth and raked the hair back horizontal on my head. I was descending, but the white sun rose no higher. It hung over the suspended waves of the hills, an insentient pivot without which the world would not exist.
>
> A small, answering point in my own body flew towards it. I felt my lungs inflate with the inrush of scenery — air, mountains, trees, people. I thought, "This is what it is to be happy."
>
> I plummeted down past the zigzaggers, the students, the experts, through year after year of doubleness and smiles and compromises, into my own past.
>
> People and trees receded on either hand like the dark sides of a tunnel as I hurtled on to the still, bright point at the end of it, the pebble at the bottom of the well, the white sweet baby cradled in its mother's belly.

---

*Nancy Hunter Steiner also noticed this pattern and suggested that Sylvia "was driven, periodically, to stage a symbolic salvation with herself as the suffering victim . . . almost as though only by being snatched from the brink of death could she confirm her worth."

In *The Bell Jar* Esther Greenwood declares that she broke her leg deliberately to pay herself back for being a heel, that is, for deserting Buddy Willard when he was ill and needed her. But Sylvia Plath, who at this moment takes over from Esther, perceived that she also broke her leg to get back, through the tunnel of her birth and past, to the sweet pure baby in her mother's womb. Getting back to that baby was apparently the only escape from responsibility Sylvia could envisage. And the nature of that responsibility? To pay her mother back (by marrying someone like Dick) for the sacrifices she had made on her daughter's behalf.

Sylvia remained in Ray Brook as the guest of Dick's doctor and his wife (Dr. Lynn was so smitten that he eagerly foisted upon her the enormous manuscript of his surrealistic novel) until her leg healed enough to permit her to return home. She sent her mother a witty telegram, as if to celebrate her deliverance from Dick and at the same time from whatever apologies might be called for in Wellesley: "BREAK BREAK BREAK ON THE COLD WHITE SLOPES OH KNEE ARRIVING FRAMINGHAM TUESDAY NIGHT 7:41. BRINGING FABULOUS FRACTURED FIBULA NO PAIN JUST TRICKY TO MANIPULATE WHILE CHARLESTONING . . ." It was signed, "YOUR FRACTIOUS FUGACIOUS FRANGIBLE SIVVY."

By January 9 she was writing to her mother from Smith that the break had been a positive boon:

> All in all, my leg has made me realize what a fool I was to think I had insurmountable troubles. It is a sort of concrete symbol of limitations that are primarily mental, or were. And now that I see how foolish I was in succumbing to what I thought were mental obstacles, I am determined to be as cheerful and constructive about my mental difficulties as I am going to be about this physical one.

By February she was less optimistic. The leg took a long time to mend, and when the cast came off on the nineteenth and she saw "the hairy yellow withered corpse" underneath it, the emotional shock was considerable.

It was while her leg was in plaster that Gordon Lameyer, a senior English major at Amherst who had heard of Sylvia from his mother in Wellesley, made a date to meet her in a Northampton coffee shop. He was "somewhat taken aback when a large blondish girl hobbled down the stairs on crutches . . . full of the enthusiasms of a college girl on her first date." She talked, a little too intensely, even naively, Gordon thought, of her "mad" passion for Dylan Thomas, her admiration for Auden — then at Smith — and her prospective thesis on James Joyce.

To her mother Sylvia wrote gleefully, "Gordon is utterly lush . . . I have a sneaking suspicion that the prognostication for the coming spring will be more than favorable!" Gordon, like Myron, was an ideal man, and although Dick continued to pelt her with letters full of *Buddenbrooks* and *The Magic Mountain* (his tastes were now earnestly literary), Sylvia was more and more disenchanted.

Meanwhile her first-semester grades occasioned mercurial high spirits: an A in science, A– in writing, and from Mr. Patch the only A in the medieval literature class. For the first time in her college career Sylvia's academic record was unblemished by a single B. In the second term, having proved herself in physics, she successfully petitioned merely to sit in on chemistry while enrolling for credit in a course on Milton. Otherwise she was free to concentrate "heart and soul" on creative writing and modern poetry with Elizabeth Drew (Auden occasionally an inspiring, awesome visitor). She was studying nothing in which she could not easily excel, and high grades throughout the term brought accustomed triumphs at the end: election as a junior to Phi Beta Kappa and the next year's editorship of the *Smith Review*. Outside college she rejoiced in three poems accepted by *Harper's*, two praised (but not taken) by one of her "unclimbed Annapurnas," *The New Yorker*, and a coveted *Mademoiselle* guest editorship.

All spring, despite her lame leg, she was taken up with visits to Yale and Myron Lotz. In May, Gordon Lameyer encountered her again after one of Auden's poetry readings. Since they both lived in Wellesley, he suggested they meet after exams. After his finals Gordon would be leaving for two years in the Navy, but he hoped to see a good deal of Sylvia before then. Jubilantly Sylvia told him of her success with *Mademoiselle*, which meant working in New York City all June. Could they meet during the two weeks early in July when they would both be home?

In a memoir Lameyer quotes Sylvia as having called him "the major man in [her] life" from the spring of 1953 until April 1956. His long, literary letters to her, together with the passionate correspondence of several other young men (who also thought they were "major" in her life), all in the Lilly Library collection, indicate that throughout her last, broken years as a Smith student, Sylvia was adept at playing different roles with at least two "major men" at the same time. To all her male admirers she wrote voluminously, warmly inviting their trust. Men who were attracted by her energy and dazzled by her brilliance usually fell in love. Yet eventually they recoiled from her intensity or from her inconsistency — or else they were summarily dismissed.

In fact, in the spring of 1953 Sylvia was chiefly preoccupied with Myron (Mike) Lotz. She indulged in invidious comparisons: in a letter home she wrote, "Dick is barely 6 feet & weighs 190, Myron is 6′4″ and weighs 185," and in her journal she dismissed another friend by saying that he "revolts me physically; I would vomit if he tried to kiss me" but that Myron "combines my favorite elements of Perry with a sort of clever observant worldliness . . . Do I want to crawl into the gigantic paternal embrace of a mental colossus? A little, maybe. I'm not sure."

Sylvia continued, nevertheless, to write to Dick at Saranac, responding to his worried letters right through to the time of her breakdown in August. She also kept up her correspondence with Eddie Cohen, who like Dick Norton expressed concern at the frantic tone of "intense unrest" in her letters. She seems consistently to have needed two kinds of men: a good, safe, homebred boy like the athletic, but not imperceptive, Dick (or, during the ensuing year, Gordon Lameyer) to please her mother, and at the same time a radically original, nonconformist soul mate with whom to fulfill, whether in correspondence or in the flesh, her full sensuous and intellectual nature.

Until she met Richard Sassoon in April 1954, Eddie Cohen seems to have represented a rebarbative alter ego to set up in opposition to Dick, Gordon, Myron, and her genteel Wellesley-Smith façade. One letter to Cohen, written in May 1951, six weeks after she had turned him from her mother's door, tried to make him out as "lovely, immoral and radical." He responded, ironically admitting the "lovely" but defining his "immorality" as that of an old-fashioned liberal (live-and-let-live) and defending his radicalism as a belief that existing states of affairs were not always for the best. In many ways Cohen was the most mature, most balanced, most intelligent of her correspondents, the quickest to recognize her habits of self-deceit and the frankest in expressing his disapproval.

◄　◄　◄

As the second semester of Sylvia's junior year drew to a close, she was too pressed getting papers written between *Mademoiselle* assignments, taking exams, paying weekend visits to Myron at Yale, and rejoicing in Warren's full scholarship to Harvard to realize how tired she was. After only two days at home in Wellesley — which were spent polishing up postal interviews with five young (male) poets on American campuses for the magazine — she reached the "plushy air-conditioned offices" of *Mademoiselle* in the company of nineteen other aspiring editors and fashion designers. Lodged on Lexington Avenue in the Barbizon Hotel for Women (the Amazon of *The Bell Jar*), she confidently expected to have the time of her life.

With the exception of a significant entry on the electrocution of the Rosenbergs — an event that occurred while she was in New York, pointedly situated in the very first sentence of *The Bell Jar* — Sylvia seems to have kept no journals for June 1953, but the substance of the novel's early chapters is confirmed by her correspondence. An unpublished letter of June 13 to her mother shows that the facts very roughly resembled the fiction:

> Thursday night, on the way to the New York City Center ballet, our taxi was stopped in traffic, and a very genial tall man came over, leaned in, paid the fare, and said to the four of us: "Too many pretty girls for one taxi. I'm Art Ford, the disc jockey. Come in for a talk." So we got out, went into a café, were treated by Art Ford (written up by *Mlle* as one of the bright young men in New York) to Greenwich Village after his night show got over at 3 a.m.

Either Sylvia expurgated the real story in this letter or the comparable scene with Lenny and Doreen in the novel is a brilliant fabrication. What both the letters and *The Bell Jar* undoubtedly reflect is Sylvia's huge mood swings. Feverishly adrift in a bewildering and unnatural world, she was clocking up experiences so quickly she had neither time nor energy to write them down — for Sylvia, a dangerous state of affairs. Several breathless accounts of her assignments went off to Aurelia, describing her guest editorship under Managing Editor Cyrilly Abels (Jay Cee in *The Bell Jar*) as "valuable" and "all-inclusive," rejoicing in meetings with famous "intellectually stimulating" writers such as Vance Bourjaily and Santha Rama Rau. Eventually she chose Elizabeth Bowen for the subject of an interview, and got on very well with her. To Warren, just graduated from Exeter, she wrote frankly of her state of shock:

> I have learned an amazing lot here: the world has split open before my gaping eyes and spilt out its guts like a cracked watermelon [a favorite simile with Sylvia]. I think it will not be until I have meditated in peace upon the multitude of things I have learned and seen that I will begin to comprehend what has happened to me this last month . . . I've realized that the last weeks of school were one hectic

running for busses and trains and exams and appointments, and the shift to NYC has been so rapid that I can't think logically about who I am or where I am going. I have been very ecstatic, horribly depressed, shocked, elated, enlightened, and enervated — all of which goes to make up living very hard and newly.

The letter went on to recount some of her experiences, many of them familiar to readers of *The Bell Jar*. In the space of six days, she had toured advertising agencies, seen television kitchens, listened to speeches, been poisoned by crabmeat salad, spent an evening in Greenwich Village with a simultaneous interpreter (Mrs. Willard's acquaintance, Constantin, in the novel), fought with a "wealthy, unscrupulous" Peruvian at a tennis club dance (in *The Bell Jar* he all but rapes her), and got lost on the subway, where, with fascinated horror, she had observed "deformed men with short arms that curled like pink, boneless snakes around a begging cup."

New York, in short, caught Sylvia off her guard and shook her confidence in her Smith façade. When asked much later about the impression Sylvia had made in the *Mademoiselle* office that summer, Cyrilly Abels, who admired Sylvia, is said to have remarked that she had never met anyone less spontaneous, less capable of departing from a rigid standard of polite behavior. Sylvia's version of an encounter with Mrs. Abels, hardly fictionalized in her novel, has Esther Greenwood hearing "terrible things" from Jay Cee and barely standing up to the blows.

The truth was that Sylvia did not like guest editing for *Mademoiselle*. The job looked glamorous from the outside, but in fact it was servile and demeaning. Her puritan fastidiousness was as much repelled as attracted by the Doreens and Lennys and even by the self-confident Jay Cee, who was all the more threatening because she represented authority — and so stood in lieu of a mother — offering a magnificent career that Sylvia/Esther rudely, helplessly, seemed to be rejecting. The entire New York experience was like her initiation to that high school sorority, but a hundred times worse. Sylvia would never have admitted to turning her back on these arbiters of fashion, but neither did she want to eat cake with them and cat about the Saturday night date. Eating poison crabmeat at the *Mademoiselle* banquet, and swallowing with it the whole corrupt cake of the fashion world, made her literally and psychologically sick.

Despite her revulsion, however, Sylvia emerged triumphant, and when the college '53 issue came out in August, there she was at the top of the human star that filled a full page of the magazine. Twenty all-American students, identically dressed in white shirts and tartan skirts, joined hands to be photographed at the apex of their college careers. Their identical smirks approved a felicitous present and happily-ever-after future. The final word was contributed by Guest Managing Editor Sylvia Plath, Smith '54:

> We're stargazers this season, bewitched by an atmosphere of evening blue. Foremost in the fashion constellation we spot *Mlle*'s own tartan, the astronomic versatility of sweaters, and men, men, men — we've even taken the shirts off their backs! Focusing our telescope on college news around the globe, we debate and deliberate. Issues illuminated: academic freedom, the sorority controversy, our much labeled (and libeled) generation. From our favorite fields, stars of the first magnitude shed a bright influence on our plans for jobs and futures. Although horoscopes for our ultimate orbits aren't yet in, we Guest Eds. are counting on a favorable forecast with the send-off from *Mlle*, the star of the campus.

◄　◄　◄

While Sylvia was experiencing and rejecting "life" in New York City, Aurelia Plath sat at home in Wellesley typing up her daughter's stories to submit to Frank O'Connor's summer writing class at Harvard, on which Sylvia had set her heart. When she returned, exhausted and unsmiling, to Wellesley, her mother had bad news to break. Although Sylvia's prizewinning "Sunday at the Mintons' " was one of the stories submitted, she had not been accepted. As they drove from the station Mrs. Plath watched Sylvia's face pale in the rearview mirror. Now all her prizes, her superb grades, her confidence as a winner dissolved in minutes. At Smith that spring the great W. H. Auden had dismissed her poems as too glib. She was ready to believe she was not, after all, appointed by fate to be a writer. Disillusioned with one dream world, she had come home to be vanquished by another.

Back at 26 Elmwood Road, Sylvia tried to take herself in hand. Should she spend her small amount of scholarship money on some other course — probably of dubious value — at Harvard, or should she sensibly stay at home, help her mother, learn shorthand, and read James Joyce in preparation for her honors thesis? "I must make choices clearly, honestly, without getting sick so I can't eat, which is in itself a defense mechanism that wants to revert to childhood tactics to get sympathy and avoid responsibility," she wrote, rationalizing in her journal while sinking into a wholly irrational morass.

The story of Sylvia's first suicide attempt and the nightmarish events that led up to it is told in the thinly disguised autobiographical passages of *The Bell Jar*. Her mother's shorter, kinder version of these painful weeks can be found in *Letters Home*. After Sylvia returned from New York Mrs. Plath became aware of "a great change in her; all her usual *joie de vivre* was absent." She ought to have rested, but, as in *The Bell Jar*, her attempts to read or sunbathe ended in self-accusatory numbness. Ten, twenty, thirty nights almost without sleep, and Sylvia began to believe she was going mad. She started to write fiction in that dreamlike state of disconnectedness experienced by people deprived of oxygen to the brain. At first her new floating, regressing condition filled her with tenderness, but as day passed into day without anything having been accomplished, she began in panic to watch words twist awry on the page. If writing and reading were impossible, she would learn shorthand; at least she could fall back on that marketable skill when she flunked out of college. A few lessons with her mother were enough to convince her she never could master "those senseless curlicues," and having failed again, she began to channel self-hatred into an exaggerated resentment of her mother.

According to Mrs. Plath, one morning Sylvia appeared with purplish gashes on her legs. On being questioned she replied, " 'I just wanted to see if I had the guts!' Then she . . . cried passionately, 'Oh, Mother, the world is so rotten! I want to die! *Let's die together!*' " Mrs. Plath thought it was time to call the family doctor, Dr. Francesca Racioppi. Concerned, she prescribed sleeping pills and recommended a psychiatrist — unfortunately one to whose vain, dandified manner Sylvia took an instant dislike. The nightmare of her breakdown, years later to be recounted with perfect recall in *The Bell Jar*, had begun.

Outwardly, incredible as it seems, Sylvia was evidently going through the motions of sociability. Gordon Lameyer insists he saw her all day every day for two weeks until he left Wellesley for his naval officers' training course in mid-July. They listened to records: Beethoven and Brahms symphonies, Dylan Thomas reciting his poems, James Joyce reading from *Finnegans Wake*, Edith Sitwell's *Façade*. Sylvia told Gordon she was preparing to write her honors thesis on *Ulysses*, and according to Lameyer's memoir, they read some Joyce aloud. Even in August, when he twice met her on weekends, he was unaware that anything was amiss or even that Sylvia was by that time undergoing electroconvulsive therapy (ECT) as an outpatient of a doctor who in *The Bell Jar* is maliciously named "Dr. Gordon."

In fact, ECT may have substantially contributed to her cool, logically-arrived-at decision to do away with herself. As she later explained it in a letter, never sent, to Eddie Cohen:

Pretty soon, the only doubt in my mind was the precise time and method of committing suicide. The only alternative I could see was an eternity of hell for the rest of my life in a mental hospital, and I was going to make use of my last ounce of free choice and choose a quick clean ending. I figured that in the long run it would be more merciful and inexpensive to my family; instead of an indefinite and expensive incarceration of a favorite daughter in the cell of a State San, instead of the misery and disillusion of sixty odd years of mental vacuum, of physical squalor, I would spare them all by ending everything at the height of my so-called career while there were still illusions left among my profs, still poems to be published in *Harper's*, still a memory at least that would be worthwhile.

Perhaps Sylvia kept the letter as a record of how it felt to live in "the snake pit."* The almost-boasting tone of the writing foreshadows *The Bell Jar*. To Cohen she explained that she had tried drowning, swimming out, as Esther does in the novel, with her heart beating "I am I am" while her body refused to stay underwater. Between writing letters abounding in Joycean puns to Gordon ("God on la mer. Or filial reward for the mother: e.g. Guerdon la mère"), the desperate girl was buying paperbacks on abnormal psychology, talking wildly to sailors on the Boston Common, trying to find a way to kill herself so her family, as she had told Eddie Cohen, would be spared the expense of her lifelong hospitalization.

In her unsent letter Sylvia described what she did. On August 24, a stiflingly hot day, she broke into her mother's household safe, where Mrs. Plath, tacitly admitting the gravity of the situation, kept Sylvia's sleeping pills. Aurelia was watching a film of Queen Elizabeth's coronation at a friend's house, and the Schobers were relaxing in the garden. With the pills and a glass of water, Sylvia crept down to the basement; she knew there was a narrow crawlspace under the porch. Stealthily she removed the firewood stacked at the mouth of the hole, hoisted herself into the womblike cave with the bottle and the water, carefully replaced the firewood, and proceeded to swallow as many pills as she could. *The Bell Jar* describes these measures so lovingly that the reader is all but persuaded of the sweetness of the act:

> Cobwebs touched my face with the softness of moths. Wrapping my black coat round me like my own sweet shadow, I unscrewed the bottle of pills and started taking them swiftly, between gulps of water, one by one by one.

---

*The Snake Pit by Mary Jane Ward was a best-selling novel of the era. Sylvia would later consider it a model for early work on *The Bell Jar*.

At first nothing happened, but as I approached the bottom of the bottle, red and blue lights began to flash before my eyes. The bottle slid from my fingers and I lay down.

The silence drew off, baring the pebbles and shells and all the tatty wreckage of my life. Then, at the rim of vision, it gathered itself, and in one sweeping tide, rushed me to sleep.

Not to be defeated, Sylvia had "drowned" after all.

Aurelia Plath tells the story without embellishment. Watching a film of the coronation — as she must have remembered much later, when Sylvia wrote to her from England of the Queen's visit to Cambridge — she was seized suddenly by horrible premonitions. The moment the film was over, she begged to be driven home; there she found a note propped against a bowl of flowers in the dining room: "Have gone for a long walk. Will be home tomorrow." Aurelia informed the police. Warren, then eighteen, helped to comb the woods around Wellesley with a number of anxious neighbors. Headlines appeared in the Boston papers: "BEAUTIFUL SMITH GIRL MISSING AT WELLESLEY"; "TOP RANKING STUDENT AT SMITH MISSING FROM WELLESLEY HOME." A report in the *Boston Herald* carried a photograph of Sylvia looking like a successful tennis champion and an article describing her as "nervous" and under a doctor's care. Further reports quoted Mrs. Plath's attempted explanation of her daughter's obsession with attaining unbelievable standards in her work and fulfilling what she believed to be her responsibility to her sponsors. More headlines and a family photo appeared when the broken safe, minus the bottle of sleeping pills, was discovered. The drama went on for two days.

Finally, while the family was at lunch (the atmosphere can be imagined), they heard a groan. Warren rushed down to the basement to find his sister struggling to raise herself in the crawlspace. She had taken too many pills and in her coma had vomited them up. Within minutes the ambulance arrived and rushed Sylvia to the Newton-Wellesley Hospital, where she regained consciousness. Mrs. Plath recollected her first words: " 'Oh, no!' When I took her hand and told her . . . how we loved her, she said weakly, 'It was *my* last act of love.' . . . [Then she said,] 'Oh, if I only could be a freshman again. I so wanted to be a *Smith* woman.' " Later that summer, exercising her talent for rewriting life to suit the audience, she told Gordon Lameyer that her first words had been, "Do we still own the house?"

Except for an ugly abrasion under her right eye, Sylvia was physically uninjured. Two weeks later she was transferred to the psychiatric wing of Massachusetts General Hospital, where her cheek healed but her will to live failed to reassert itself. On the contrary, the conditions of her hospitalization brought out all her latent paranoia, and she refused absolutely to cooperate with the staff or reconcile herself to her mother's visits. Letters poured in from Smith and elsewhere. "You are by far the best student in English in the college," wrote Elizabeth Drew, "and you don't have to strain to be." Her adviser, Evelyn Page, affirmed, "We are very proud of you, with the kind of pride that makes no demands on you." Gordon Lameyer sent fond, concerned letters from his Officers' Candidate School in Rhode Island.

When news of Sylvia's breakdown and attempted suicide reached Mrs. Prouty, on holiday in Maine, she telegraphed that she wanted to help, soon afterward writing with an offer to pay for treatment at McLean Hospital in Belmont. Mrs. Prouty herself had suffered a nervous breakdown many years before, and it had taught her, she said, to value life. She would see to it that Sylvia recovered in the best mental institution in the country.

McLean, indeed, is famous in Massachusetts as that part of Massachusetts General Hospital to which Robert Lowell would retreat during his manic periods and where Anne Sexton would periodically be a patient. Sylvia was there nearly four months before she was "cured." Her psychiatrist, Dr. Ruth Beuscher, was a young woman with whom Sylvia established a trustful relationship that lasted the rest of her life. Under Dr. Beuscher's care she submitted to a second, less horrific course of electroconvulsive therapy and was given insulin treatment, which fattened her but seemingly did no lasting harm.

The kind of psychiatric treatment Sylvia Plath received in the 1950s now seems almost as barbaric as the rituals of eighteenth-century Bedlam. Certainly the experience of shock treatment during her prolonged summer breakdown and again during the purgatory of her "cure" affected Sylvia more deeply than anyone understood at the time. It may be that she never really recovered from it, that it changed her personality permanently, stripping her of a psychological "skin" she could ill afford to lose. Attributable to her ECT is the unseen menace that haunts nearly everything she wrote, her conviction that the world, however benign in appearance, conceals dangerous animosity, directed particularly toward herself. Sylvia's psychotherapy also certainly opened up the dimensions of her Freudian psychodrama, revealing the figure of her lost, "drowned" father, master of the bees, whose death she could neither forgive nor allow herself to forget; psychotherapy also intensified the presence of her much-loved yet ultimately resented mother, whose double she had to be, for reasons of guilt or ego weakness, and to whom she was tied by a psychic umbilicus too nourishing to sever.

Outside of the convoluted variations of her private myth, Sylvia scarcely knew what to write about. The outer world was there, of course; she saw it, and badly wanted to write about it. Yet both before and after her suicide attempt it seems it remained unattainable, on the other side of a transparent but nevertheless distorted wall of glass, the bell jar she herself identified and described as the imprisoning house of her madness. When the bell jar lifted, she could be optimistic and happy, rejoicing in the radiance of the sun she loved. But the least misfortune was likely to bring it back: a rejection slip, a bad review, an imagined slight from a rival, competition from other women for her "man" or her deserved fame. And once the bell jar had closed down, escape seemed impossible, however valiantly she battled to achieve freedom of mind and imagination. Her poetic power developed as her will, her intellect, her ingenuity, her great gifts wrestled with the enigma of her plight, defining and refining it, always within the same constricting arena. When her late poems finally emerged, they were winged with furious resentment and honed like fine steel. At their strongest, they should have shattered the bell jar forever, as she must have hoped. That they did not is one of the most disturbing circumstances of Sylvia Plath's story.

Sylvia remained at McLean at Mrs. Prouty's expense and under the supervision of an eminent psychoanalyst, Dr. Erich Lindemann, from mid-October until early February, with a private room and every advantage that one of the best mental hospitals in the country could confer. She had plenty of visitors. Mrs. Prouty came by every week or so, bemoaning the hospital's lack of a disciplined framework; she felt that Sylvia was making little progress without it. Among the Wellesley faithful was her former English teacher Wilbury Crockett. Mrs. Cantor, Sylvia's affectionate employer of the previous summer, drove Mrs. Plath to visit Sylvia every Saturday. A part of Sylvia sturdily hated all these visits. The only sympathetic character in *The Bell Jar* is Dr. Nolan (a straightforward portrait of Dr. Beuscher), who forbids visitors after the scene — which actually occurred — in which Esther Greenwood hurls the roses brought by her mother for her twenty-first birthday into the wastebasket.*

---

*Mrs. Plath later commented on the actual incident: "I brought her her favorite flowers: yellow roses . . . I knew in my bones she would in her depressed, negative state of mind find fault with that; but I also knew that if I ignored the day, she would write, 'Mother saw fit to ignore my 21st birthday' and make much of that. So I did what *my* heart prompted me to do."

Finally, in December, Sylvia had a positive reaction to the insulin treatment and thereafter to a short course of ECT. By the twenty-eighth, writing to Eddie Cohen, she was half looking forward to getting out. The hospital director had written earlier to Mrs. Prouty, offering to meet Sylvia's expenses if she failed to recover by the end of the year. She went home for a day at Christmas but returned to McLean for yet another month. Early in February Warren drove her back to Smith through the winter's worst blizzard. Near Paradise Pond on the Smith campus, the car slid into a 180-degree skid, an event Sylvia construed symbolically as a "death." Her rebirth was now an inevitability.

◄　　◄　　◄

At Lawrence House Sylvia was received as a golden girl. Although she had arranged a reduced work schedule, her third term as a junior sounds challenging: American literature, European intellectual history, and a course in Russian literature with her next-year's thesis supervisor, George Gibian. It seems she also went to lectures on medieval art. Having arranged to graduate with the class of 1955, a year later than her Smith friends Marcia Brown, Enid Epstein, and others, Sylvia was in something of a limbo. Her first need was for a *belle amie* other than Marcia, now preoccupied with graduation and marriage. Her second was for sexual adventure.

For a time, a girl who had transferred to Smith from Wooster College in Ohio, Nancy Hunter, was chosen for the first role. Nancy Hunter Steiner's vivid memoir of Sylvia sets her in the context of her time, showing just how much Sylvia's fragile ego depended on conforming to the Smith pattern. Like others, Nancy was at first astonished at Sylvia's apparent normality. There *were* a few nonconformists at Smith. A small group in Lawrence House, led by "Gloria Brown," rejected the warm-weather campus uniform of Bermuda shorts, button-down collars, and loafers, appearing in bare feet and tattered jeans. Sylvia highly disapproved of these girls and, according to Nancy, waged a sort of running war against them, seeking ways to bring them before Honor Board for infringement of rules; meanwhile, they set themselves to annoy her, raiding her neatly arranged drawers and in other ways trespassing on her sacred territory.

Before the end of term, Nancy says, she and Sylvia were like "Siamese twins, joined at the ego." Nancy shared with another girl the suite of rooms Sylvia would have had as a senior, while Sylvia had a room of her own but still used the small vestibule outside Nancy's room; therefore they saw a lot of each other — Sylvia blond and German, Nancy equally tall but black-haired and Irish. They were drawn together by common interests and a shared taste for adventure. For a few months their friendship flourished.

It was partly through Nancy and partly through Marcia Brown that Sylvia met Richard Sassoon in April 1954. A junior at Yale, Sassoon shared rooms in Calhoun College with a friend of Marcia's, Melvin Woody, and also with a former flame of Nancy's, Dick Wertz. Woody had been drawn to Sylvia when they met in New York while she was guest editing for *Mademoiselle*. His or Dick's glowing account of this extraordinary Smith poetess so intrigued their roommate, Sassoon, that he persuaded Wertz to drive up with him to Northampton in April. The meeting between Sylvia and Richard was an instantaneous success. At midnight, wandering together into the Mount Tom reservation "under a plethora of stars," they climbed the firetower "in hegelian dialectical spirals up into the dark unknown"— thus went Sylvia's first letter to Sassoon, on April 20. To Sylvia, Sassoon wrote even more wildly (sometimes while drinking) in hectic, spiky handwriting, as illegible in English as in French.

They had agreed to disagree, evidently, about the nature of nature, Sylvia holding forth in a romantic, Wordsworthian vein, Sassoon insisting that without art nature was abominable and vile. "I am God. I damn you for my pleasure," Richard began his first letter, switching into French to insert, "Voilà! C'est l'amour. (On va à l'esprit — après)," before commanding, "Amour! Primordial-egotistical. Battle!" Here was a correspondent even more radical and far more "immoral" than Eddie Cohen. Moreover, she found Richard's slender, sinuous body and dark-ringed eyes (like those of an absinthe addict, she unwisely told her mother) compellingly attractive. Sassoon's only drawback was that he matched her in height and weight; she could not wear high heels when out with him.

A distant relative of the English poet Siegfried Sassoon, Richard had been brought up on the Continent, and, although only nineteen, he had European tastes that were far more sophisticated than those of his American peers. At Yale, where he was studying history and philosophy, he affected a tone of cynical decadence and Nietzschean hauteur, pretending to despise alike the intellects of his professors and the select clubs of his fellow undergraduates — though in reality, probably, he was lonely. His exotic tastes in sex, wine, food, and philosophy were exactly calculated to impress Sylvia, still anxiously a virgin. Her romantic entanglements with the baseball-playing Myron and the upright, record-playing Gordon had scarcely prepared her for the lovemaking of a French existentialist, albeit a very young one.

Richard's letters to Sylvia throughout 1954 and 1955 — scores of which are in the Lilly Library — as a whole leave an impression of someone intelligent, proud, and certainly passionate, but at sea in an alien world. He posed when threatened by a relationship he could not always control, but though his early letters consist mostly of bombast and boasting, later ones give evidence of sensitivity and considerable insight. Sylvia was possibly the first woman he really loved. And once his defenses were down, he proved exceptionally vulnerable to her perplexing volatility.

On Sylvia's side, there seems no doubt that she loved being loved by Sassoon, but in 1954 she was quite unready to choose among her many admirers. She still felt under obligation to Gordon, who throughout the spring sent long letters from Europe. By now a full-fledged ensign, he was touring the seas in his ship, rejoicing (or re-Joycing) in his role as an apprentice Ulysses. From Yale, Melvin Woody was also inundating her with love letters that often arrived in the same post as Richard Sassoon's. Nearer at hand was an Amherst scientist, George Gebauer, with whom, in March, she spent a few glorious days in New York. Finally, there was Myron Lotz, now more a friend than a lover, who kept in touch with Sylvia, occasionally driving up to Northampton to see her and talk about his "problems."

And life was no less gratifying on other fronts. Late in April, in time for her mother's birthday, Sylvia learned that Smith had voted her the largest scholarship ever given to an undergraduate, $1,250; it would leave only $300 to pay the next year. In May, *Harper's* published one of her poems, "Doomsday," bringing exclamations of approval from an amazed Richard Sassoon ("It is Art! . . . And I did not know you were capable of t's and k's. Or had such a strong fist. You will crack poor nature yet!") as well as rather puzzled compliments from Mrs. Prouty. With her end-of-term grades all A's and B's, Sylvia was set to graduate from Smith as the top girl of her year.

The only discordant note came from Eddie Cohen, now married to a divorcée and stepfather to a child of nine. After Sylvia had asked for her letters back, Eddie wrote expressing astonishment at her sudden upsurge of joy and energy but bitterly castigating her for her egotism. Perceptively, he — not for the first time — went right to the heart of the matter. "Has it ever occurred to you that you might make carbon copies of your personal letters?" he blazed. "The principle seems to be about the same, and would indicate in either case that you wrote them for the sake of your own ego rather than the illumination of, or contact with, the addressee. What you are asking, in effect, is the act of a woman who gets a great deal of pleasure from looking into a mirror. A very flattering mirror at that."

Sylvia must have made it plain to Eddie that she was no longer interested in him, for his letters of April and May 1954 ring with pained anger. He advises against cherishing too many ideals because "when reality intrudes, as it eventually must, you will merely bounce back to where you so recently returned hence." Suggesting that he himself had reached a "sensible conformity," he goes on to observe (May 6) that "when a person cannot adjust to reality, it is because they are already too fiercely committed to some other reality. They see themselves in some other light. When this cannot be, *they can only retreat into a world of their own making* — which is not the world in which the rest of us live!" (my italics). What, one wonders, did Sylvia write to Cohen to spark off the most penetrating assessment of her psychological blindness that has yet come to light among her papers?

◄   ◄   ◄

At the end of that triumphant semester of 1954, Sylvia brought Nancy Hunter home to Wellesley to meet her mother and visit Mrs. Prouty in her grand colonial house in Brookline. The girls drove out to Sylvia's cherished Nauset Beach on Cape Cod and "double-dated" glamorously in Boston, agreeing, finally, to attend Harvard Summer School together. Mrs. Plath, still ill from the strains of the previous summer, made no secret of her relief. Together with two other Smith girls, Sylvia and Nancy sublet a student apartment at the unfashionable end of Massachusetts Avenue, deciding not to take their studies too seriously. Gordon Lameyer was back but still in the Navy; Sassoon was in Europe; and Nancy's David Furner was in Ohio. They agreed to accept any dates that came their way, as long as dinner or the theater was thrown in. Sylvia, who had peroxided her hair and passed for a dizzy blond, soared into a dangerous high, boasting of a smoldering relationship with a Harvard professor whose wife called her "the blond bitch."

In his memoir Gordon Lameyer lays some of the blame for Sylvia's sexual frenzy that summer on Nancy Hunter. It seems more likely that Sylvia was approaching men with a deliberate plan. When, in May, she had accompanied Richard Sassoon to New York, he had wined and dined her like a mistress; it is not clear whether she was.

Afraid to be found wanting in sexual savoir faire should the great moment arrive in the fall, it would have been characteristic of Sylvia to decide on a practice run in Cambridge. Gordon, of course, would not do; he was far too noble, the kind of man Sylvia admired for his good looks but could not desire. No, she would have to find somebody experienced, to whom she felt no emotional attachment. Nancy, witnessing this great event, would not be shocked; she had, after all, been chosen *belle amie* and double.

At home in the apartment, Nancy and Sylvia agreed to do the cooking, since the two other girls had full-time jobs. Sylvia produced gourmet dinners out of the housekeeping funds, choosing to ignore, says Nancy, such uninteresting necessities as detergent and paper towels. Strangely protective about her possessions, after a party to which she contributed the snacks Sylvia carefully inscribed her name on every leftover box and bag to store in a back cupboard for her private use. Nancy also relates with astonishment that when both girls bought identical bottles of nail polish, Sylvia painstakingly labeled her bottle lest Nancy accidentally use it instead of her own. "The exclusiveness," Nancy writes, "was becoming a familiar symptom." On an earlier occasion Nancy ran into Sylvia fuming with rage in Harvard Yard: " 'Did you see her?' she demanded . . . 'That awful, audacious girl . . . just came up to me and said, "I see you've got my hairdo." Imagine that! She thinks I've got her hairdo!' "

These seemed like minor incidents, but to Nancy they were of a piece with the crisis at the end of the summer. She and Sylvia had encountered a tall, balding, myopic-looking man on the steps of Widener Library; Nancy Steiner in her memoir calls him Irwin, as does Sylvia in her version of him in *The Bell Jar*. Irwin taught biology at an Eastern college and looked like a genius, but whatever the caliber of his mind, the nature of his intentions soon became clear.

First he attempted to seduce Nancy. Meeting with rebuff, he turned his attentions to Sylvia, who was more responsive. Here, perhaps, was the scientist-father who would wisely preside over her initiation into womanhood. After seeing him platonically for some time, Sylvia went to Irwin's apartment for dinner one evening and stayed the night. The next day Irwin phoned Nancy to say Sylvia had been unwell, had hemorrhaged, but a doctor had seen her and she was all right. Sylvia returned in the early evening looking "dreadful." Soon she was again drenched in vaginal blood, still hemorrhaging. Nancy phoned the doctor of the night before, after Sylvia tried in vain to remember the fictitious name she had used, and he gave her instructions about how to stop the flow. These not succeeding, Nancy summoned Irwin, who drove them both to the hospital emergency ward; there the hemorrhage was finally arrested.

Though shaken herself, Nancy was surprised by the force of Sylvia's terror. As she lay in a pool of blood on the bathroom floor, fear invaded the room "like a third person." When the mantle of self-possession fell apart, "all the stored-up fear and vulnerability came pouring out in a confusing helter-skelter of words and sobs."

As summer drew to a close and Sylvia, amazingly, still continued to see Irwin, Nancy began to withdraw. Sylvia was asking too much. It was inconceivable, for instance, that she undergo hospital checkups or even live through a headache without her friend at her side. As Nancy came to understand her, Sylvia wanted to embody her Smith-girl image and at the same time experience life at turbulent extremes. The conflict was excruciating and unremitting. Nor was it resolved that summer, when she told Gordon she had suffered a "vaginal tear" and went on seeing him as if nothing had happened. At last Nancy refused the role of savior and deliverer, and although she and Sylvia roomed together the following year, they were never again doubles.

◀   ◀   ◀

Sylvia began work on her honors thesis, a study of the double in Dostoevsky, shortly after she returned to Smith in September. "The Magic Mirror" — appropriately titled — is a detached, competent study of the crisis of identity in nineteenth-century romantic fiction, which in many ways anticipated the schizoid diagnoses of twentieth-century psychoanalysis. Unfortunately, Sylvia adopted for her thesis the wooden, academic style approved by her supervisor, and no one would guess from reading it that the author of this well-mannered, well-researched academic paper had invested the least bit of emotional capital in it. The logic is impeccable, the notes impressive, the writing studious.

While Sylvia was at work on her senior thesis, she also took entrance exams for Oxford and Cambridge in England, her first choices for graduate study if, as she hardly dared hope, her application for a Fulbright grant was successful. With Mary Ellen Chase strenuously backing her for Cambridge (she was accepted by both British universities) as well as for the Fulbright and a Woodrow Wilson scholarship,* Sylvia made contingency plans to go to Radcliffe and Columbia.

---

*One of her oral exams included a question about several contemporary British

For a time, too, she seriously contemplated taking a teaching job in Morocco, along with her latest *belle amie,* Sue Weller.

In October Sylvia was invited to join a small writing class taught by Alfred Kazin. Finding him more sympathetic to her efforts than Mr. Auden, she produced a number of lively short stories, among them "Superman and Paula Brown's New Snowsuit" and "The Day Mr. Prescott Died" (both rooted in her memories of Winthrop) as well as "Tongues of Stone," her first fiction to use as material those long months of mental deadness in McLean. Typically, she also turned out some sentimental popular fiction to submit for a Christopher Prize* and went in for the *Vogue* Prix de Paris, a competition for college seniors.

In the second semester of her senior year, Sylvia was the sole pupil of Alfred Fisher — "a very strict man, and a brilliant professor"— in a special course in poetics she had been allowed to set up for herself. With her schedule tailored exactly to suit her, she was free to take Kazin's reading course in modern American literature and a course in Shakespeare. German, always her bête noire, in which she got persistent B's, finally had to give way altogether to creativity. Every week she typed out new poems for "handsome middle-aged" Mr. Fisher to criticize in his tiny, illegible handwriting. He seems to have approved her tight, eclectic style: the contrived stanzas, the Dylan Thomas-like locution, the endless villanelles. For Fisher she wrote scores of poems, a technically precocious and extraordinarily copious output. Many of these poems were simply exercises, but for years Sylvia remained proud of "Mad Girl's Love Song" (written for Myron Lotz in 1953), "Go Get the Goodly Squab," "Doomsday," "Circus in Three Rings," and "Two Lovers and a Beachcomber by the Real Sea." Some were published in *Mademoiselle, Harper's,* or *The Atlantic Monthly,* as well in the *Smith Review;* many others have never been published.

"Circus in three rings" describes Sylvia's whirlwind senior year with wonderful accuracy. She seems never to have stopped. Working, winning, spiraling higher and higher in a manic upswing that was threatened only once — when she was refused a Woodrow Wilson scholar-

---

novelists, among them C. P. Snow. Sylvia had never heard of Snow, and according to Nancy Hunter Steiner, she was incredulous that there existed a notable novelist of whom she had never heard. She went to the library immediately to look him up.

*In *Letters Home* Mrs. Plath explains that the Christopher Movement, founded in 1945, stressed "the importance of personal responsibility and individual initiative in raising the standards of government, education, literature, and labor relations."

ship late in January — she was, almost unbelievably, carrying on a torrid affair with Richard Sassoon throughout the year.

After November, it seems, they spent several weekends in New York hotels, though Sylvia told her mother she was visiting a newly married classmate, Clairborne Handleman. Early in February, during one of these hectic times, Sylvia's suitcase, full of her favorite clothes, was stolen from Sassoon's Volkswagen. On this occasion Richard had to slap her out of hysteria. Sylvia happily wrote a poem about it, but she invented a story for Mrs. Plath, telling her she had sold her clothes to cover Smith expenses. The result? An offer from her mother of a monthly loan until the end of the year.

Richard attempted to teach Sylvia how to love, defy authority, enjoy wine, and respond wholehearted to the artist in her divided nature. It was with Richard, late in February 1955, that Sylvia visited the Museum of Modern Art, seeing there a silent French film, *The Temptation of Saint Joan,* which impressed itself indelibly on her:

> The burning at the stake was incredibly artistic and powerful, but the very lack of sensationalism, just the realism of fire licking at sticks, of soldiers bringing wood, of peasant faces watching, conveyed by the enormity of understatement the whole torture of the saint.
>
> After it was all over, I couldn't look at anyone. I was crying because it was like a purge, the buildup of unbelievable tension, then the release, as of the soul of Joan at the stake.

It was a scene, like her visit to the lying-in hospital with Dick Norton, that would recur in Sylvia's poems of the Ariel period. Sylvia saw herself, in one of her incarnations, *as* Joan.

In November 1954, when she had begun to be deeply involved with Richard, Sylvia told Gordon Lameyer, then stationed in Virginia, that Dostoevsky was absorbing her weekends. After the thesis was completed in January (it tied at the end of the year for a Marjorie Hope Nicholson Award, with highest commendations), she claimed to be writing stories and poems — as indeed she was. It was not until May that she summoned confidence enough to break their semi-engagement. Nothing had been official, but the previous autumn Gordon had been looking forward to a future of knowing Sylvia "for what we call forever," and at that time Sylvia was also writing of their married future. Although Sassoon knew all about Gordon (a rival who sometimes worried him), Gordon, apparently then as later, knew almost nothing of Sassoon. How could he anticipate that the Sylvia *he* knew would opt for sex with "a weird little chap" with a sickly constitution, especially one who posed as arrogantly sadomasochistic? "I teach girls to be women," Richard wrote, "and teach them how to taunt me . . . I have wished to please and punish."

Richard was twenty, Sylvia twenty-two, but he had found a way of attracting her and keeping her interest. It appears they were acting out, innocently enough, a mutually exciting melodrama of love and art. Sylvia, however, was able to keep this relationship quite separate from her life at Smith. After every "wicked" weekend in New York, Sylvia snapped back to her "good" student personality, picturing herself as a nun returning to her convent. Before setting off for New York during spring vacation in March 1955, Sylvia wrote to her mother of needing "a respite from the daily round of classes and waitressing." She was looking forward, she said, to a few days of peace at home. "There is nothing like an alternation of work and play to keep one fresh and spirited. Fortunately, I am building up a list of outlets and tonics for my periodic slackening times. In the summer, it will be tennis, swimming, sunning and sailing. In the winter, New York is a help, and I hope to add skiing in the Alps next year!"

This was how "bright-eyed Sivvy" reconciled healthy activities with lots of healthy sex, without having to explain too much to her mother. Richard's letters may swagger, but Sylvia's imply that what mattered was work; everything else, including romantic encounters in New York, had to be "outlets" or "tonics" for "slackening times." This formulation clearly did not always work, and she must often have been torn between irreconcilable facets of her personality.*

Work, in the spring of 1955, certainly brought Sylvia the rewards she coveted. In May she learned that her application for a Fulbright grant had been successful and that, with the backing of Mary Ellen Chase, Alfred Kazin, and Elizabeth Drew, she would be enrolling as a foreign student at Cambridge. She phoned her mother at the Newton-Wellesley Hospital, where Mrs. Plath was about to undergo a subtotal gastrectomy. After Sylvia's breakdown in 1953, Mrs. Plath had suffered so many ulcerous hemorrhages that her doctor advised the removal of most of her stomach. When Sylvia phoned to announce her latest triumph, a nurse answered that her mother was too ill to speak. "Tell my mother," cried Sylvia, "that my news will help her more than anything else could." Accordingly, Aurelia was wheeled

---

*Author's note: Many women who, like myself, were students in America in the 1950s will remember duplicities of this kind. Sylvia's double standard was quite usual, as was the acceptable face she assumed in letters to her mother. My own letters home of the time were not dissimilar.

to the telephone to hear from Sivvy's own lips that she had been awarded a Fulbright to study at Cambridge University in England.

Although the Fulbright was the most glorious, other prizes fell into Sylvia's lap all spring. At the Glascock poetry contest at Mount Holyoke College — within a few miles of Smith and Amherst — Sylvia competed with five other aspiring young poets from New England. After all six had read to a panel of judges consisting of Marianne Moore, John Ciardi, and Wallace Fowlie, Sylvia was given first prize, tying with a student from Wesleyan. Afterward, she chatted with John Ciardi over Scotch and had herself photographed with Marianne Moore for the *Christian Science Monitor*. The contestants spent the night at Mount Holyoke, and it was then that she got to know Lynne Lawner, a sophomore at Wellesley College, to whom Sylvia later wrote a number of bracing, elder-sister letters from England and Boston.

On May 21 Sylvia wrote to her mother from the sunroof of Alumnae Gym at Smith. There was *more* good news. Edward Weeks, editor of *The Atlantic Monthly*, had accepted "Circus in Three Rings," which would be published in August. Weeks had also been "charmed" by her three-page "The Princess and the Goblins," which unfortunately was too long to print in *The Atlantic*. To cheer Mrs. Plath further, Sylvia listed her year's prizes:

$30 Dylan Thomas honorable mention for "Parallax," *Mlle*
$30 For cover of novel symposium, *Mlle* [an assignment in March]
$5 *Alumnae Quarterly* article on Alfred Kazin
$100 Academy of American Poets Prize (10 poems)
$50 Glascock Prize (tie)
$40 Ethel Olin Corbin Prize (sonnet)
$50 Marjorie Hope Nicholson Prize (tie) for thesis
$25 *Vogue* Prix de Paris (one of 12 winners)
$25 *Atlantic* for "Circus in Three Rings"
$100 Christophers (one of 34 winners)
$15 *Mlle* for "Two Lovers and a Beachcomber by Real Sea"

$470 TOTAL, plus much joy!

Mrs. Plath was allowed to leave the hospital and travel on a mattress to Sylvia's commencement exercises. She watched Alfred Kazin wave to her daughter as she returned with her *summa cum laude*, nodding in relieved agreement when Sylvia breathed in her ear, "My cup runneth over." The Smith girl had graduated; the Cambridge woman was about to begin.

PURSUIT

1955-1956

in my head I know it is too simple to wish for war, for open battle, but one cannot help but wish for those situations that make us heroic. living to the hilt of our total resources. our cosmic fights, when I think the end of the world is come, are so many broken shells around our growth.

> — *Journals*, excerpt from a letter
> to Richard Sassoon,
> January 15, 1956

> There is a panther stalks me down:
> One day I'll have my death of him.
> — "Pursuit," 1956

AFTER GRADUATION, faced with another unstructured summer at home, Sylvia might have "ricocheted" from peak to pit had she not been looking forward to England and Cambridge in the fall. By now she had learned to manipulate the tidal swings of mood, grooming herself to suit whichever personality seemed appropriate to the task in hand. At Smith she had allowed her hair to return to its natural brown, writing to Gordon Lameyer at the beginning of her senior year:

I'm rather sure that my brown-haired personality will win out this year . . . gone is the frivolous giddy gilded creature who careened around corners at the wheel of a yellow convertible and stayed up till six in the morning because the conversation and bourbon-and-water were too good to terminate . . . here is a serious, industrious, unextracurricular unswerving creature who, if you looked closer, might admit to being me!

The summer of 1955 found Sylvia gilded again, the sole leading lady in a sizable cast of devoted, often puzzled admirers. Chief among them still was Richard Sassoon, who had graduated from Yale with "one or two small prizes" and was working in New Haven as a furnace salesman before setting off for Europe in the autumn. Dazzled like everyone else by Sylvia's achievements, Richard wrote letters that, though still passionately patronizing, no longer affected the flamboyance of his first outbursts. Like Gordon Lameyer, from whom a stream of correspondence also arrived, Richard was at the crossroads between youth and maturity, making important decisions about the future and appealing to Sylvia for understanding.

The more serious Richard became, the greater was Sylvia's anxiety lest he satisfy only one dimension of her complex personality. Her friends were getting married with alarming rapidity. Sylvia had been a bridesmaid for Marcia Brown a year previously, becoming hysterical after drinking too much champagne. Now, in June 1955, she was maid of honor for her childhood friend Ruth Freeman. With Richard writing in strong, pleading language of "many possible paths for the future," Sylvia now withdrew. Competitive and not to be outdone by her girlfriends, she wanted a "mate"; on the other hand, she was not sure Richard fulfilled her requirement for a physical and intellectual colossus. It is clear from Sassoon's letters that her way of blowing hot and cold produced a reaction of baffled distress.

One problem was undoubtedly her mother, back in Wellesley after several weeks on Cape Cod, where she had gone to recuperate from her stomach operation. Mrs. Plath could not approve of Richard as she had of Gordon Lameyer, though after a visit from Sassoon over the Fourth of July weekend, Sylvia wrote to Warren: "Mother revised her former picture of him, and I think found him okay. Anyway, I cooked like mad . . ."

Although it is impossible to deduce from their letters the precise nature of their relations, it is clear that by August they had reached a crisis. Sylvia accused Richard of "laughing faithlessness," provoking in reply two very serious letters warning her to be careful. In what was possibly a reference to Sylvia's carelessness about contraceptives, Richard wrote, "What can I say but that you are one of the most foolish and irresponsible girls that ever roamed about freely . . . I tell you strongly that you must never again place so much irresponsibility in the hands of chance. Either accept it or put it on me . . . Sylvia, you are a great big, healthy, powerful woman!" His tone is that of a man pushed to the limit of patience.

The same letter expresses concern at the amount of "hatred and frustration" in the air at 26 Elmwood Road, advising Sylvia to patch things up with her mother "at least superficially," and showing a maturity that Sylvia did not possess: "Believe me, it is no good to leave a home with a foul taste in the air." Richard Sassoon was beginning to sound like Eddie Cohen, facing reality and asking Sylvia to do the same. She no doubt found his letters less exciting when they advised her to "smile and relax" and stop being "so proud and stoic and tense" than when they threatened her with spankings for disobedience.

While accusing Richard Sassoon of faithlessness, Sylvia was temporarily distracted by a new love affair with a young man who had just become assistant to the director of Harvard University Press. Peter Davison had met Sylvia in her final months at Smith through Alfred Kazin, who thought they would have tastes in common. Davison moved to Cambridge (from New York) in June, when he looked up Sylvia again in Wellesley. His autobiography, *Half Remembered*, devotes several pages to his impressions.

Sylvia, it seems, was drawn to Peter chiefly for reasons advantageous to herself. Having studied in Cambridge on a Fulbright some years before, he would tell her all about "abroad"; even more glamorous was his rising star as a publisher. The son of an English poet, brought up among writers and literary people Sylvia considered influential — Robert Frost among them — Davison was just the man to prepare her for Cambridge and her glittering future as a writer. She arrived for her first dinner at Peter's apartment "in a white dress, with a deep suntan and thick hair turned blonde by the sun," Davison recalls. "She asked more and more questions, she seemed strangely elevated, and she hardly waited to be asked to slip into my new bed."

Between July 24 and August 23, when Sylvia broke off the affair, he saw her ten times; she read him her poems and took him home to meet her mother (who put herself out to impress him), but usually he picked her up for dinner and drove her back to Wellesley late at night. "Her quest for knowledge was voracious," he writes. "I felt as though I were being cross-examined, drained, eaten; yet when she told me about her life, her previous love affairs, her successes at Smith, it was as though she were describing a stranger to herself, a highly trained circus horse." Though the poems she showed him were imitative, they were promisingly adroit; he was taken aback mainly by the forced pace of her eagerness and her impersonal appetite for experience. "What she said, what she alleged, the ways she loved, lacked credibility. She was too exigent for me. I could not seem to hold my own with her, though I was older and presumably more experienced. Her friends," Davison adds, "seemed as baffled by her, yet as fascinated, as I."

Only once did Davison feel he was approaching something like the real girl when, toward the end of the summer, "lying rigid . . . as though she were being fueled from within," she related the story of her breakdown and suicide attempt. The version Davison heard then was "a simpler, less poised and more touching story" than the semi-fiction of *The Bell Jar*; "the episode still seemed to be the only period of her life that she could invest with any real emotion in retrospect." Afterward, though they would spend a weekend together on Martha's Vineyard, she seemed to want to shrug him off; when they parted at the end of August, Davison was left feeling "used," even "despised."*

Throughout the summer of 1955, Sylvia masterminded a veritable "circus in three rings." Before she left for England, her list of men accepted or rejected was indeed considerable: Gordon Lameyer, Richard Sassoon, Peter Davison, George Gebauer ("a very conservative and conventional scientist," she told her brother, "who seems to like to take me out"), plus, doubtless, a number of other, more casual dates. Before setting off for Cambridge she enrolled in the Fred Astaire Dance Studio in Boston, preparing herself to meet the ballroom requirements of those passengers on board who might qualify intellectually as potential "mates." (Alas, for all its medieval splendor, Cambridge was to have little to offer in the way of tango-dancing intellectuals.)

In mid-September, after a brief visit to Sue Weller in Washington (Gordon Lameyer obligingly drove her back), Sylvia bade a tearful farewell to her family, Mrs. Prouty, Mary Ellen Chase, and all her "wonderful" Wellesley neighbors and set sail on the *Queen Elizabeth* for Europe. On the boat she met "a genial versatile Jewish physics major from New York" (bound for the University of Manchester) with whom she danced, had "bull sessions," and, in accordance with her mores at that time, probably slept. "Carl" was a suitable partner to share "the most enchanting afternoon of my life" when the boat

---

*In March 1959 Peter Davison would marry Sylvia's Smith classmate Jane Truslow, whose study of American women and their domestic expectations, *The Fall of a Doll's House* (New York: Holt, Rinehart and Winston, 1980), mentions Sylvia's phenomenal ambition at college, which included an overpowering desire to become one of the world's "wizard housewives and homemakers." The two girls never much liked each other.

stopped for a day in Cherbourg; later he made a useful escort in London, where in five days they went together to no less than four plays, including *Waiting for Godot*, then very new and avant-garde.

With others, Sylvia was entertained one evening by the American ambassador. On another occasion, at Bedford College in Regent's Park, Sylvia was annoyed when a body of illustrious figures was assembled but not introduced. "I only met David Daiches, who will be lecturing at Cambridge and is a well-known critic," she wrote to her mother. "Imagine my chagrin when I found out that Stephen Spender (the poet), John Lehmann (brilliant head of BBC [*sic*] and editor of the *London* magazine, a literary review) and C. P. Snow himself (!) had been in the crowd! . . . Even T. S. Eliot had been invited, but couldn't make it at the last moment."

By October 2 Sylvia was writing to her mother from Cambridge, a cloistered community sprawled gracefully along the fennish banks of the Cam, scarcely, in the 1950s, the thriving city it is today. Sylvia was enchanted with its groomed courts and crooked streets. As a foreign graduate at Newnham, she was an "affiliated" student and lived with other outsiders and older students in Whitstead, a small building set apart from the college, on Barton Road. Soon after her arrival, her director of studies, Kathleen Burton, advised her to read for Part II of the English tripos. Exams, however, lay two years ahead, and at first she was astonished at her freedom to study without obligations to specific courses. Apart from writing two essays a week for this supervisor, there were no academic hurdles to leap. She was conscious of being in many ways ill prepared. At Smith it had been too easy to escape from the drudgery of languages and history into art and creative writing; at Cambridge no supervisor would care whether she was "creative" or not. The English girls who shared her supervisions were at least three years younger than she was; it was provoking that they were able to date passages of poetry and prose she had never considered in a historical context.

Taking a program "which should slowly spread pathways and bridges over the whistling voids of my ignorance," as she told her mother, she excitedly chose from among a "miraculous smorgasbord of lecturers," arranging to go to F. R. Leavis on criticism ("a magnificent, acid, malevolently humorous little man who looks exactly like a bandy-legged leprechaun"), Basil Willey on the moralists, David Daiches on the modern English novel, and, in her second term, Dorothea Krook (known in Cambridge as Doris), who was later to become Sylvia's favorite supervisor.

Mrs. Krook recalls seeing Sylvia for the first time, in the Mill Lane lecture room, "a conspicuously tall girl standing in one of the aisles ... staring at me intently." Struck by the "concentrated intensity of her scrutiny," Mrs. Krook wondered suddenly if she was Jewish, and although she never again caught that particular expression, she remembered it when she read Sylvia's poems after her death.

Indeed, Sylvia cut a conspicuous figure at Cambridge. Dressed in archetypal American college clothes — sweaters, skirts, loafers — she seemed unaware that these stood out oddly in the generally understated, if not dowdy style of other university women. Tall, slim (though not thin), good-looking rather than beautiful, she set off her vivid face with the jamlike smear of lipstick fashionable in those days. Her brown hair, streaked with bleached blond strands, was shoulder-length, tidily held back by a broad hairband or *bandeau*. She had come to Cambridge with a new set of white and gold Samsonite luggage, together with a bicycle she had imported, and was often seen pedaling furiously around the town, her black gown billowing out behind like an undisciplined shadow.

Jane Baltzell, another American, in Cambridge on a Marshall scholarship, was struck by Sylvia's bumptious insensitivity to the kind of behavior the British found ridiculous. Self-conscious about any appearance of naiveté or gushiness, Jane was embarrassed when Sylvia rode up to a bobby to ask in her twangy American accent for directions to "somewhere really picturesque and collegiate" in which to eat. Like Nancy Hunter at Smith, Jane began by admiring Sylvia's resourcefulness, her professionalism, and her ability to make any room she lived in her own. Later she was amazed when Sylvia defended her possessions with a rapacity that, in the end, injured their friendship. No one at Whitstead knew anything about her 1953 breakdown, so Sylvia's peculiarities — her physical restlessness, her habit of sitting with one leg crossed over the other, impatiently swinging her foot while her hands locked and unlocked in her lap, the two thumbs "stabbing each other with their nails" — were regarded simply as the mannerisms of a very intense, very ambitious overachiever.

Social life was much easier than at Smith. A ratio of ten or more men to every woman meant that Sylvia was, if anything, overprovided with escorts who ferried her around to tea parties and wine parties until she tired of them. She made her debut by joining the Amateur Dramatic Club, taking part in an eighteenth-century farce about a cuckold and, later, in a large-scale production of *Bartholomew Fair* in which she took the small part of a whore in a yellow satin dress. In letters to her mother and Mrs. Prouty, Sylvia made much of her interest in acting, but in truth, after a week of performing a little part in a big production, she pulled out. In her journal she was unrepentant. She had been stricken with sinusitis, but more than that, "knowing I could not be big, refusing to be small, I retreated to work."

Letters home during these first Cambridge weeks scintillate with enthusiasm, describing with characteristic bravado the men she met (she took an instant dislike to the ubiquitous "fair-skinned, rather hysterical and breathless . . . English girl[s]"), parties she attended, the "activities" she "went out for," her triumphs on the stage. On October 14, having met a "tall, rather handsome, dark-haired chap, named Mallory Wober . . . a brilliant pianist" reading natural sciences,* she decided to make a list of activities through which she could meet influential people — theater groups, newspapers, political clubs — and start from the top. On October 24 the Queen and the Duke of Edinburgh visited Cambridge, stopping at Newnham on their way to open a veterinary laboratory. Sylvia described with archetypal American gusto their procession into the dining hall. Cycling to the ADC for a rehearsal later in the evening, she preceded the royal car (by a few minutes) in her red mackintosh, raising a titter from the waiting crowd. Such anecdotes, together with the mention of "brilliant" new men — the American Nathaniel LaMar, "a lovely, light-skinned Negro"; the actor David Buck; Mallory Wober (who moved a Hammond organ into her room so he could play to her); John Lythgoe; Dick Gilling; and such old friends as Dick Wertz from Yale — showed her at the center of events and of male attention, and reveling in it:

> Yesterday was most amazing. I was, as I said, to have gone to Ely with John, but Mallory had invited me to lunch, and it was a bad day, so I left a note on my door, telling whoever read it to come to tea . . . Well, Mallory took me and some of his Jewish friends from Israel around King's and the chapel, which was exquisite at dusk with all the colored stained-glass windows (which Mallory explained the stories of and the history and architecture) and myriads of candles and lacy fan-vaulted ceiling.
> . . . We were biking back to my place with sandwiches for tea-lunch when John pulled up on his motorcycle . . . Well, nothing remained but to have them both for tea . . . Believe it or not, they both stayed from 4 till 10 at night, talking about everything from "Is there a purpose to the universe" to the Belgian Congo — no mention of supper! . . . My first "salon," and most stimulating.

---

*Twenty or so letters from Sylvia Plath to Mallory Wober have recently been donated to the Kings College Library in Cambridge.

Just as when Sylvia had come back from dances in high school, she felt she had to share all these "great moments" with her mother. Yet there was something frenetic about all this joy, as if she had to cram it in hard before it got away. On December 5 she reported a visit from Richard Sassoon, who had flown from Paris to see relatives in England. He took her to lunch in town, after which she gave him and Dick Wertz tea in her room at Whitstead. She and Richard must then have been planning to meet in Paris for Christmas, though, as she told her mother, she was already "dulled with a cold." On December 12 she went riding with Dick Wertz in Cambridge. Her hired horse, Sam, reputed to be old and gentle, took it into his head to bolt with the inexperienced Sylvia clinging to his back.*

Toward the end of the autumn term Sylvia had indeed begun to slump. The "wonderful" boys she had so "enjoyed" at first were far too young for her, hardly the sexually experienced sophisticates she had anticipated. She would crouch to study by a woefully inadequate gas fire to which she fed shillings in return for scant, uneven heat. The bathroom was so icy her breath came in puffs when she bathed. The soggy, sludgy Newnham food nearly gagged her, while the dowdy lady dons, however brilliant, struck her as a "caricature series from Dickens." Was that what you became if you refused marriage and devoted your life to learning? The marriage question began to weigh heavily on her mind, and although she wrote of Mallory Wober to Mrs. Prouty, "My favorite man is a tall, handsome raven-haired red-cheeked boy . . . who looks like a young Hercules . . . a giant of earth strong as the Rock of Gibraltar," she began to make unfavorable comparisons between the young men around her and Richard Sassoon. Certainly her journals for her first two terms in Cambridge show her as obsessed by Sassoon. Letters, or draft letters she may or may not have sent while he was at the Sorbonne, ring with the hyperbole she specialized in when writing to or about potential "mates":

> in the beginning was the word and the word was sassoon and it was a terrible word for it created eden and the golden age back to which fallen eva looks mingling her crystal tears with the yellow dahlias that sprout from the lips of her jaundiced adam.
>
> be christ! she cries, and rise before my eyes while the blue marys bless us with singing. and when, she asks (for even eva is practical), will this resurrection occur?

---

*In July 1958 Sylvia used this experience in her poem "Whiteness I Remember," with, in its final lines, a foretaste of that other poem about horse-riding, "Ariel."

These letters (some must have been sent) were bait, clever, succulent, and surrealistic, with which to prepare Richard — who probably answered in the same vein — for her visit at Christmas.

◄　　◄　　◄

Jane Baltzell Kopp writes wittily of crossing to France with Sylvia on December 20. They had met by chance in the London terminal of a "shady" airline that was to have flown them to the Continent. Bad weather having grounded the planes, the two girls embarked instead on a traumatic voyage by boat (the subject of "Channel Crossing," a heavily overwritten poem Sylvia must have blushed about later). Nearly everyone on board was seasick. Sylvia and Jane crouched on deck under a raincoat, staving off sickness "despite the fact that pans of vomit repeatedly clanged down the deck nearby where we were huddling, wind-ripped away from their users and flinging out their contents as they flew along."

It was ten or eleven at night when they got to Paris. Nathaniel LaMar or Richard Sassoon had booked a room for Sylvia, but Jane, who had expected to arrive in the afternoon, had made no arrangements. Sylvia suggested they share her room (and expenses), an offer Jane accepted with relief.

Both girls were young and terribly excited. They oohed and ahed to each other about finally, actually being in Paris before Jane, exhausted, dropped into bed. Sylvia said she wanted to go out and explore right away. It was one o'clock in the morning when she handed Jane the only key and disappeared. Having used the key to lock the door from the inside, Jane fell so deeply asleep she failed to hear Sylvia's knock an hour or so later. The next day, there was Sylvia, incandescent with rage in the corridor. She had spent the night in the concierge's office, she said,* and was now so spectacularly furious that Jane was taken aback. It was as if Jane had locked her out on purpose.

Sylvia had told her mother she would be spending Christmas "having a whirl in London and Paris with John, Nat, and Sassoon and Mallory," but in Paris she chiefly saw Sassoon. He escorted her to Notre Dame, showed her Sacre Coeur and Montmartre, pointed out the "painted whores" in the Place Pigalle — these were of great fascination to Sylvia — and took her to a performance of Charles Peguy's

---

*Sylvia told her mother that she had shared a bed that night with "two very vivacious, friendly girls from Switzerland."

Jeanne d'Arc at the Comédie Française. In the Louvre, the Wingèd Victory may have given Sylvia the image of the "white Nike" and other stony museum statues that haunt her late poems.

On New Year's Eve they were rushing through France, sitting up on the overnight express. In one of her ecstatic highs, Sylvia scribbled in her notebook while Richard slept "fitfully" on her breast. Delirious in this Dali landscape, she described it in language that foreshadowed the possessed surrealism of the Ariel poems — but this time her impetus was an exalted and exaggerated joy:

> On the train: staring hypnotized at the blackness outside the window, feeling the incomparable rhythmic language of the wheels, clacking out nursery rhymes, summing up the moments of the mind like the chant of a broken record: saying over and over: god is dead, god is dead, going, going, going: and the pure bliss of this, the erotic rocking of the coach. France splits open like a ripe fig in the mind; we are raping the land, we are not stopping.

Compare this with the nightmare of "Getting There," written nearly seven years later:

> The train is dragging itself, it is screaming —
> An animal
> Insane for the destination,
> The bloodspot,
> The face at the end of the flare . . .
> The carriages rock, they are cradles . . .

As their train reached the Mediterranean at dawn on New Year's Day, Sylvia must have achieved a cathartic crisis, a point at which, for her, death resurrected itself into life — eventually the leitmotif of her poems. Just as images of the sun rising are central to *Ariel*, so, on January 1, 1956, she was writing in her notebook: "Red earth, orange tiled villas in yellow and peach and aqua, and the blast, the blue blast of the sea on the right. The Côte d'Azur. A new country, a new year: spiked with green explosions of palms, cacti sprouting vegetable octopuses with spiky tentacles, and the red sun rising like the eye of God out of a screaming blue sea." The manic violence of this passage, with its powerful verbs and vivid colors, again prefigures Sylvia's mature writing.

From Nice, Sassoon piloted Sylvia by motor scooter to Vence, where she was eager to visit what she calls the Matisse cathedral (in fact, a chapel); she crammed a description of it onto a postcard to her mother. Her rapture conspicuously excluded any mention of Sassoon, but the day was "about the most lovely in my life." She found the chapel "small, pure, clean-cut. White, with blue tile roof sparkling in the sun. But shut!" Then a miracle occurred. Although rich people were daily turned away, she had been chosen, she told her mother, set apart. As she stood crying with her face pressed to the barred gate, she heard a voice, "Ne pleurez plus, entrez," and the Mother Superior let her in, "after denying all the wealthy people in cars. I just knelt in the heart of the sun and the colors of the sky, sea, and sun, in the pure white heart of the Chapel." In many of her letters home Sylvia exaggerated or suppressed her true feelings, but her experience in the "pure white heart" of the Matisse chapel must have been as she described it — something holy, the radical purity she sought all her life to make permanent.

Back in Cambridge on January 10, she retained for a while the glow of confidence she had found in France with Richard, moralizing to her mother:

> My New Year mood is so different from the rather lonely, weary, depressed and slightly fearful state in which I left Cambridge a mere three weeks ago. Coming "back" here for this first time made me feel *this* is truly home, and my vacation has given me an invaluable perspective on my life, work and purpose here which I had lost in the complex overstimulation of the first semester. I now feel strong and sure.

But in spite of her determination to begin writing again, abandoning theatricals and parties to devote herself to the pure memory of "her" Richard, inevitably her spirits fell as the winter grew colder and her inflamed sinuses tormented her. Although she met Christopher Levenson, the editor of the Cambridge magazine *Delta*, and through him Stephen Spender (at last she was moving in a literary rather than theatrical Cambridge), her English loves were all "stillborn children"; nothing could come of them after Richard.

One Monday night at the end of January she was woken by "excruciating pains," was violently sick, and fainted. A doctor summoned by the college sent her to the hospital for observation, but she returned after her "appendicitis" was diagnosed as "colic." Back at Whitstead, she was stunned to read a mocking review by one Daniel Huws of two poems she had published in *Chequer*, a student magazine.*

---

*The poems were "Epitaph in Three Parts" and "Three Caryatids Without a Portico by Hugh Robus: A Study in Sculptural Dimensions," neither of which is in the *Collected Poems*. Typical of the convoluted, hyperaesthetic style she affected at this time,

Such troubles would probably have affected her less were it not that Sassoon was distancing himself from her. Either during their time together in France or in a letter (now lost) after her return, he persuaded her that she must not contact him until he said so. He seems to have been quite open with her about other women in his life. In a journal outpouring dated February 19, Sylvia reiterates her love for him but adds, "Meanwhile you are probably sleeping exhausted and happy in the arms of some brilliant whore, or maybe even the Swiss girl who wants to marry you." And she wonders, "Will Richard ever need me again? Part of my bargain is that I will be silent until he does . . . If ever, in the next five years."

Sylvia's long letters to Sassoon, some seemingly unposted, indicate that she doggedly refused to believe that their affair was over. Was it only herself she was trying to deceive? Letters to her mother continue for some months to imply that all was well between them:

Actually, as you probably know, Richard Sassoon is the only boy I have ever loved so far; he is much more brilliant, intuitive and alive than anyone I've ever known. Yet he pays for this with spells of black depression and shaky health which means living in daily uncertainty and would be hard over any long time. But he is the most honest, holy person I know. And, in a sense, I suppose I will always love him, together with his faults. Ironically enough, he "looks" not at all like the kind of man I could be fond of; but he is, and that's that.

Despite her decisive tone, Sylvia must have doubted herself, for the pendulum of her ups and downs was again set in motion. It is clear that throughout February Sylvia was sinking into a very serious depression. On the nineteenth and twentieth she poured her grief into her journal. "To whom it may concern: Every now and then there comes a time when the neutral and impersonal forces of the world turn and come together in a thundercrack of judgment. There is no reason for the sudden terror, the feeling of condemnation, except that circumstances all mirror the inner doubt, the inner fear."

Walking over the Mill Lane Bridge on February 19, "smiling that smile which puts a benevolent lacquer on the shuddering fear of strangers' gazes," she had been a target of some small boys' snowballs. These boys, suddenly the agents of opposing forces, seemed to accuse

---

one can see why they provoked her critics to mirth. Christopher Levenson, who published only one ("Winter Words") of Sylvia's poems in *Delta*, thought the poems she submitted to him "too tricksey and self-consciously clever," though he liked and admired her personally.

her of the sickness, the oddness that shut her out of ordinary life. She was now sorry she had told her Cambridge followers about Richard in France, for Chris and Nat and John and Mallory were looking for company elsewhere. The girls at Whitstead — she knew it — were whispering of her madness behind her back. She recognized this "morbid fear." How was it that "all the edges and shapes and colors of the real world . . . built up again so painfully with such a real love [could] dwindle in a moment of doubt, and 'suddenly go out' "? She determined to see the university psychiatrist, "just to meet him, to know he's there . . . I feel I need him. I need a father. I need a mother. I need some older, wiser being to cry to." The entry continues: "I feel like Lazarus: that story has such a fascination. Being dead, I rose up again, and even resort to the mere sensation value of being suicidal, of getting so close, of coming out of the grave with the scars and the marring mark on my cheek which (is it my imagination?) grows more prominent."*

When Sylvia was at her most despairing that winter, she made a ritual of visiting by moonlight a sculptured boy with a dolphin that stood in the Newnham garden. Taking to the "blessedly neutral" dark trees —"so much easier than facing people, than having to look happy, invulnerable, clever"— she poured out her grief to the moon, that neutral, impersonal force to which she was drawn in these black moods because it did not "smite her down." The "bronze boy" represented her romantic dream of Richard Sassoon as she brushed the clots of snow from his "delicate smiling face."

Yet Sylvia also desired power: "The vampire is there, too. The old, primal hate. That desire to go round castrating the arrogant ones who become such children at the moment of passion." In such moods, anger and hatred were positives to set against the negative of her loneliness. "I fight all women for my men. My men. I am a woman, and there is no loyalty, even between mother and daughter. Both fight for the father, for the son, for the bed of mind and body." Between contempt for men and jealousy of women, she heard ticking at her back the mocking clock of an approaching doomsday: "A Life Is Passing. My Life."

The unloving world was still closing in on her when Sylvia wrote to her mother on February 24, deploring the lack of "someone to bring me hot broth and tell me they love me." Her journal complains of

---

*This refers to the quite noticeable scar on Sylvia's left cheek, a reminder of her first suicide attempt.

a lousy sinus cold that blunted up all my senses ... And atop of
this, through the hellish sleepless night of feverish sniffling and
tossing, the macabre cramps of my period (curse, yes) and the wet,
mussy spurt of blood ... This was Friday, the worst, the very worst.
Couldn't even read, full of drugs which battled and banged in my
veins. Everywhere I heard bells, telephone not for me, doorbells
with roses for all the other girls in the world. Utter despair.

The next morning, on Saturday, February 25, Sylvia went to see
the university psychiatrist. To her relief, he was fatherly and sympathetic. Talking to him, she realized how much she missed intelligent
companions of her own age. The boys she knew at Cambridge were
at least three years her junior, as was Jane Baltzell. English girls were
of little interest to her, although around the time Sylvia was at Cambridge, Hilary Bailey (whom she met), Margaret Drabble, A. S. Byatt,
and Joan Bakewell were all there; the future Cambridge scholar Isobel
Murray Henderson, a close friend of Jane's, lived in Whitstead.

Back after her morning session with the psychiatrist, Sylvia felt
much better. She sent off a second, more positive letter to her mother,
mentioning that she was going to a party that evening to celebrate
the publication of a new literary magazine, *St. Botolph's Review*.
That morning she had bought a copy from an American, Bert Wyatt-
Brown (now an eminent historian), and read in it poems by Ted
Hughes and E. Lucas Myers which impressed her more than any others
she had seen in Cambridge. Returning to ask Bert where she could
meet these poets, she had been told that they would be at the party
that night at the Women's Union in (what was then) Falcon Yard.
Seemingly, a Canadian named Hamish had offered to take her,* for
that afternoon she was "cleansed, and once again stoic, humorous."
Since this party was to be a turning point in Sylvia's life and something
of a landmark in Cambridge literary history, it is worth going into
the particulars of its genesis.

◂   ◂   ◂

In the autumn of 1954, a year before Sylvia arrived in Cambridge, a
young man from Tennessee named E. Lucas Myers, a cousin of the
American poet Allen Tate, had come to Cambridge to study English
with F. R. Leavis.† While a merchant mariner he had written two

---

*Sylvia wrote in her journal: "Then, too, a boy named Hamish ... asked me out
next week, and, quite by chance, said he'd take me to the *St. Botolph*'s party (tonight)."
†Like Ted Hughes, he eventually studied social anthropology.

shipboard poems that, after he arrived in Cambridge, were published in *Chequer* along with work by two other young poets, Ted Hughes and Daniel Huws. Luke Myers decided that if he could get to know these two he might feel less lonely. One autumn night, standing in the dinner line at Peterhouse, Daniel Huws introduced himself. Then in January one of the *Chequer* editors brought Ted Hughes around to meet Luke in his room at Downing.

Hughes had by then graduated and was working at odd jobs, making enough money to return to Cambridge from time to time; when in town he stayed with friends and read in the library. As Myers recalls, Hughes was an inch or two taller than the six-foot Huws and habitually clad in a brown leather greatcoat that had been issued to an uncle in World War I. "His brown hair fell across the right side of his forehead and his voice modulated curiously at certain significant points in his speech," writes Myers. "His eyes and mouth were powerfully expressive."

Sometime in January or February 1955 — while Sylvia was accumulating prizes at Smith — Luke Myers wearied of his college rooms and, as he says, "failing to rent a disused water tower, put a classified advertisement in the undergraduate newspaper, *Varsity*, for a 'shack or shed.' " The advertisement was answered "by a courtly note on blue letter paper from a Mrs. Helen R. Hitchcock of St. Botolph's Rectory." The widow of a former rector, Mrs. Hitchcock let rooms to students. Luke happily arranged to live in a disused chicken coop in her garden in return for stoking her Aga boiler in the kitchen.*

One of Luke's first guests in the chicken coop (after the room had been furnished with a bed, a desk, and a chair, the door opened to about seventy degrees) was Ted Hughes. Myers recalls:

> The first night Ted stayed there, I thought he should sleep in the bed and I under it because he was the guest, but he refused out of hand. Years later, in the course of giving me some hints on a story in which I had the hero falling in some droppings in a zoo, he

---

*Author's note: Mrs. Hitchcock's establishment in Cambridge was well known to me since she was for seven years my mother-in-law. It was surely one of the most unclerical "digs" in Cambridge. Temperamentally flighty but robust and once one of the beauties of New Zealand, Mrs. Hitchcock delighted in turning a blind eye to the capers, bibulous and otherwise, of her undergraduate lodgers, of whom she was very fond. The Rectory was a poets' haven, anarchic and unjudgmental. Mrs. Hitchcock exercised her prerogative as landlady by occupying the bath for two hours each morning and the kitchen from lunchtime to dinner — that is, from the time the late risers had finished breakfast until the pubs closed in the evening. Mrs. Hitchcock died in London, aged ninety-two, while this book was being written.

claimed that his green pullover still smelled of chicken soil, but he didn't admit to discomfort at the time. In any case he soon bought a tent and pitched it near the hut.

After a student escapade described in detail in his memoir, Luke Myers, with Ted Hughes, David Ross, Daniel Huws, Danny and George Weissbort, and Than Minton, resolved to publish a literary review named after their "spiritual home," the St. Botolph garden. Those involved in the magazine were part of a large convivial group, mainly students (they had their own jazz band), who met regularly at the Anchor pub. When it finally appeared in February 1956, *St. Botolph's Review* was more like a pamphlet than a magazine, the deep crimson of its card binding like a rich lining under a plain ivory slipcover. Its contents page listed the five artists responsible for its creation, while the austere dignity of the design permitted no mention of a price. Its only advertisement, if it can be so called, was a spare inscription on the back: "This review is published occasionally. All correspondence and contributions should be sent to the Editor . . ."

So it came about that on the very morning Sylvia Plath first went to see the university psychiatrist, teams of *St. Botolph's* supporters, among them Luke's friend Bert Wyatt-Brown, were selling the magazine throughout Cambridge. Sylvia excitedly read, admired, and even, apparently, memorized several poems by Ted Hughes and E. Lucas Myers, determined to meet these poets at the party that evening and force them to recognize her. Glad as she was to accept Hamish as an escort, she set out, dressed in the reds and blacks she favored for sexual conquest, in a mood to catch bigger game:

> I long so for someone to blast over Richard; I deserve that, don't I, some sort of blazing love that I can live with. My God, I'd love to cook and make a house, and surge force into a man's dreams, and write, if he could talk and walk and work and passionately want to do his career. I can't bear to think of this potential for loving and giving going brown and sere in me. Yet the choice is so important, it frightens me a little. A lot . . .

Sylvia's account of meeting Ted Hughes at the *St. Botolph's* party in Falcon Yard is heatedly described in a long journal entry, written (with a bad hangover) the next day. As might be expected, she made the most of its dramatic potential, relating how she stood drinking whiskey and ginger for Dutch courage in Miller's Bar, listening to the tedious gabble of "some ugly gat-toothed squat grinning guy" before arriving late for the party, with Hamish. Daniel Huws confirms that the first thing she did was to approach him with "great verve," archly to defend the poems he had unkindly attacked in his review. (He is not quite sure if she ever forgave him afterward.) She then danced with a rather drunk Luke Myers while quoting lines from his poems, to little effect — except to annoy his girlfriend.

None of the *St. Botolph's* crowd had met Sylvia before, but they had read several of her poems in university magazines and on the whole disapproved of them. Sylvia disciplined her verse in the manner approved by Sassoon, who had once written to her that he preferred "les pyramids du mal" to "les fleurs du mal" because man had made them. Myers believed more romantically that poetry "should come down on the poet from somewhere." Only Ted in the group had not commented.

At the *St. Botolph's* party Sylvia was determined to meet Ted Hughes, force for force, to "melt" the walls between them. After "slobbing around" with Luke, whom she forgave for his "blub, maundering"* because he had "raped" the lines of his sestina to some purpose, she moved on through the crowded hall. The next day she wrote in her journal:

Then the worst thing happened, that big, dark, hunky boy, the only one there huge enough for me, who had been hunching around over women, and whose name I had asked the minute I had come into the room, but no one told me, came over and was looking hard in my eyes and it was Ted Hughes. I started yelling again about his poems and quoting: "most dear unscratchable diamond" and he yelled back, colossal, in a voice that should have come from a Pole, "You like?" and asking me if I wanted brandy, and me yelling yes and backing into the next room past the smug shining . . . face of dear Bert, looking as if he had delivered at least nine or ten babies, and bang the door was shut and he was sloshing brandy into a glass and I was sloshing it at the place where my mouth was when I last knew about it.

We shouted as if in a high wind, about the review, and he saying Dan knew I was beautiful, he wouldn't have written it about a cripple, and my yelling protest in which the words "sleep with the editor" occurred with startling frequency. And then it came to the fact that I was all there, wasn't I, and I stamped and screamed yes, and he had obligations in the next room, and he was working in London, earning ten pounds a week so he could later earn twelve pounds a week, and I was stamping and he was stamping on the floor, and then he kissed me bang smash on the mouth and ripped

---

*From a line in a poem of Myers's: "The fools came maundering, blub, behind."

my hair band off, my lovely red hairband scarf which had weathered the sun and much love, and whose like I shall never again find, and my favorite silver earrings: hah, I shall keep, he barked. And when he kissed my neck I bit him long and hard on the cheek, and when we came out of the room, blood was running down his face.

Although the general configuration of this story is true, most of the yelling and stamping seems to have been a drama of the Plathian interior. This was how she envisaged giving herself "crashing and fighting" to her ideal lover. (Hughes himself has always said this account of their meeting was ridiculously exaggerated.) Certainly Hughes must have been taken aback by this energetic, extremely excited, very drunk American girl who could quote his poems verbatim. They talked about the magazine and he told her about his job in London. He had a girlfriend, Shirley, to whom Sylvia thought he had "obligations" — or perhaps the obligations referred to were merely those of a host at the party. He kissed her and she bit him, but at such a party the incident caused little stir. He was amazed, attracted enough to want to see her again. For Sylvia, of course, the symbolism of the "raped" hairband and the rent cheek confirmed that the melodrama had proceeded along Sassoonian lines. The slave of passion in her own Baudelairean rite, Sylvia must have known she was casting Ted in the role of demon lover. It was for him to bestow the erotic martyrdom Sassoon was withdrawing from her. The next day she wrote: "And I screamed in myself, thinking: oh, to give myself crashing, fighting, to you. The one man since I've lived who could blast Richard."

This was Sylvia's Ted. The Ted his Cambridge friends knew was quite different. Every one of them testifies to his essentially quiet, equable temperament in which shyness played a fair part — although his skeptical attitude to the Cambridge establishment had made Ted something of a legend, particularly among women who, like Sylvia, responded to his sexual magnetism. In a letter Luke Myers contradicts Sylvia's version in a few telling sentences:

Now let me tell you how I and everyone else who knew Ted well saw him. Ted was always the first to buy his round of drinks at the Anchor. Ted rarely drank to excess. In fact, he never allowed himself to lose control of himself in any way. He also never gave expression to an insincere sentiment even if it created some social awkwardness . . . Ted was a most considerate guest. He stayed with me for weeks in small quarters. He was the most considerate intellect in our circle and never did anything violent that I saw. He never even made a violent gesture. There was violence in his poetry — it expressed the violence of the universe.*

In 1956, when he met Sylvia Plath, Ted Hughes was certain that he wanted to devote his life to writing poetry; other matters, such as jobs, money, girls, were secondary. After leaving Cambridge in 1954, he had worked as a night watchman and a rose gardener, and at the time of the *St. Botolph's* party he was working for J. Arthur Rank, although the prestige Sylvia hinted at to her mother hardly attached to the job; he was employed to find novels or other fictional material suitable for turning into film scripts.

Hughes has written little about himself, but his family is an interesting one. Born in 1930, he was the youngest of three children. Gerald, ten years his senior, emigrated to Australia. His sister, Olwyn, took an arts degree from the University of London; after that she worked as a secretary in various organizations in Paris, where eventually she joined a theater and film agency run by Hungarians.

The family came from the upper Calder Valley in West Yorkshire. Ted Hughes's mother was a Farrar, from a family centered on Ewood (Mytholmroyd). In the sixteenth century it had produced the father of Nicholas Ferrar, the founder of Little Gidding, the religious community celebrated by T. S. Eliot in *Four Quartets*. Nicholas Ferrar's brother John emigrated to the American colonies and was an ancestor of Thomas Jefferson. Subsequent Farrars intermarried with Norfolk and Yorkshire farmers and fell to more modest stations in life.

The Hughes side of the family is more obscure. Ted's grandmother was half Spanish or Moorish; his half-Irish father, William Henry Hughes, served with the Lancashire Fusiliers in the First World War. In 1938, when Mrs. Hughes had inherited a little money, they bought and refurbished a large newspaper-and-tobacco shop in the mining town of Mexborough in South Yorkshire, moving there from the spectacular country in the Calder Valley. Ted was eight at the time. At school in Mexborough he had two remarkable English teachers who encouraged his talent, becoming friends of the family as well as mentors to the boy. When Ted went up to Cambridge he was better read than Sylvia, for all her Smith education, and at ease with literature in a way she was not.

When Ted and Sylvia met, then, their passion for poetry made a bridge between two very different worlds. As Luke Myers perceptively

---

*Jane Baltzell Kopp, whose memoir of Sylvia suggests that Ted Hughes was of a violent temperament, seems to have taken this view from Sylvia herself. Jane barely knew Hughes at Cambridge.

puts it, "What Ted and Sylvia shared was an unsurpassed single-mindedness about their art. They were quite determined to put into words the best that was in them, but, I thought, in somewhat different ways. Sylvia was determined that it should be read. Ted was determined that it should exist."

After they met at the *St. Botolph's* party, Sylvia had no idea whether she would see Hughes again. She had crept back into Whitstead at three in the morning after more adventures, including climbing with Hamish over the Queens College gates so the two could make love in his room. The next morning, having written down the whole story, she recoiled: "Somehow these sluttish nights make me have a violent nunlike passion to write and sequester myself." Such a reaction was predictable. For Hughes, Sylvia immediately (on February 27) wrote a full-page poem, which she called "Pursuit," about "the dark forces of lust." What it invoked, in fact, was not so much lust as her own libidinous double, the deep self full of violence and fury she was suppressing under her poised and capable appearance. As with a volcano, pressure from within had for some time been pushing for an explosion. Ted Hughes had unwittingly provided its occasion. Now that the eruption had taken place, all turned calm again on the surface, with five or six pages of journal and a poem to prove it had happened. A letter Sylvia wrote to her mother on March 3 was the offering of a guilty conscience to the "good" double on the other side of the Atlantic. So long as Mrs. Plath stayed in America, letters home could tell the "truth" both mother and daughter wanted to hear:

> I do want to tell you now how much your letters mean to me . . . Isn't it amazing what the power of words can do? . . . I don't know if you've felt how much more mellowed and chastened I've become in the last half year, but I certainly have gotten beyond that stage of "not listening" to advice and feel that I have been confiding in you through letters more than ever before in my life and welcome all you think wise to tell me. Perhaps you still don't realize . . . how very much I have admired you: for your work, your teaching, your strength and your creation of our exquisite home in Wellesley, and your seeing that Warren and I went to the Best colleges in the United States.

What seems peculiar about Sylvia's swing from violent vampire to virtuous nun is that most of her "bad" behavior was quite innocent. She was twenty-three years old, had gone to a party where she had drunk too much and clutched at a man she was attracted to. No one in Cambridge — not even the Victorian dons who so alarmed her — would have been surprised. Much worse had been known to happen; had it been discussed at all, the biting episode would have been regarded as a joke. But Sylvia, nervous lest people condemn her, feared they had found out she was really a whore, a vampire, a nymphomaniac — all the things, in fact, she loved to *imagine* she was, while acting the part of a nice, bright, neat, gushy American student.

Although Sylvia had been violently attracted to Ted, the whole experience was too dreamlike to build hopes on, and, in any case, she still held to the habit of longing for Richard Sassoon. Since January, when she returned from her idyll in France with Sassoon, she had been counting the days till spring vacation, when she planned to hunt him out even though she had been forbidden to communicate with him. On March 6 she wrote in her journal, "I got a letter from my Richard this afternoon which shot all to hell." Suddenly she realized how very much she loved him: "to hell and back and heaven and back, and have and do and will." She typed a long, wailing letter, recapitulating moments when she had felt most desperate and alive: on the Adirondack ski slope with Dick Norton; in Cambridge when Sam, the hired horse, had run away with her; in ecstasies of "fury and death" in Sassoon's lovemaking. Near the end she summed up in an astonishing revelation what she thought her purpose in living to be:

> I am inclined to babies and bed and brilliant friends and a magnificent stimulating home where geniuses drink gin in the kitchen after a delectable dinner and read their own novels and tell about why the stock market is the way it will be and discuss scientific mysticism (which, by the way, is intriguing: in all forms: several tremendous men in botany, chemistry, math and physics, etc., here are all mystics in various ways) — well, anyhow, this is what I was meant to make for a man, and to give him this colossal reservoir of faith and love for him to swim in daily, and to give him children; lots of them, in great pain and pride.

This is only a fragment of what she wrote (but presumably did not mail) to Sassoon. To Hughes she had already written "Pursuit." To her mother, on March 13, she posted the most extraordinary of all these testimonies, posing the surely obsolete dilemma of a choice between Gordon Lameyer, who was about to arrive in Paris, and Richard Sassoon. She loved Sassoon, but would the "Our Town" community of Wellesley ever accept him? Gordon, on the other hand, was "physically beautiful and really my match outwardly." Gordon had the body, Richard the soul. And how was she going to reconcile the two worlds they represented?

◀   ◀   ◀

Love, with its tribulations, was Sylvia's chief preoccupation in that most fraught of Marches, but there were other matters to trouble her. There was bad news from Wellesley. Grammy, for some time thought to be ill with gastritis, was now known to be dying of cancer. Sylvia was devastated. Closer at hand, Jane Baltzell brought down the wrath of the avenging angel when she underlined in pencil some passages in Sylvia's books. Sylvia's journal (for the same date on which she received Sassoon's letter) breathes out that note of relief which usually followed an explosion:

> *March 6* . . . had marvelous cathartic blowup with Jane on Sunday [March 4]. After she had underlined five of my new books in pencil with notes; evidently she felt that since I'd already underlined them in black, nothing further could harm them; well, I was furious, feeling my children had been raped, or beaten, by an alien* . . . And this led to other things: to France (where I realize that I threw myself at Richard, making her feel superfluous: I was so desperate then! . . .) To St. Botolph's Review: and the evidence that [Jane is in] no league [at] all [with] the two I admire, Luke and Ted . . . [she] also felt clumsy in my presence, even as I felt obtuse in hers.
>
> Turns out we're too much alike, too much the same, ironically, to be friends closely here: One American girl who writes and is humorous and reasonably attractive & magnetic is enough in any group of Englishmen . . . When we are together, it is a mutual grabbing for queenship . . . we overlap in too many places . . . So that at least is that. And the hydra is slain. Thank God.

Meanwhile, Ted Hughes had returned to Cambridge and with Luke had inquired of Bert Wyatt-Brown the whereabouts of Sylvia's room in Whitstead. That night they tried to wake her by throwing stones at her window, but they got the wrong window. Moreover, Sylvia was out drinking with Hamish. The next day (March 10), on the way

---

*The remark is very similar to Sylvia's comment, years before, to Nancy Hunter in Cambridge. When Nancy remarked on "the neat, almost mechanical arrangement of the contents of her drawers," Sylvia replied, "If anyone ever disarranged my things I'd feel as though I had been raped intellectually." Hunter goes on: "The reaction was extreme, and it frightened me."

back from a second appointment with the psychiatrist, she met Bert by accident. "HE" was back in Cambridge. "A huge joy galloped through me; they remembered my name . . . Please let him come," she prayed in her journal,

> let me have him for this British spring. Please, please . . . and give me the resilience & guts to make him respect me, be interested, and not to throw myself at him with loudness or hysterical yelling; calmly, gently, easy, baby, easy . . . Oh, he is here; my black marauder; oh hungry hungry. I am so hungry for a big smashing creating burgeoning burdened love: I am here; I wait; and he plays on the banks of the river Cam like a casual faun.

Ted returned to London without seeing Sylvia, but shortly afterward, Luke Myers invited her to supper in his new digs on Barton Road. He remembers her smooth skin, "like cellophane," her general effusiveness, and a way she had of talking of Wallace Stevens in one breath and *Mademoiselle* in the next. Sublimely unaware of his misgivings, Sylvia chatted on from a cushion on the floor while he prepared the meal on a gas ring. Over supper Luke told Sylvia he intended to spend several days in a flat Daniel Huws's father kept in Rugby Street, near Queen Square in Bloomsbury. Would Sylvia be interested in joining him and Ted for a drink at The Lamb before she left to spend her Easter vacation in France? Sylvia, who had waited in "hell" for the sound of Ted's fateful footsteps on the Whitstead stairs, eagerly accepted.

Through all this erotic turbulence Sylvia had not abandoned her need for a safe, meat-and-potatoes American to hold her hand when the world split open around her. She had promised to meet Gordon in Paris, but in Cambridge she was seeing a good deal of a "sweet, if pedantic, Fulbright student from Yale," Gary Haupt. Writing of him in her journal, she admits that at first he might have been put off by her "emotional, irresponsible gushing."*

In the last week of the term, a splinter of grit lodged in Sylvia's eye, causing intense pain. Luckily Haupt was on hand to sit with her in the casualty ward of Addenbrooke's Hospital while a doctor froze the eye and removed the splinter. Again, this relatively minor event prompted major emotions. To her mother she reported "listening to screams and seeing blood-stained people being wheeled by on stretchers." While the doctor operated, she babbled on "about how Oedipus

---

*Elsewhere she speaks of "my absurd overflowing enthusiasms. They *are* absurd, and I *am* acting — because I feel peculiar . . ."

and Gloucester in *King Lear* got new vision through losing eyes, but I would just as soon keep my sight and get new vision, too." Afterward, Gary was a great consolation, plying her with wine and reading Thurber aloud while she recovered in her room at Whitstead. The experience was the source of her poem "The Eye-mote," written two years later.

On Friday, March 23, Sylvia went up to London by train to meet Ted and Luke. She spent the night with Ted in Rugby Street, in a flat without running water and a WC three flights down, in the basement. It says a good deal for the impression Ted had made on her that Sylvia accepted these conditions without a murmur.* The next day, exhausted, she made the tedious journey to Paris by car and ferry with a Fulbright student and his girlfriend, finding a room in the evening in the Hotel Béarn, near Les Invalides. Tired as she was when she wandered out of the hotel on the evening of her arrival, she was excited to meet an Italian journalist named Giovanni Perego. In her naive American way she borrowed a map from him and accepted "steak tartar[e] and wine and meringue at a little *brasserie*." They talked in French, which especially pleased her. A few days later she wrote in her journal: "The guy turned out to be, interestingly enough, the Paris correspondent for . . . *Paese Sera* . . . an Italian Communist journalist, no less! Hence the Olivetti which he loaned me for today."

On Sunday, March 25, Sylvia rose, still tired, and set off to find Richard Sassoon in the rue Duvivier. Presenting herself at number 4, where he had rooms, she was admitted by "the dark and suspicious concierge," who told her Sassoon was away (as he had forewarned her) and would not be back until after Easter. Writing the next day of her baffled disappointment, for some reason she was as much amazed as distressed:

> I had been ready to bear a day or two alone, but this news shook me to the roots. I sat down in her living room and wrote an incoherent letter while the tears fell scalding and wet on the paper and her black poodle patted me with his paw and the radio blared: "Smile though your heart is breaking." I wrote and wrote, thinking that by some miracle he might walk in the door. But he had left no address, no messages, and my letters begging him to return were

---

*She *did* mind, though, when Michael Boddy, the ex-Marlborough School, 280-pound trombonist of the student jazz band at The Anchor, interrupted them. Sylvia's journal refers to this episode later as one of her reasons for not fleeing Paris sooner than she did.

lying there blue and unread. I was really amazed at my situation. Never before had a man gone off to leave me to cry after . . .

No miracle occurred, and Sylvia realized she was alone. Part of the rest of her time in Paris she spent on romantic pilgrimages to the places she had been with Richard. She could only hope that Gary Haupt, Gordon Lameyer, or *somebody* would turn up to save her. On the twenty-sixth "a good-looking chap . . . with a Slavic bone structure and diabolical green eyes" fell into step with her as she was walking to the American Express. She wondered if he was a gigolo. "Toyed with idea of sleeping with whoever took my fancy," she wrote in her journal, "in a kind of aesthetic fashion: there have been many handsome strong faces, probably some with sinewy minds." Obviously she was in a very unsinewy state of mind herself when she lunched at the Tour Eiffel with an Oxford man named Tony and his sister, missing Richard's purse as much as his presence. Paris without an escort was expensive.

After a few days Gary Haupt showed up and they walked together to the Pont Royal, where it seems she exchanged him for Tony, whose sister had gone back to England. The weather was golden and spring-like. She and Tony strolled through Montmartre, lunching in a café off the main square where Tony became "increasingly attentive" and she "mellowed to fondness." By late afternoon they were in bed in the Hotel Béarn. Tony, however, apparently had second thoughts about making love to her, and rather suddenly "dressed and with the layers put on his decorum."

Sylvia wondered what to do: about Tony, about men, about herself. She wanted to go back to Ted in London but decided against it. She was afraid of Cambridge gossip and he had not written; "he can come to me, and call me Sylvia not Shirley [the name of his former girl-friend]." Determined to be "chaste and subdued" in the next term "and mystify those gossipmongers by work and seriousness!" on April Fool's Day she set down a list of commandments:

Don't drink much — (remember misfortunes w. Iko after St. John's party, Hamish — 2 dates, *St. Botolph's* party and London night); stay sober.
Be chaste and don't throw self at people (c.f. David Buck, Mallory, Iko, Hamish, Ted, Tony) . . .
Be friendly and more subdued — if necessary, smog of "mystery woman," quiet, nice, slightly bewildered at colored scandals. Refuse ease of Sally Bowles act.

Work on inner life to enrich — concentrate on work for Krook
[Doris Krook was to be her supervisor in the next term] — writing
(stories, poems, articles for *Monitor* — sketches) — *French daily.*
Don't blab too much — listen more; sympathize and "understand"
people.
Keep troubles to self.
Bear mean gossip and snubbing and pass beyond it — be nice and
positive to all.
Don't criticize anybody to anyone else — misquoting is like a tele-
phone game.
Don't date either Gary or Hamish — be nice but *not too enthusiastic*
to Keith et al.
Be stoic when necessary and *write* — you have seen a lot, felt deeply,
and your problems are universal enough to be made meaningful —
WRITE.

With her superego in the ascendant once again, Sylvia was relieved
the next evening when she accidentally ran into Gordon Lameyer at
the American Express. She was too sick of the "small dark sleazy
men" who dogged her wanderings to refuse Gordon's "orange-juice-
and-broiled-chicken solidity." Over ham and eggs they planned their
week of travel: Munich, Venice, and Rome. Reluctantly Sylvia realized
that to tour Europe with Gordon "like brother and sister" was by
now her only option. Richard had "deserted" her, Whitstead was
closed, and she dared not descend on Ted. Her journal for April 5
debates the question, "Can I be good for a week [with Gordon]? No
acidity, or lemon looks . . . oh my God, what is it what is it? Why
does one not learn to love and live with the . . . daily bread that is
good for one, that is comfortable, convenient and available?"

The alternatives indeed were revolving "in a fatal dance." She sent
a postcard to her mother informing her of her trip to Rome with
Gordon, and another, Rousseau's *Snakecharmer*, to Ted, who had
written her a note, in London.

On April 6 Sylvia and Gordon were pulling out of the Gare de
Lyon, acidly quarreling over whether John Malcolm Brinnin was or
was not to blame for not having saved Dylan Thomas's life in New
York. They continued to quarrel over one thing and another throughout the five days of their tour. When they got to Rome they separated,
but after an accidental meeting in the Vatican Museum in Rome, on
Friday the thirteenth Gordon bought Sylvia an air ticket and put her
on the plane to London. It bore her out of Gordon's life forever,
bringing her straight to Heathrow, Rugby Street, and Ted Hughes.

▶ 5 ◀

F I R E

A N D   F L O W E R

1956-1957

Dear Sylvia,
There is no end to the thrilling things happening. It frightens
me a little. I am very proud of you, Sylvia. I love telling your
story. Someone remarked to me after reading your poem "Pursuit" in the *Atlantic*, "How intense." Sometime write me a little
poem that isn't intense. A lamp turned too high might shatter its
chimney. Please just *glow* sometimes . . .

— Letter from Olive Higgins
Prouty, March 1957

SYLVIA HAD BEEN AWAY from Cambridge for only three weeks
when she returned to Whitstead in mid-April. By all accounts she was
a new person, as she herself would later declare: "I took a plane from
Rome through the mist-shrouded sky of Europe, to London — re-
nounced Gordon, Sassoon — my old life — and took up Ted." There
was room for no one else. Nathaniel LaMar, who had been one of
Sylvia's favorites at Cambridge, recalls that when Ted entered her life
"the door closed on our friendship." When he first knew her she had
many lovers. Ted now eclipsed all friendships.* No longer her "black
marauder," Ted was "the strongest man in the world, ex-Cambridge,
brilliant poet whose work I loved before I met him, a large, hulking,
healthy Adam . . . with a voice like the thunder of God — a singer,

---

*LaMar says that, to those she trusted, Sylvia used to talk about herself "with a
rapt clinical objectivity, like a lepidopterist dissecting an impaled butterfly."

story-teller, lion and world-wanderer, a vagabond who will never stop."

Once Sylvia had begun describing Ted to her mother in terms like these, as she did on April 17, it may have occurred to her that her mother must be wondering what had happened to her "great love" for Sassoon, so characterized only a month before. She reported, "Richard went off to Spain for a month and was miserable alone and wrote long letters which I didn't receive till I got back here, too late, after feeling terribly deserted in Paris."

But no such letters from Richard survive. On April 18 she drafted a cryptic letter to him in her journals and possibly sent it:

> Something very terrifying too has happened to me, which started two months ago and which need not to have happened, just as it needed not to have happened that you wrote that you did not want to see me in Paris . . . When I came back to London there seemed only this one way of happening, and I am living now in a kind of present hell and god knows what ceremonies of life or love can patch the havoc wrought.

The letter goes on to accuse him of utter and brutal desertion. Now her vacation was "spent too, brutally, and I am spent, giving with both hands, daily, and the blight and terror has been made in the choice and the superfluous unnecessary and howling void of your long absence."

It is possible to construe this as her reply to a note from Richard written after he read the tearful letter she had left at his Paris address. Perhaps he had reminded her that he had already "brutally" told her how his holiday was going to be "spent." Whether or not Sassoon's "long letters" from Spain actually existed, only one last letter (or so it seems: his letters are undated) survives among Sylvia's papers. It seems to respond to Sylvia's April 18 outpouring, and it signals the end: "Your letter was not the letter of a happy woman . . . I shall have to live my years with the specter of loss, in regret and even in shame. For the angel is dead, the red god dead and I am like a carcass from which the interior has been taken."

But it was too late. Now that Sassoon had been disposed of, Sylvia had little inclination to mourn him. On April 19 she wrote:

> It is this man, this poet, this Ted Hughes. I have never known anything like it. For the first time in my life I can use *all* my knowing and laughing and force and writing to the hilt all the time . . . Daily I am full of poems; my joy whirls in tongues of words . . . I do not merely idolize, I see right into the core of him . . . I know myself,

in vigor and prime and growing, and know I am strong enough to keep myself whole, no matter what . . . I have never been so exultant . . . What a huge humor we have, what running strength!

Ted's friends looked on in perplexity as Ted too showed increasingly that he was falling in love. "To our circle," writes Lucas Myers, "poetry was the single claim and any kind of ongoing commitment to flesh and blood an unfaithfulness, an abandonment. Sylvia was in love, eager to marry Ted, eager to have children, to engage any experience which might come her way . . . They both were writing a lot." But Myers was also concerned that Sylvia might "pull him into a struggle for income, shoes, tableware, functioning appliances, perhaps into the American English Literature Establishment, a shallow sea hostile to his happiness." That, in fact, never happened; it was Ted who persuaded Sylvia to be true to her gift rather than to her ambition.

Myers goes on to say that Ted left his job in London in May and came to live with Myers in Tenison Road, Cambridge. He and Sylvia met every day, sometimes with Luke, who shared their delight in quoting poems, one of the three beginning with a few lines and calling on the others to finish the quote. Being wholeheartedly in love gave Sylvia energy for other activities. She joined *Varsity* and traveled up to London to report on a reception for Bulganin and Khrushchev at Claridges. She modeled bathing suits and ball gowns for May Week. She went with Ted for long walks in the fens. There was only one shadow to cloud her ecstasy, and that was Grammy's approaching death in Wellesley.

Grammy died on April 29, three days after Aurelia Plath's fiftieth birthday. As it happened, on the same day Sylvia wrote rapturously of her newfound happiness:

> The reason why you must be at ease and not worry about my proud growing this time is because I have learned to make a life growing through toleration of conflict, sorrow, and hurt. I fear none of these things and turn myself to whatever trial with an utter faith that life is good and a song of joy on my lips. I feel like Job and will rejoice in the deadly blasts of whatever comes. I love others, the girls in the house, the boys on the newspaper, and I am flocked about by people who bask in my sun. I give and give; my whole life will be a saying of poems and a loving of people and giving of my best fiber to them.
>
> This faith comes from the earth and sun; it is pagan in a way; it comes from the heart of man after the fall.

Loving Ted made it easy to love the world while not for a moment abandoning her ambition. Her letter continues:

> I know that within a year I shall publish a book of 33 poems which will hit the critics violently . . . My voice is taking shape, coming strong. Ted says he never read poems by a woman like mine; they are strong and full and rich — not quailing and whining like Teasdale or simple lyrics like Millay; they are working, sweating, heaving poems born out of the way words should be said . . .

With her letter Sylvia enclosed three poems: "Firesong," "Strumpet Song," and "Complaint of the Crazed Queen."

Despite her grandmother's death, the tone of Sylvia's letters to her mother throughout April and May never once lowers from a fevered, ecstatic crescendo. Outsiders who knew her at the time comment on her very evident intellectual as well as personal happiness. In May, Mary Ellen Chase visited Cambridge with her companion, Eleanor Shipley Duckett —"both of them," Sylvia assured Mrs. Plath, "making fabulous money on new books and articles and radio broadcasts!" Sylvia met them over coffee and during their talk gleaned that she might very well be asked back to teach at Smith after taking her degree, a pleasing prospect. Dorothea Krook remembers discussing Sylvia with Miss Chase shortly afterward, the latter pretending much exasperation: " 'Plato and Mrs. Krook, Mrs. Krook and Plato, Mrs. Krook on Plato, Plato on Mrs. Krook . . . It's hard to know *which* she's talking about, whether it's Plato or Mrs. Krook she admires most.' "

Sylvia had not, of course, brought Ted Hughes into the conversation, but Smith or no Smith, she wanted to marry him. Ted had been planning to join his elder brother in Australia the following year. Now, Sylvia told her mother, he was willing to book a passage to America with her after a year's teaching in Spain. "If we got married," she wrote on May 10, ". . . do you suppose it would be possible for us both to get part-time or full-time summer jobs and a cottage down the Cape . . . so we could travel and write all over America the next year? This is just one of the little pots cooking in my head, but you might talk to the Cantors or anyone who has an 'in' at the big hotels."

By May 18 Sylvia was sending batches of Ted's poems to American magazines so that American editors would be "crying for him" when he arrived. She persuaded Ted to accompany her to a "Fulbright blast" in London, where she introduced him to the American ambassador. The Duke of Edinburgh addressed the assembly, after which he stepped down to chat with Sylvia, asking her about her studies before turning inquiringly to Ted. Ted, in his eight-year-old suit, grinned and said he was "chaperoning Sylvia." "Ah, the idle rich," quipped the Duke.

Meanwhile, Ted's circle of friends watched with concern. Commenting on the marriage into which Sylvia was hastening Ted, Luke Myers observes that Ted was attracted chiefly to her vitality:

> Ted and Sylvia were a united couple, and they complemented each other. Without Sylvia, Ted might have had to work in rose gardens and warehouses for quite a few more years. Competent and organized in the American, specifically the Eastern seaboard, manner . . . Sylvia always had Ted's poems, like her own, meticulously typed and out at English and American magazines. A number, both of his and hers, were being published, and those that weren't accepted the first time went right out again. It was Sylvia who got Ted's first book, *The Hawk in the Rain*, to the Harper contest, which it won, making his name. I don't think Ted would have heard of the Harper prize on his own.

Myers continues perceptively:

> Ted responded to Sylvia's vitality and her appetite for life; he needed this in his wife and friends. He was not put off by the unselfconscious expression of qualities which made her well-disposed English friends uncomfortable and gave the ill-disposed an opportunity to condescend. At that time, in the 1950s, Americans hadn't yet been exposed much to television or acquired its secondhand cosmopolitanism. Americans were rich; the products of Europe's long traditions and ruined wealth had to watch crowds of untutored but confident Yanks eat in the best restaurants and tramp through their museums making ludicrous observations. American universities, in the English Departments at least, were nursery schools compared to Cambridge. Sylvia's effusiveness, which disguised her intelligence, and her seemingly commercial approach to literature . . . exposed her to mockery at Cambridge. While I was still there, she had published some enthusiasms about a vacation visit to Paris . . . I was convinced that the editor [of *Varsity*] had mousetrapped her into giving him an article that would allow his readers to condescend to Americans. Ted shared this view, and his touching defensiveness on her behalf was the first sure index I had to the depth of his feelings for her. As it happened, the editor later gave her some good assignments on the paper, so my suspicions may have been unjust.
>
> It would have been unlike Ted to have said to her, "Look, they're making a fool of you." He always let his friends, and doubtless Sylvia too, come at their own epiphanies.

Lucas Myers presented this picture long after what in retrospect seems a curiously abrupt decision. Soon after Mrs. Plath arrived at Waterloo Station, she apparently endorsed Ted and Sylvia's decision to marry in London before all three set off for Paris on June 22. The idea was probably Sylvia's, catalyzed by Aurelia's temporary presence in England and her approval of Ted. Marriage, since the couple planned to spend the summer in Spain together, would make traveling easier. They were in love, sure of each other's dedication to writing; and for Sylvia a romantic wedding may have been the only way of securing their future partnership. She was convinced, too, that the college authorities would disapprove; by no means could her tutor at Newnham be informed, nor the Fulbright Commission, which might, she feared, cancel her scholarship forthwith. The marriage was therefore a secret, shared only with Sylvia's mother and brother. Not even Hughes's parents were told about it, although the day after the wedding Ted returned to Yorkshire to store his belongings in their house in Heptonstall.

The marriage, which was made possible by a special license from the Archbishop of Canterbury,* took place at 1:30 P.M. on June 16, in the eighteenth-century church of St. George the Martyr, Blooms-bury. Writing to Warren in Austria (he was enrolled in an American good-neighbor project called the Experiment in International Living), Sylvia describes the circumstances without stating quite why it had to take place so hastily and how Mrs. Plath came to acquiesce in the scheme: "When Ted and I see you in Europe this summer, we'll tell you all the fantastic details of our struggle to get a license (from the Archbishop of Canterbury, no less), searching for the parish church where Ted belonged and had, by law, to be married, spotting a priest on the street, Ted pointing, 'That's him!' and following him home and finding he was the right one." The sexton was about to drive off with a bus full of children to visit the zoo when they prevailed on him to be a witness. The bus sat, with all the children on board, until the ceremony was over.†

Sylvia preceded her description with a hectic explanation of her reasons for the marriage:

---

*The Archbishop of Canterbury's right by special license — given only in exceptional circumstances — to authorize a marriage to be celebrated at any time or place derives from Henry VIII's time. For the Hughes marriage one can speculate that the license was essential as requiring neither a residential qualification nor a waiting period.

†Ted Hughes, the source of this information, recalls that the sexton, not the curate (as Sylvia reported in her letter to Warren), was a witness to the marriage.

Why two weddings? Why a secret wedding? Why anyhow? Well, it so happens that I have at last found the one man in the world for me, which mother saw immediately (she and Ted get along beautifully, and he loves her and cares for her very much) and after three months of seeing each other every day, doing everything from writing to reading aloud to hiking and cooking together, there was absolutely no shred of doubt in our minds. We are both poverty-stricken now, have no money, and are in no position to have people know we are married. Me at Newnham, where the Victorian virgins wouldn't see how I could concentrate on my studies with being married to such a handsome virile man, the Fulbright, etc., etc. Also, he is getting a job teaching English in Spain next year to earn money to come to America with me next June, so we'll have to be apart while I finish my degree for three long 8-week periods (I must do very well on my exams). I'll fly to be with him for the 5-week-long vacation at Christmas and Easter. So this marriage is in keeping with our situation: private, personal, legal, true, but limited in its way. Neither of us will think of giving up the fullest ceremony, which will be kind of folk festival in Wellesley.

Clearly Sylvia wanted to secure Ted before he went alone to teach in Spain — a scheme that never materialized. Her letter to Warren continues with an account of breathless days preparing for the wedding:

We rushed about London, buying dear Ted shoes and trousers, the gold wedding rings (I never wanted an engagement ring) with the last of our money, and mummy supplying a lovely pink knitted suit dress she brought (intuitively never having worn) and me in that and a pink hair ribbon and a pink rose from Ted, standing with the rain pouring outside in the dim little church [today it is a cheerful, well-lit church], saying the most beautiful words in the world as our vows, with the curate as second witness and the dear Reverend, an old, bright-eyed man (who lives right opposite Charles Dickens' house!) kissing my cheek, and the tears just falling down from my eyes like rain — I was so happy with my dear, lovely Ted.

After the wedding on James Joyce's Bloomsday — June 16 having been chosen for its literary association — the Hugheses spent their wedding night in Rugby Street, a "slum" (as she called it) that she hoped to leave behind forever. Then Ted moved his belongings to Yorkshire while Sylvia showed her mother Cambridge. On the twenty-first they met once more for a night in London before flying to Paris the next morning. A week's exhausting sightseeing saw Mrs. Plath off on a tour of Europe while Ted and Sylvia lingered happily in Paris;

to Luke Myers, who met them there, they looked "happy, happier than I had ever seen them." They were writing every day —"a necessity to our personal self-esteem" —when they set off for Spain with a rucksack, a battered portable typewriter, and a sturdy determination to succeed.

◄　◄　◄

In mid-July they settled in Benidorm, a still-undeveloped fishing village on the Mediterranean coast. After a week in the seafront villa of the widow Mangada, whose inadequate plumbing (shades of Rugby Street!) and unwelcome intrusions became the subject of a story Sylvia later wrote, they shook themselves free and set up housekeeping in a pleasant, inexpensive house a little way from the beach. Despite the exaggerated panegyrics she sent to her mother, Sylvia was not at ease in Spain. Its intense heat and scorched hills, its mood of suppressed passion, the casual violence that emanated from its cities' streets were too close to her own nightmares. Many years later Ted Hughes recalled her apprehensive panic in his poem "You Hated Spain":

> You saw right down to the Goya funeral grin
> And recognized it, and recoiled
> As your poems winced back into chill, as your panic
> Clutched back towards college America . . . Spain
> Was the land of your dreams: the dust-red cadaver
> You dared not wake with, the puckering amputations
> No literature course had glamorized . . .

In Madrid they saw a bad bullfight. Sylvia recoiled in shocked disgust, full of sympathy for the bull. To her mother she wrote:

> I'd imagined that the matador danced around with the dangerous bull, then killed him neatly. Not so. The bull is utterly innocent, peaceful, taunted to run about by the many cape-wavers. Then a horrid picador on a horse with a strawmat guard about it stabs a huge hole in the bull's neck with a pike from which gushed blood, and men run to stick little colored picks in it. The killing isn't even neat . . . The most satisfying moment for us was when one of the six beautiful doomed bulls managed to gore a fat, cruel picador, lift him off his horse; . . . he was carried out, spurting blood from his thigh.

The cruel scene gave her a good poem, "The Goring": "Arena dust rusted by four bulls' blood to a dull redness, / The afternoon at a bad end under the crowd's truculence . . ."

Although Sylvia could not like Spain, she was nonetheless fascinated. Passages in her journal exclaim over the wealth of color, the abundance of fruit in the market, the intense blue of the Mediterranean, while complaining bitterly of the widow Mangada's "bad dirty bathroom, ant-infested kitchen . . . to be shared with . . . the piggy Spaniards" and the terrace overlooking "the honking staring gawking crowds on the boulevard." Olwyn Hughes remembers Sylvia's describing in an especially horrified voice, "as though she had in truth found it all hateful and obscene," the amputated beggars who had waylaid her in filthy lanes, the dirt and dust, the fearful smells and ugly poverty. During their stay Sylvia picked up a stomach bug. She lay in a fever, occasionally delirious, insisting that only if she climbed into the well of the house would she ever get cool.

Things improved after they moved inland, away from the seafront, yet her moods seemed to soar and sink with alarming rapidity. Sylvia recorded in her journal her volatile and intense reactions to some unmentioned incident, possibly arising out of her husband's surprise at the rancor she displayed in a running tiff with the house owner, who wanted to raise the rent, or perhaps arising out of an evening when they had drinks with some English people who upset Sylvia. These moods, Ted found, were largely unaccountable: they began and ended like electric storms, and he came to learn simply to accept their occurrence. Suddenly Sylvia found herself at the center of a melodrama:

> Alone, deepening. Feeling the perceptions deepen with the tang of geranium and the full moon and the mellowing of hurt; the deep ingrowing of hurt, too far from the bitching fussing surface tempests. The hurt going in, clean as a razor, and the dark blood welling. Just the sick knowing that the wrongness was growing in the full moon. Listening, he scratches his chin, the small rasp of beard. He is not asleep. He must come out, or there is no going in.
>
> . . . It is very quiet. Perhaps he is asleep. Or dead. How to know how long there is before death. The fish may be poisoned, and the poison working. And two sit apart in wrongness.
>
> What is wrong? he asks as the sweater is yanked out, wool slacks, and raincoat. I'm going out. Do you want to come? The aloneness would be too much; desperate and foolish on the lonely roads. Asking for a doom. He dresses in dungarees and shirt and black jacket. We go out leaving the light on in the house into the glare of the full moon . . . We sit far apart, on stones and bristling dry grass. The light is cold, cruel and still. All could happen: the willful drowning, the murder, the killing words. The stones are rough and

clear, and outlined mercilessly in the moonlight. Clouds cross over;
the fields darken, and a neighboring dog yaps at the two strangers.
Two silent strangers. Going back, there is the growing sickness, the
separate sleep, and the sour waking. And all the time the wrongness
is growing, creeping, choking the house, twining the tables and
chairs and poisoning the knives and forks, clouding the drinking
water with that lethal taint. Sun falls off-key on eyes asquint, and
the world has grown crooked and sour as a lemon overnight.

Everything became grist for Sylvia's writing. Suppressing the nightmarish, grotesque aspects of Spain, she captured the unspoiled water-
front and town in several pen-and-ink sketches the *Christian Science
Monitor* accepted with an article in the autumn. Throughout most of
July and August both writers worked continually, Ted writing a book
of animal fables (published many years later as *How the Whale Became*), Sylvia laboring over stories she planned to sell to *McCall's* or
the *Ladies' Home Journal.* Both writers were still, of course, beginners.
By the end of the summer Sylvia's sales putsch had produced only
two American acceptances, for Ted's "Bawdry Embraced" from *Poetry* (Chicago) and "Hag" from *The Nation*. Rigorously they disciplined themselves to follow the schedule Sylvia needed to keep herself
working. A letter to Mrs. Plath written on July 25 details "a day in
the life of the writing Hugheses":

> We wake about seven in the morning, with a cool breeze blowing
> in the grape leaves outside our window. I get up, take the two litres
> of milk left daily on our doorstep in a can and heat it for my café-
> con-leche and Ted's brandy-milk . . . [to accompany] delectable wild
> bananas and sugar. Then we go early to market, first for fish . . .
> every day brings a different catch. There are mussels, crabs, shrimp,
> little baby octopuses, and sometimes a huge fish which they sell in
> steaks . . . Then we price vegetables, buying our staples of eggs,
> potatoes, tomatoes and onions . . . If only you could see how fan-
> tastically we economize. We go to the one potato stand that sells a
> kilo for 1.50 instead of 1.75 pesetas and have found a place that
> charges a peseta less . . . for butter. I hope that never again in my
> life will I have to be so tight with money. We will one day have a
> great deal, I am sure of it.
> For the rest of the morning Ted and I write, he at the big oak
> table, I at the typewriter table by the window in the dining
> room . . . from 8:30 to 12. Then I make lunch and we go to the
> beach for two hours for a siesta and swim when the crowds are all
> gone home and [we] have it completely to ourselves. Then two more
> hours of writing from 4 to 6, when I make supper. From 8 to 10

we study languages, me translating *Le Rouge et Le Noire* and planning to do all the French for my exams this summer; Ted working on Spanish.

As usual when writing to her mother, Sylvia exaggerated her happiness and idealized her surroundings, but in her journal she revealed both sides. One side of her reached back for a harmonious home life and commercial success; another abandoned itself to moony fantasies, black, silent furies, or imaginary scenes of violence.

Toward the end of August, after sixteen hours on the train, they reached Paris, where Sylvia introduced Ted to Warren, on his way home to Wellesley and a final year at Harvard after a summer in Austria. Ted had written to his family from Benidorm, announcing his marriage, and as soon as they were back in England they went up to Heptonstall, to Ted's family home, The Beacon, on the outskirts of the village.

Picturesque, black, and ancient, Heptonstall straggles along a steep slope near the top of a hill. Its gnarled old stone houses, slate-roofed, seem to lean over the narrow main street — still cobbled when Sylvia knew it — that runs crookedly down through the village toward Hebden Bridge in the valley bottom. Near the summit, set back slightly from the road, stands a handsome church alongside the ruins of a much earlier one. Bill and Edith Hughes received Sylvia warmly. Though she never told them so, Edith Hughes was hurt not to have been told of the wedding, or invited to it — particularly as Aurelia Plath had been present. Ted and Sylvia were by now completely out of money, so the Hugheses put them up until Sylvia returned to Cambridge.

A greater contrast to Spain could not have been imagined. Writing (inevitably) to her mother on September 2, Sylvia described "an incredible, wild, green landscape of bare hills, crisscrossed by innumerable black stone walls like a spider's web in which gray, woolly sheep graze, along with chickens and dappled brown-and-white cows. A wicked north wind is whipping a blowing rain against the little house, and coal fires are glowing."

To Sylvia this was Brontë country, undeniably romantic. Ted's parents, to whom she rather condescended, were "dear, simple Yorkshire folk," his mother "plumpish and humorous," his Uncle Walter (a prosperous small-factory owner) a "millionaire." She indulged her passion for cooking in Mrs. Hughes's tiny kitchen, envisioning how one day she would luxuriate in an American one "with orange juice and egg beater and all my lovely supplies for light cookies and cakes!"

With Ted and his uncle she walked across the moor to "Withins," reputedly the site of *Wuthering Heights*, and made a sketch of it.

While in Heptonstall Sylvia received a letter from Edward Weeks, editor of *The Atlantic Monthly* in Boston, accepting her poem "Pursuit"—"a fine and handsome thing"— and enclosing a check for $50. It was Sylvia's first professional acceptance that year, a good omen. Her Smith friend Elly Friedman, with whom she had planned to travel before she met Hughes, arrived for a visit with flattering rumors from Northampton: almost certainly Sylvia would be asked to teach at Smith the following year. For herself, Sylvia was pleased. It seems, however, that she actually took steps to prevent Ted's teaching at a women's college, perhaps out of jealousy in advance. Toward the end of their stay in Heptonstall, Ted and Sylvia took a bus to London, where Ted auditioned for part-time work reading poetry for the BBC. They then returned to Yorkshire for some quiet, happy days together before Sylvia's Cambridge term began. By September 30 she was back at Whitstead; there she found a letter from Peter Davison, now working for the Atlantic Monthly Press.

Sylvia could not believe her luck. Here was a personal link with a journal and publishing house of the first importance. In a four-page reply she described Hughes as her English discovery of the year (only at the very end mentioning that she was *going* to marry him), begging Davison to advise them both about publishers and agents in America. Where could Ted publish his animal fables? Where could she publish a novel? poems? England was hopeless, she added (spiteful after a summer of rejections), its old-fashioned values "sick, sick, sick. I have never been so disappointed and disgusted by anything as the London literati, with their outposts in Oxford and Cambridge." The young English poets were to a man "incredibly malicious, vain, and with no sense of music, readableness or, for that matter, deep honest meaning."

Together with Davison's letter was one from *Poetry* (Chicago) accepting no less than six of her new poems: "Two Sisters of Persephone," "Metamorphosis" (published as "Faun"), "Wreath for a Bridal," "Strumpet Song," "Dream with Clam-Diggers," and a love poem begun on the beach at Benidorm, "Epitaph for Fire and Flower." They would appear in the same issue as Ted's "Bawdry Embraced." Such a coup alleviated her gloom at being parted from her husband, and with renewed determination she set to work on a novel about Cambridge life and a book of poems.

Shortly after the beginning of the term, Ted heard from the BBC that they wanted him to record a number of Yeats's late poems for

a broadcast that autumn. It involved his coming down from Heptonstall to London to make the recording, and he and Sylvia, in a drama
of missed connections, met briefly to debate the wisdom of living
apart. Previously, alone in Cambridge, Sylvia had suffered what she
described to her mother as a "hectic suffocating wild depression."
After meeting Ted in London she went to look up the list of women
Fulbright scholars and discovered that three were married. If she could
enlist Dorothea Krook's sympathy, the Newnham dons might be persuaded to apply their rule to the effect that an undergraduate who
married could continue her course if granted permission by the council. She decided to take the risk and announce her marriage. On the
last day of October she traveled up to London to put her case to the
Fulbright Commission. To her amazement, she was received not with
disapproving shakings of hoary heads but by a young man who offered
congratulations on her having so successfully cemented Anglo-
American relations.

On returning to Cambridge she and Ted found a flat almost immediately on the ground floor of a dilapidated but pleasantly situated
house at 55 Eltisley Avenue, close to Grantchester Meadows.* Ted
would be able to move in as soon as they had got the "ghastly yellow"
walls painted a soft gray and got their books into bookcases. Sylvia
had still to break the news to the authorities at Newnham College.

Mrs. Krook recalls Sylvia's coming to one of her supervisions in
an exaggerated state of agitation in which the older woman glimpsed
for the first time "the passionate *rage* which has since come to be
recognized as a dominating emotion of her poetry." In the circumstances, it seems the rage was uncalled for. I. V. Morris, Sylvia's tutor
(at Cambridge the tutor is responsible for the student's moral welfare),
remembers Sylvia's phoning to say she had a terrible confession to
make. Anticipating the worst, Miss Morris was relieved to discover
that this "confession" concerned only her legal and quite acceptable
marriage. The college council, Miss Morris was sure, would raise no
objections. Sylvia's only fault lay in her having concealed her married
status from the Senior Member at Whitstead, who needed notice that
the room she occupied was available for another student. At this point,
Miss Morris has written, Sylvia threw her arms about her neck, protesting that she was "the dearest, most understanding Tutor." Miss
Morris's letter to the *Newnham College Roll* (January 1975) contin-

---

*Curiously enough, living above them were George Sassoon, son of Siegfried, and
his Scottish wife. George Sassoon remembers the Hugheses from this period but says
that Sylvia never mentioned Richard to him.

ues, "Needless to say I was not accustomed to such demonstrative behaviour." She concluded the interview with an invitation to Sylvia and Ted for sherry.

The "Victorian virgins" of Newnham had mercifully turned out to be inventions of Sylvia's strong imagination. Officially she had to postpone her move to the Eltisley Avenue flat until December 7, but in fact she moved in with Ted in mid-November while still retaining her attic room at Whitstead. Life together in their first home was overshadowed by the specters of the Hungarian revolution and the Suez crisis. The world in the autumn of 1956 indeed seemed mad. To her mother Sylvia described walking "stunned and sick" by the river Cam and talked gloomily of "the crass materialistic motives of [Britain's] attack on Suez" with its devastating effect on Russian propaganda in Budapest. Her letter reflects her keenly personal response to the wrongs of the world — a concern with morality she was later to bring into her poetry, as if evil intimately threatened an immutable vision of the right and the good. In 1956 she confidently expected the American jobs she and Ted hoped to get to provide sufficient money to facilitate a retreat to nature,

> some island or other . . . to live a creative, honest life. If every soldier refused to take arms . . . there would be no wars; but no one has the courage to be the first to live according to Christ and Socrates, because in a world of opportunists they would be martyred. Well, both of us are deeply sick. The creative forces of nature are the only forces which give me any peace now, and we want to become part of them; no war, after these mad incidents, has any meaning for us. All I think of are the mothers and children in Russia, in Egypt, and know they don't want men killed.

The Cambridge flat was not ideal. They had to share a bathroom with their neighbors upstairs. But they had a living room, bedroom, dining room, and cavelike kitchen to themselves, and the rent was only £4 a week. Sylvia's sinusitis had returned with the English winter; *The New Yorker* had turned down all the stories and poems she had sent from Yorkshire, and *The Atlantic*, too, despite Peter Davison, had returned politely worded rejections to Sylvia, keeping only a powerful lyric of Ted's, "The Hawk in the Storm." With worry about war, money, and rejection slips and the Cambridge damp to exacerbate her sinusitis, Sylvia's moods, as usual, fluctuated.

Shortly after Ted had moved into Eltisley Avenue, while Sylvia was still officially living in Whitstead, Ted's sister, Olwyn, returning to her job in Paris after a visit to Yorkshire, stopped in Cambridge to meet her new sister-in-law. She had missed them in Paris in the summer, having been at a conference in Cannes on their way to Spain and on holiday in Ravenna on their way back. In Cambridge, Sylvia surprised Olwyn by seeming the epitome of the well-groomed middle-class American so often seen in Europe in the 1950s. Olwyn remembers that

> her clothes were American-classic: casual and well mannered, with long uncluttered lines. Her hair, blonded at the time, and fair skin set off the brown eyes — deep, watchful and intelligent — that were, with her elegant limbs, her best feature. Her voice was attractive: low-pitched, deepening engagingly when she was amused. She seemed poised and controlled, with a hint of reserve or constraint.

That evening Sylvia produced an excellent three-course dinner from "the somewhat stygian kitchen which she bemoaned," and they ate in the living room, where there was a shabby velvet-covered sofa on which Olwyn later slept. Sylvia talked, with bursts of enthusiasm, about writers, painters, places, lacing her conversation with almost jubilant attacks on various acquaintances and delivering scathing views on the nunlike bigotry of the lady dons. These Olwyn privately thought too sweepingly dismissive, finding what she calls "the primary colours" of some of Sylvia's attitudes disconcerting. "I imagine I shared with the British women students with whom she seemed to have found little common ground, a more ironical, philosophical approach to life."

The next day they all three wandered around Cambridge, where Sylvia bought an impressive pile of books from Heffers with her generous Fulbright book allowance. Olwyn writes:

> She selected the heavy volumes and completed her purchase with a deliberate concentration. It was my first glimpse of her thus totally engaged, curiously impressive, as though she'd switched to some private, highly efficient gear. The implication of my perception was that she had *not* been so engaged up to this point . . . She had powerful priorities and easily grew impatient of activities that did not engage them, or that simply went on too long and interfered with her programme — as, I suspect, was the case this second day of my visit. We had tea at Newnham, where she still had a room. I remember her curled in her window seat there, in tartan slacks and a navy roll-neck sweater, the afternoon sun lighting up her bright face and hair.

This programmed concentration and impatience with anything that interfered with it was doubtless one reason Ted's friends found Sylvia difficult to know. Danny Weissbort remarks in a letter that he suspected she never found him interesting enough to talk to. Nonwriters of the Rugby Street circle such as Michael Boddy and Joe Lyde were given short shrift.

In a letter to her mother written on November 21, Sylvia reported on Olwyn, combining enthusiasm and spite in an oddly forced appraisal:

> Olwyn, Ted's sister, stopped by this weekend on her way from a stay at home to her job in Paris. She is 28 and very startlingly beautiful with amber-gold hair and eyes. I cooked a big roast beef dinner, with red wine and strawberries and cream. She reminds me of a changeling, somehow, who will never get old. She is, however, quite selfish and squanders money on herself continually in extravagances of clothes and cigarettes, while she still owes Ted 50 pounds. But, in spite of this, I do like her.

Ever watchful where money was concerned, Sylvia was unforgiving about a small family debt (£20 of which Olwyn had left, together with a key to her tiny flat, for Ted in Paris the summer before). The exaggerated description, "startlingly beautiful with amber-gold hair and eyes," was due to Olwyn as Ted's sister; the reservations were similar to those she harbored, off and on, for almost all Ted's friends and relations.

When they met, Sylvia had promised Ted to get at least fifteen of his poems in print within a year. From Yorkshire she had sent out a huge pile of his manuscripts; now, discouragingly enough, they were coming back to her in Cambridge. Nevertheless, she retyped them, shifted them into new groups, crammed them into fresh packets, and sent them off again. Throughout the Hugheses' eight months in Eltisley Avenue she kept twenty or so manuscripts by each of them in circulation all the time — an act of postal juggling Sylvia prided herself on being able to keep up even as she studied for her tripos exams and experimented with cooking on the ancient, thermostatless stove she had inherited with the flat. At the time she was also writing and making notes for a novel while regularly attending lectures and supervisions.

Dorothea Krook, who has written a short, moving memoir of Sylvia, lived close to the Hugheses in Grantchester Meadows. After the problem of the "illicit marriage" was resolved, Sylvia invited her to dinner in Eltisley Avenue, an invitation Mrs. Krook had to turn down as, she explained, the claims of her teaching permitted her little time for society. Sylvia's eyes gleamed with admiring understanding.

To have little time for socializing meant total commitment to work. Sylvia approved.

Dorothea Krook had arranged for a South African friend, Wendy Christie (now Campbell), a widow living in Cambridge with her two children, to sit in on Sylvia's supervisions. A pleasant older woman who gave interesting parties, Mrs. Christie fitted into Sylvia's category of motherly friends who offered companionship and support without provoking her jealousy. It was Wendy Christie who, on March 17, came around to the flat in Eltisley Avenue with a *Sunday Times* in which Harold Hobson had reviewed Sylvia's poem "Spinster," published in the Oxford-Cambridge student magazine, *Gemini*. She seems, with Dorothea Krook, to be the only woman Sylvia genuinely liked in Cambridge. Neither knew Sylvia very well. They admired the earnest scholar and radiant young wife, someone who held herself apart from most people with a queenly fastidiousness not unlike that of the spinster of her poem. Mrs. Sylvia Hughes was indeed quite a different person from the garish, sexually rapacious man-chaser of her first terms. Having let love in, she closed herself off within it:

> . . . Let idiots
> Reel giddy in bedlam spring:
> She withdrew neatly.

Sylvia told Wendy Christie that "Spinster" referred to a Newnham student who seemed unable to amalgamate healthily the life of feeling and that of the mind; yet in many ways the poem reflects Sylvia's own compulsive orderliness, her profound terror of an inner chaos she constantly suppressed. Sylvia's poems of the Cambridge period, for instance, resembled nothing so much as her spinster's house:

> And round her house she set
> Such a barricade of barb and check
> Against mutinous weather
> As no mere insurgent man could hope to break
> With curse, fist, threat
> Or love, either.

No one who knew Sylvia in Cambridge had any notion of what she was to become. Mrs. Krook, though, having observed Sylvia's joy in her marriage, had a fearful insight:

What would happen (I said, or half-said, to myself) if something should ever *go wrong* with this marriage of true minds? Nothing of course would, nothing *could*, go wrong: I was sublimely sure of

this. Yet if, inconceivably, it should, she would suffer terribly; I held
my breath to think how she would suffer. That was as far as my
momentary fear carried my imagination; nor was it possible it
should go further, in the face of her serenity, her tranquillity, her
confidence, and (most of all) her marvelous vitality, which seemed
a guarantee of limitless powers of resistance.

Though Sylvia would not have allowed ambition to cloud the confident image she presented to her supervisor, she was, of course, very
ambitious, both for her husband and for herself. In November she
learned that Harper Brothers Publishers in New York was sponsoring
a competition through the New York Poetry Center for a best first
book of poems. Since Sylvia judged her own book unready, she typed
up forty of Ted's poems and sent them off under the title *The Hawk
in the Rain*. Marianne Moore, Stephen Spender, and W. H. Auden
were to be judges — three big poets, as she wrote to her mother, who
wouldn't be able to help accepting Ted's book, "the most rich, powerful work since Yeats and Dylan Thomas." Her own book, *Two Lovers
and a Beachcomber*, was growing well, she added, and she hoped to
have fifty poems to submit by the end of February 1957 to the Yale
Series of Younger Poets.

They spent Christmas vacation in Yorkshire. Olwyn came over from
France for a few days' break but quickly realized that it was a working
holiday for Ted and Sylvia. Sylvia was studying for her exams and
writing poems. Ted too kept busy. Yet Sylvia loved the countryside,
and she was clearly relaxed with Edith Hughes and always chirpy
and pleasant with Bill. There were some good evenings together and
outings visiting various relatives. Aunt Hilda, Edith's sister, particularly liked and approved of Sylvia.

It was on this visit that Olwyn first noticed the scar high on Sylvia's
cheek and asked her about it. Sylvia, growing quite tense and excited,
talked at length about her suicide attempt at her mother's house and
the shock treatments afterward. Olwyn says:

Sylvia spoke about it as though it were some quite amazing feat —
rather like having climbed Everest and wondering afterwards how
and whyever you'd done anything so mad. I got the impression it
had all happened and been recovered from within about a week,
assuming it must have had something to do with a boyfriend. Sylvia
seemed too healthy and composed for it to have been more than an
unlucky stage in her growing up. I had absolutely no idea of the
gravity of her illness, nor of all those months she suffered with it,
and remained in ignorance until I read *The Bell Jar*. Ted joined her

in telling me about it, and I don't think he knew any more of it than I did.

Back in Cambridge, Sylvia again suffered from the English weather. (There is no colder place in England than Cambridge in winter.) Learning that Sylvia was affected by the raw indoor damp, Dorothea Krook lent her a paraffin heater. Well before Christmas Ted found a job in a secondary modern school under an enlightened headmaster who encouraged him to employ any method of teaching he wished. Although he took the job for money and was hired to teach English, Ted liked the boys and followed up subjects that interested them, seeking out books on Russian history, the Jews, and the Nazis for his classes. To her mother Sylvia wrote with tender enthusiasm: "We have such lovely hours together . . . We read, discuss poems we discover, talk, analyze — we continually fascinate each other. It is heaven to have someone like Ted who is so kind and honest and brilliant — always stimulating me to study, think, draw and write. He is better than any teacher, *even fills somehow that huge, sad hole I felt in having no father*" (my italics).

For financial reasons, among others, Sylvia aimed to have a first novel drafted, or partly drafted, before she left Cambridge. She seems to have been writing it on and off since meeting Ted the year before. The heroine, Dody Ventura (named after a high school friend — possibly the underprivileged "Tracy" of her 1952 story "Initiation"), was to be an American ingénue like herself whose adventures among the Cambridge literati were to enliven a light, satirical but nonetheless penetrating (surely autobiographical) social comedy. Writing fiction, however, proved difficult, and it was not until the following year, after she had been teaching at Smith, that she completed the only part of this novel she preserved. Her problem, as always, was to escape from herself. For all her will power, immense vitality, intelligence, and passion to give order to life through art, she was helplessly tied to events that pressed themselves on her limited experience. She could exaggerate, distort, caricature, remodel, and interpret, but she could not easily invent.

The very title she gave the chapter she kept, "Stone Boy with Dolphin," provides evidence of how her imagination worked in a painterly way around a given image, endowing it with symbolic significance but nevertheless remaining faithful to the object observed. As a sophomore at Smith in 1951, she had written a poem extolling a bronze boy she associated with Constantine, her glamorous dancing partner at Maureen Buckley's coming-out party:

The bronze boy stands kneedeep in centuries
and never grieves,
remembering a thousand autumns . . .

In 1955 she had sent Peter Davison a postcard from the Victoria and
Albert Museum depicting the statue of a faun. In 1956, at Whitstead,
Sylvia had paid tributary visits to the small baroque statue of a winged
boy with a dolphin in the Newnham gardens, seeing it as a symbol
of her passion for Richard Sassoon. It stands there still, on a dais
overlooking the rose garden just by the dining hall; it is not bronze
or stone but, somehow fittingly, of garden-statue plaster.

Even after meeting Hughes, she was roughing out love letters to
Sassoon in her journal: "I thought that your letter was all one could
ask; you gave me your image, and I made it into stories and poems;
I talked about it for a while to everyone and told them it was a bronze
statue, a bronze boy with a dolphin, who balanced through the winter
in our gardens with snow on his face, which I brushed off every night
I visited him." To express the pathos of her passion she had to find
an image near at hand. Later, as if in bondage, she pleaded with her
lover to "break your image and wrench it from me." Her first thought
about Hughes was that he was "the one man since I've lived who
could blast Richard," by which she meant physically destroying his
image. She had to dissociate one man from her idol and replace him
with another. Doubtless the real idol was the Colossus, her dead
father, and every man she chose for a lover had to be somehow cast
in his mold.

"Stone Boy with Dolphin," published in *Johnny Panic and the Bible
of Dreams*, is a barely fictionalized account of Sylvia's meeting with
Hughes; it was intended to be the pivotal chapter of her novel. After
this appearance the bronze/stone boy vanishes from Plath's mythology, or is taken over by the figure of the drowned seagod, the Man
in Black, the Colossus, and finally the black paper Nazi of "Daddy"—
at once a persecutor and a figure she can repudiate with the increasing
authority of her wronged and embittered voice.

Late in February 1957, almost a year to the day from that dramatic
meeting in Falcon Yard, a telegram arrived from New York. *The
Hawk in the Rain* had won the New York Poetry Center competition
and would be published by Harper in the summer. Although it was
ten-thirty in the morning and some unconscionable hour in New
England, Sylvia rushed to telephone the wonderful news to her
mother. Then she and Ted took a whole day off to celebrate. (Did it
seem odd to Hughes that nothing could be real to Sylvia until she

had shared it with Mrs. Plath?) Writing to her the next day, Sylvia expressed delight that Ted would be first to make his name. "It will make it so much easier for me when mine is accepted," she gloated, "— if not by the Yale Series, then by some other place. I can rejoice then, much more, knowing Ted is ahead of me."*

In March Sylvia received official confirmation of the instructorship at Smith which Mary Ellen Chase had been negotiating for her. As of September she would be an untenured full-time teacher, with three classes, three hours each per week, for a yearly salary of $4,200 — to Sylvia, an immense sum. Family friends on Cape Cod had offered to rent the Hugheses their cottage for seven weeks of the summer. Sylvia was eager enough to get back to America. In Cambridge, the raw climate, the grimy flat, the stuffy politics, the antiquated class system (so she told her mother) exasperated her. Although she published a good deal that year in Cambridge magazines, she now looked with distaste on the once-glamorous English literary scene. As always with any major change, Sylvia was full of repudiations of the old and dazzled by the promise of the new.

Between Christmas and the beginning of February Sylvia had written a good many poems, among them "Sow," "Hardcastle Crags," "The Thin People," "On the Difficulty of Conjuring Up a Dryad," "The Other Two," and, at the end of January, "The Lady and the Earthenware Head." The last was the enactment of a very Plathian superstition. A roommate at Smith had made a model of her head in red clay which the superstitious Sylvia, like a savage guarding her soul, was in terror of throwing away; it was a sort of double. Finally Ted suggested they carry it out to Grantchester Meadows, where they walked daily, and give it a home in a willow tree. This they did, and until they left Cambridge (and probably long afterward) Sylvia's "sanguine effigy" lay "Vaulted by foliage" in a "crotched willow," safe from marauding boys and corrupting weeds. It seems to have been singularly important to Sylvia that the head not be drowned. She must, many times, have dreamed of a drowned skull, for the image occurs in her next poem, written in April, "All the Dead Dears," in connection, one supposes, with her father. Much later it became a powerful image in "Words." Stanzas from all three poems uncannily

---

*Aurelia Plath writes in *Letters Home*: "In her diary, written when she was a seventh-grader, she described coming in second in the Junior High School spelling contest — a boy came in first. 'I am so glad Don won,' she wrote. 'It is always nice to have a boy be *first*. And I am second-best speller in the whole Junior High!'"

echo one another, the pool and the drowned skull already epiphanous emblems as early as 1957.

Grantchester Meadows became almost sacred to Sylvia as spring approached. On February 8 she described an early walk lyrically to her mother, "the sky a seethe of grey clouds and eggshell blue patches, the dark bare trees along the river framing brilliant green meadows." In simple prose, Sylvia caught the colors and mood of Cambridge better than in any of her poems of the time. Two years later, in Boston, by which time she had modified her mannerisms, she wrote the lovely poem "Watercolor of Grantchester Meadows."

Spring arrived, lush and enticing, but Sylvia had exams ahead of her and by April 28 reported "living at the University library from morning to night" cramming for them. For most undergraduates the English tripos consisted of a three-year course, of which two years were spent on Part I and one year on Part II. For affiliated students like Sylvia who already had a degree, the course lasted two years and consisted of Part II only. Three out of the six subjects to be taken were compulsory: essay; criticism and composition (passages of English prose and verse for critical comment, exercises in English composition, translation, and so on); and tragedy. Of these, criticism and composition was Sylvia's bane. Tragedy, in contrast, was "marvelous for me," for over the two years of her course she had read the classics right up through the modern European playwrights Pirandello and Cocteau. Sylvia was studying, then, for these three exams and for a further three she had chosen in the English Moralists (Dorothea Krook's specialty, with the Platonists among them), the history of English literary criticism, and, as a special subject, Chaucer. She had also elected to submit a typescript of her poems under the title *Two Lovers and a Beachcomber* to the English faculty.

Writing in March to Lucas Myers, who was with Daniel and Helga Huws in Rome that year, Sylvia admitted to being "rather oppressed by my colossal ignorance of traditional lit. — I ignored everything except poets & novelists who were of use to my writing & now it looks as if I have to swallow all of English lit. before the end of May." A month later she was writing to Mrs. Plath of "enjoying my work, really, steadily reading tragedy now, the Greeks, then on through 2,000 years up to Eliot, concentrating on several major figures: Corneille, Racine, Ibsen, Strindberg, Webster, Marlowe, Tourneur, Yeats, Eliot."

On fine mornings she and Ted took walks together, sometimes rising before dawn to watch the sun rise. On one such occasion she stood on a stile, reciting all she knew of Chaucer's *Canterbury Tales* to a circle of astonished cows. Sylvia took her exams from May 27 to May 31, reporting on the ordeal to her mother on the twenty-ninth:

> I am taking time early this sunny morning to limber up my stiff fingers in preparation for my Tragedy exam this afternoon . . . I have honestly never undergone such physical torture as writing furiously from 6 to 7 hours a day . . . with my unpracticed pen-hand. Every night I come home and lie in a hot tub, massaging it back to action. Ted says I'm a victim of evolution and have adapted to the higher stage of typing and am at a disadvantage when forced to compete on a lower stage of handwriting!

So far the essay exam had gone well, but the exam on dating, "that black terror of Americans who have no sense of the history of language," had taken "half an hour simply to read." As for the Moralists, a "mean, vague, fly-catching mind" had been behind the paper, but she had got back at him by writing on a story by D. H. Lawrence close to her heart — "The Man Who Died."*

Sylvia had wanted to do very well on her exams, but in the event she achieved a respectable but not dazzling II-1, the equivalent of an American B or B+. She had already decided, in any case, not to try for higher degrees but to concentrate on her writing, even while teaching at Smith. By June 1957 Sylvia was well known as a Cambridge writer. In her last year she published two stories in *Granta* ("The Day Mr. Prescott Died" and "The Wishing Box") as well as numerous poems, including "Ella Mason and Her Eleven Cats," "Two Lovers

---

*As early as March 1956 Sylvia recorded in her journal: "Ran to catch Krook . . . who went on to D. H. Lawrence & incredible fable: *The Man Who Died*. She read sections, felt chilled, as in last paragraph of [James Joyce's] "The Dead," as if angel had hauled me by the hair in a shiver of gooseflesh: about the temple of Isis bereaved, Isis in search. Lawrence died in Vence, where I had my mystic vision with Sassoon; I was the woman who died [in August 1953], and I came in touch through Sassoon that spring [with] that flaming of life, that resolute fury of existence. All seemed shudderingly relevant: I read in a good deal; I have lived much of this. It matters." As a child, Sylvia had experienced similar gooseflesh, hearing her mother read Arnold's "The Forsaken Merman," that Victorian tale of the great depths. The story of Isis in search of the dismembered Egyptian god Osiris affected her similarly. With Sassoon she had imagined herself as a sort of Christ-woman resurrected through the power of sexual love — as Jesus in Lawrence's story. With herself as heroine of the tale, Sylvia identified, too, with the bereaved votary, patiently awaiting her lost father/lover. Isis, in later Greek mythology, became a composite goddess, uniting Ceres and Proserpina, Venus and Hecate. When Sylvia and Ted moved to London in 1960 they filled a recess in their sitting room with an enlarged print of Apuleius' Isis, "Magnae Deorum Matris" (great mother of the gods), a polymorphous demon.

and a Beachcomber by the Real Sea," "Dream with Clam-Diggers," "Mad Girl's Love Song," and "Black Rook in Rainy Weather." In the Oxford-Cambridge magazine, *Gemini*, she published "Spinster," "Vanity Fair," and "All the Dead Dears." Most of these Cambridge poems also appeared in *Poetry*, *Mademoiselle*, and other periodicals in the United States. Her last letter home from Cambridge (May 29, 1957) concludes, typically, with some verbal finger-crossing over her poems sent to the Yale Series of Younger Poets:

> I . . . got a note from the Yale Press, saying my book had been chosen among the finalists for the publication prize, but Auden wouldn't have judged them till some time in early summer. My heart sank as I remember his judgments on my early Smith poems, but I do hope my book, "Two Lovers and a Beachcomber," shows growth and would give anything to have it win; Auden would have to write a foreword to it then . . .

▸ 6 ◂

DISQUIETING

MUSES

1957-1958

Mother, mother, what illbred aunt
Or what disfigured and unsightly
Cousin did you so unwisely keep
Unasked to my christening, that she
Sent these ladies in her stead
With heads like darning-eggs to nod
And nod and nod at foot and head
And at the left side of my crib?

— "The Disquieting Muses,"
1957

All my life have I not been outside? Ranged against well-meaning
foes?

— *Journals*, January 22, 1958

I myself am the vessel of tragic experience.

— *Journals*, February 20, 1958

IMMEDIATELY AFTER Sylvia's exams the Hugheses left Cambridge
for Yorkshire. They spent their first wedding anniversary, June 16,
walking on the moors. After seven years of higher education (her
entire adult life), Sylvia at last felt strong enough to break away from
the sustaining routine of academic study. At Smith and even at Cambridge, her tense, vulnerable nerves had craved an external structure
within which to work and write. Now Ted, highly disciplined as a

writer but calmer and more self-possessed than Sylvia, could supply
that structure, from both within and without. As in Spain, they created
for themselves a rare world of their own; they read and walked together, corrected the American proofs of *The Hawk in the Rain*,
enjoyed large, nourishing meals. Olwyn Hughes, home for a short
holiday from Paris, remembers Sylvia's fish chowder and other tasty
dishes and her sheer delight in both cooking and eating. Ted and
Sylvia, she recalls, worked mornings and took long afternoon walks
usually *à deux*; they spent time with the rest of the household only
in the evening. When not actually working, Sylvia seemed to need to
be with Ted, almost as a timid child needs to be with its mother
among strangers. He could not so much as collect a bottle of milk
from the nearby farm without Sylvia's throwing on her coat and
running after him.

Just before Olwyn returned to France a curious incident gave rise
to some unease in the Hughes family. In Olwyn's words:

> John and Nance Fisher (John had been Ted's English master at
> Grammar School and they were family friends) drove the 40 miles
> from Mexborough one afternoon to visit us all — the first time since
> schooldays. I remember Sylvia was very "gushy" when they arrived.
> This clearly disconcerted the Fishers, and possibly their inadequate
> response offended her. Well on in the afternoon, when the talk was
> deep in reminiscences, she suddenly rose and left the room. We
> heard the outside door opened and banged shut. When she didn't
> return after about ten minutes, during which time Ted had become
> rather silent, he rose in turn and said he'd better go and see where
> she was. Quite a while later they returned, Sylvia rushing straight
> upstairs. Everyone was embarrassed by this . . . and it certainly put
> a damper on the afternoon. She made no attempt at apology.

It must have been of this incident that Ted wrote to Olwyn from the
Queen Elizabeth, attempting to explain Sylvia's behavior:

> After her exams etc. I suppose she felt nervy — she did, that was
> obvious . . . Her immediate "face". . . when she meets someone is
> too open and too nice — but that's the American stereotype she
> clutches at when she is in fact panic-stricken. Or perhaps — and I
> think this is more like it — her poise and brain just vanish in a kind
> of vacuous receptivity — only this American stereotyped manner
> keeps her going at all. She says stupid things then that mortify her
> afterwards. Her second thought — her retrospect — is penetrating,
> sceptical and subtle. But she can never bring that second thinking

mind to the surface with a person until she's known them some time.

Their weeks with the Hugheses, however, on the whole passed swiftly and pleasantly. Without rejecting Yorkshire, which at that time she loved with passion, Sylvia was looking forward to adding Ted to her own strong family matrix in Wellesley, confidently expecting him to find a campus job in New England while she was at Smith. With two salaries they would be able to visit Heptonstall during summer vacations.

A few days after their anniversary, Ted and Sylvia traveled with all their luggage to Southampton, where on June 20 they boarded the *Queen Elizabeth*. A week later they were sailing into New York Harbor. The day before the ship docked, Sylvia had been violently seasick, so it was Ted who saw their huge boxes, mostly of books, off the boat into the customs; there, to Sylvia's distress, a "customs man, fat, sweating & suspicious," made them break into one of their crates. Pawing over Sylvia's D. H. Lawrence, he pulled out *Lady Chatterley's Lover* and waved it in her face. On being sarcastically questioned about her teaching job, Sylvia "melted into salt sobs," as she wrote to Lynne Lawner, but at last they were released to fall into the arms of her Smith friend Elly Friedman and several Amherst acquaintances. To Lynne — the young poet she had met two years previously at the Glascock competition, who now in her turn was struggling to find her feet in Cambridge — Sylvia described everything as looking "immensely sparkling & shiny & fast-paced & loud after my bucolic existence on the Backs and the Brontë moors."

By June 29 they were in Wellesley for the large garden party Mrs. Plath had arranged instead of a superfluous second wedding. There, a radiant Sylvia introduced her Yorkshire husband to over seventy relatives and friends. A few days later Warren drove the couple to Eastham, Cape Cod, two bicycles festooning the roof of his car. In the Spauldings' cottage, rented by Mrs. Plath for seven weeks (her wedding present to them), Ted and Sylvia were free at last to resume their disciplined writing lives.

At Eastham they spent a marvelously relaxing summer, sunbathing, swimming, fishing, and generally enjoying themselves. On most days Sylvia was up with the sun and out on the beach. One day almost ended in disaster. They had taken a rowboat out to fish; the sea was rougher than usual, and the fish were not biting. They realized with horror that they were being swept out to sea. With much maneuvering and luck they managed to get onto a long reef on the outside of the channel, and they stayed there, stranded, until a motorboat on its way to the dock spotted them and towed them back to safety. Rowing back to the beach from the dock via a backwater, they ran into a school of fish and returned with a fine catch.

Few of these adventures and delights found their way into Sylvia's journal. Although that summer she rarely spent more than an hour or two of the day writing, her journal gives the impression of a strained time spent struggling to write marketable stories. When she considered her work, she must indeed have felt gloomy. She had intended to get on with her Cambridge novel, warming up on short stories for the *Saturday Evening Post* and the *Ladies' Home Journal.** When her stories were returned without so much as a note from the editor, she sank into dejection. The novel refused to be written. Her most interesting piece of work was a long poem she may have finished at a later date, "Dialogue Over a Ouija Board."†

One sultry day in August, Sylvia's manuscript of *Two Lovers and a Beachcomber* came back, rejected by the Yale Series of Younger Poets. Her misery was the greater because she had just lived through a "black lethal two weeks" when she feared she was pregnant. The plan was to have three or four babies, but not until she and Ted had made their names: "I will write until I begin to speak my deep self, and then have children, and speak still deeper. The life of the creative mind first, then the creative body." The missed period turned out to be a false alarm, but her overreaction to a dreaded pregnancy that would bang shut all the "glittering and coming realities" left her ill prepared for disappointment.

Sylvia picked through her rejected manuscript ruefully, discarding

---

*Sylvia's journal entry for July 18, 1957, records the enthusiasm with which she embarked on a story about a mother-daughter relationship, "The Trouble-Making Mother." By August 9 it had been rejected by the *Saturday Evening Post*, while "a flashy light one about a mother's helper which I consider artificial and not worth rewriting" and a short sketch, "Laundromat Affair," were expected back daily from the *Ladies' Home Journal*. In the light of these failures, Sylvia accused herself of not having worked at all.

†First published by Rainbow Press in 1981 and then in the notes to *The Collected Poems* (pp. 276–286). During the Hugheses' year together in Cambridge, Sylvia had begun to take an interest in astrology and the supernatural. For her twenty-fourth birthday Ted had given Sylvia a pack of tarot cards. She already regarded herself as "psychic" and a dreamer of presentiments. Occasionally the two played with a home-made Ouija board — a wine glass upturned on a table with cut-out letters set in a circle around it. With fingers lightly balanced on the bottom of the glass, they summoned a spirit called Pan to predict, in the first instance, the winning numbers in the football pools. Pan obliged, forecasting accurately enough but unfortunately anticipating each draw by just one match.

weak poems, tinkering with the title. The resolutions she had made earlier to be "stronger" than Virginia Woolf, to live not "for life itself: but for the words which stay the flux," began to pale before her growing panic at her poor output that summer and her lack of success in publishing what she had written.

Matters were hardly helped when two young writers, sent over by Mrs. Cantor to meet them, rubbed salt in Sylvia's wound. Both had just completed three-hundred-fifty-page first novels. To her journal Sylvia swore that next summer there would be no idle, expensive holiday "with the beach & the sun always calling"; instead she would sweat it out at home and have a novel to show for her time. But even as she wrestled with her desperate need to publish, in calmer moods she realized she must "write every story, not to publish, but to be a better writer — and ipso facto, closer to publishing . . . And Ted will be proud of me, which is what I want. He doesn't care about the flashy success, but about me & my writing. Which will see me through."

Before leaving the Cape, Sylvia recorded an event in her notebook which, some months later, gave her an unusual poem, her first to be published in *The New Yorker*. She had gone one morning with Ted to collect mussels for fish bait in the mud flats off Rock Harbor. There, with ghoulish fascination, she watched "the weird spectacle of fiddler crabs . . . like an evil cross between spiders and lobsters and crickets" creeping in their sideways fashion, each balancing an outsize green claw. Stirred as always by the mavericks of nature, Sylvia wrote "Mussel Hunter at Rock Harbor" in the syllabics she had learned from Marianne Moore. The poem — stylistically an adroit imitation — describes a world utterly alien to her own. At first the poet expresses curiosity without investing it with emotion. Only at the end does she, by evoking the grim courage of a possible "recluse or suicide" crab, recognize an affinity. In the "dense grasses" was a dried husk:

> The crab-face, etched and set there,
>
> Grimaced as skulls grimace: it
> Had an Oriental look,
> A samurai death mask done
> On a tiger tooth, less for
> Art's sake than God's . . .

In these final stanzas Plath is back in her own territory; the "relic saved" from the mass grave of water's "friendly element" is the hero-martyr left to face "the bald-faced sun," a surrogate self even among the not unhumorously depicted crabs.*

◀   ◀   ◀

At the end of August Sylvia and Ted moved into the top back apartment of a white frame house at 337 Elm Street in Northampton. Sylvia had anticipated teaching at Smith College as "bliss" after the frustrating, unproductive summer, but as it happened, her job commenced with a crisis in confidence, a black, self-lacerating mood that lasted all autumn. At first teaching terrified her. The reception she received from Smith's English faculty was cool and appraising. Although she liked her students, she felt ill at ease and watched at faculty meetings. The gods of her former pantheon — particularly Mary Ellen Chase (who had retired) and Elizabeth Drew — seemed diminished or remote. Whatever grounds existed for her paranoia were, of course, magnified by her imagination, and soon she was writing feverishly in her journal:

> Last night I felt the sensation I have been reading about to no avail in James: the sick, soul-annihilating flux of fear in my blood switching its current to defiant fight. I could not sleep, although tired, and lay feeling my nerves shaved to pain & the groaning inner voice: oh, you can't teach, can't do anything. Can't write, can't think. And I lay under the negative icy flood of denial, thinking that voice was all my own, a part of me, and it must somehow conquer me and leave me with my worst visions: having had the chance to battle it & win day by day, and having failed.

Never had Sylvia written more honestly about the battle she waged constantly with her dark self. Her journal entry for October 1, 1957, with its long "letter to a demon," reveals her enormous intelligence coping rationally with the powerful forces of the irrational which dogged her, sleeping and waking. The entire passage is in many ways a key to understanding her and needs to be quoted at length. It continues:

> I cannot ignore this murderous self: it is there. I smell it and feel it, but I will not give it my name. I shall shame it. When it says: you shall not sleep, you cannot teach, I shall go on anyway, knocking

---

*For a definitive reading of this poem, see Seamus Heaney, "The Indefatigable Hoof-taps," in *The Government of the Tongue* (London: Faber, 1988; New York: Farrar, Straus & Giroux, 1989).

its nose in. Its biggest weapon is and has been the image of myself as a perfect success: in writing, teaching and living. As soon as I sniff nonsuccess in the form of rejections, puzzled faces in class when I'm blurring a point, or a cold horror in personal relationships, I accuse myself of being a hypocrite, posing as better than I am, and being, at bottom, lousy.

I am middling good. And I can live being middling good. I do not have advanced degrees, I do not have books published, I do not have teaching experience. I have a job teaching. I cannot rightly ask myself to be a better teacher than any of those teaching around me with degrees, books published and experience. I can only, from day to day, fight to be a better teacher than I was the day before. If, at the end of a year of hard work, partial failure, partial dogged communication of a poem or a story, I can say I am easier, more confident & a better teacher than I was the first day, I have done enough. I must face this image of myself as good for myself, and not freeze myself into a quivering jelly because I am not Mr. Fisher or Miss Dunn or any of the others.

I have a good self, that loves skies, hills, ideas, tasty meals, bright colors. My demon would murder this self by demanding that it be a paragon . . . I can learn to be a better teacher. But only by painful trial and error. Life is painful trial and error. I instinctively gave myself this job because I knew I needed the confidence it would give me as I needed food: it would be my first active facing of life & responsibility: something thousands of people face every day, with groans, maybe, or with dogged determination, or with joy. But they face it. I have this demon who wants me to run away screaming if I am going to be flawed, fallible. It wants me to think I'm so good I must be perfect. Or nothing. I am, on the contrary, something: a being who gets tired, has shyness to fight, has more trouble than most facing people easily. If I get through this year, kicking my demon down when it comes up, realizing I'll be tired after a day's work, and tired after correcting papers, and it's natural tiredness, not something to be ranted about in horror, I'll be able, piece by piece, to face the field of life, instead of running from it the minute it hurts.

The demon would humiliate me: throw me on my knees before the college president, my department chairman, everyone, crying: look at me, miserable, I can't do it. Talking about my fears to others feeds it. I shall show a calm front & fight it in the precincts of my own self, but never give it the social dignity of a public appearance, me running from it, & giving in to it. I'll work in my office roughly from 9 to 5 until I find myself doing better in class . . . I'll keep myself intact, outside this job, this work. They can't ask more of me than my best . . .

If Sylvia *had* run crying to the department chairman or thrown herself on her knees before President Wright, her fellow teachers might have penetrated her veneer and put themselves to some trouble to reassure her. But apparently none of her colleagues, young or old, had the least inkling of her personal distress. She put up her calm front and admitted no one but Ted behind it. Naturally, she suffered, continuing to fight the "sick naked hell" of her depression and the demon of her perfectionist pride. No one had told her that teaching is difficult, and beginning as a teacher most difficult of all. She taught three freshman English classes three times a week where she was responsible for nearly seventy girls.* Her students had to be introduced to an array of writers, from Hawthorne and Henry James to D. H. Lawrence and Virginia Woolf. They were required to write competent weekly essays (on which they were graded) and interviewed from time to time about their work. As their papers flooded in, reducing the time available for class preparation, Sylvia began to fear she would never have the time or energy to write again. Inevitably her anxiety rubbed off on Ted, though he did his best to reassure her. Because their social life was confined to members of the faculty, it was difficult to get away from Smith even in the evenings and on weekends. Northampton, in short, became for her a too-genteel, soul-killing prison in which she could neither create nor feel justified in not creating.

By November Sylvia was writing to her mother, "I can't be really frank with [other Smith teachers] or say how I begrudge not sitting and working at my real trade, writing, which would certainly improve rapidly if I gave it the nervous energy I squander on my classes." To Warren, then on a Fulbright in Austria, she was more open:

> My ideal of being a good teacher, writing a book on the side, and being an entertaining homemaker, cook and wife is rapidly evaporating. I want to write first, and being kept apart from writing, from giving myself a chance to really devote myself to developing this "spectacular promise" that the literary editors write me about when they reject my stories, is really very hard.

In fact, by November Sylvia and Ted had agreed to get clear of academic life the following year and risk freelancing in Boston.

---

*In letters to his sister, Ted Hughes described Sylvia working twelve hours a day, often "cracking under the strain."

It was in late 1957 that the Hugheses met the American poet W. S. Merwin and his English wife, Dido, through John L. Sweeney, then director of the Woodberry Poetry Room at Harvard's Lamont Library. Jack Sweeney, as Dido Merwin confirms,* liked nothing better than to bring poets together in his home on Beacon Street in Boston. Merwin, who had hailed *The Hawk in the Rain* in the *New York Times Book Review* of October 6, 1957, was living in Boston for a while and naturally wanted to meet Hughes. Dido Merwin remembers the Sweeneys' dinner party for six. Ted, who had fractured a bone in his right foot (by leaping out of a chair when the foot was asleep), arrived limping with his foot in plaster. "He didn't say much and appeared to be watching attentively from the touch line," writes Dido Merwin. "Sylvia, on the other hand, was all outgoing sociability." Ted, writing his first impressions of them in a letter to Olwyn, found Merwin a "composed" figure and commented that Dido was "very amusing, a sort of young Lady Bracknell."

They all met again soon afterward, at the Merwins' fifth-floor walk-up on West Cedar Street, described by Sylvia as a "high Boston apartment [opening] its wide-viewed windows like the deck of a ship." Dido Merwin remembers:

> Ted had a job getting up the stairs, but the moment he hobbled in the door he opened up. There was talk about lots of things, but the all-absorbing topic was the sixty-four-thousand-dollar question of how to survive without having to teach. Bill had proved it was possible. He was just then, to all intents and purposes, the only One That Got Away, and as such, an authentic and experienced refusenik — not only on account of what he had managed to avoid so far (including the plummy position of Poetry Consultant to the Library of Congress) but also because he had actually done what Ted and Sylvia claimed they wanted to do: travelled, light and footloose with a ruthless disregard for inessentials, picking up whatever was to be had by way of a living, in no less than three European countries . . . besides England.

The son of a Presbyterian minister in Union City, Pennsylvania, Merwin had attended Princeton and given himself to writing with enviable single-mindedness. He was a few years older than Ted and knew how to survive as a poet by freelancing. It was Merwin's advocacy of the BBC in England that weighed heavily in the balance when Ted and Sylvia considered returning there. In November 1957

---

*See Appendix II.

Merwin's example was like manna to the hungry and reinforced the Hugheses' plan to make all the money they could by teaching that year in order to be free to write in Boston the next. Sylvia's letters to Warren and her mother at this time put forth a view (also held by Ted) that was identical to Merwin's. "Every time you make a choice you have to sacrifice something," she told Warren on November 5,

> and I am sacrificing my energy, writing and versatile intellectual life for grubbing over 66 Hawthorne papers a week and trying to be articulate in front of a rough class of spoiled bitches . . .
>
> How I long to write on my own again! When I'm describing Henry James' use of metaphor to make emotional states vivid and concrete, I'm dying to be making up my own metaphors. When I hear a professor saying: "Yes, the wood is shady, but it's a *green* shade — connotations of sickness, death, etc.," I feel like throwing up my books and writing my own bad poems and bad stories and living outside the neat, gray secondary air of the university. I don't like talking *about* D. H. Lawrence and about critics' views of him. I like reading him selfishly for an influence on my own life and my own writing.

The writer's as opposed to the academic's view of English studies has never been better put. Having made the decision to abandon teaching, Sylvia returned to her classes with renewed energy, observing to her mother in a letter written on December 8:

> Although it is extremely painful for me not to write, knowing how even more painful it will be when I start to write in June, I've decided to make the best of a bad job and make them sorry to lose me. I have had several teachers say to me they've "heard" from students and visiting teachers . . . that I'm a "brilliant teacher," so in spite of my obvious faults, I can't be bad. One thing, I'm hardly ever dull, and since it's my first year, I think I'm doing about all I could ask of my ignorant self.

Sylvia, in fact, *was* a brilliant teacher, and as she became more realistic about the demands she made on herself she grew more relaxed in the classroom.

Five days before they were expected in Wellesley for Christmas, Sylvia and Ted appeared at Elmwood Avenue, Sylvia flushed from what could have been the high wind but was actually a high fever. A doctor was summoned who diagnosed viral pneumonia exacerbated by physical exhaustion. Put on a course of antibiotics over Christmas, she was well enough by early January to return to Smith, from where she wrote to her mother of building up "pretty good relation[s]" with most of her students.

At the very beginning of the new year she felt only relief. "Air lifts, clears," she wrote on January 4. "The black yellow-streaked smother of October, November, December, gone and clear New Year's air come — so cold it turns bare shins, ears and cheeks to a bone of ice-ache." As usual, the tiniest things had helped to lighten her mood: a Chinese red shirt to wear against light blue walls, sunlight lying on the fresh white paint of a door. Of more significance was Ted's chance to teach at the University of Massachusetts at Amherst for the spring semester. He would be able to bring in $1,000 to $2,000 "clear savings for Europe" (for by then they had decided to return to England after their year in Boston).

By January 7, however, the black lid had fallen again. As she wrote in her journal it was snowing, an "auspicious" beginning to the term after a sunny week. "And my lectures as usual, to prepare tomorrow morning — felt and feel mad, petulant, like a sick wasp — cough still [after her pneumonia] and can't sleep . . . feel grogged and drugged till noon."

The day before, she had informed her department chairman, Charles Hill, of her decision to leave Smith at the end of the academic year. Normally a new instructor would be expected to teach for two years before coming up for reappointment. Hill, in Sylvia's words "blue and squinch-toothed," had been his "icy self," but her former poetry tutor, Alfred Fisher, had that morning tried to talk to her. As always when under attack (or imagined attack), Sylvia fought back viciously:

A call from Mr. Fisher and my stupid discussion this morning in the high white atticky study, all book-crammed, and his 7 volume novel in black thesis books with white lettering that I know must be so ghastly. The gossip. One gets sick trying to conjecture it. The eleven o'clock coffee break and the gossip. All the inferences: The Institution will regard you as irresponsible. Two-year conventions. Rot. I am in a cotton-wool wrap. All is lost on me — all double entendres. "I have divided loyalties," I say. "I am your friend," he says . . . "It's all in your mind," he says, "about anxiety. I have it from various sources." If they deal in inference, hint, threat, double entendre, gossip, I'm sick of it. They mean vaguely well, somehow. But have no idea what is for my own good, only theirs. "What do you need to write?" Gibian asks over tea. Do I need to write anything? Or do I need time and blood?

Sylvia was especially resentful of her superiors' well-meaning attentions because at that time she truly did not know why she had to write. She knew only that she had somehow to find herself. The entry continues, significantly:

> First know myself, deep, all I have gathered to me of otherness in time and place. Once Whitstead was real, my green-rugged room with the yellow walls and window opening onto Orion and the green garden and flowering trees, then the smoky Paris blue room like the inside of a delphinium with the thin nervous boy [Sassoon] and figs and oranges and beggars in the streets banging their heads at 2 A.M., then the Nice balcony over the garage, the dust and grease and carrot peels of Rugby Street on my wedding night, Eltisley Avenue, with the gloomy hall, the weight of coats, the coal dust. Now this pink-rose-walled room. This too shall pass, laying eggs of better days. I have in me these seeds of life.

This is such excellent writing that a hypnotized reader will easily overlook its premise. What Sylvia implies here is an inevitable ascension from the discarded past into "better days" of the future. The philosophy is childlike, American to the core. Once Smith had epitomized all her aspirations. Now she despised it, longing for the higher echelons of freedom. It seems never to have occurred to her that the seeds of life she cherished were not necessarily destined to sprout more vigorously once she was free. In the past she had always known what to do and whom to please to achieve success. The future would be amorphous. Yet she embraced it, certain that something within her needed to find its way out in the form of art. Nothing if not courageous, Sylvia had decided, in fact, to take the most challenging route.

Sylvia had mentally left Smith at Christmas, but the academic year continued and she went on teaching until May. Among her colleagues she felt herself to be an outcast. The fury she poured into her journal in January took on an exaggerated intensity like that she must have experienced in Yorkshire during the tea with John and Nance Fisher. No longer at war with her "demon" self, she now galvanized her energies to defend her pride from (mostly imaginary) attacks. On January 12, feeling "fumings of humiliation," she relived a minor scene in a coffee shop, dealing with her rage in the only way she could, forging it out "grit into pearl. Grit into art." Sylvia's molten journals, more than her labored poems of this period, augur the fierce violence of *Ariel*:

Blundering, booted, to the little coffee shop table, past muffled chairs, braced under draped coats. The intimate group of three, James leaving, black-haired, squinting, not speaking, air sizzling with unspoken remarks, "Do you really hate it here so much?" The pale British Joan, green-rimmed spectacles, green-painted finger-nails, furred, with great dangling gold Aztec earrings, shaped like cubist angels, meaning remarks and meaning looks — Sally's great flat pale hands, like airborne white-bellied flounders, backs freckled, gesturing, stub-nails enameled with gilt paint. Superior. Conde-scending. Rude pink white-mustached [Alfred] Fisher: "Shame on you," grinning foolishly, pointing to red lipstick caked in a crescent on a coffee cup — "The mark of the beast." All the back references to common experience . . . Parties. Dinners. Lady with fishy eyes. "It's all in your mind," Fisher says. "I have it from various sources." In polite society a lady doesn't punch or spit. So I turn to my work. Dismissed without a word from the exam committee, hearing Sally superciliously advising me not to tell my students questions, I am justifiably outraged. Spite. Meanness. What else. How I am exor-cising them from my system. Like bile . . . Saturday exhausted, nerves frayed. Sleepless. Threw you, book, down, punched with fist. Kicked, punched. Violence seethed. Joy to murder someone, pure scapegoat. *But pacified during necessity to work. Work redeems.* [My italics.]

Throughout January and February Sylvia alternately fumed and sulked under the pressures of teaching, but what chiefly worried her was not feeling able to write. How she longed for the fountaining fluency of her teens, words whirling in her head. On January 14 the manuscript of her poetry book bounced back from a $1,000 contest, its second defeat. She rid herself of gloom by typing Ted's new poems, living in him until she was ready to live on her own. In despair with poetry, she again took up her Cambridge novel, working the "kernel chapter" about meeting Ted at the *St. Botolph's* party into a story. Her summary in her journal shows how close she still was to her old romantic yearnings: "A girl wedded to the statue of a dream, Cin-derella in her ring of flames, mail-clad in her unassaultable ego, meets a man who with a kiss breaks her statue, makes man-sleepings weaker than kisses, and changes forever the rhythm of her ways."

"Stone Boy with Dolphin" filled her once more with ambition to publish. Between semesters she read *Saturday Evening Post* stories until her eyes ached. But she read poetry, too, poring over a recently published anthology, *New Poets of England and America*, edited by

Donald Hall, Robert Pack, and Louis Simpson, "green-eyed, spite-seething" with the envy of the overlooked as she noted that of the six women poets, "except for May Swenson and Adrienne Rich, not one [is] better or more-published than me." Spurred by jealousy and "righteous malice" she lashed herself again into the breach. "Wait till June," she swore to her journal. "Somehow, to write poems, I need all my time forever ahead of me — no meals to get, no books to prepare. I plot, calculate: twenty poems now my nucleus. Thirty more in a bigger, freer, tougher voice: work on rhythms mostly . . . No coyness, archaic cutie tricks. Break on them in a year with a book of forty or fifty — a poem every ten days."*

Between fumings, bitter envy, and frustration, Sylvia went on teaching, learning how to manage, stockpiling money for her free year in Boston. For pay she undertook some extra grading for Newton Arvin in the English Department, finding time, too, to sit in on an art course taught by a Mrs. Van der Poel. Although her former heroes, Alfred Fisher and George Gibian, were now "enemies," she and Ted made new friends, among them the poet Anthony Hecht of the Smith faculty and the British poet and classicist Paul Roche and his American wife, Clarissa, who were also at Smith that year. Paul was becoming known in academic circles for his verse translations of Greek drama, and as a couple they were as close to bohemians as staid Northampton could produce. Sylvia delighted in describing them in her swelling notebook: Paul, gilded and blue-eyed, with "commercially . . . curled blond hair on his erect, dainty-bored aristocrat head looking as if it had been struck on a Greek coin," and "blond witchy . . . Clarissa, her red mouth opening and curling like a petaled flower or a fleshly sea anemone."† Sylvia's portraiture was acute but complicated, with ambiguous feelings. She could be merciless, describing one unfortunate member of the English faculty as "pale with a mouth like [a] snail spread for sliding — a man who always keeps the expression on his face for a moment too long."

In May Sylvia and Ted would be introduced to the painter and

---

*Whenever Sylvia felt cornered, as at Smith that year, her imagination brooded on private horrors. Her current list of subjects for new writing: "Hospitals and mad women. Shock treatment and insulin trances. Tonsils and teeth out. Petting, parking, a mismanaged loss of virginity and the accident ward, various abortive loves in New York, Paris, Nice. I make up forgotten details. Faces and violence. Bites and wry words. Try these."

†Sylvia wrote (and apparently talked) very bitchily indeed about Paul Roche. She liked Clarissa but was at first fairly dismissive of her. She felt Paul was dangerous — he drew her and repelled her at the same time. She was a bit of a puritan, and Paul was both sophisticated and rather *louche*.

sculptor Leonard Baskin, his wife, Esther, crippled by multiple scle-
rosis, and their little son, Tobias. A close friendship was to develop
over the next year, leading to collaborations between Hughes and
Baskin that have continued to the present time. Sylvia's poem "Sculptor," written the following summer and dedicated to Baskin, had its
origins in pleasant days spent visiting the Baskins, wandering round
his studio, and having tea with Esther and the baby in their garden.
Six months later Sylvia would write "Goatsucker" for an anthology
Esther was editing. The Baskins, deeply committed to art, home, and
family, represented an ideal to Sylvia, with her scant sympathy for
lesser mortals: "How I love the Baskins. The only people I feel are a
miracle of humanity and integrity, with no smarm."

Toward the end of January Sylvia received a letter from a magazine
called *ARTnews* asking for a poem on some aspect of art and offering
an "honorarium" of $50 to $75. Sylvia leaped at the chance. Mrs.
Van der Poel's art course was already an inspiration. Sylvia went to
the art library and came back with heavy volumes of reproductions
by Paul Klee, Henri Rousseau, and, most compellingly, the early surrealist Giorgio de Chirico. It came to her during a lecture on African
heads — inspirational to Klee — that "the right title, the only title"
for her book of poems was *The Earthenware Head*.

It was not until spring vacation that Sylvia's broodings and false
beginnings broke suddenly into a frenzy of writing. Between March
20 and March 28 she produced not one but eight poems based on
paintings. To her mother she wrote on March 22: "I've discovered
my deepest source of inspiration, which is art: the art of primitives
like Henri Rousseau, Gauguin, Paul Klee, and De Chirico. I have got
out piles of wonderful books from the Art Library . . . and am overflowing with ideas and inspirations, as if I've been bottling up a geyser
for a year." Her journal for March 28 sings with jubilation:

> I was taken by a frenzy a week ago Thursday, my first real day of
> vacation, and the frenzy has continued ever since: writing and writ-
> ing: I wrote eight poems in the last eight days, long poems, lyrical
> poems, and thunderous poems: poems breaking open my real ex-
> perience of life in the last five years: life which has been shut up,
> untouchable, in a rococo crystal cage, not to be touched. I feel these
> are the best poems I have ever done.

Writing sharpened her appetite not only for art but for something
in life that would fulfill her longing for action. A late-night brush fire
in the neighborhood caused her to burst out suddenly in the same
journal entry: "I longed for an incident, an accident. What unleashed

desire there must be in one for general carnage. I walk around the streets, braced and ready and almost wishing to test my eye and fiber on tragedy — a child crushed by a car, a house on fire, someone thrown into a tree by a horse. Nothing happens: I walk the razor's edge of jeopardy."

Sylvia's art poems consisted of two on paintings by Rousseau, four on etchings by Klee, and two on surrealistic paintings by de Chirico, whose diaries, she noted, "have unique power to move me." As it happened, the two de Chirico poems related to her parents. "On the Decline of Oracles" was the first of her "lost father" poems, associating the dead Otto Plath with the sea; and "The Disquieting Muses" was the first specifically to explore her relationship with her mother. The epigraph to "On the Decline of Oracles" — after de Chirico's early painting *The Enigma of the Oracle* — came from lines by de Chirico himself which she copied into her journal:

1) "Inside a ruined temple the broken statue of a god spoke a mysterious language."
2) "Ferrara: The old ghetto where one could find candy and cookies in exceedingly strange and metaphysical shapes."
3) "Day is breaking. This is the hour of the enigma. This is also the hour of prehistory. The fancied song, the revelatory song of the last, morning dream of the prophet asleep at the foot of the sacred column, near the cold, white simulacrum of god."
4) "What shall I love unless it be The Enigma?"

De Chirico opened to Sylvia a whole range of oneiric imagery: ruined statuary, vaults, trains, and shadows cast by unseen figures, subconscious symbols similar to those of her own dreams. While the poem "On the Decline of Oracles" owes something stylistically to Yeats, its three sinister male figures clearly balance the female trio of "The Disquieting Muses." Both poems were important to Sylvia beyond their debt to de Chirico's paintings, but "The Disquieting Muses" bears particularly on her development.

Introducing this poem on a radio broadcast in 1961, Sylvia drew attention to its painterly origin:

All through the poem I have in mind the enigmatic figures in this painting, de Chirico's *The Disquieting Muses* — three terrible faceless dressmaker's dummies in classical gowns, seated and standing in a weird, clear light that casts the long strong shadows characteristic of de Chirico's early work. The dummies suggest a twentieth-century version of other sinister trios of women — The Three Fates, the witches in *Macbeth*, de Quincey's sisters of madness.

Sylvia's poem, however, has less to do with classical mythology than with the fairy tale of Sleeping Beauty. A daughter is cursed in her cradle of blessings by a "disfigured and unsightly" witch who sends to the christening in her stead three ladies

> With heads like darning-eggs to nod
> And nod and nod at foot and head
> And at the left side of my crib.

The "my" gives the speaker-daughter away; she is recognizably Sylvia. The rest of the poem consists of vignettes from childhood carefully distorted to suit her purpose. While all the details are rooted in Sylvia's family history, certain "violation[s] of actual circumstances" (to borrow from Richard Wilbur) have rearranged the truth. In the fourth stanza the speaker describes schoolgirls dancing with flashlights, singing the glowworm song — a scene taken not from Sylvia's childhood but from her mother's:

> When on tiptoe the schoolgirls danced,
> Blinking flashlights like fireflies
> And singing the glowworm song, I could
> Not lift a foot in the twinkle-dress
> But, heavy-footed, stood aside
> In the shadow cast by my dismal-headed
> Godmothers, and you cried and cried:
> And the shadow stretched, the lights went out.

The child in the poem, in fact, is neither Aurelia Schober, who took ballet lessons and loved them, nor Sylvia Plath, who, though not a ballerina, nevertheless took pride in acting the prima donna throughout her life. She is instead a pathetic version of Sylvia's furious, wronged demon, the dark, deprived, and vengeful source of her real poems. Although "The Disquieting Muses" is deceptively light in tone, in it Sylvia said good-bye to illusion. Insofar as Aurelia Plath represented a never-never land of soap-bubble happiness, she had to be ridiculed and rejected, while Sylvia's muse-mothers stood their vigil "in gowns of stone,"

> Faces blank as the day I was born,
> Their shadows long in the setting sun
> That never brightens or goes down.

The lines derive from de Chirico, but the finale of the poem is straight Sylvia Plath and takes the form of a confession — and a resolution to deceive:

> And this is the kingdom you bore me to,
> Mother, mother. But no frown of mine
> Will betray the company I keep.

Midway through this week of feverish creativity Ted Hughes wrote to his sister: "[Sylvia] sits and writes for about 12 hours at a stretch, and gets too excited to sleep. What she'll do when she's doing nothing but writing for month after month, I don't know." Yet there was to be no comparable flood of inspiration until the Ariel poems unleashed themselves in the autumn of 1962. In spite of its decorous tone, "The Disquieting Muses" is an aggressive poem, drawn from Sylvia's seething unconscious.

Nine months later, when she was undergoing psychotherapy in Boston, Sylvia was to analyze her driving ambition to succeed as a writer as the "old need of giving Mother accomplishments, getting reward of love." She would come to recognize that, by extension, her mother stood for all editors, all readers, all persons in a position to accept or reject her. She began to suspect, too, that what seemed to her a writing block might in fact be a manifestation of an unconscious will *not* to write, not, that is, to present her mother with beautiful work in order to earn her love. In connection with her 1953 suicide attempt, Sylvia confessed in her journal entry of December 27, 1958: "I felt I couldn't write because she would appropriate it. Is that all? I felt if I didn't write nobody would accept me as a human being. Writing, then, was a substitute for myself: if you don't love me, love my writing and love me for my writing."

It seems that in writing "The Disquieting Muses" Sylvia for the first time discovered a way to fulfill two warring subconscious drives in a single subversive poem. Her resentment, instead of blocking the gift intended to win love, was enfolded within it. In her unrelenting bid both for unqualified love and for complete self-realization, Sylvia had at last hit on what was to be a secret mechanism of her finest work: she offered an exquisitely wrought, poisoned chalice. It was as if the only way open to her for free expression in her poems was to write pleas for love whose themes were subtle shafts of hate. The enigma that gave rise to the creative uprush behind "The Disquieting Muses" remained hidden from her for some years to come.

Sylvia, with reason, was pleased with her art poems, confiding to her journal on March 28:

Arrogant, I think I have written lines which qualify me to be The Poetess of America . . . Who rivals? Well, in history Sappho, Elizabeth Barrett Browning, Christina Rossetti, Amy Lowell, Emily Dickinson, Edna St. Vincent Millay — all dead. Now: Edith Sitwell and Marianne Moore, the aging giantesses, and poetic godmother Phyllis McGinley is out — light verse: she's sold herself. Rather: May Swenson, Isabella Gardner, and most close, Adrienne Cecile Rich — who will soon be eclipsed by these eight poems.

Arrogance or hope? Sylvia's much-plucked book now stood at thirty poems; she needed thirty more if she was to have a publishable collection by the end of the year. She sent off two on Klee's etchings ("Virgin in a Tree" and "Perseus") to *ARTnews* and the rest to *The New Yorker*. A month later *The New Yorker* sent them back.

Hughes had been asked to give a reading of his poems at Harvard in April, and on the eleventh he and Sylvia drove down in the car they had borrowed from Warren Plath during his Fulbright in Austria. There was a sleet storm that day and the streets of Cambridge were rivulets of icy water, but enough people came to the reading in Longfellow Hall to make a responsive audience. Ted read mainly to friends: Aurelia Plath and Mrs. Prouty (who was heard to exclaim "in loud, clear tones: 'Isn't Ted *wonderful!*' "), Gordon Lameyer, Marcia Brown Plumer, Mrs. Cantor (the "Christian Science lady" for whom Sylvia had babysat on Cape Cod), Sylvia's former Wellesley confidant Phil McCurdy, and Peter Davison. There were two poets Ted and Sylvia met for the first time: Philip Booth, just awarded a Guggenheim, and — at last — Adrienne Cecile Rich, Sylvia's dreaded but admired rival. "Little, round and stumpy," Sylvia wrote later, "all vibrant short black hair, great sparkling black eyes and a tulip-red umbrella."

After the reading the Hugheses were invited with others for drinks with Jack and Maire Sweeney on Beacon Hill and then dinner at the Boston restaurant Felicia's. Among strangers, Sylvia was suddenly gagged. She sat "feverish in lavender tweed," feeling out of things, in the Sweeneys' sitting room, where she nonetheless noted two Picassos, a Juan Gris, and an oil by Jack Yeats on the walls. The restaurant proved to be an icebreaker. At dinner, sitting next to Adrienne Rich's husband, Alfred Conrad, she found herself talking to him earnestly about "tuberculosis, deep, deeper, enjoying him." She and Ted spent the night with Mrs. Plath at Elmwood Road and returned the next day, heartened, to Northampton.

At last May arrived, and with it, end-of-term exams to interrupt

Sylvia's writing for the last time. She set about finishing her work, tying up uncomfortable social ends at Smith, impatient to begin her new free life. Before the end of term she completed the chapter of *Falcon Yard* ("Stone Boy with Dolphin") on which she had been working before writing her eight art poems, and dispatched it to *New World Writing*. (It was rejected.) She wrote a new poem that pleased her. An entry for May 11 in her journal records:

> Another title for my book: *Full Fathom Five* [the title of the new poem] . . . It relates more richly to my life and imagery than anything else I've dreamed up: has the background of *The Tempest*, the association of the sea, which is a central metaphor for my childhood, my poems and the artist's subconscious, of the father image — relating to my own father, the buried male muse and god-creator risen to be my mate in Ted, to the sea-father Neptune — and the pearls and coral highly-wrought to art; pearls sea-changed from the ubiquitous grit of sorrow and dull routine.

Perceiving how a godlike image of Otto Plath (whom Ted had replaced) needed to rise from the sea, Sylvia composed "Full Fathom Five" — Hughes has written — while reading Jacques-Yves Cousteau on the submarine world, holding the book open on her knees as she wrote. The poem was one of a chain she was to wrestle with for years, linking the image of a drowned, Poseidon-bearded father with the undertow of her undeniable death wish. For, wildly as Sylvia loved life, in her poems death predominates, as if she could not embrace one without acknowledging the pull of the other.

In her journal of May 11 she rehearsed the relevant lines from James Joyce's *Finnegans Wake*: " 'And it's old and old it's sad and old it's sad and weary I go back to you, my cold father, my cold mad father, my cold mad feary father . . .' — so Joyce says, so the river flows to the paternal source of godhead." Joyce's lines read like an epigraph to "Full Fathom Five":

> Old man, you surface seldom.
> Then you come in with the tide's coming
> When seas wash cold, foam-
>
> Capped: white hair, white beard, far-flung,
> A dragnet, rising, falling, as waves
> Crest and trough . . .

Like many poems of this period, "Full Fathom Five" ends with a fully orchestrated *Liebestod* that states her predicament:

You defy questions;

You defy other godhood.
I walk dry on your kingdom's border
Exiled to no good.

Your shelled bed I remember.
Father, this thick air is murderous.
I would breathe water.

◄   ◄   ◄

The year at Smith ended in crisis and another outburst of paranoia, recorded in bewildering detail in Sylvia's journals. By the end of the spring term she was exhausted, her nerves frayed from overwork; as always when she had to fight herself as well as the world around her, she grew depressed. Sleeplessness, brought on by a painful nervous itch, enclosed her in "a transparent lid" of aloneness (one of many early intimations of the bell jar), and she dreamed again her recurrent nightmare: "Joan of Arc's face as she feels the fire and the world blurs out in a smoke, a pall of horror."

Two events stand out among the journal's Medean eruptions in May. Paul Roche directed a public reading of his translation of Sophocles' *Oedipus* and invited Hughes to read the part of Creon. Ted, who had somewhat grudgingly agreed to do it, intimated to Sylvia that he'd prefer her not to come. Scandal was in the air at Smith that spring, rumors and catty gossip relating to adulteries in the English Department. In her nerve-peeled state, Sylvia feared that the nastiness might be contagious and would eventually corrupt her husband. "Superstitious about separations from Ted, even for an hour," Sylvia rushed through marking her papers and then ran off through the "heavy lilac-scented May dark" to the reading in Sage Hall. Having slipped into a seat in the back, she sensed immediately that, on stage, Ted "was ashamed of something." In a long journal entry written on May 22 she rehearsed her impressions, seething with disgust, disillusion, and excruciating jealousy. Listening to the *Oedipus* reading, she "felt like hawking and spitting." When, afterward, she went backstage, she found Ted "with a mean wrong face" at the piano, "banging out a strident one-finger tune . . . I'd never heard before."

Ted was unaware of Sylvia's interpretation of his mood. After he had agreed to do the reading, it had dawned on him that he had inadvertently become involved in a production he was not happy with. He felt embarrassed during the performance, for which there had been no rehearsals and in which he felt he didn't belong. Sylvia, perceiving his discomfiture, had radically misjudged its cause.

The next day was the last day of classes. Having arranged to meet Ted after her final lecture and "armed with various poems by Ransom, Cummings and Sitwell," she sallied forth. From each group she received, she recorded, "applause in the exact volume of my enjoyment of the class — a spatter at 9, a thunderous burst at 11, and something in between both extremes at 3." Afterward, hurrying to meet Ted in accordance with their plan, she somehow missed him. As irony would have it, she had been lecturing "about the joy of revenge, the dangerous luxury of hate and malice, and how, even when malice and venom are 'richly deserved,' the indulgence of these emotions can, alas, be ruinous." In the parking lot she found their empty car but no Ted; nor was he in the library. Then, as she came "striding out of the cold shadow of the library, my bare arms chilled," she had one of her "intuitive visions":

> I knew what I would see, what I would of necessity meet, and I have known for a very long time, although not sure of the place or date of the first confrontation. Ted was coming up the road from Paradise Pond, where girls take their boys to neck on weekends. He was walking with a broad, intense smile, eyes into the uplifted doe-eyes of a strange girl with brownish hair, a large lipsticked grin, and bare thick legs in khaki Bermuda shorts. I saw this in several sharp flashes, like blows. I could not tell the color of the girl's eyes, but Ted could, and his smile, though open and engaging as the girl's was, took on an ugliness in context. His . . . smile became too white-hot, became fatuous, admiration-seeking. He was gesturing, just finishing an observation, an explanation. The girl's eyes souped up giddy applause. She saw me coming. Her eye started to guilt and she began to run, literally, without a good-bye, Ted making no effort to introduce her . . . She hasn't learned to be deceitful yet in her first look, but she'll learn fast. He thought her name was Sheila; once he thought my name was Shirley: oh, all the twists of the tongue; the smiles.

Sylvia's journal entry goes on in much the same vein to attack members of the English Department whom she considered lecherous — "Why is it I so despise this brand of male vanity?" — before declaring bitter independence:

> No, I won't jump out of a window or drive Warren's car into a tree, or fill the garage at home with carbon monoxide and save expense, or slit my wrists and lie in the bath. I am disabused of all

faith and see too clearly. I can teach, and will write and write well.
I can get in a year of that, perhaps, before other choices follow.
Then there are the various — and few — people I love a little. And
my dogged and inexplicable sense of dignity, integrity that must be
kept. I have run too long on trust funds. I am bankrupt in that
line.*

Remarkable about this entire entry is the lightning quickness with
which Sylvia made her deductions. One day Ted was her godlike
father risen to be her mate; the next, he was a scurrilous adulterer
hiding behind a façade of fake excuses, vague confessions, and lies.
Ted was a handsome man, and no doubt girls made passes at him.
Sylvia's overreaction to seeing him once talking to a student was
fueled, no doubt, chiefly by her exhaustion, but it blazed up, as always,
in the theater of her terror, her paranoia, and her ever-ignitable imagination. The girl was in fact one of Hughes's students from the University of Massachusetts who just happened to be crossing the Smith
campus as he went to meet Sylvia; he had caught up with the girl
only minutes before Sylvia saw them. After a cathartic battle from
which Sylvia emerged with a sprained thumb and Ted with a clawed
face, she realized that her reaction had been absurd. By June 11 her
diary reports a reconciliation: "Air cleared. We are intact. And nothing — no wishes for money, children, security, even total possession — nothing is worth jeopardizing what I have, which is so much
the angels might well envy it."

Sylvia's American journals never again attack Ted in this way,
although his leaving her for a more glamorous or seductive woman
was a perennial fear of hers. Only once did she broach the subject,
and this was in December 1958, while she was undergoing therapy
with Dr. Beuscher in Boston. "I identify him [Ted] with my father at
certain times," she wrote thoughtfully,

> and these times take on great importance: e.g., that one fight at the
> end of the school year when I found him not-there on the special
> day and with another woman. I had a furious access of rage. He
> knew how I love him and felt, and yet wasn't there. Isn't this an
> image of what I feel my father did to me? I think it may be. The
> reason I haven't discussed it with Ted is that the situation hasn't
> come up again and it is not a characteristic of his: if it were, I would
> feel wronged in my trust of him. *It was an incident only that drew
> forth echoes, not the complete withdrawal of my father, who de-*

---

*This outburst against her husband, extended to include most of the men she knew,
continues for several pages and is to be found in the published *Journals*.

serted me forever . . . images of his faithlessness with women echo my fear of my father's relation with my mother and Lady Death. [My italics.]

It was beginning to bear in on Sylvia how closely a Freudian explanation fitted the enigma of her strangeness.

► 7 ◄

E L E C T R A   O N
A Z A L E A   P A T H
1958-1959

I am the ghost of an infamous suicide,
My own blue razor rusting in my throat.
O pardon the one who knocks for pardon at
Your gate, father — your hound-bitch, daughter, friend.
It was my love that did us both to death.

— "Electra on Azalea Path," 1959

WITH THE TERM OVER and the last papers in, Sylvia and Ted took a week's holiday in New York. On June 10 Sylvia wrote to her mother of seeing publishers, dining at the Biltmore, going to parties thick with literary pundits, and, best of all, visiting Marianne Moore in her Brooklyn home. In a confidential aside she mentioned an odd coincidence: "Coming down in the subway ... I almost ran into Dick Wertz, Nancy Hunter's old flame, who was at Cambridge when I was and is marrying a Smith girl from my class ... I was about to speak to him, as his back was turned to me, when, talking to him, I saw Richard Sassoon. I kept quiet and passed by and probably only I ... knew about it. Of all the people in NYC!" The next day, in a long letter to Warren, she skipped lightly over the final agonizing weeks at Smith. "On the whole, my colleagues have depressed me," she remarked dismissively; "it is disillusioning to find the people you admired as a student are weak and jealous and petty and vain ... which many of them are."

With the exception of a two-week holiday on Cape Cod, the Hugheses spent the rest of the summer in their hot apartment on Elm

Street in Northampton, testing themselves as professional writers. Although their university salaries were still coming in ($70 a week through August), they were anxious to make money. Ted's application for a Saxton grant had been turned down, ironically because his publishers were trustees for the grant, making him ineligible. Sylvia decided to apply instead; Ted would try for a Guggenheim. Marianne Moore, with whom both poets had chatted amiably in New York, had been Ted's referee for the Saxton. Now Sylvia sent her a group of poems, requesting a reference for herself.

In July, to Sylvia's surprise and keen distress, Miss Moore sent her in reply what Sylvia saw as "a queerly ambiguous spiteful letter . . . 'Don't be so grisly,' " she commented; " 'you are too unrelenting.' " And she added "certain pointed remarks about 'typing being a bugbear.' " Sylvia concluded that Miss Moore was annoyed because she had been sent carbon copies instead of fresh top sheets. That seems unlikely. While Marianne Moore usually admired Ted's work, she never warmed to Sylvia's, disliking the early traces of the very elements that later were to carry her to fame: macabre doom-laden themes, heavy with disturbing colors and totemlike images of stones, skulls, drownings, snakes, and bottled fetuses — hallmarks of Sylvia's gift.

For most of the summer Sylvia gritted her teeth against depression: "It is as if my life were magically run by two electric currents: joyous positive and despairing negative — which ever is running at the moment dominates my life, floods it. I am now flooded with despair, almost hysteria, as if I were smothering. As if a great muscular owl were sitting on my chest." She set to work, however, to complete her book of poems. On June 25 her diary records a "starred day" — the date is decorated with asterisks — when a letter brought her first acceptance from *The New Yorker*:

Seated at the typewriter, I saw the lovely light-blue shirt of the mailman going into the front walk of the millionairess next door, so I ran downstairs. One letter stuck up out of the mailbox, and I saw *The New Yorker* on the left corner in dark print. My eyes dazed over. I raced alternatives through my head: I had sent a stamped envelope with my last poems, so they must have lost it and returned the rejects in one of their own envelopes. Or it must be a letter for Ted about copyrights. I ripped the letter from the box. It felt shockingly hopefully thin. I tore it open right there on the steps, over mammoth marshmallow Mrs. Whalen sitting in the green yard with her two pale artificially cute little boys in their swimsuits jumping in and out of the rubber circular portable swimming pool and bouncing a gaudy striped ball. The black thick print of Howard Moss's letter banged into my brain. I saw "MUSSEL HUNTER AT ROCK HARBOR seems to me a marvelous poem and I'm happy to say we're taking it for The New Yorker . . ." — at this realization of ten years of hopeful wishful waits (and subsequent rejections) I ran yipping upstairs to Ted and jumping about like a Mexican bean. It was only moments later, calming a little, that I finished the sentence ". . . as well as NOCTURNE ["Hardcastle Crags" in *The Colossus*], which we also think extremely fine." TWO POEMS — not only that, two of my *longest* — 91 and 45 lines respectively: They'll have to use front-spots for both and are buying them *in spite* of having [a] full load of summer poems and not for filler. This shot of joy conquers an old dragon and should see me through the next months of writing on the crest of a creative wave.

The entry is characteristic. Transported with joy over her success, Sylvia could not resist a gratuitous dig at Mrs. Whalen and her "artificially cute little boys" or forget that there was a "millionairess" next door. She wrote immediately to her mother (on the pink memorandum paper that had by that time become a fetish) to give her the good news, rejoicing that it would mean $350, enough to cover three months' rent in Boston. She went on, "You see what happens the minute one worships one's own god of vocation and doesn't slight it for grubbing under the illusion of duty to Everybody's-Way-Of-Life!"

However boldly the *New Yorker* acceptance refuted her mother's arguments against risking a freelancing life, the god of vocations soon proved fickle, and Sylvia's summer work bogged back into depression. Giving up for the moment her quest for the enigma, she begged Ted to give her marketable poem subjects. With his encouragement she completed "Owl," "Child's Park Stones," and "Fable of the Rhododendron Stealers," the third about an occasion in the park that had caused a white-hot rage.

Sylvia delighted to walk in the evening with her husband in nearby Child's Park, where she made a ritual of picking a single rose to give its "prodigal scent" to their living room. One evening they heard rustlings in the rhododendron grove; three high school girls were tearing armfuls of blossoms from the bushes. They wanted them for a dance, they said. Sylvia, overwhelmed with indignant fury, outstared the "sassy" leader before she and Ted pursued the girls through the evening drizzle to a waiting car. It was a minor incident, but like all such incidents, it left Sylvia wondering at her capacity for extreme reactions. She herself had stolen two individual rosebuds, but surely there was a difference between aesthetically savoring roses one by one and stealing truckloads of blossoms for a high school dance. Chiefly it was the girls' greedy insensitivity that incensed her. "I have a violence in me," she wrote afterward, "that is hot as death-blood. I can kill myself or — I know it now — even kill another. I could kill a woman, or wound a man. I think I could. I gritted to control my hands, but had a flash of bloody stars in my head as I stared that sassy girl down, and a blood-longing to [rush] at her and tear her to bloody beating bits."

On the third of July, for the first time in America, the Hugheses summoned their telepathic messenger, Pan, with their makeshift Ouija board. In an important essay on his wife's art, Ted Hughes later wrote about the significance of these sessions:

> She would describe her suicide attempt [of 1953] as a bid to get back to her father, and one can imagine that in her case this was a routine reconstruction from a psychoanalytical point of view. But she made much of it, and it played an increasingly dominant role in her recovery and in what her poetry was able to become. Some of the implications might be divined from her occasional dealings with the Ouija board, during the late Fifties. Her father's name was Otto, and "spirits" would regularly arrive with instructions for her from one Prince Otto, who was said to be a great power in the underworld. When she pressed for a more personal communication, she would be told that Prince Otto could not speak to her directly, because he was under orders from The Colossus. And when she pressed for an audience with The Colossus, they would say he was inaccessible. It is easy to see how her effort to come to terms with the meaning this Colossus held for her, in her poetry, became more and more central as the years passed.

In her journal Sylvia showed herself intrigued and entertained by these sessions, the overturned brandy glass responding admirably and with "charming humor": "Even if our own hot subconscious pushes it (it says, when asked, that it is 'like us'), we had more fun than a movie. There are so many questions to ask it. I wonder how much is our own intuition working, and how much queer accident, and how much 'my father's spirit.'" Some of Pan's predictions came true. He informed them Sylvia's book would be published by Knopf (to be), and forecasted two sons, Owen and Gawen (not to be), and a daughter, Rosalie (they would name her Frieda). He also recited a poem of his own called "Moist," reporting that "Pike" was his favorite of Ted's poems, "Mussel Hunter" of Sylvia's. The journal entry continues:

Among other penetrating observations Pan said I should write on the poem subject "Lorelei" because they are my "own kin." So today for fun I did so, remembering the plaintive German song Mother used to play and sing to us beginning "*Ich weiss nicht was soll es bedeuten . . .*" The subject appealed to me doubly (or triply): the German legend of the Rhine sirens, the sea-childhood symbol, and the death-wish involved in the song's beauty. The poem devoured my day, but I feel it is a book poem and am pleased with it.

"Lorelei," a companion piece to "Full Fathom Five," was composed on Independence Day of 1958; it was one of several she wrote that summer good enough, she considered, for her slowly growing book. In her heart she probably guessed that many of her "exercises" were pastiches: "I Want, I Want" smacks of Theodore Roethke, "Poems, Potatoes" imitates Wallace Stevens, and "The Times Are Tidy," W. H. Auden. Enthusiastic about anything she had just finished, Sylvia packed each poem off immediately to an editor. If it came back, either she impatiently rejected it herself or defiantly sent it elsewhere.

Meanwhile, writing prose was becoming a bugbear. For days she wrestled unsuccessfully with a story about an injured fledgling she and Ted had rescued from under a tree in Child's Park. After a week of nursing the bird in a shoebox, Ted had to gas it, at Sylvia's insistence: she couldn't bear for its neck to be wrung. It was for her a traumatic event. She fought herself into a crisis over the story, finally collapsing in tears. After a long talk with Ted, who questioned her habit of taking stories directly from experience, she set limits to her ambition and, temporarily abandoning fiction, returned to poems. The honeymoon in Benidorm now provided her with two ("Old Ladies' Home" and "The Net-Menders"), and she based another, "Whiteness I Remember," on Sam, the horse that had run away with her in Cambridge, an experience that was later to return, heightened and transformed, in "Ariel."

It was at about this time that symbolic colors entered Sylvia's poems, to disturbing effect: white suggesting the purity of annihilation, red signifying the blood and pain of continuing life. The macabre "Moonrise," set in a cemetery, would provoke Marianne Moore to comment, "I only brush away the flies," but to Sylvia it was a book poem:

> Berries redden. A body of whiteness
> Rots, and smells of rot under its headstone
> Though the body walk out in clean linen.

I smell that whiteness here, beneath the stones
Where small ants roll their eggs, where grubs fatten.
Death may whiten in sun or out of it.

Sylvia's notebooks for the summer of 1958 show that she followed
a psychic pattern not unlike that of the year before. Initial enthusiasm
hardened into writing block which climaxed in hysteria. The only
way forward was to work slavishly to schedule through spells of
paranoia and self-doubt. On August 9 "Mussel Hunter at Rock Harbor" came out in *The New Yorker*, a day after Sylvia had dreamed
about its being there. But by August 27 she was again furious after
a "venomous blowup" with her landlady, Mrs. Whalen, who had
removed their living room rug while the Hugheses were on vacation
on Cape Cod. Any trespassing on her territory drove Sylvia wild, but
it seems she was learning to use this wildness. "Fury jams the gullet
and spreads poison," she wrote, "but, as soon as I start to write,
dissipates, flows out into the figure of the letters: writing as therapy?"
She read Oesterreich's *Possession: Demoniacal and Other*, noting that
in primitive cultures demons are often "the objective figures of angers,
remorse, panic."

◄　◄　◄

In early September Sylvia and Ted moved, via Wellesley, from Mrs.
Whalen's house in Northampton to a tiny, two-room apartment at 9
Willow Street on Beacon Hill in Boston. A letter from Ted to Olwyn
Hughes described the flat as "very small. Each main room (of the
two) had a little bay window — 5th floor — looking out over the
rooftops (very jumbled and ancient and interesting) onto the Charles
river one way, down the other way [onto] Louisburg Square, where
all the characters in Henry James lived . . . and directly below, opposite our front door . . . the view down Acorn Street."

The setting was exhilarating, and soon Sylvia and Ted were seeing
the city with Lucas Myers, briefly in Boston en route from Tennessee
to a teaching job in Paris. They walked on the Boston Common,
where Ted could name all the birds and trees, and went down to the
docks, where fishing boats were unloading crabs. Ted and Sylvia
cheered on the few that escaped back to sea. Luke found Sylvia
changed: she was now

> very sober at times, hanging back in conversations, standing back,
> looking different, not like the pretty American girl of the *St.
> Botolph's* party, but more interesting and more thoughtful. I was

surprised by the sober-sidedness and doubt that it was her inevitable manner that year. It probably had something to do with me, for, though I thought of them abstractly at that time almost as an amalgam, the fact was that Ted was my close friend and I wasn't as close to her, and the fact must have asserted itself.

Sylvia's sobriety may also have had something to do with the looming depression that overwhelmed her later in the month. Boston in 1958 was packed full of poets; that may have threatened Sylvia as much as it excited her. She and Ted began to see a good deal of Stephen Fassett (who had recorded poems by both of them for the archives at Harvard's Lamont Library the previous Christmas) and his Hungarian wife, Agatha (a pianist who would write a memoir of Béla Bartók), and also the friendly and generous Sweeneys, who lived nearby on Beacon Street. The Merwins had recently left for Europe, but Robert Lowell was teaching at Boston University, and he and his wife, Elizabeth Hardwick, met the Hugheses at dinner parties.

Other notable poets and literary figures lived within a fifteen-mile ring around Boston. Archibald MacLeish was the Boylston Professor at Harvard, while Robert Frost lived in Cambridge on Brewster Street, a few doors away from Sylvia's archrival Adrienne Rich (who surely did not suspect she was a rival). Richard Wilbur and Philip Booth had been teaching at Wellesley, though Wilbur departed in 1957. George Starbuck lived close by on Pinckney Street and worked at Houghton Mifflin on Park Street. Anne Sexton, like Sylvia raised in Wellesley, lived with her family in the suburbs of Boston, as did Sexton's close friend Maxine Kumin. Other embellishments of this lively poetic scene included I. A. Richards at Harvard, Dudley Fitts at Andover, and John Holmes at Tufts University. Cambridge was, in this heyday of the drama of T. S. Eliot, renowned for its theater: the Brattle Theater Repertory Company and the tiny Poets' Theatre, at that time aided by the Rockefeller Foundation, which handed out fellowships to such visiting poet-playwrights as Frank O'Hara and Merwin. Donald Hall, Richard Eberhart, Kenneth Koch, John Malcolm Brinnin, John Ashbery, V. R. Lang, Alison Lurie, Edward Gorey, William Alfred, and Peter Davison were at various times associated with the Theatre, which would in later years present plays by both Sylvia and Ted.

Sylvia's journal at the time is surprisingly uninformative about known meetings with such luminaries. Almost all she recorded about a dinner party she put on for Robert Lowell and Elizabeth Hardwick was what she gave them to eat. Her journals are more likely to give wicked prose portraits of people she hardly knew, like the woman she met at a party (anticipating the damning portraits of women that figure so prominently in her later poems) who talked in "raucous, shrill tones, which allowed of no interruptions: a woman who never listens, a horrible woman, shaped in hard round bullet shapes, squat, unsympathetic as a dry toad. Dirty decaying teeth, hands with that worn glisten of flesh unmarried old ladies have: a glitter of rhinestones somewhere, a pin, or chain."

The women Sylvia seemed most at ease with in Boston were on the whole friends from previous incarnations: Perry Norton's wife, Shirley, from whom she learned to braid rugs between bouts of writing panic, and her favorite college roommate, Marcia Brown Plumer, now living domestically in Cambridge next door to Peter Davison, who would soon be marrying Sylvia's Smith classmate Jane Truslow. Both Marcia and Shirley had babies,* representing the world of young womanhood Sylvia hankered after almost as much as she yearned for success as a writer. "How odd," she remarked in her journal for January 28, "men don't interest me at all now, only women and women-talk. It is as if Ted were my representative in the world of men."

All the same, one of the first people to whom Sylvia wrote in Boston was Peter Davison at *The Atlantic Monthly*, who had responded favorably to the poems on art subjects Sylvia had sent him in April. As she had heard nothing since, her letter was a friendly nudge, and Davison soon came to tea. *The Atlantic* was hoarding a backlog of unpublished manuscripts left over from its centennial issue the previous year. After hesitating, the editors accepted Ted's "Dick Straightup," but Edward Weeks turned down Sylvia's "The Disquieting Muses" and "Snakecharmer" with a stiff apology Sylvia branded as "snotty." She was pleased for Ted, happy to add his check for $150 to the $800 Guinness Prize he had won that month in England for "The Thought Fox," but Sylvia herself was deeply discouraged.

With panic "sitting firm" on her back, she began to reiterate all her old futile questions — Who am I? What shall I do? — contemplating a retreat to Harvard or Yale to start a Ph.D., "anything — only to take my life out of my own clumsy hands." Repeatedly she resisted the impulse to run back to external academic structures, recognizing that dependency as a lure to more deadly illusions. Out of school, she saw herself as a "soldier, demobbed." "I am going to

---

*Marcia Plumer had adopted twins to whom Sylvia wished to dedicate her *Bed Book*, written in May 1959.

work, doggedly, all year, at my own pace," she determined on September 27, "being a civilian, thinking, writing, more and more intensely, with more and more purpose, and not merely dreaming, ego-safe, about the magnificent writer I could be."

With time a welter of unstructured days, Sylvia's journals for September stumble from depression to self-examination to panic to odd bursts of joy. On September 18, after days wasted in the "vicious circle" of being too much alone with herself or with Ted, she suddenly felt much better. Why? The seed of a story had been sown after a visit with her husband to a tattooist's shop in Scollay Square (Boston's effort at a red-light district) where she had recognized in the tattooist a macabre and bizarre double of herself. Here was "life" at last:

> I got the man talking — about butterfly tattoos, rose tattoos, rabbit-hunt tattoos — wax tattoos — he showed us pictures of Miss Stella — tattooed all over — brocade orientals. I watched him tattoo a cut on his hand, a black, red, green and brown eagle and "Japan" on a sailor's arm, "Ruth" on a schoolboy's arm — I almost fainted, had smelling salts. The pale, rather excellent little professorial man who was trying out new springs in the machine, hung round about. Rose tattoos, eagle tattoos spin in my head — we'll go back. Life begins to justify itself.

The next day Sylvia was happily writing "The Fifteen-Dollar Eagle," but within the week she was back in the doldrums, so much so that she finally decided to get a job. She found one almost immediately, on October 8, typing records in the psychiatric clinic of Massachusetts General Hospital while acting as a secretary, "answering phones, meeting and dispatching a staff of over twenty-five doctors and a continual flow of patients." The job, she thought, would structure her days and give her unending subjects. "Paradoxically," she rather too hopefully concluded, "my objective daily view of troubled patients through the records objectifies my own view of myself. I shall try to enter into this schedule a wedge of writing — to expand it. I feel my whole sense and understanding of people being deepened and enriched by this: as if I had my wish and opened up the souls of the people in Boston and read them deep."

The heroine of Sylvia's next story, "Johnny Panic and the Bible of Dreams," was, not surprisingly, just such a secretary as herself, daily combing the records of the psychiatric clinic for evidence that fear was indeed the chief god of the mentally disturbed, "fear of elevators, snakes, loneliness" — but for Sylvia, chiefly fear of electroconvulsive therapy. To write the story she used her first traumatic, unforgettable experience of fear as an outpatient at Valley Head Hospital prior to her suicide attempt in 1953. A passage from Defoe's *Journal of the Plague Year* gave her a seminal image: "It was the opinion of others that it [the plague] might be distinguished by the party's breathing upon a piece of glass, where, the breath condensing, there might living creatures be seen by a microscope of strange, monstrous and frightful shapes, such as dragons, snakes, serpents and devils, horrible to behold."

It was only a small step from Defoe's dragons of infected breath to Plath's monsters in the Sargasso of the world's dreams as described by the narrator-secretary of the story, herself a self-appointed, self-educated "connoisseur of dreams":

> I've a dream of my own. My one dream. A dream of dreams.
>
> In this dream there's a great half-transparent lake stretching away in every direction, too big for me to see the shores of it, if there are any shores, and I'm hanging over it, looking down from the glass belly of some helicopter. At the bottom of the lake — so deep I can only guess at the dark masses moving and heaving — are the real dragons. The ones that were around before men started living in caves and cooking meat over fires . . .
>
> It's into this lake people's minds run at night, brooks and gutter trickles to one borderless common reservoir . . . the sewage farm of the ages.

Like Sylvia, the narrator of "Johnny Panic" leads a double life. While her superficial persona, jaunty and sourly clever, types up records for the clinic, her secret self has contracted with the devil — Johnny Panic, god of fear — for whom she works under cover of respectability. In her public role she bluffs; privately she pursues her true calling as a spy and collector of dream-evidence for Johnny Panic's accumulating files. Throughout the story she is shown as delighting in duplicity, having people on, taking them in, putting them off, "pursuing a vocation that would set these doctors on their ears."

Sylvia believed, with reason, that she had at last got her life into her writing in "Johnny Panic," regarding the story as "queer and quite slangy" and thus not unsalable. Did she realize just *how* queer, with its rigorous dreamlike logic? Given her premise that fear really *does* rule the world and that doctors are adherents to a false doctrine of health, the narrator's devious plan to spend the night reading and memorizing sick dreams from the record book seems perfectly reasonable. When she is caught by the villainous Clinic Director and strapped down for shock treatment by the huge-breasted Miss Milleravage, the message is that the psychiatrists are mad and the victim-adherents to Johnny Panic sane. The reader is half persuaded to believe the heroine's rhetoric — *half* persuaded because by the end no one in the story, a tour de force of poetic prose, appears to be "real" at all. All the characters are dreams, the final scene pure nightmare from which a reader wakes wondering how much to credit as symbol, how much to toss away with the rubbish of the subconscious. Only for Sylvia was the nightmare real, for it was, in fact, based on her own experience. The narrator says:

> They extend me full-length on my back on the cot. The crown of wire is placed on my head, the wafer of forgetfulness on my tongue. The masked priests move to their posts and take hold . . .
> From their cramped niches along the wall, the votaries raise their voices in protest. They begin the devotional chant:
>
> > The only thing to love is Fear itself.
> > Love of Fear is the beginning of wisdom.
> > The only thing to love is Fear itself.
> > May Fear and Fear and Fear be everywhere.

The "moral" of the story, its didactic effect, is wholly ironical. The priest-doctors who administer "cure" to the patient are mere instruments of Johnny Panic's will:

> At the moment when I think I am most lost the face of Johnny Panic appears in a nimbus of arc lights on the ceiling overhead. I am shaken like a leaf in the teeth of glory . . . His Word charges and illumines the universe.
> The air crackles with his blue-tongued lightning-haloed angels.
> His love is the twenty-story leap, the rope at the throat, the knife at the heart.
> He forgets not his own.

In May 1959 Sylvia's by-then-abandoned hospital job gave her a second story, originally titled "This Earth Our Hospital," later changed to "The Daughters of Blossom Street." Here again is that hospital world of hers, populated by people chiefly preoccupied with death. The style, bleak yet bitterly humorous, is the one she would later perfect for *The Bell Jar*. The unnamed narrator is an early version of Esther Greenwood, with Dotty as a proto-Doreen — tough, tenderhearted, and artificially cheerful amid a continuous rain of corpses. The story begins as the narrator opens a record book stamped "DEAD. DEAD. DEAD" and develops as the death agony of a cancer-stricken spinster foreshadows the fatal fall of a necrophilic messenger boy,

Billy, who for breaking his neck in the course of duty is awarded a posthumous gold medal and a full spread in the newspapers. In language vigorous with sarcasm and glittering with caustic irony, Plath manages to convey icy contempt for her characters while permitting her narrator hardly a wisp of sympathy for herself. Yet the irony again inadequately disguises a weird philosophy: that in this sick world death is a good bet for fame and happiness.*

Sylvia's job in the psychiatric clinic lasted two months. Jobs were useful only so long as they were writing-block breakers, and although she took other typing jobs later in the year — one for a professor of Indian studies at Harvard — Sylvia was by temperament ill suited to work for anyone but herself. In mid-December, moreover, her interest in psychiatry swerved in a new and wholly preoccupying direction. On Wednesday, December 10, she went to see her former McLean psychiatrist, Dr. Ruth Beuscher, without telling either her husband or her mother of the appointment. By that Friday she was determined to "pay money for her time & brain as if I were going to a supervision in life & emotions & what to do with both, I am going to work like hell, question, probe sludge & crap & allow myself to get the most out of it."

One sentence spoken by Dr. Beuscher in the course of Wednesday's therapy had gone home "like a shot of brandy": "I give you permission to hate your mother." Sylvia had returned to Willow Street "a new person." Her reaction was that of a grown girl let out of boarding school, a prisoner released from an invisible prison. "So I feel terrific," she wrote. "In a smarmy matriarchy of togetherness it is hard to get a sanction to hate one's mother especially a sanction one believes in." Sylvia believed in Dr. Beuscher, she admitted, because she admired her, could tell her anything without fear of being scolded, and because Dr. Beuscher herself represented "a permissive mother figure." Hating her mother was a lesser factor; what mattered was the *permission*. Someone older and wiser than Sylvia had told her coolly that hating was a permissible emotion. It was like being taught to breathe with two lungs instead of one, like being able to use a hitherto dark side of her brain.

Sylvia's weekly therapy with Dr. Beuscher continued throughout the six or seven months that remained to the Hugheses in Boston.

---

*Amazingly enough, "Johnny Panic and the Bible of Dreams" failed to find a publisher during Sylvia's lifetime. "The Daughters of Blossom Street," having been turned down by *The Atlantic Monthly*, was published in the *London Magazine* in May 1960, a year after it was written. "Johnny Panic" was finally published in *The Atlantic* in 1968.

Sylvia soon mapped out the principal areas of her panic-cum-writing-block and was tackling them one by one in long, analytical passages in her journal. After the first session with Dr. Beuscher she worked through her resentments. Society, represented by her mother, Mrs. Prouty, Mary Ellen Chase, and all the "hag"-mothers whom she saw as expecting her to conform and pay them back for sacrifices rendered, was pressing her into a mold which she justifiably hated. Why? Because it conflicted with the writing she did partly out of gratitude (the mothers would appropriate and judge her stories) but mainly because writing for her, as for her husband, was "a religious act . . . an ordering, a reforming, a relearning and reloving of people and the world as they are and as they might be." So, on one level, Sylvia was bogged down in guilt. "*Mother:* What to do with your hate for . . . all mother figures?" she wrote speculatively. "What to do when you feel guilty for not doing what they say, because, after all, they have gone out of their way to help you?" Dr. Beuscher could not solve the problem but only help her to recognize it. It was the same with her writing block:

> *Writing:* My chain of fear-logic goes like this: I want to write stories and poems and a novel and be Ted's wife and a mother to our babies. I want Ted to write as he wants and live where he wants and be my husband and a father to our babies.
>
> We can't now and maybe never will earn a living by our writing, which is the one profession we want. What will we do for money without sacrificing our energy and time to it and hurting our work?

Guilt on this level — for not taking steady jobs, for refusing to teach and provide for a probable family — was something Sylvia shared with most serious writers. Yet there was a level beneath this, personal and even more insoluble, which differed from dissatisfaction with herself (for not working hard enough) and from the anger she was directing at her mother and all the mothers who had wanted her to be "what I have not felt like really being" — that is, a success on society's terms.

Searching for reasons for "hating" her mother in her entry for December 12, Sylvia lists causes for guilt. Her mother had a "lousy" life but sacrificed all so that her daughter could have an ideal one. Her daughter should marry for "love love love," almost as though this were owed her mother. But this daughter brought up in a family full of women —"So many women, the house stank of them" — had never known a father. With her competitive brother away at boarding school, she had had her pick of boys whom she thought she liked but in fact "hated." The only man she might have loved was the one who, had he not died when she was eight, would have loved her "steady through life." But her mother had come in to her one morning with "tears . . . in her eyes and told me he was gone for good. I hate her for that."

Then her mother had had bad luck. Despite her loyalty, goodness, love, and self-sacrifice, things had gone wrong. Her husband died; her mother died of cancer; her daughter tried to commit suicide. Why had life been so unjust? Wasn't it her daughter's fault, partly? Didn't this ideally good mother really blame her daughter for her terrible life, and if this was so, didn't she really hate her daughter — as much as her daughter really hated her mother? Such was Sylvia's argument, backed up by a dream (sadly, undated) that she attributes in her journal to Aurelia Plath:

Her daughter was all gaudy-dressed about to go out and be a chorus girl, a prostitute too, probably . . . The husband, brought alive in dream to relive the curse of his old angers, slammed out of the house in rage that the daughter was going to be a chorus girl. The poor Mother runs along the sand beach, her feet sinking in the sand of life, her money bag open and the money and coins falling into the sand, turning to sand. The father had driven, in a fury, to spite her, off the road bridge and was floating dead, face down and bloated, in the slosh of ocean water by the pillars of the country club. Everybody was looking down from the pier at them. Everyone knew everything.

As Sylvia saw it, guilt was clearly the family curse, and she and her mother shared it, hating both themselves and each other. Being a poet and a Germanic one at that, she easily made guilt pivotal to her evolving psychodrama. At the end of her long December 12 entry she methodically listed her "Main Questions," among them:

What to do for money & where to live: practical.
What to do with fear of writing: why fear? Fear of not being a success? Fear of world casually saying we're wrong in [through] rejections?
Ideas of maleness: conservation of creative power (sex & writing).
Why do I freeze in fear my mind & writing: say, look: no head, what can you expect of a girl with no head?
Why don't I write a novel?
Images of society: the Writer and Poet is excusable only if he is Successful. Makes Money.
Why do I feel I should have a Ph.D., that I am aimless, brainless

without one, when I know what is inside is the only credential necessary for my identity?

NB: I do not hit often: once or twice.

How to express anger creatively?

Fear of losing male totem: what roots?

R[uth] B[euscher]: You have always been afraid of premature choices cutting off other choices.

To most of these and other, related questions Sylvia addressed herself for the remainder of her life. With Ruth Beuscher she had laid out the grounds of her quest at last.

The very next day, on December 13, the postman arrived with "a charming warm admiring letter from John Lehmann" of the *London Magazine*, accepting "Lorelei," "The Disquieting Muses," and "The Snakecharmer." The jinx of a long autumn of rejections — from *Harper's*, *Encounter*, *The Atlantic Monthly*, World Publishing (for her next book of poems), and the Saxton Fellowship trustees — had been broken. Christmas came and went between therapy sessions with Sylvia gaining more and more insight into her fears and blockages.

Clearly in some respects she identified Hughes with her dead father — as when he wasn't there on her last teaching day at Smith, or when she was jealous of other women — while in other respects she depended upon her husband as she had formerly on her mother.* She was more and more drawn to psychology and to Freudian explanations of her behavior. "Read Freud's *Mourning and Melancholia* this morning . . ." she noted on December 27.

An almost exact description of my feelings and reasons for suicide: a transferred murderous impulse from my mother onto myself: the "vampire" metaphor Freud uses, "draining the ego" that is exactly the feeling I have getting in the way of my writing: Mother's clutch. I mask my self-abasement (a transferred hate of her) and weave it with my own real dissatisfactions in myself until it becomes very difficult to distinguish what is really bogus criticism from what is really a changeable liability.

On December 28 she recorded, with a touch of awe:

Went to library yesterday afternoon with Ted. Looked up requirements for a Ph.D. in psychology. It would take about six years. A

---

*Her journals record "two acrid fights" with her husband, one about sewing on his buttons, the other about her wish to change seats at a Truman Capote reading. But she realized that the worries that caused such moments of stress between them had really to do with their financial and professional uncertainties.

prodigious prospect. Two years for prerequisites, languages for M.A. Four years for the rest . . . The work of applying, figuring out programs, etc., and not to mention money, a formidable thing. Awesome to confront a program of study which is so monumental: all human experience.

It was too late to start again, so she turned with "a kind of relief" to Frank O'Connor's stories, which she was studying for technique, and the autobiography of Saint Theresa, which she admired for its "pure soul," critical only of a "horrid self-satisfied greed for misfortune" that she detected in nuns and saints. "The only way to stop envying others is to have a self of joy," she burst out in a sudden revelation. "All creation is jammed in the selfish soul."

On Saturday, January 3, after an hour with Dr. Beuscher, she wrote of feeling cleansed and exhausted as after "watching or participating in a Greek play":

> All my life I have been "stood up" emotionally by the people I loved most: Daddy dying and leaving me, Mother somehow not there. So I endow the smallest incidents of lateness, for example, in other people I love, with an emotional content of coldness, indication that I am not important to them. Realizing this, I wasn't angry or bothered she [Dr. Beuscher] was late. The terror of my last day of teaching last May . . . especially with the face of that girl. If it happened more often, I would find it a character fault, but it doesn't seem to have happened.

She goes on, significantly:

> At McLean I had an inner life going on all the time but wouldn't admit it . . . I needed permission to admit I lived. Why?
> Why, after the "amazingly short" three or so shock treatments, did I rocket uphill? Why did I feel I needed to be punished, to punish myself. Why do I feel now I should be guilty, unhappy: and feel guilty if I am not? . . . My need to punish myself might, horribly, go to the length of deliberately and to spite my face disappointing T[ed] in this way or that. That would be my worst punishment. That and not writing.

Opening her eyes to the "great, stark, bloody play acting itself out over and over again behind the sunny facade of our daily rituals, birth, marriage, death," Sylvia began to feel her way toward her real subject. The writer was beginning to identify with the woman, the woman with the writer; there could be no true distinction between them. Her characters were archetypes, "the dark, cruel, murderous

shades, the demon-animals, the Hungers" of her readings in Oesterreich and in what she found in psychology. On January 7 she reported
reading Ainu tales, "primitive: all at penis-fetish, anus-fetish, mouth-
fetish stage. Marvelous untouched humor, primal: bang, bang you're
dead."

Yet throughout these explorations she craved the outward appurte-
nances of success: "I need to have written a novel, a book of poems,
a *Ladies' Home Journal* or *New Yorker* story." Complaining of lack
of ideas, lack of know-how, she wrote a story, "The Shadow," a less
impressive evocation of her Winthrop childhood than her earlier
"Superman and Paula Brown's New Snowsuit." She was afflicted with
nightmares connected with her half-formed desire for a baby:

> Very bad dreams lately. One just after my period last week of
> losing my month-old baby: a transparent meaning. The baby,
> formed just like a baby, only small as a hand, died in my stomach
> and fell forward: I looked down at my bare belly and saw the round
> bump of its head in my right side, bulging out like a burst appendix.
> It was delivered with little pain, dead. Then I saw two babies, a big
> nine-month one, and a little one-month one with a blind white-
> piggish face nuzzling against it . . .

In another dream she was walking with Stephen Fassett through a
cemetery, dragging away the stones with a rope. There appeared

> a corridor, with dead corpses being wheeled down it, half decayed,
> their faces all mottled and falling away, yet clothed . . . We got
> pushed into the stream, and horror, the dead were moving. A dead
> corpse, all grinning and filth being propelled along standing by
> another man almost as bad, then a lump of flesh, stunted, round,
> with black cloves, or nails stuck in all over it, and only one long
> apish swinging arm, reaching out for alms.

While Sylvia was making painful forays into her subconscious,
emerging each Wednesday from sessions with Dr. Beuscher purged
and streaming with tears, she was struggling to find a place for herself
in some community. "I feel, am mad as any writer must in one way
be," she wrote on January 8; "why not make it real? I am too close
to the bourgeois society of suburbia: too close to people I know: I
must sever myself from them, or be part of their world: this half-and-
half compromise is intolerable. If only Ted wanted to do something.
Saw a career he'd enjoy . . ."

In some such mood of frustration, and because, as a practical matter, she wanted outside reaction to her work, Sylvia decided to follow

the example of two other poets of roughly her age and experience and attend Robert Lowell's writing seminar at Boston University. With Anne Sexton and George Starbuck she spent Tuesday afternoons "auditing" the class, which she at first found disappointing. "I said a few mealymouthed things," she commented in her journal on February 25, and

> a few B.U. students yattered nothings I wouldn't let my Smith freshmen say without challenge. Lowell good in his mildly feminine ineffectual fashion. Felt a regression. The main thing is hearing the other students' poems & his reaction to mine. I need an outsider: feel like the recluse who comes out into the world with a life-saving gospel to find everybody has learned a new language in the meantime and can't understand a word he's saying.

In a short memoir of Sylvia, Anne Sexton set down her impression of their brief period of association when they met, as she put it, as "suicides sometimes meet" in the bar of the Ritz-Carlton Hotel. After each Lowell class, writes Sexton, she, George Starbuck, and Sylvia would "pile into the front seat of [Sexton's] old Ford" and drive to the Ritz, where she would park illegally in a loading-only zone, explaining that it was all right because they were only going to get loaded. The memoir continues:

> Often, very often, Sylvia and I would talk at length about our first suicides; at length, in detail, and in depth between the free potato chips. Suicide is, after all, the opposite of the poem . . . We talked death with burned-up intensity, both of us drawn to it like moths to an electric light bulb. Sucking on it! She told the story of her first suicide in sweet and loving detail and her description in *The Bell Jar* is just the same story . . . We talked death and this was life for us, lasting in spite of us.

For Sylvia, Anne Sexton had an ease of phrase and an honesty that served as a model of how to unclench herself, though in Lowell's class they were rivals as well as collaborators. Perhaps they were too much alike temperamentally to be close friends. Sexton's memoir continues frankly:

> I have heard since that Sylvia was determined from childhood to be great, a great writer at the least of it. I tell you, at the time I did not notice this in her. Something told me to bet on her but I never asked it why. I was too determined to bet on myself to actually notice where she was headed in her work. Lowell said, at the time, that he liked her work and that he felt her poems got right to the

point. I didn't agree ... I told Mr. Lowell that I felt she dodged the point and did so perhaps because of her preoccupation with form. Form was important for Sylvia ... [but she] hadn't then found a form that belonged to her. Those early poems were all in a cage (and not even her own cage at that).

This was good criticism, reflecting the "criticism of rhetoric" Sylvia heard in Lowell's class, where, as she noted on March 20, "he sets me up with Anne Sexton, an honor I suppose. Well, about time. She has very good things, and they get better, though there is a lot of loose stuff." It is clearer now than it would have been in 1959 that Sylvia Plath and Anne Sexton were different kinds of poet. For Sexton, to tell the whole story was indeed "the whole point," and she was foremost among Lowell's disciples in furthering the concept of confessionalism. Sylvia, on the other hand, though patently a poet of her "self," was more a surrealist of internals, seeking to reveal the archetypes and patterns working within or behind them. Nevertheless, she realized the pitfalls of rhetoric and determined to overcome her faults. Covertly she was working out a style of her own, walking a razor's edge between Sexton-like directness and the lyricism she may have envied in Adrienne Rich's early work. A paragraph in her journal for February 25 shows how she went about teaching herself to be herself:

Ted's thinking idea good. I listed five subjects and got no farther than Egg Rock. Wrote a ghastly poem in strict varying line lengths with no feeling in it although the scene was fraught with emotion. Then did it over, much better: got something of what I wanted. Pulled. To the neat easy A[drienne] C[ecile] R[ich]–ish lyricism, to the graphic description of the world. My main thing now is to start with real things: real emotions, and leave out the baby gods, the old men of the sea, the thin people, the knights, the moon-mothers, the mad maudlins, the Lorelei, the hermits, and get into me, Ted, friends, mother and brother and father and family. The real world. Real situations, behind which the great gods play the drama of blood, lust and death.

Besides "Suicide off Egg Rock," Sylvia mentions writing with greater or lesser success that winter "The Ravaged Face" (after a tearful session with Ruth Beuscher), "Point Shirley," "Watercolor of Grantchester Meadows" (specifically for *The New Yorker*, where it appeared on May 28, 1960), "Man in Black" (also published in *The New Yorker*, on April 9, 1960), "The Bull of Bendylaw," "Goatsucker" (for Esther Baskin's anthology of night animals), "The Hermit at Outermost House," and, most significantly, two poems relating to her father, "Electra on Azalea Path" and "The Beekeeper's Daughter."

On March 8, for the first time, Sylvia paid a visit to her father's grave in the Winthrop cemetery, an event she placed in *The Bell Jar* just before Esther's suicide attempt. The notes Sylvia took on the occasion were clearly useful when she came to write her novel:

> Three graveyards separated by streets, all made within the last fifty years or so, ugly crude block stones, headstones together, as if the dead were sleeping head to head in a poorhouse. In the third yard, on a flat grassy area looking across a sallow barren stretch to rows of wooden tenements, I found the flat stone, "Otto E. Plath: 1885–1940," right beside the path, where it would be walked over. Felt cheated. My temptation to dig him up. To prove he existed and really was dead. How far gone would he be? No trees, no peace, his headstone jammed up against the body on the other side. Left shortly. It is good to have the place in mind.

The comparable passage in *The Bell Jar*, written in the spring of 1961, revives the event with wry partiality but few changes of fact:

> I had a great yearning, lately, to pay my father back [note the double-entendre] for all the years of neglect, and start tending his grave. I had always been my father's favorite, and it seemed fitting I should take on a mourning my mother had never bothered with . . .
>
> The graveyard disappointed me. It lay at the outskirts of the town, on low ground, like a rubbish dump, and as I walked up and down the gravel paths, I could smell the stagnant salt marshes in the distance . . .
>
> The stones in the modern part [of the graveyard] were crude and cheap, and here and there a grave was rimmed with marble, like an oblong bathtub full of dirt, and rusty metal containers stuck up about where the person's navel would be, full of plastic flowers . . .
>
> Then I saw my father's gravestone.
>
> It was crowded right up by another gravestone, head to head, the way people are crowded in a charity ward when there isn't enough space. The stone was of a mottled pink marble, like tinned salmon, and all there was on it was my father's name and, under it, two dates, separated by a little dash.
>
> At the foot of the stone I arranged the rainy armful of azaleas I had picked from the bush at the gateway of the graveyard. Then my legs folded under me, and I sat down in the sopping grass. I couldn't understand why I was crying so hard.
>
> Then I remembered that I had never cried for my father's death.

Writing in 1961, Sylvia had mastered her plot and could control the casual, almost blasé tone of the novel. She had also learned to capitalize on her gift for mocking pathos. Two years earlier her touch, particularly in poetry, had been less sure. Where, she asked herself on March 20, 1959, soon after writing the Electra poem, is "that casual, gay verve? Alas alas. I maunch on chagrins." Still, here is the graveyard scene again, rendered in recognizable particulars in the midst of the highly wrought mythos of "Electra on Azalea Path" (not only the name of the path where Otto Plath is buried but also a sly echo of Aurelia Plath's name):

> The day I woke, I woke on Churchyard Hill.
> I found your name, I found your bones and all
> Enlisted in a cramped necropolis,
> Your speckled stone askew by an iron fence.
>
> In this charity ward, this poorhouse, where the dead
> Crowd foot to foot, head to head, no flower
> Breaks the soil. This is Azalea Path.
> A field of burdock opens to the south.
> Six feet of yellow gravel cover you.
> The artificial red sage does not stir
> In the basket of plastic evergreens they put
> At the headstone next to yours, nor does it rot,
> Although the rains dissolve a bloody dye:
> The ersatz petals drip, and they drip red.

Sylvia was dissatisfied with "Electra on Azalea Path," which, after criticism from Lowell and Anne Sexton, she discarded from her book as too rhetorical. Yet the poem marked a transition for her, and was written, interestingly enough, on the same day she completed the delightful little pregnancy poem "Metaphors," which, despite or perhaps because of its self-conscious form (nine lines, nine syllables in each), is still memorable. More successful than "Electra" was "The Beekeeper's Daughter," in which Freudian symbolism replaces "the stilts" of the old Greek tragedy, incest here prevailing over revenge. The "maestro of the bees" among his "many-breasted hives" is unmistakably Otto tending to his forbidden "garden of mouthings" in some womblike land of death. Throughout the spring of 1959 Sylvia labored to use the nuggets she was digging up in her therapy directly in new poems. Her growth as a person and development as a writer were inseparable. In her journal she wrote:

> [What can I] do to sift out grown self from contracted baby feelings, jolting jealousies[?] . . . I am worried about being lazy if happy,

worried about being self-deluding if working on anything. So little myself all other identities threaten me. [January 27]

What inner decision, what inner murder or prison break must I commit if I want to speak from my true deep voice in writing . . . and not feel this jam-up of feeling behind a glass-dam fancy-facade of numb dumb wordage . . . I think success would be heartening now. But, most heartening, the feeling [as if] I were breaking out of my glass caul. [February 19]

What good does talking about my father do? It may be a minor catharsis that lasts a day or two, but I don't get insight talking to myself. What insight am I trying to get to free what? If my emotional twists are at the bottom of misery, how can I get to know what they are and what to do with them? She [Dr. Beuscher] can't make me write, or if I do write, write well. [March 20]

And finally the lessons of confessionalism and psychiatric counseling came together in an opportunistic notion for a novel just as the summer was coming to take Sylvia away from Boston: "And a story, a novel even. Must get out SNAKE PIT. There is an increasing market for mental hospital stuff. I am a fool if I don't relive it, recreate it."

All this time, of course, ordinary life had been going on in Boston. Between struggles and depressions, was Sylvia enjoying it? Peter Davison recalls an encounter of the previous autumn:

On Monday, 11 November, Ted and Sylvia came to my attic apartment in Cambridge to meet Robert Frost. It was a curious occasion: a photographer and a reporter from *Life* magazine were present, in the process of compiling a story about my life as a bachelor, little knowing that before the week was out I would meet Jane Truslow, Sylvia's Smith classmate, whom I would marry in March 1959. (*Life* never published the story.) The Hugheses, with me and my girlfriend of the moment, sat with drinks while Frost, a little cautiously at first, discoursed on poetry and experience, gradually losing any consciousness of the camera. The evening became relaxed, and when it was over, Ted and Sylvia and I walked towards Frost's house with him, shuffling through the deep drifts of autumn leaves in the midnight streets. Frost clearly took a shine to Ted, but Sylvia kept very quiet while the two spoke of Edward Thomas and the English countryside, of Ezra Pound and T. S. Eliot.

In Sylvia's journals domestic questions sit cheek-by-jowl with anguished self-analysis. On the day she went to the library to look up requirements for a degree in psychology — December 28, 1958 — she noted:

> Ted labored all yesterday afternoon and evening making a wolf-mask out of Agatha [Fassett]'s old, falling-apart sealskin. It is remarkably fuzzy and wolfish. About the party tonight [evidently a costume affair]: the sense of not wanting to go: the Unknown, everybody buying fabulous costumes and toys to go with them. I haven't even got a red hood or a basket, which is all I need, but can't see spending even a couple of $$.

Again, on January 27, 1959, after worrying about her work, her "contracted baby feelings," and her guilt for not working, she remarks prosaically that "Robert Lowell and his wife and the Fassetts are coming to dinner this week. I am wondering what to serve them all in one dish. Lemon meringue pie." Three weeks later, on February 19, having written "a Grantchester poem of pure description," she castigates herself: "I must get philosophy in. Until I do I shall lag behind A[drienne] C[ecile] R[ich]." She was obviously worried that she was unable to write what she really felt because of "an anesthetizing of feeling." In the next paragraph she reported, "Dinners and parties all this week, which I am glad to forgo from now on." Clearly the journals were a catchall mainly for dissatisfactions and cannot be taken as evidence that Sylvia was morose all winter.

Late in January the Hugheses acquired a "playful, adventurous" tiger-striped kitten they named Sappho; she was a granddaughter, on one side, of Thomas Mann's cat. There were plays and poetry readings in plenty. Sylvia records a reading by Truman Capote in December 1958: "Big head, as of a prematurely delivered baby . . . big white forehead, little drawstring mouth." She added perceptively, "Men hated the homosexual part of him with more than usual fury. Something else: jealousy at his success? If he weren't successful there would be nothing to anger at."

In April, with the arrival of spring, came "joyous news." After a query or two and some "paltering over the budget," the Guggenheim trustees awarded Ted a $5,000 grant on April 10. "Financial worries for the next year were over," wrote Hughes to his sister, "so joy. The chance to come to Europe, so easily — with all the usual worries etherized — overpowered me when I got the letter." Ted and Sylvia had decided, the previous year, to return to England after the year in Boston. Nevertheless, in the spring they accepted an invitation to spend the autumn at Yaddo, the artists' colony in Saratoga Springs,

New York. Between Boston and Yaddo they would tour the United States in Mrs. Plath's Plymouth. Everything was coming right at last.

Rejoicing in the *New Yorker* acceptances of "Watercolor of Grantchester Meadows" and "Man in Black," Sylvia gathered together the "40 unattackable poems" she had completed for her book. This time she felt sure she would be at least a runner-up for the Yale Series of Younger Poets, though she wished there were "more potent ones" and fewer "miserable death wishes." Meanwhile she set about writing a poem for children. On May 3 she noted in her journal: "I wrote a book yesterday. Maybe I'll write a postscript on top of this in the next month and say I've sold it. Yes, after half a year of procrastinating, bad feeling and paralysis, I got to it yesterday morning, having lines in my head here and there."

The upshot was *The Bed Book*, a clever eight-page rhyme she sent off immediately to Emilie McLeod, children's editor for the Atlantic Monthly Press. Mrs. McLeod wrote back that she liked it, suggesting that Sylvia omit the two cute children, Wide-Awake Will and Stay-Uppity Sue, and simply describe ten fantastic beds. Sylvia agreed and cut the book to its present length. It begins:

> Most Beds are Beds
> For sleeping or resting,
> But the *best* Beds are much
> More interesting!
> Not just a white little
> Tucked-in-tight little
> Nighty-night little
> Turn-out-the-light little
> Bed.*

Although Emilie McLeod warmly recommended it, the editor at Little, Brown (which published Atlantic Monthly Press books at the time) sent it back with a curt dismissal: the text seemed forced, and without illustrations the book made little sense, she said. Ted Hughes's children's book *Meet My Folks!* met with an equally cool reception in America after it had been accepted by Faber in England.

Sylvia's poetry manuscript, titled *The Bull of Bendylaw*, was not finally accepted by the Yale Series of Younger Poets. Dudley Fitts wrote to say that her book had missed selection "by a whisper," principally because of her lack of technical finish. Justifiably, Sylvia

---

*Amazingly, this charming little book failed to find a publisher until 1976, when Harper & Row brought it out in New York and Faber in England.

was furious. "My main flaw," she expostulated on May 20, "is a machinelike syllabic death blow. Will I ever be liked for anything other than the wrong reasons?" On the same day she noted, again in "green-eyed fury," that Anne Sexton's *To Bedlam and Part Way Back* had been chosen over her own *The Devil of the Stairs* (a more recent title for *The Bull of Bendylaw*) for publication by Houghton Mifflin. ("But A[nne] S[exton] is there ahead of me, with her lover G[eorge] S[tarbuck] writing *New Yorker* odes to her and both of them together: felt our triple-martini afternoons at the Ritz breaking up.") George Starbuck was Sexton's editor at Houghton Mifflin. As the ultimate insult, *he* had won the Yale award. Sleepless, furious, jealous, Sylvia was stopped in her tracks, resolving amid "hostile silences" to consult with Dr. Beuscher:

> What to do with anger, ask her. One thing to say: Yes, I want the world's praise, money & love, and am furious with anyone, especially with anyone I know or who has had a similar experience, getting ahead of me. Well, what to do when this surges up and over & over? Last night I knew that Mother didn't matter — she is all for me, but I have dissipated her image and she becomes all editors and publishers and critics and the World, and I want acceptance there, and to feel my work good and well-taken. Which ironically freezes me at my work, corrupts my nunnish labor of work-for-itself-as-its-own-reward. Hit this today.

Despite self-lashings, self-searchings, and disappointments, Sylvia had accomplished a great deal in her first year of freedom. She had six stories to her credit: "Johnny Panic and the Bible of Dreams," "The Fifteen-Dollar Eagle," "The Shadow," "Sweetie Pie and the Gutter Men," "Above the Oxbow," and "This Earth Our Hospital," the last three composed in the spring. In addition, she had written a fine children's book and put together a substantial collection of poems.

More than this, she had confronted her demons of helpless fear and self-abasement. Her ambition was unrelenting, but she had gained some understanding of how buried feelings for her mother caused writing blocks. Moreover, she was beginning to recognize her intense jealousies as destructive. Her deep inner anger, however unappeased, could be harnessed like energy to drive her talent. On May 31 she was writing in her journal: "I feel that this month I have conquered my Panic Bird. I am a calm, happy and serene writer . . . I have done, this year, what I said I would: overcome my fear of facing a blank page day after day, acknowledging myself, in my deepest emotions, a writer, come what may."

Before they left their Boston apartment in June, Sylvia suffered another setback that threatened her achieved equilibrium. Having been alarmed by false pregnancies all year, she visited the hospital and was told that she was temporarily infertile. Everything suddenly had "gone barren"; she was "part of the world's ash, something from which nothing can grow, nothing can flower or come to fruit." Fighting overreaction, tears, despair, she went for checkups, where it was discovered that she was failing to ovulate. "How can I keep Ted wedded to a barren woman?" she moaned. But her barrenness was short-lived. After treatment — more horror, more hospitals — she and Ted set off for California in Mrs. Plath's car, with her blessings. Sylvia was to become pregnant on the trip.

POEM FOR A

BIRTHDAY

1959

I shall perish if I can write about no one but myself.
                            — *Journals,* November 4, 1959

The IDEAS kill the little green shoots of the work itself.
                            — *Journals,* November 15, 1959

THE AMBITIOUS driving and camping tour around North America
that Ted and Sylvia took in the summer of 1959 opened new territory
to them both, for although Sylvia had traveled in Europe she had
never before ventured out of her own continent's cozy New England
corner. Their route cast a wide circle — first north into Ontario, west
to Wisconsin and the Dakota Badlands, across Montana to Yellowstone Park, and on to Lake Tahoe and San Francisco; then south to
Los Angeles, east across the Mojave Desert and, via the Grand Canyon, to New Orleans; then northeast to Tennessee, Washington, D.C.,
and Philadelphia; and finally back home to Boston.

At Rock Lake, Ontario, they stopped for two or three days' fishing.
A poem about their stay there, "Two Campers in Cloud Country,"
shows how this tour of the huge land mass of North America, with
its extremes of scenery and climate and its wide, magical skies, was
absorbed by the poet in Sylvia and became a main source for the big,
dramatic effects of land and sky in the Ariel poems. After three days'
driving, she says in the poem, they at last found

> . . . a cloud
> The polite skies over Boston couldn't possibly accommodate . . .

> The horizons are too far off to be chummy as uncles;
> The colors assert themselves with a sort of vengeance.
> Each day concludes in a huge splurge of vermilions

> And night arrives in one gigantic step.

From Rock Lake they drove to the tip of the Wisconsin peninsula that protrudes north into Lake Superior east of Duluth. They spent a marvelous four or five days there, where they were befriended by a Polish family, the Nozals (with the most northerly telephone in Wisconsin). In her impulsive way, Sylvia took to them with an immediate feeling of kinship. Mr. Nozal was a professional fisherman, and they used to take his little daughter with them when they fished on the lake. Sylvia started sketching again, drawing the boats at the wharf. Their visit had its dramatic moment when one night a hoodlum set fire to a nearby house.

There was more drama at Yellowstone Park. One evening, after sightseeing all day, they were heading toward camp on a long, circular road through the forest when they noticed that their car was nearly out of gas. Just as Sylvia was beginning to panic, a huge elk bounded out in front of them, casting grotesque shadows among the trees. Sylvia was sick with fear. Finally their scant supply of gas got them to their campsite, where they fished and caught cutthroat trout, but the night was eerie and tense. In the middle of the night they were woken by a shuffling noise outside their tent. They peered out to see a bear rip out the window of a rear door of the car, lift out everything edible, and eat it. Outraged but not particularly alarmed — they were used to seeing tourists feed the bears — they watched for some hours. The first thing next morning, however, a terrified Sylvia dashed back from the washroom. She'd met a woman there who had just driven over from a neighboring camp with news that a man who'd tried to shoo a bear away from his stores had been killed in one blow that very night. "We've got to get out of here!" cried Sylvia. "The bears are killing people!" She was so upset that they left that morning.

Sylvia's story "The Fifty-ninth Bear," written two months later at Yaddo, merges these events. A high-strung neurotic wife called Sadie plays a game of counting bears in Yellowstone with her husband, Norton,* finally willing him to die when he confronts the bear at-

---

*Note the significant names: Sadie, suggesting sadist, and Norton, the surname of a still-resented boyfriend.

tacking their car. Sylvia came to dislike the story, not because it seemed to reveal ill will against her husband — his family and friends were appalled when it appeared in the *London Magazine* in February 1961 — but because she found it "a stiff artificial piece . . . [with] none of the deep emotional undercurrents gone into or developed." Her ambition to produce a publishable story or poem seemed to cancel out any normal regard for people's sensibilities, however dear to her the people were. It was a blind spot of Sylvia's; the problem was to arise again with what seemed cruel caricatures of people close to her in *The Bell Jar* and in some of the poem-portraits of the Ariel period.

Having left Yellowstone, Sylvia and Ted continued their journey. Arriving at the Pacific at last, they dashed straight into the ocean to swim, then slept under the stars on Stinson Beach, wrapped in a blanket, to wake drenched with dew in a cold fog. In San Francisco they stayed for a day or two and got the window replaced in their car before driving on to Big Sur, where they camped and fished. After seeing Los Angeles, they relaxed in some comfort in Pasadena with Otto Plath's sister, Aunt Frieda (after whom, with Frieda Lawrence, the baby Sylvia was carrying was to be named), and her husband, a retired surgeon.

From Pasadena they crossed the Mojave Desert. Sylvia's impressions were captured in her poem "Sleep in the Mojave Desert," and again we see how America's huge, uncozy spaces contributed to the surrealistic landscapes characteristic of the Ariel poems:

> . . . It is dry, dry.
> And the air dangerous. Noonday acts queerly
> On the mind's eye, erecting a line
> Of poplars in the middle distance, the only
> Object beside the mad, straight road
> One can remember men and houses by.

After the panoramas of the Grand Canyon they headed east and south across Texas to New Orleans, where they swam in the sweltering heat in Lake Pontchartrain and enjoyed the city. Turning north again, they visited Lucas Myers's family home in Tennessee; then, after sightseeing in Washington, they drove to Philadelphia, where they stayed with Sylvia's adored Uncle Frank. They reached home on August 28, having been away for ten weeks.

Before their trip Sylvia had left her collection of poems with her mother along with instructions to send its contents out to a long list of magazines and book publishers. She returned to a heap of rejection slips but with the promise of two calm months of uninterrupted writing at Yaddo in Saratoga Springs in upstate New York.

◀   ◀   ◀

Yaddo began as a magnificent private estate — handsome buildings set in fine, extensive grounds. In 1926 it was converted into an artists' colony under the direction of Elizabeth Ames. For those invited to work there, it provides spacious living quarters as well as a private studio and excellent meals. It was here that Ted and Sylvia lived and worked from September 10 to late November. In those eleven weeks Sylvia wrote the final poems for her first book, *The Colossus,* completing the process of internal growth and self-discovery as an artist that she had undertaken so determinedly in Boston.

At Yaddo Ted was provided with a conservatory-like studio in the surrounding woods, while Sylvia's workroom was on the top floor of West House, an annex to the grand mansion and hardly less sumptuously furnished. The poet May Swenson, also a Yaddo guest that autumn, describes Sylvia's study as "high and sunny . . . overlooking pines." Sylvia's first Yaddo notes evoke "air clear enough for angels. The wet dews gleaming on the rusty pine needles underfoot, standing on the looped plant stems in pale drops." The gardens were studded with marble statuary, pools, fountains, and wooded walks by the Yaddo lakes, where Ted, and often Sylvia too, fished in the morning. On the ground floor of West House they shared an enormous bedroom, bigger than their entire Boston apartment. By the end of their stay its whiteness came to seem sterile, hospital-like, to Sylvia.

During the summer there were thirty or so artists working in the colony, but with the closing of the mansion at the end of September only ten or twelve guests stayed on, mostly visual artists or composers. In the Hugheses' first weeks at Yaddo a young Chinese composer, Chou Wen-Chung, struck up a friendship and working relationship with Ted. Although Chou left before the end of September, over the next year the two men collaborated on an oratorio based on the Tibetan Book of the Dead (*Bardo Thödol*), a project they never completed.

At first Sylvia was enthralled by the elegance and peace of Yaddo. Breakfast and dinner were served at the outset in the mansion's great dining room under a beamed ceiling, at mammoth tables surrounded by carved mahogany chairs. Later, when the summer guests had left, the smaller group ate more intimately in a small dining room above the estate's garages. Thermoses and box lunches were provided each day so that the artists could work to their own schedules. Sylvia's plan was to write stories such as "The Fifty-ninth Bear" as a warm-up for marketable fiction. She also began, for the umpteenth time, to study German — that language so dangerously linked with her past that she never did properly master it.

In the mansion there was a well-stocked library on which she took notes before the building closed at the end of September. The authors she chiefly read, however, were those on the bookshelves of West House, most of whom wrote for *The New Yorker,* including Mavis Gallant (whose "novel on a daughter-mother relation, the daughter committing suicide" Sylvia read), Eudora Welty, Jean Stafford, Katherine Anne Porter — all successful senior writers of literary fiction over whose works Sylvia enviously pored, looking for a way into "otherness." She read May Swenson's poems with interest, noting their virtuosity and independence. For the first time, too, Sylvia read Elizabeth Bishop with full attention, approving her "fine originality, always surprising, never rigid, flowing, juicier than Marianne Moore, who is her godmother."

At Yaddo Sylvia was also reading Jung's *Symbols of Transformation,* and Ted Hughes has recorded that she was much impressed by Paul Radin's *African Folktales,* which is still, according to Grace Schulman, on the shelves of West House, along with Theodore Roethke's *The Waking.* Jung, Radin, and Roethke all played their part in the work she produced there.

Although it is impossible to say, finally, what brought about the creative leap Sylvia experienced at Yaddo in October 1959, it seems certain it had to do with the inner turmoil she had struggled to face all year, focusing on traumatic childhood events and her breakdown and suicide attempt at twenty. Sylvia had long been confusing two very different battles within herself. One was with an artificial Sylvia, modeled on her mother, driven by ambitions she believed Aurelia harbored for her and ideals she thought Aurelia projected. This battle was occurring on a comparatively superficial level. Beneath it, so to speak, raged an altogether more serious war, where the "real" Sylvia — violent, subversive, moonstruck, terribly angry — fought for her existence against a nice, bright, gifted American girl. This "real" self may have been created, and gone underground, at the time of her father's death in November 1940. It had emerged in August 1953, before her suicide attempt, and it remained in charge during the months of her slow recovery at McLean. It would be too simple to say that the nice girl wanted to live while the vengeful, deserted daughter wanted to die. But it was probably the case that Sylvia's powerful buried self was deadly in its determination to emerge at any cost.

She supposed she was wrestling with the "never-satisfied gods" of her mother's presumed expectations, those ideals of success, security, and conventional domesticity which were embedded in her culture and which she uncompromisingly attacked in The Bell Jar. But these little gods were relatively easy to identify and mock. They are part of all of us, particularly those who were young in the 1950s — they whisper their threats of failure, blame us for selfish egoism, exhort us to improve ourselves. In attacking them Sylvia was striking at familiar panicmongers, which many of her readers would subsequently identify and condemn.

Some of her poems, even early ones such as "Spinster" and "Two Sisters of Persephone," give evidence that her divided loyalties, good girl versus bad girl, ran so deep they muddled her purpose. The poems present dichotomies of mutually exclusive types of women, yet Sylvia can be identified with both. Though she said she intended "Spinster" to criticize the unwedded, bloodless intellectuals she had rejected as models at Newnham, the poem also defines the "barb and check" of her own barricaded soul — which became, after she married, a barricade behind which she defended her marriage as well as herself. The rosy fertility queen and the gray scholar of "Two Sisters of Persephone" are again twin aspects of herself.

These poems, setting up opposites, mirror images of self and other self, reflect Sylvia's strange perception of the world and go some way toward explaining her preoccupation with doubles, or doppelgängers. Life in the bell jar was impossible without the total support of another human being. Thus she repeatedly chose to see those close to her as doubles and soul mates: Nancy Hunter, Jane Baltzell, and, in her novel, Joan Gilling, killed off by the plot to enable Esther to live. When such doubles showed their autonomy, as they inevitably did, they became hated rivals, causing Sylvia immense anguish as they threatened the frail construct of her ego. They, of course, recoiled from what appeared to be monstrous egotism, a self-absorption that negated the reality of their own lives.

Sylvia seemed egotistical, however, not because her ego was strong, but because it was perilously weak. Between her rigid, genteel-mother construct, on the one hand, and the suppressed Medean furies of a "real self," on the other, her ego was ground between upper and nether millstones, allowing her only two options for action. Either she could remain a pathetic victim, a homunculus with barely a chance of survival, or she could fight back with all the bitterness of deeply aggrieved injury — which in her writing is mostly what she did. All through 1959, first with Dr. Beuscher in Boston and then with herself at Yaddo, she was struggling to find a means, which for her had to be an art, to defend her right to live, her right to *be*.

After the first few days Sylvia's Yaddo journal shows her increasingly depressed, dissatisfied with her work, baffled by her inability to break out of her glass cage or caul into self-expression. She wrestled to bring into play the self-knowledge so painfully won from her therapy with Dr. Beuscher. With so much insight she ought to have been able to come to grips with the outer world and write like the authors she admired. But every time she set off on the road out of Ego-land, like Alice through the looking glass, she found it leading straight back to the spot of her setting forth. Within a week Johnny Panic again had established his feverish kingdom at the magnetic center of her consciousness. Even the meals she so characteristically relished — "sweetbreads, sausages, bacon and mushrooms; ham and mealy orange sweet potatoes; chicken and garden beans" — filled her with guilt. What had she produced to deserve them? Clearly there was a further area of repression, deeper and more deadly than she knew, that she would have to dig up and confront before she was free to write about anything else.

Nightmares oppressed her. On September 25 she woke with a dream of giving birth, "with one large cramp, to a normal-sized baby, only it was not quite a five-months baby. I asked at the counter if it was all right . . . and the nurse said: 'Oh, it has nest of uterus in its nose, but nothing is wrong with the heart.' " Awake, she had a vision of her mother, dead, having her eyes cut out in the Eye Bank. Another dream was of her father "making an iron statue of a deer, which had a flaw in the casting of the metal. The deer came alive and lay with a broken neck. Had to be shot. Blamed father for killing it, through faulty art."

By September 30 Sylvia woke feeling "cured" of an abnormal heartbeat that had plagued her for days, and full of an idea for a story she then wrote, called "The Mummy."* She described it as a "diatribe against the Dark Mother" and as "the monologue of a madwoman . . . really a simple account of symbolic and horrid fantasies." Afterward, she was "electrified" to read in Jung a case history echoing its disturbing images:

---

*"The Mummy" was finished and sent off to *New World Writing,* which turned it down. It has since been lost.

The child who dreamt of a loving, beautiful mother as a witch or animal: the mother going mad in later life, grunting like pigs, barking like dogs, growling like bears, in a fit of lycanthropy. The word "chessboard" used in an identical situation: of a supposedly loving but ambitious mother who manipulated the child on the "chessboard of her egotism"; I had used "chessboard of her desire." Then the image of the eating mother, or grandmother: all mouth, as in Red Riding Hood (and I had used the image of the wolf).

On October 6 Sylvia's poetry manuscript came back for the fifth time, rejected by Henry Holt. She wept and raged but sent it off to the next publisher on her list, Harcourt, Brace. Ted suggested that she start a new book, an idea Sylvia took up with a gleam of hope. She wrote a "syllabic exercise" on dream images, called "Polly's Tree" (Polly Hanson, also a poet, was secretary to the director of Yaddo and acting director while Sylvia and Ted were there), but Sylvia was still hankering to write stories: "Is it because the avenue of memory is so painful that I do not walk down it, gray, laden with sorrow, vanished beauties and dreams?" Increasingly nights were raked with vivid images:

October 3 . . . Last night I lived among Jews. Religious service, drinking milk from a gold chalice & repeating a name: the congregation drank milk also at the same time from little cups, I wished they put honey in it. Sitting with three pregnant women. My mother furious at my pregnancy, mockingly bringing out a huge wraparound skirt to illustrate my grossness . . . Shaving my legs under table: father, Jewish, at head: you will please not bring your scimitar to table. Very odd . . .

There were a few bright interludes: *The New Yorker* accepted a Christmas poem, "A Winter's Tale," and the *Christian Science Monitor* accepted two "exercises," "Magnolia Shoals" and "Yaddo: The Grand Manor." Still, by October 13 Sylvia had hit a nadir. Her journal entries while at Yaddo are in fact a long, depressed monologue on a single theme: her dilemma as a prose writer. Her arguments with herself have the muffled persistence of someone tied in a sack, patiently trying to get out. She acknowledges the primacy of writing in her life: "Writing is my health." Only achievement can "get rid of the accusing, never-satisfied gods who surround me like a crown of thorns." But, paradoxically, the desperate need for success stands in the way of success: her "commercial American superego," her "jealous queen-bitch superego," her "cold self-consciousness," prevent her enjoying things — "for their own sake, not for what presents and acclaim I may receive." She can't properly write about the world, about people, because "the idea of a Novel" is more important to her than any group of people. Her interest in others is always one of comparison, never of "pure intrigue with the unique otherness of identity." She nurses "a horror that *I am really at bottom uninterested in people*" (my italics). Despairingly, she suspects that all she can create are "a few psychological fantasias."

She deplores her need for a framework in life, to be a student again, authorized and guided in her pursuits. Should she learn French or German, to give herself self-respect? she wonders. Why has she no real spontaneous separate identity or interests of her own? Why the constant "traces of passive dependence: on Ted, on people around me"? She envies Ted, working away "unencumbered by any fake image of what the world expects of him." Ted, "so rare, so special," is her salvation; "how could anyone else stand me!" "How many couples could stand to be so together?" While still in Boston she wrote in her journal: "I would bear children until my change of life if that were possible. I want a house of our children, little animals, flowers, vegetables, fruits. I want to be an Earth Mother in the deepest richest sense." But at Yaddo she reflects: "Children might humanize me. But I must rely on them for nothing. Fable of children changing existence and character as absurd as fable of marriage doing it. Here I am, the same old sourdough."

Through all these questionings Sylvia craves to become "a vehicle, a pure vehicle of others, the outer world." Instead she is "outcast on a cold star, unable to feel anything but an awful helpless numbness. I look down into the warm, earthy world. Into a nest of lovers' beds, baby cribs, meal tables, all the solid commerce of life in this earth, and feel apart, enclosed in a wall of glass."

At Yaddo the key to her puzzle at first evaded Sylvia. It was to be some time before she fully realized the nature of the genius within, struggling to get out. Only then could she abandon her envied models and sing the song of herself alone, under her bell jar. And, paradoxically again, this was to be her only route of escape toward self-expression and worldly success. The portrayal of others in her work would only then reflect what they truly represented artistically to her: projections and reflections of her own powerful subjectivity.

But her struggles were to be rewarded. A breakthrough was to occur into the shadowy unknown where lay the roots of her torments. On October 19, after trying some breathing and concentration exercises suggested by Ted, she wrote two poems that pleased her. One, to the baby she was carrying, was called "The Manor Garden." The

other was on "the old father-worship subject. But different. Weirder.
I see a picture, a weather, in these poems." This second poem gave
her a title for her new book, "The Colossus."

In "The Manor Garden" the "difficult borning" she was approaching in her work was embodied by the embryo in her womb, her old
death-into-birth theme delicately structured to suggest the end of one
era cradling the beginning of another. "The Colossus," on the other
hand, boldly transformed the figure of her seagod-father, a "poeticized,"
heavily Gothic presence in "Full Fathom Five," into a vast, disintegrating statue. Sylvia's verve, her old "audacity" and "brazenness," had
come back to her in the wry, comic impatience of the first stanza:

> I shall never get you put together entirely,
> Pieced, glued, and properly jointed.
> Mule-bray, pig-grunt and bawdy cackles
> Proceed from your great lips.
> It's worse than a barnyard.

Much heartened by these poems, Sylvia was able to take in stride
a sixth rejection of her "old" book, from Harcourt, Brace. As she
walked before breakfast on October 22 in the Yaddo grounds, her
despondent mood continued to disperse. "The sheer color of the trees:
caves of yellow, red plumes. Deep breaths of still frosty air. A purging,
a baptism. I think at times it is possible to get close to the world, to
love it." Having returned from her walk, lines for "Poem for a Birthday" already forming in her head, she noted in her journal: "Ambitious seeds of a long poem made up of separate sections: Poem on
birthday. To be a dwelling on madhouse, nature: meanings of tools,
greenhouses, florists shops, tunnels, vivid and disjointed. An adventure. Never over. Developing. Rebirth. Despair. Old women. Block
it out."

Once Sylvia had achieved this open-nerved state, everything became
material for poems. That same morning she observed two dead moles
in the road, the origin of "Blue Moles," written some days later.
Suddenly her whole being was absorbed into her writing and she
knew exactly how to do it, step by logical step. Proceeding to the
Yaddo greenhouse, she drew "a surgical picture" of the stove, flow-
erpots, and the accumulation of tools. "That greenhouse is a mine of
subjects," she wrote, taking a leaf from Theodore Roethke's book.
"Must get more intimate with it . . . Watering cans, gourds and
squashes and pumpkins. Beheaded cabbages inverted from the rafters,
wormy purple outer leaves. Tools: rakes, hoes, brooms, shovels. The
superb identity, selfhood of things."

By the next day, "an exercise begun, in grimness," was "turning into a fine, new thing: first of a series of madhouse poems. October in the toolshed. Roethke's influence, yet mine."

◄　◄　◄

Between October 23 and the beginning of November, a period that embraced her twenty-seventh birthday on October 27, Sylvia completed the seven parts of "Poem for a Birthday." During this time she was cheered by a letter from James Michie, an editor at Heinemann, in England, expressing admiration for her poems in the _London Magazine_. On November 1 she dreamed of "having a five-months . . . old blond baby boy named Dennis riding, facing me, my hips, a heavy sweet-smelling child. The double amazement: that he was so beautiful and healthy and so little trouble." Ted thought the dream represented the rebirth of her deep soul. It also showed her that when she wrote naturally, from instinctive feeling, her poems, also, gave her little trouble. Yet at first she hardly knew what to make of them.

In "Poem for a Birthday" Sylvia re-creates her attempted suicide and breakdown. "Who," the first section, begins in the Yaddo greenhouse, already the threshold of an underworld:

> The month of flowering's finished. The fruit's in,
> Eaten or rotten. I am all mouth.
> October's the month for storage.

"All mouth," taken from Jung, becomes the All-mouth of "Dark House," the second section, which takes place in the "mummy's stomach" of preconscious, insatiable hungers. In "Who," the underworld Sylvia has set out to explore opens into the corridors of a madhouse: "These halls are full of women who think they are birds." As for herself, shrunk to "a root, a stone, an owl pellet," she desires only to be embraced by the Great Mother — the Mummy of her lost story, the Dark Mother, the Mother of Shadows, Lady Death:

> Mother, you are the one mouth
> I would be a tongue to. Mother of otherness
> Eat me. Wastebasket gaper, shadow of doorways.

Inevitably, she is attacked by ECT:

> Now they light me up like an electric bulb.
> For weeks I can remember nothing at all.

All seven parts of "Poem for a Birthday" — seemingly incoherent on a first reading — are skillfully contained in a frame of the first and last poems. "Who" takes the poet from breakdown to her mummy's (Mummy's) cellar, where "Dark House," "Maenad," and "The Beast" take place. These are poems of nightmarish regression comparable to Roethke's "mad sequences," attempting to reproduce in infantile images and language the mute appetites of babies and beasts. Sylvia wrote from her own experience, recognizing in Roethke a fellow digger, but her work is more than imitative; rather, she writes from a shared root, in a parallel quest. Both Roethke and Plath sought lost parents. For Roethke the father was fierce and terrifying in the greenhouse of his myth:

> Fear was my father, Father Fear.
> His look drained the stones . . .

In Plath's madhouse, the father, once the source of all wisdom, has betrayed her; he "shrank to a doll" while she grew "too big to go backward" into childhood, when she

> Sat by my father's bean tree
> Eating the fingers of wisdom.

In "Maenad" the poet undergoes a shamanistic transformation in the course of which she rejects the Dark Mother:

> Mother, keep out of my barnyard,
> I am becoming another.

From this moment on, a process of self-"borning" takes place, first in the "moon's vat" and later (in "The Beast") in a swamp where the now-disintegrated soul shape-shifts among lowly, primitive forms of being: Mumblepaws, Fido Littlesoul, Mud-sump, Hogwallow. Here, in a squirming, Hieronymous Bosch-like hell, the poet housekeeps "in Time's gut-end / Among emmets and mollusks, / Duchess of Nothing, / Hairtusk's bride" until, in "Flute Notes from a Reedy Pond," a rumor of resurrection reaches her at the bottom of what now appears to be a teeming pool. This pool, a recurrent Plathian image for her father's death, resembles the pond into which "the daft father went down" in "All the Dead Dears." It represents a higher stage of evolution than the swamp of worms and mollusks, but is still safer than air. Among fish and frogs the soul hides like a pupa:

> This is not death, it is something safer.
> The wingy myths won't tug at us any more.

Yet the possibility of rebirth, mooted by tongueless molts singing from the reeds, brings about the soul's emergence into human form. There it instantly undergoes martyrdom in "Witch Burning," a subject Sylvia had brooded over since watching the film of Joan of Arc in New York early in 1955, but also, no doubt, suggested by the burning of fallen autumn leaves at Yaddo — "In the month of red leaves I climb to a bed of fire." In this section the shape-shifting proceeds at such a pace that the poem scarcely makes sense. The newborn soul is at once a witch-spirit and the wax image persecuted by witches — a doubled woman, one of whom has to be killed to release the other. Here, of course, is Sylvia's perennial motif of the double, later to be integral to *The Bell Jar* and identified as a red flag in "Witch Burning": "Sickness begins here." A "black-sharded lady" (the Mummy) keeps the child-entity (seen as a witch's familiar) in a parrot cage among the dead, where she is "intimate with a hairy spirit" but rendered little and harmless as a rice grain. Only when the burners are turned up — again an image of ECT — can the rice-grain girl be hurt into "truth," swelling eventually into a beetle in a candle flame, begging longingly for rebirth in her own shape even as the fire consumes her, in a splendid Plathian line: "I am lost, I am lost, in the robes of all this light."

Despite its difficulty, "Witch Burning" can be seen as central to this strange opus. It epitomizes Plath's weird myths, cramming them into a veritable echo chamber of images, as do, to a greater or lesser extent, all seven sections of "Poem for a Birthday." The most artistically satisfying of the seven, however, is the last poem, "The Stones," which at once rounds off the sequence and restates all its motifs.

"The Stones" takes place in a hospital, "the city where men are mended," where the poet lies on "a great anvil" to suffer her cure. Recalling the "stomach of indifference" of "Who," where she lay in the "wordless cupboard" among the peaceable stones, she rehearses the stages of her rebirth. Life is still there; the mouth (red, wet) would not succumb:

> Only the mouth-hole piped out,
> Importunate cricket
>
> In a quarry of silences.
> The people of the city heard it.
> They hunted the stones, taciturn and separate,
>
> The mouth-hole crying their locations.

There follows the process of being brought back to life. First the mouth-fetus-body takes food:

> Drunk as a foetus
> I suck at the paps of darkness.

Next comes the swabbing of the stone eyes, the prying open of the lips and ears. Since this is a rebirth, a pseudo-birth, not the birth of a baby, the world is recognized and unwelcome: "daylight lays its sameness on the wall." The torturers are cheerful as they set about the rituals of ECT:

> Heating the pincers, hoisting the delicate hammers.
> A current agitates the wires
> Volt upon volt . . .

But gradually, painfully, the hospital world exerts its power, and in "the city of spare parts" life is rendered acceptable, finally desirable:

> Here they can doctor heads, or any limb.
> On Fridays the little children come
>
> To trade their hooks for hands.
> Dead men leave eyes for others.
> Love is the uniform of my bald nurse.
>
> Love is the bone and sinew of my curse.
> The vase, reconstructed, houses
> The elusive rose.

This is the nub of the poem. The nature of love is to be perishable, as the nature of the rose is to die.

> My mendings itch. There is nothing to do.
> I shall be as good as new.

These final lines of "Poem for a Birthday" foreshadow the mournful irony toward the end of *The Bell Jar:* "There ought, I thought, to be a ritual for being born twice — patched, retreaded and approved for the road." Like *The Bell Jar,* "Poem for a Birthday" is a fascinating but flawed work by a writer just beginning to come to grips with her subject, her own self, and to find her voice. Both grapple with the same obsessive, traumatic events, and both end on a dubious note of hope.

◀   ◀   ◀

After Sylvia had written "Poem for a Birthday" she began to find the enclosed world of Yaddo stifling. Paralysis set in again in early November as she felt "a terrific blocking and chilling go through me like anesthesia." Would she ever be free of Johnny Panic? Ten years away from the easy flow of her *Seventeen* stories, and what had she accomplished? "One or two unpleasant psychological stories" and a handful of poems worth keeping. By now, her "old" book was dead to her, sent off on November 4 to a seventh publisher. Unless Dudley Fitts decided to relent and at last give her the Yale award, she would try to publish it in London. The Mummy story came back from *New World Writing* with a mimeographed rejection. She was beginning to feel oppressed by her constant proximity to Ted, as if she had "no life separate from his." With a baby coming and her reputation not yet established, she realized: "I will hate a child that substitutes itself for my own purpose: so I must make my own." Drained of creative energy and weary of the restricted company at Yaddo, Sylvia was beginning to look for new directives. She watched May Swenson enviously: "My old admiration for the strong, if lesbian, woman. The relief of limitation as a price for balance and surety." At the same time May was also watching Sylvia. Taken to meet the Hugheses toward the end of their two months at Yaddo, she gives a vivid glimpse of Sylvia, at that time suffering from one of her sinus colds:

> She was not up to coming to the dining room, and Ted was bringing her food on a tray. We found her sitting up in bed among pillows in the shadowy room under the hooded yellow light of a floor lamp, with pine boughs outside the windows turning the twilight a vivid rainy green. Books and notepads, papers, pens, magazines, a box of tissues, a bowl of apples and grapes, nestled among the blankets. Sylvia, in a flannel bed jacket . . . A handshake and the flash of a smile, then Sylvia's head drooped, her dark eyes lidded, and she looked down into her lap.

Actually Sylvia had accomplished a good deal at Yaddo — more than most poets would have expected to in the time. For her new book she had "The Manor Garden," "The Colossus," "Blue Moles," "Medallion," and the seven birthday poems. In the second week of November she would write "The Burnt-out Spa," and on November 13, as an exercise, the excellent "Mushrooms." Although her three stories disappointed her and what she called "a bad, impossible children's book" had been laid aside, she felt prepared for a novel once she got to England. She and Ted were eager to go. "When I think of living in America," she wrote on November 11, "I just can't imagine where: hate suburbs, country too lonely, city too expensive and full of dog turds." In London she pictured herself living in a quiet square (without dog turds?), taking her children to the parks, and driving out into the country whenever the urge came upon her.

By the time Sylvia and Ted left Yaddo, Sylvia was noticeably pregnant. They spent Thanksgiving in Wellesley and stayed for two weeks. Ted worked on the play he had begun at Yaddo. Sylvia, relieved to be free of her writing demons, sorted out her clothes and packed. In *Letters Home* Mrs. Plath remarks wistfully, "This was really leaving home — apartment hunting in London lay ahead, as well as making arrangements for the baby, due at the end of March." With her hair in a single braid down her back, Sylvia looked painfully young — "like a high school student." On their last day Mrs. Plath drove them to the station; as the train pulled out, Ted called out, "We'll be back in two years."

Above: Warren, Aurelia,
and Sylvia Plath
Left: Sylvia Plath,
spring 1954

Martha's Vineyard, August 1955. *Left to right:* Roger Baldwin, Eleanor Besse, Peter Davison, Sylvia Plath

A sketch by Sylvia Plath of fishing boats

At Cambridge, 1957

The Anchor Inn, Cambridge, sketched by Sylvia Plath

Lucas Myers at Cambridge, 1957

Dorothea Krook at
Newnham College,
Cambridge, 1953

Sketches by Sylvia Plath of Benidorm, Spain, where the Hugheses honeymooned, 1956

9 Willow Street, Boston (the tall stone building), 1989

Sylvia Plath and Ted Hughes at Willow Street, 1959

Oluyn Hughes

A sketch by Sylvia Plath, probably made in Hawley, Massachusetts, near Northampton

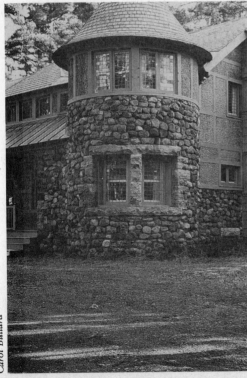

Carol Bullard

West House at Yaddo

Above: The house on Rugby Street, London, 1988
Below: The house in Chalcot Square, London, 1988

Dido Merwin

Sylvia and Ted Hughes with Frieda in the Merwins' kitchen,
London, 1960

Dido Merwin

Above: Dido Merwin at
Lacan de Loubressac,
1961
Right: W. S. Merwin at
Lacan, early 1960s

Left: Richard Murphy at Cleggan, 1962
Below: Letter from Sylvia Plath to Murphy, September 1962

September 8

Dear Richard,
   Thank you so much for your good letter. We have got a nanny for the babies so can leave here with easy heart. We plan to take the train to Holyhead Tuesday night, cross to Dublin by night, say hello to Jack Sweeney & come by rail to Galway Wednesday eveningish. Shall call as soon as we arrive. We would love to stay in your cottage. I don't know when I have looked so forward to anything. Warmest good wishes,
                                Sylvia

Manuscript from
Sylvia Plath's
journal, 1950

A draft of "Elm" and
notation for *Three
Women*, 1962

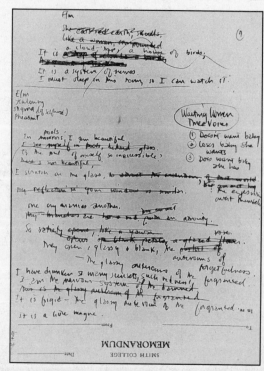

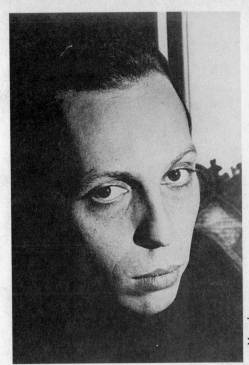

Helder and Suzette
Macedo in the 1960s

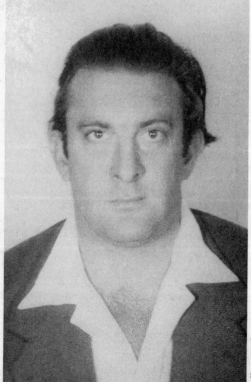

Above: Jillian Becker
with Madeleine, 1962
Right: Gerry Becker

Frieda, Nicholas, and Sylvia Hughes, 1962

Oluwyn Hughes

Right: The engraving of Isis, "great mother of the gods," that hung on the wall of Sylvia Plath's home

Below: The house at 23 Fitzroy Road where Sylvia Plath's life ended

Penguin Books

► 9 ◄

A R I E L
I N   T H E   T R E E
1959-1960

A woman is dragging her shadow in a circle
About a bald, hospital saucer.
It resembles the moon, or a sheet of blank paper
And appears to have suffered a sort of private blitzkrieg.
> — "A Life," November 18, 1960

How shall I tell anything at all
To this infant still in a birth-drowse?
Tonight, like a shawl, the mild light enfolds her,
The shadows stoop over like guests at a christening.
> — "Candles,"
> November 17, 1960

UP TO THE TIME Sylvia left Yaddo in late November 1959, her journal — that "litany of dreams, directives and imperatives," as she
termed it — yields to the biographer its full, fluctuant image of the
poet's inner life, an interior "Sargasso" almost as despairing, angry,
and determined as the poems of her last years. Seldom has a poet of
comparable gifts left such detailed documentation of the creative matrix of her work. But for the years after 1959, although Sylvia continued to keep her "book" up to date, the journals are no longer
available.*

---

*As Ted Hughes explains in his foreword to the American selection of 1982, the
mature notebooks for the years up to 1959 are in the Neilson Library at Smith Col-

The loss of these last journals robs us of a valuable source. Through her journals we have been able to follow Sylvia's inward struggles, realizing with every entry just how difficult it was for her, at times, to sustain ordinary existence even for a day. After her return to England in December 1959, the only written evidence of her suffering lies in the deepening and disturbing quality of her poems. Letters home continue to paint an externally joyous picture of dreams fulfilled and anticipated successes achieved. These cannot be wholly false; in 1960 Sylvia's daughter Frieda was born, her first collection of poems, *The Colossus,* published, and her faith in Ted confirmed by the increasing recognition of his work. All these events gave Sylvia satisfaction and joy.

At the same time, there is evidence that outsiders found Sylvia difficult to know, perverse in her habit of keeping her husband to herself, sometimes unreasonable to the point of rudeness in her dealings with friends and family. So, while paying wary attention to the liveliness of the life she describes to her mother, we have to assume, too, that her self-preoccupation increased as she matured, and that the tension between the outer Sylvia, characterized by Robert Lowell as "a brilliant tense presence embarrassed by restraint," and the inner woman, fraught with fears and aggressions, continued to divide her.

A first glimpse of Sylvia in England comes from Olwyn Hughes, who vividly remembers arriving in Heptonstall for Christmas of 1959:

> Ted and Sylvia were standing at the door of the sitting room to welcome me. Sylvia's hair was no longer blonded but mouse brown without the "body" that the bleach had given it, and she was pale, not rosily sunburnt as I had last seen her. I was taken aback (I'd had no idea that she was not naturally blonde) and said tactlessly, "But your hair! You look different!" Sylvia, too, had one of her unguarded reactions. She stepped back, glaring alarmingly, like an animal at bay. "But it suits you!" I cried hastily, and to my great relief she then relaxed. I wasn't sure it suited her at all just then. But as I got used to it, it seemed an outer reflection of her increased

---

lege. He goes on, "Two more notebooks survived for a while, maroon-backed ledgers like the '57–'59 volume, and continued the record from late '59 to within three days of her death. The last of these contained entries for several months, and I destroyed it because I did not want her children to have to read it (in those days I regarded forgetfulness as an essential part of survival). The other disappeared." Journal notes Plath kept separate from the main volumes do remain, and her 1962 notes on neighbors in Devon and a record of her time in the hospital in 1961 are both in the Neilson Library.

maturity; she was less a good-looking girl, more a contained individual.

That evening the family passed some pleasant hours around the fire while Sylvia and Ted related tales of their adventures in the States. Olwyn, however, remembers a bizarre confrontation with Sylvia a day or two later:

I had asked my mother if there was a spare dressing gown I could use. She lent me a new one she had made herself (she was an excellent dressmaker), cut from a pattern made from an old worn and torn blue dressing gown Sylvia had thrown out before leaving for the States two years before. It was in a mauve tweedy wool, soft, warm and very pretty. I came down for breakfast wearing it. But the next time I looked for it on the hook behind my bedroom door it was not there. I wandered around and found it hanging behind Ted and Sylvia's door with their dressing gowns. Thinking I must have left it lying about and someone had absent-mindedly put it there, I thought nothing of it. Next day, exactly the same thing occurred. This was getting quite mysterious. I mentioned it to Sylvia over my morning coffee. She and Ted had already had their usual full breakfasts and she was sitting reading the paper with my mother also in the room. To my astonishment, Sylvia abruptly rose to her feet and, back very stiff, eyes straight ahead, rushed out of the room, saying in a mocking, sing-song voice, "My blue dressing gown has become a mauve dressing gown."

Mother and I eyed each other in dismay. Was Sylvia trying to appropriate her hostess's new dressing gown? Had she spent the last two or three days fuming that I was using it, determined to have it for herself? It all seemed quite outrageous. My mother calmly took charge of the situation and said she still had the pattern and if Sylvia wanted a new dressing gown she would make her one. Next day she went and bought the cloth, and by the time I returned to Paris Sylvia had pronounced herself pleased with the first fitting. She refers to it in a letter to her mother of 16 January: "I am sitting in the big warm bathrobe Mrs. Hughes made me." She never apologized for her behaviour or gave any sort of explanation of it and the incident was never mentioned again.

However slight and even comical, this episode illustrates Sylvia's peculiar aggressiveness, observed on a number of occasions by friends not only in England but in America. Eddie Cohen, Nancy Hunter Steiner, Jane Baltzell Kopp, and Gordon Lameyer, in their various ways, record similar incidents. Perhaps the dressing gown episode and other events of that kind were recrudescences of sibling rivalry, something to which Sylvia alerted herself in her journals of January 1959 when she made a note to "ask Dr. B[euscher] what I can do to sift out grown self from contracted baby feelings, jolting jealousies."

On the whole, that first Christmas back in Yorkshire was a happy time. Sylvia had brought a pack of tarot cards from America with which in the evenings she taught Ted and Olwyn the game of tarok, learned from her grandmother. Olwyn remembers that her cousin Vicky, twenty-one and an art teacher, joined them for sessions "which proceeded with a good deal of excitement and merriment." At first Sylvia entered into the game with gusto, letting down her usual guards, and Olwyn found herself for the first time truly at ease and liking her without reservation. Olwyn continues:

> But it didn't last very long. One evening as Vicky and I prepared to play, Sylvia announced very tensely, with Ted's help, that she couldn't play any more as gambling (we played for sixpences) made her too strung up to sleep. I remember feeling irritated. I had no inkling then of the terrible depressions and nervous states she was prone to, and she never confided in me about them. As the games ended, so did the new closeness . . . Indeed, throughout the years I knew her and in spite of her cordial letters, when we actually met, any increase in friendship between us I felt had been attained evaporated as though it had never been.

When *Letters Home* was published in 1975, Olwyn was struck by a comment Sylvia made about her in a letter of December 26, 1959: "I get along with her much better now that she's really accepted me as Ted's wife and like her immensely." To Olwyn the phrase "accepted me as Ted's wife" missed the point:

> I had wanted to get to know *her,* as a person, as a friend, not approve or disapprove of her as a wife. I'd no idea what a wife should ideally be — except perhaps happy. Maybe she saw her role in Yorkshire as showing us all what a worthy wife she was, and thus acquiring our approval and allegiance. Maybe that's where part of the ambient unease lay — that she was acting out some bizarre conception of a role rather than relating naturally to us.

As Sylvia told her mother, two weeks in Yorkshire free of house-hunting worries gave her time to type up the manuscript of her new poetry book, *The Colossus and Other Poems,* to send to James Michie, the editor at Heinemann who had admired her poems in the *London Magazine* that autumn. Combining the new Yaddo poems with the best of her old book (soon to be rejected by Farrar, Straus in New York), Sylvia abandoned any idea of arranging the poems in chronological order. Instead, she distributed her new work among the old, setting the text within the frame of two Yaddo poems relating to birth. The collection began with "The Manor Garden," an evocation of the child she was carrying, and ended with the seven sections of "Poem for a Birthday," which, as we have seen, recorded in her new voice the stages of her breakdown and rebirth six years before.

◄ ◄ ◄

Early in January the Hugheses arrived in London to look for a flat. After a few days in "a cold, cheerless room-and-breakfast place" at £2 a day, they welcomed an invitation from Daniel and Helga Huws to move into a spare room at 18 Rugby Street, where Ted had been staying when he and Sylvia first met. The flat had undergone an improvement since they had last been there. According to Daniel Huws, "The landlord had provided each flat with a sink and running water in its tiny kitchen (which was perforce also the bathroom). Previously one had fetched water from a communal tap on the stairs and emptied slops into a bucket. The only WC for the house was still down in the basement under the pavement." For all its sanitary inconveniences, Rugby Street had its dignities. Huws writes:

> Number 18 still stands, its interior much revamped in the 1970s . . . [It is] a small early Georgian house, the odd one out at the end of a terrace of larger ones. On each floor was a living room with two windows facing south onto a lively street, a tiny kitchen beside it and, at the back, a small bedroom. The rooms still had their original wooden panelling, covered in many coats of paint. When Sylvia and Ted were there Helga and I had the use of the bedroom in the flat above. Sylvia and Ted slept in the second floor bedroom in a sagging net of a bed which might have tested any relationship.

Daniel Huws clearly recalls Sylvia's "indefatigable home-hunting. She would come back after a long day on the streets, obviously exhausted yet still good company." Helga Huws remembers differently. Pregnant, eager, determined, Sylvia warmed to the Huwses, especially because Helga already had a baby daughter and was coping stoically with primitive plumbing. "But as time wore on," writes Helga, "she became visibly downcast and tired. She often looked [so] despondent that you could not help feeling warmly towards her. Her daily assessment of the flats they had seen sounded like something out of Dickens."

Sylvia's expectations were, of course, American. Helga, who had lived through wartime and postwar Germany, found "those slightly dilapidated yet functional London tenements" a "haven," having by then adjusted to the British phlegm "in particular towards the aesthetics (or perhaps, athletics?) of living." Helga adds:

> But not all was gloom in those days. At times she would talk with great animation about their travels in America and her family. One's similar origins [Helga being a Prussian Pole] would make this an inexhaustible subject. [Sylvia's] cooking skills were quite impressive and I still feed my family on some of Grandmother Schober's recipes. I still see her adorned with my huge grey apron explaining the intricacies of German fish soup.

Helga Huws remembers that Sylvia also wrote a lot, notes and letters, confessing "to a dire need to keep in contact with her mother, although when near each other this closeness would become disagreeable and oppressive — a quite natural phenomenon between daughters and mothers, I thought." Since the Rugby Street flat was on the outskirts of Bloomsbury and therefore fairly central, old friends were apt to drop in, some of them unwelcome to Sylvia. Occasionally the men would go off to the pub while the women cooked together. Only once, according to Helga, did they turn someone away. This was Joe Lyde, an amusing but sometimes crude friend of Ted's of whom (with Michael Boddy) Sylvia could not approve.

Clearly, with the baby three months away and a panicky need to make all things perfect before its arrival, Sylvia was impatient to leave Rugby Street and get settled as soon as possible. Fortunately, W. S. Merwin and his wife, Dido, determined to help Ted and Sylvia professionally and practically in any way they could, had preceded them from Boston. The Merwins were living in their comfortable flat in St. George's Terrace overlooking Primrose Hill, near Regent's Park. At that time, although Regent's Park Road was fashionable, the little village behind it, to the east of Primrose Hill, remained unexploited. Ted and Sylvia looked at two unfurnished flats in the area. One was on the ground floor of a large house, "unbelievably big and beautiful," but the landlord had stipulated no children. The other, suggested to them by Dido Merwin, was on the third floor of a five-story house that was being refurbished in Chalcot Square. It was too small, with only one bedroom and no study, but comparatively cheap at six guineas a week, within convenient distance of shops, and, importantly, close to Dido's friend Dr. Horder. This smaller flat Sylvia and Ted finally agreed to take on a three-year lease. Dido almost immediately introduced Sylvia, now nearly six months pregnant, to Dr. Horder, and the obstetrician in the group practice took her on as a patient. Much relieved, Sylvia and Ted returned to Yorkshire on January 15 to collect their books and belongings from the Hugheses' home, The Beacon.

Helga Huws remembers that all through their "gruelling search" Ted was gentle and protective toward Sylvia. "After finding the Chalcot Square flat, her exuberance was indescribable," writes Helga, "and in the following weeks she really won my admiration (however quietly critical I was of her perfectionism as to all things) by working incredibly hard." They returned from Yorkshire to find workmen still in the house; the floors had to be sanded and, with the walls, painted before their books could be moved in on February 1. They splurged on a huge new bed, a refrigerator, and a cooking stove, rather to Dido Merwin's surprise. Dido, who with her husband was able to furnish temporary tables, chairs, curtains, and rugs from their attic in St. George's Terrace, remembers recommending secondhand shops where a bed frame and kitchen equipment could have been bought very cheaply. (Bill Merwin had furnished their Boston "pad" almost entirely from the Salvation Army, and both of them were connoisseurs of "trouvailles.") But Sylvia, who had had her fill of the "sagging net" at 18 Rugby Street, wanted at least her bed and her kitchen to meet American standards of comfort and convenience.

Sylvia was feeling heavy with pregnancy but full of happy energy when she and Ted moved into the barely redecorated flat at 3 Chalcot Square at the beginning of February 1960. Rested, as she told her mother just before leaving Yorkshire, she could cope with anything; tired, she felt "very homesick and blue." But whatever her condition or state of mind, "what was planned for the day," as Helga Huws put it, "had to be met at all costs." Even when she was very pregnant, Sylvia was never seen to sit quietly, hands in her lap, just resting.

In three months Sylvia had written almost no poetry. With the exception of the lighthearted pregnancy poem "You're," she wrote nothing more serious than entries in her journal and letters home in the period between "Mushrooms" on November 13, 1959, and "The Hanging Man" on June 27, 1960, her creative focus centering instead on the nest she was building. It was a time of disturbing transition: leaving Wellesley, journeying by boat across the Atlantic, traveling up and down to Heptonstall, flat-hunting from the Huwses' menage in Rugby Street, and, finally, preparing for their move, with all the arrangements still remaining to be made for the baby's birth. Although Ted helped generally and did most of the heavy labor — all the lifting and carrying of furniture — by February Sylvia was desperate for time and peace. After Ted received his Guggenheim they had blithely planned to travel in Italy. Now they were relieved to stay in London and establish their family. Sylvia wrote to Lynne Lawner in Rome soon after moving into 3 Chalcot Square:

> I haven't even had time to fully take in the fact I'm pregnant & find it amazing that I'm to produce a child in 5 weeks. After traipsing all over the great area of London & seeing filthy, cheerless, lightless, bathless places for $25 and up a week . . . the poet W. S. Merwin & his older, very energetic, very British, very thrice-married wife found us an unfurnished flat . . .
>
> We've invested in a marvelous bed, stove & refrigerator, & the Merwins have furnished us with tables & chairs out of their Victorian attic.

However "bourgeois" and in contradiction to Sylvia's stated priorities they seemed to Dido Merwin, Sylvia's pragmatic, American-good-housekeeping aims would have struck Lynne Lawner, and of course Mrs. Plath, as perfectly in keeping with her ambitions as a writer. To start a family in a small London flat near the zoo was a first step toward buying a house in the area. It was with such a plan in mind that Sylvia, who a month before had cursed "blue & black at everything Londonian," began to realize the advantages of having a baby in her new home (she still dreaded hospitals), where, with luck, she would soon be writing stories and poems in a new role as a mother.

London was in those days a nourishing environment for writers. Merwin, for whom the BBC was already a dependable source of income, introduced Ted to Douglas Cleverdon, the producer of Dylan Thomas's *Under Milk Wood* and soon to be invaluable to both Ted and Sylvia. Dido Merwin, in her memoir of Sylvia, refers to the "galaxy of talent" that had been attracted by the liberal policies of the Third Programme in the 1960s: a "rich, quirky mix of poets . . . , novelists . . . , journalists, historians, communists, avant-garde mavericks, drama producers of the calibre of McWhinney, and above all the incomparable Douglas Cleverdon had a track record that has never been equalled in the history of broadcasting."

Meanwhile, Ted was on the verge of expanding the reputation made by *The Hawk in the Rain* with the publication of his second book, *Lupercal,* which would come "along with the baby" at the end of March 1960. His children's book, *Meet My Folks!,* much admired by Sylvia, would be out the following winter, while three of his short stories were soon due to appear in a Faber anthology, "The Rain Horse" having already been published in *Harper's* in January. Far from being jealous of her husband's success, Sylvia partook of it and vicariously enjoyed it, confident that her own hour was approaching.

Of more substantial significance to Sylvia's art than any of these "successes" was the rich vein of foreign influence that, in the late 1950s, had been opened up by such poets as Robert Bly and Merwin in the United States and Michael Hamburger in Britain. Robert Lowell, too, became preoccupied with translation, publishing *Imitations* in 1961. This general interest in the poetry of other languages eventually produced international festivals in London and elsewhere in the 1960s and gave rise to such magazines as *Modern Poetry in Translation,* edited by Daniel Weissbort, founded in 1965 with Ted Hughes as co-editor.* Ted and Sylvia collected all they could of this sort of material, including sheafs of Merwin's translations — some of his superb Neruda translations among others — and they occasionally made their own from French, Italian, and Spanish. A. Alvarez brought back the first translations of various Eastern European poets in 1962, among them Zbigniew Herbert. Ted Hughes contends that by 1962 Sylvia regarded Rilke and Herbert much more as her "fellow countrymen" than other English-language poets. She revered Rilke and used poems of his in her efforts to learn German.

In London, then, although at first Sylvia was not writing, she would have been intensely aware of new excitement in this area of modernist literature. The presence of W. S. Merwin with his large library in St. George's Terrace, three minutes' walk from Chalcot Square, together with her impression that London literary life was reaching out to embrace not only Ted but herself as well, to some extent alleviated her dire apprehensions of childbirth. *Letters Home* shows Sylvia delighting in her new home, cooking apfelkuchen and chicken stew in her shining kitchen, decorating her sitting room with a poster-sized enlargement of an old print of Isis† (mother-goddess both of fertility

---

*It is now in its fiftieth issue. The title was recently changed to *Poetry World.*

†The print of Isis was taken from a little French astrology book on the sign of Cancer, published by Editions Le Seuil. The print is in the Bibliothèque Nationale in Paris, captioned "Oedipus Aegyptiacus, Isis." Presumably one "Oedipus the Egyptian" was the artist.

and of the underworld, a combination of Ceres and Persephone), which, with a print of Ted's "Pike" and their woodcuts by Leonard Baskin, made the flat their own.

On February 10, enormous with child but "resplendent in black wool suit, black cashmere coat, fawn kidskin gloves from Paris (Ol- wyn's Christmas present) and matching calfskin bag (from Italy)," Sylvia proceeded triumphantly to the York Minster pub on Dean Street, Soho, where she signed a contract with James Michie of Heine- mann for the publication of *The Colossus* while Ted waited in a nearby pub to take her for a celebration lunch at Bianchi's. James Michie recalls their first meeting:

> She appeared carefully pleasant, shy, rather silent, quick to agree with you — which I now recognize as a sign of danger later on. She did not dress to be seen. She neither wanted to look, nor looked, "sexy." She was a well-bred, apple-cheeked New England girl. I thought that some of her poems took a new form, which broke beyond form. It wasn't an outpouring, like most new poetry. She was out of the literary instant. I was able to persuade her that I understood her work. I may have persuaded her to drop some weaker poems. I was never sure whether she was grateful that I was making these decisions.

With luck, Sylvia wrote her family, the book would be out by her birthday, October 27. "They do very few, very few poets at Heine- mann," she went on, "and will do a nice book . . . It is dedicated to that paragon who has encouraged me through all my glooms about it, Ted." Later that month she accompanied her husband to Oxford, where he read to the Oxford Poetry Society; it was the first time she had been to the "other" university. Michael Horovitz remembers joining the Hugheses for dinner, with Ian Hamilton — who was then running the society — and three or four others. His impression is that "Sylvia was relaxed and witty and exuded girlish good humor — perhaps it was a simplicity they were sharing, Ted's slightly gruff directness tempering her apparently more brittle sensitivity. They seemed very much in love."

With her home established and W. S. Merwin nearby to supply her with books while she waited, Sylvia looked forward to giving birth and then "living and writing in seclusion and skimming the cream off London periodically . . . Now we are 'at home,' London is a de- light."

Despite her assertions of calm self-sufficiency to her mother, there is evidence that life in Chalcot Square was somewhat tense. Lucas

Myers, briefly in London on his way back to the United States from Corsica, remembers an uncomfortable visit to their flat shortly before a reunion of the *St. Botolph's* group on Leap Year Day, February 29. "The flat was so small," writes Myers, "that Ted did his writing in a little hallway by the entrance door . . . Sylvia was preparing a meal when I arrived and Ted and I went to a pub to get some beer. I suggested we have a drink there, and we left Sylvia, cooking supper and eight months pregnant, alone for forty minutes." In the pub Ted mentioned that it was difficult to write in the flat because Sylvia was constantly interrupting. This was the first time Luke had heard Ted say anything even mildly critical of Sylvia. Myers's memoir continues:

> I doubt if [Ted] ever told her, "Look, I can't work like this." I don't think that is the way the marriage functioned; otherwise it probably would have ended early on. All this may have been the effects of pregnancy, the return to England, the search for and move into a flat, but instinctively I disbelieve this explanation. At the time, my assessment was even more unkind. I was thinking something about the demanding style of some American women of the period.

When Ted and Luke returned to the flat that evening, Sylvia was, as Myers recalls,

> standing in the dining space, which was on a sort of rise, and staring down at us seated on the couch. What I remember is not the tall, gravid figure, but the eyes, boring down at us. When we went to the table we found three bowls of clam chowder somewhat less than half full. Full stop for supper. Ted and I washed and cleaned every crumb and corner, ostentatiously trying to make amends, but it was no good.

Like many a wife, Sylvia would have resented the men's going to the pub and leaving her to get supper alone. Yet Sylvia's implacability was extreme, even for a very pregnant woman. Was Ted to be confined to quarters entirely? No doubt it was Luke's visit that prompted a curt remark from Sylvia to her mother on March 3: "I really put my foot down about visitors now. I get tired easily and like the house to myself so I can cook, read, write, or rest when I please . . . I have no desire for people sleeping in my living room or causing me extra cooking or housework."

On the following Saturday, March 5, Olwyn came to lunch at Chalcot Square, bringing with her Janet Crosbie-Hill, a friend she had known in Paris with whom she was staying for the long weekend. When they arrived, having got lost finding the house, Lucas Myers was there, standing silent and moody in the background while Ted and Sylvia put the finishing touches on the meal. Olwyn remembers Ted "studiously sieving applesauce through a Mouli as Sylvia testily told us we were late." From the outset, Sylvia seemed possessed by some seething aggression. Both Luke and Olwyn were immediately aware of it, Luke commenting in his memoir that it was the only time he ever saw Olwyn disconcerted. Both noted with acute embarrassment that Sylvia addressed neither look nor word to Janet throughout the afternoon. Her silent animosity was all but tangible while the other four — Ted for his visitors' sake and they for his — tried to proceed as though nothing were amiss. Periodically Sylvia would rise and violently slam the window open, not an inch or two but as wide as it would go. Both girls smoked a little, but because Sylvia made no reference to disliking it, they did not connect this with her fury. Mystified, sooner or later someone would ask for the window to be closed (it was a cold day), but after a time Sylvia would again slam it up. "Had Sylvia said the smoke annoyed her," Olwyn writes, "we both would have desisted. (The occasional cigarette in 1960 was by no means held in the horror it is now.) Had she said she was tired, it would have been easy for her to withdraw for a nap or suggest the others take a stroll and leave her to rest. Yet she seemed not at all tired, but rather highly animated."

Over ten years later, in a letter to the *New Review,* Janet Crosbie-Hill recalled the shock of the occasion: "As Olwyn had spoken only with affection of both brother and sister-in-law, I was totally unprepared for the resentment our visit seemed to cause Sylvia." Olwyn remembers, as does Janet, that when W. S. Merwin came by after lunch Sylvia's manner immediately changed, as with great warmth and vivacity she addressed herself almost exclusively to him. The conversation turned to dreams of flying, and Sylvia described the most gorgeous flying dream of all in which she floated in a brilliantly colored tropical paradise among huge exotic birds, butterflies, and dragonflies, in great harmony and joy. Evidently, too, there was some question of Merwin's taking Sylvia and Ted — at Sylvia's suggestion — for a spin in the country in his two-seater. "This not materializing," writes Janet, "there was a strained walk on Primrose Hill during which I was the unhappy witness of the sheer quantity of distress Sylvia was capable of causing her nearest and dearest. Her aggression was relentless and dominated the reactions of all present."

After the ordeal of the visit, Ted walked his sister and Janet to the Chalk Farm tube station, all three in stunned silence. As they paused for farewells, Olwyn tentatively, and for the first time, asked Ted if he couldn't make Sylvia see how upsetting such behavior was to other people. "What I had just witnessed," Olwyn writes, "had been far more alarming and sustained than any of Sylvia's brief bouts of inexplicable rudeness in Yorkshire." Hughes replied with a helpless gesture. He had tried to reason with Sylvia on similar occasions, he said, but it was no use. She adamantly refused anything that sounded like criticism and simply became hysterical.

There were other social occasions, however, that Sylvia enormously relished. She had seemed completely at ease at the *St. Botolph's* reunion a week earlier, which she described to her mother in glowing terms: "Amusing to see what paternal and familial fates have, four years later, fallen on such once-confirmed bachelors!" Families fitted her ideas of what was proper, and she felt no threat from them. David Ross and his wife, Barbara, had a little son; Helga and Dan Huws, their daughter Madelin. Even Luke Myers, soon to sail for New Orleans, was married, and his wife was expecting a baby in May. Such couples mirrored her own state of absolute concentration on her family. To be a fertile, producing wife among other wives gave her reassurance, confirming her role in the schematic structure of her life. To be a poet among other poets fulfilled another role. So long as life presented itself in a series of safe, acceptable, or desirable frames, like a gallery of paintings, Sylvia could manage it.

Alfred Kazin, who taught her at Smith, once remarked that the world for Sylvia Plath existed only for her to write about. That may have been unfair, but her inward fears did restrict a wider acceptance of that world to which she aspired. No doubt against her better judgment, she was imaginatively confined to her own approved, heavily defended areas of achievement: marriage, parenthood, and the ideal of a well-managed "home." To less settled worlds and to people with different priorities she could be fiercely antagonistic, almost as if personally attacked by realities that escaped her chosen categories. It was more than misunderstanding that isolated her in that glass cage; it was something like a blindness or incompleteness of the imagination. Olwyn Hughes, appalled by that afternoon with Janet Crosbie-Hill and further perplexed when Sylvia's expected apology failed to materialize, comments:

Whether she was blind to her fault and by some mechanism of self-justification managed to believe that others, not she, were in the wrong, or whether she considered herself above bending to apologize, or whether she was simply, for some deep-seated psychological reason, incapable of admitting her behaviour could in any way

fall short of perfection, the result was the same — a growing alien-
ation from whomever she had offended.

Yet within the bailiwick of her enclosed world, Sylvia was capable
of the warmest affection and enthusiasm. On Olwyn's last night in
London, Ted had arranged to meet Luke, Dan, and Helga in a pub
in Camden Town where there was good live Irish music. Olwyn was
surprised to see Sylvia there in the smoky, noisy atmosphere, enjoying
herself very much. Equally, Sylvia was happy to mingle with the
London literati over cocktails or at dinner parties. Letters home reel
off the famous names:

> Wednesday evening we went for cocktails with John Lehmann,
> editor of the *London* magazine, who reminisced about his memories
> of Virginia Woolf, et al. I met the popular British Oxford graduate-
> poetess, Elizabeth Jennings, a Catholic, who reads for a London
> publishing house and lives in a convent while here, returning to her
> rooms in Oxford on weekends to write (she has three volumes out).
> We got along very well. [Met] a lawyer-poet-novelist, Roy Fuller,
> and lady novelist-reviewer, Christine Brooke-Rose. I must get them
> all in my diary.

Whatever Sylvia's views on friends and family, the friends and
family began to form their own opinions. Shortly after the lunch party
Olwyn wrote to Luke Myers:

> I'm sorry I was such bad company during my stay in London but
> as you perhaps gathered the first day was so sickening that in spite
> of my pleasure in seeing you and Ted and meeting Dan and Helga
> I just retired into a wretched wish that I'd never come . . . I didn't
> discuss this with you in London partly as we were never alone and
> partly because I just hadn't the heart to. I'd really like to know,
> though, what reasons [Sylvia] gave herself for all this. (Ted phoned
> me on the Sunday and said I must come at once to be alone with
> Sylvia as she must speak to me and explain, but when we were left
> alone she just behaved as though nothing had happened at all.) I
> don't want to mention this further to Ted.

Luke replied on March 12:

> There was, as far as I know, nothing specific behind Sylvia's behavior
> and volte-faces between pleasantness and bitchiness . . . My som-
> berness when you and Janet arrived, my taciturnity, was due to the
> fact that the ambience in Sylvia's salon seemed strained to me and
> made me uncomfortable . . . I have the feeling that it is best to think
> of Sylvia as being always pretty much as she was this weekend,

although there is a good chance a baby will modify her to some degree for the better. Ted suffers a good deal more than he would ever indicate or admit, but he also loves her and I think it is best to assume he will stay with her. And she very evidently loves him in the self-interested and possessive way of which she is capable.

Ted Hughes was sympathetic to his wife's ambitions, and he had some degree of understanding of how powerfully both her antisocial behavior and her eagerness to be accepted by literary London were fueled by underlying terrors and needs. Friends were often less generous. The Merwins, for instance, were shocked when they realized that Sylvia had reserved the sitting room and bedroom in Chalcot Square for her exclusive use, relegating Ted to the vestibule for his writing. In her memoir "Vessel of Wrath" Dido Merwin comments on what she and her husband privately termed "the Black Hole of Calcutta":

> Within a few days of their moving into Chalcot Square, Ted asked me if he could borrow a beat-up old card table he'd spotted in our attic. It was rickety and moth-eaten, but he assured me it was exactly what he needed. It turned out that he was setting up a work place in the single square metre (give or take) of dark, unventilated vestibule where the coats were hung. Into this space it was just possible to squeeze the card table and a chair — provided nobody tried to open the front door.

W. S. Merwin, who regarded his study as sacrosanct, offered to lend it to Ted while he was in France in the summer. He was indignant that a poet of Ted's quality had no proper place to work; Merwin was unaware, doubtless, that Ted was quite content with his cramped quarters. (In a private letter Ted mentions that "one of the best places I ever had [in which to write] was the hallway of our flat in Chalcot Square — a windowless cubicle just big enough for a chair.") Nevertheless, with a baby on the way, Ted was happy to accept Merwin's offer.

On March 24 a telegram arrived announcing that *The Hawk in the Rain* had won that year's Somerset Maugham Award: £500 to be spent traveling in foreign countries. Sylvia was as excited as Ted, planning to rent a villa in the south of France or in Greece as soon as the baby was old enough to travel. Ideally, she told her mother, they would find a place close to a large, cosmopolitan city where she could hire "one of those foreign maid-babysitters and have at least 4–6 hours a day free to write, too."

But all this lay speculatively in the future. For the present she was daily preoccupied with her pregnancy, writing on March 28 to her mother that "since the baby did not take advantage of the significant 27th date, I am sure it will wait till April Fool's Day, just to get into the main Plath month." (Otto Plath had been born on April 13; Aurelia, April 26; and Warren, April 27.) In the same letter Sylvia wrote delightedly of having come across A. Alvarez's review of *Lupercal* in *The Observer* — a column and a half of unreserved praise.

◂   ◂   ◂

As Sylvia had predicted, the baby arrived in April: Frieda Rebecca Hughes was born in the early hours of April Fool's Day after a spectacularly speedy delivery by natural childbirth. Even Sister Mahdi, the "capable little Indian" midwife, and the doctor, who arrived just in time, were amazed at its rapidity, which allowed no time for the administration of an anesthetic. Two hours after the birth Sylvia phoned her mother, getting through to Wellesley at about 3 A.M. (New England time) only to be cut off before she could relay the good news. An hour later Sylvia's voice came through clearly: after four and a half hours of labor she had produced a seven-pound-four-ounce baby girl, *"Ein Wunderkind."* Ted had been at her side throughout, and she had experienced a minimum of pain. "Well, I have never been so happy in my life," she wrote to her mother after lunch the same day. "The whole American rigamarole of hospitals, doctors' bills, cuts and stitches, anesthesia, etc., seems a nightmare well left behind." She expanded on this theme some time later in a letter to Lynne Lawner:

> The whole experience of birth and baby seem [*sic*] much deeper, much closer to the bone, than love and marriage. Have one, it's incredible. I think being mountainous-pregnant was my favorite feeling, & I wish I could prolong it . . . Ted hypnotized me to have an easy delivery . . . At sunup precisely, 5:45 am, Frieda Rebecca sneezed & began life. I was immensely moved & heartened by the whole experience, which I had deeply feared . . . You just can't get most women to talk honestly about labor. Ironically, after reading and being disgusted with Grantly Dick Read, who at one point says "Childbirth isn't physical!" and goes ga-ga over the spiritual Nobility etc. of it all, and says you're only in pain if you're nervous, I, being as nervous as possible, had exactly 4½ hours of labor, without any anesthesia (except a barley sugar the midwife had in her pocket). A notoriously easy time for a first baby. All very violent, rapid, rather than the long-drawn-out horrors a German friend of

mine describes. After a couple of really impressive contractions the whole stage of getting the baby out is really painless & terrifically exciting.

For the next week or so Sylvia remained in a state of euphoria, holding court in her bedroom, tended by a roster of midwives while Ted did all the housework and Dido Merwin supplied casseroles. The speedy delivery had launched her into an emotional high. She was certain the birth would inspire new and better poems once she had her strength back. With Ted about to inherit Merwin's study in May, she would soon be coping with the baby, the housework, and what writing she could manage in the flat. Her letters home not surprisingly glow with pride, her only regret being that no relatives or friends from America were there to share her joy. "Ted's people and friends are dear," she wrote on April 7, "the room is full of flowers, telegrams and cards and well wishes, but it isn't the same."

The English spring arrived soon after Frieda Rebecca, and by April 21 Sylvia was writing to her mother, from a bench in Regent's Park, of a cocktail party at Faber's that evening and a dinner the following day with a visiting American poet. Her chief item of news, however, was that on Easter Sunday she and Frieda had witnessed the arrival of the Aldermaston antinuclear march in Trafalgar Square. "An immensely moving experience" she called it, explaining that Ted had gone with Dido Merwin to see Bill Merwin, who was with the ten thousand or so peaceful protesters, while she had gone with Peter Redgrove, "a poet-friend of Ted's" who had loaned her a carry-cot for Frieda. "We carried the sleeping baby easily between us," she went on, "installed the cot on the lawn of the National Gallery overlooking the fountains, pigeons, and glittering white buildings. Our corner was uncrowded, a sort of nursery, mothers giving babies bottles on blankets." Sylvia described the event in a tone of political concern:

I saw the first of the 7-mile-long column appear — red and orange and green banners, "Ban the Bomb!" etc., shining and swaying slowly. Absolute silence. I found myself weeping to see the tan, dusty marchers, knapsacks on their backs — Quakers and Catholics, Africans and whites, Algerians and French — 40 percent were London housewives. I felt proud that the baby's first real adventure should be as a protest against the insanity of world-annihilation. Already a certain percentage of unborn children are doomed by fallout and no one knows the cumulative effects of what is already poisoning the air and sea.

No doubt Sylvia did feel strongly about the march; she was fervently opposed to nuclear weapons. Nevertheless, it appears that the afternoon had not simply been the moving public occasion described in her letter. Dido Merwin's account suggests that a good deal of domestic turbulence lay behind Sylvia's smooth rendition:

> On the final day of the 1960 CND Ban the Bomb demonstration during the Easter weekend, Bill's and my goddaughter, Frieda Hughes, was sixteen days old. Bill as usual had gone on the three-day march. Ted was keen to see it come into London and I had agreed — when the two of them suggested it — to go along with him, despite my dislike of being buffeted and elbowed around.
>
> During the previous two weeks, a radiant Sylvia had been blissfully preoccupied getting to know her beautiful first-born. At no time, so far as anyone knew, had there been the slightest indication that she was interested in the march, let alone wanted to see it . . .
>
> Ted and I went to the Albert Memorial. We didn't stay long. I had soon had enough of the crowds, and he was anxious to get home, which seemed altogether natural and normal — although at that stage I didn't know the half of what was natural and normal in the Hughes menage. For instance, that even the suggestion of Ted's going anywhere with anyone automatically triggered abreactions great or small, which went double if the "anyone" was a woman.
>
> There was no sign of Sylvia and Frieda when we got back to Chalcot Square, except for a note saying that they had "gone to the march."

It seems that Sylvia had telephoned Peter Redgrove and invited him to go with her. Recovering from childbirth and more than usually vulnerable, she may have conceived that Ted, in going to the march with Dido, had given her just cause for "revenge." His "punishment" had its desired effect: when Ted returned with Dido to the flat, he had no notion of where his wife and baby were. Yet when Redgrove came back with Sylvia and Frieda, he noticed nothing amiss. He and Ted, he says, went out for a beer and talked about general matters. It would have been out of character for Ted to complain about his marriage. They got back late from the pub, and Redgrove vaguely recalls that Sylvia seemed peeved about that.

The entire Aldermaston incident could be seen as a minor tempest in a happy teapot. Nevertheless, since *Letters Home* for the whole of 1960 proclaims steadily that all was as well as possible with the Hugheses at 3 Chalcot Square, it is easy to be misled — as Aurelia Plath probably was not; she well knew her daughter's ups and downs — into believing that childbirth had resolved most of Sylvia's difficulties.

Without knowing it, Dido may indeed have posed a threat to Sylvia. Clever, very pretty in a dark-haired, petite style that may have caused Sylvia feelings of awkwardness, Dido had been brought up in what could be termed the English intellectual Squirearchy. However scanty her formal education, her conditioning had bestowed on her the advantages of an insider in the Georgian circles among which her family moved. Her uncle was Lascelles Abercrombie, poet and friend of Robert Frost. As Abercrombie's discovery in the second decade of the century, Frost had pinched Dido's cheek when she was in her pram. Reintroduced years later, Frost recalled the incident, describing how Dido had held out her arms to him, whereupon Robert Lowell said, "She's been doing that to poets ever since!" Given her innate sense of belonging (something Sylvia never had), Dido easily attracted the attention of poets by admiring them and amusing them and, above all, by her love of poetry.

To Dido, Sylvia's outlook seemed narrow and too judgmental. While acknowledging her talent (not yet so conspicuous in 1960), Dido could not forgive Sylvia for what she saw as her misrepresentations, her eagerness to build up images of those she wanted to impress and deny existence to people for whom she had no use. Dido vividly describes Sylvia's "frequently antisocial behaviour":

> Her public and/or chronic scenes, as witnessed by various people in London, Yorkshire, and France, followed a characteristic pattern which is not easy to describe, in that from the point of view of dramatic action virtually nothing happened. To call them sulks because they were conducted in silence — apart from the occasional monosyllabic shrug — would be to suggest a switched-off, withdrawn dissociation on Sylvia's part that was exactly the opposite of the inescapable blast of active hostility that she directed at each individual who happened to be involved. This nonstop dispensation of condemnatory *Schadenfreude* made for a climate of sickened bewilderment that was (and still is) unforgettable and, I suspect, not believable for anyone who never came into contact with the anger of which Sylvia wrote: "I have a violence in me that is hot as death-blood."

People suffered, to varying degrees, from her jealous self-protection, although not always in the same way. On May 5, for instance, Sylvia wrote to her mother of dining with Peter Davison and his wife, Jane Truslow, in an Indian restaurant at the expense of *The Atlantic*

Monthly. Sylvia's attitude to Davison had cooled after *The Atlantic* turned down the poems and stories she had rushed off to him while she was in Boston. Without evidence she believed him responsible for her rejections, and her letter is couched in tones of triumphant spite:

> Peter is worse than ever. He was furious (although he tried to conceal this) that I'd sent my stories and poems directly to Edward Weeks and not through him. I figured he'd been behind the rejections of my things, as since he came on, not one of my pieces has been taken and he is very jealous, as he now considers himself a real poet. Evidently his job is furthered by "bringing writers in," but I was there before he came. He also bragged about his work in the most puerile way . . . He can't bear to hear about our work, so of course we tell him nothing.

The occasion for Sylvia's scorn was an acceptance, directly from Weeks, of her poem "A Winter Ship." Not surprisingly, Davison's version of the Indian meal differs radically from Sylvia's. He says that he and his wife went to Chalcot Square, where

> we stayed long enough to have a sherry and then took a bus to Soho, where we dined at an Indian restaurant. During dinner Jane (who was herself newly pregnant and who had hung on Sylvia's story of the midwife) talked mostly to Ted, while I talked mostly to Sylvia. Jane had always relished Ted's wit, and she had a great gift of laughter, which tended to make witty people wittier. I did not notice this at the time, but the growing evidence of Sylvia's discomfort may (*pace* her *Letters Home*) have had much less to do with the literary conversation between me and Sylvia than with the nonliterary conversation between Jane and Ted. It is possible that, by Sylvia's borderguard standards, Jane was entirely *too* entertained. As Sylvia's mood grew more and more stony, I doubtless nattered about American literary and publishing gossip, which only made Sylvia more furious. But you may be sure that she never asked me a word about my own work. It was only as they were boarding the bus to return to Chalcot Square that, disarmed by the oddity of the evening, I foolishly boasted of the poems I was about to see in print, which inspired the letter home, with its pointed malice.

Sylvia was actually mistaken about Davison's influence in turning down her work. The *Atlantic* file for that period shows that all decisions were made by consensus and that no opinion, except that of Weeks, ever determined either acceptance or rejection. What puzzled the Davisons further was that Sylvia had written warmly to them shortly before their arrival in England, describing the wonders of home childbirth and urging them to make a date for dinner.

In the same letter to her mother, Sylvia described, in quite different terms, a dinner the night before at the T. S. Eliots':

> The Eliots live in a surprisingly drab brick building on the first floor — yet a comfortable, lavish apartment. His Yorkshire wife, Valerie, is handsome, blond and rosy. He was marvelous. Put us immediately at ease . . . I felt to be sitting next to a descended god; he has such a nimbus of greatness about him . . .
>
> Then the Spenders arrived; he handsome and white-haired, and she . . . lean, vibrant, talkative, lovely. Her name is Natasha Litvin, and she is a concert pianist. Talk was intimate gossip about Stravinsky, Auden, Virginia Woolf, D. H. Lawrence. I was fascinated. Floated in to dinner, sat between Eliot and Spender, rapturously, and got along very well. Both of them, of course, were instrumental in Ted's getting his Guggenheim and his book printed.

In May, after the Merwins had departed for their farmhouse in France, Ted began to work every day in Bill's study. Both Hugheses found his daily absence from the flat a relief; Ted had the peace he needed for his writing, while Sylvia, aching to see what childbirth would do for her poems, was still preoccupied with the baby. Visitors had begun to pour into London. Ann Davidow, Sylvia's friend of her first year at Smith, arrived with her fiancé, Leo Goodman, who was on a Guggenheim at Cambridge before going to Columbia as a visiting professor of mathematical statistics. Sylvia adored them both, seeing the couple as the astrological twins of herself and Ted: Leo, "that unique combination of the intellectual and loving-lovable Jew," *was* a Leo, while Ann's birthday under the sign of Scorpio was October 26, the day before her own. With these unthreatening visitors Sylvia apparently got on extremely well. *Letters Home* reproduces a snapshot taken by Ann which shows Sylvia happily cradling a contentious Frieda in a wood outside Stonehenge.

By May 30, however, writing to Wellesley to congratulate their cat, Sappho, on the safe delivery of three kittens, Sylvia begged her mother to send no more Americans their way. It was all she could do to cope with the baby's feedings, keep house, cook, and take care of Ted's "voluminous mail" while trying to carve out a few hours a day for her own writing. With "several projects going" for the BBC, Ted almost daily received requests for readings, school visits, and other paying but peripheral jobs. A visit from his mother and Aunt Hilda (they stayed in a hotel) had prompted a final scrubbing and decorating of the flat. Ted had painted the vestibule (where he still worked when not at Merwin's study) and one of the kitchen walls "a marvelous vermillion." The color like a tonic to her, Sylvia wrote: "I can hardly stop looking at it, eating it up. I am so influenced by colors and textures."

It was while Sylvia was in her most positive housekeeping-mothering phase that A. Alvarez came around to interview Hughes for *The Observer;* it was his first meeting with Ted and Sylvia. In the now-famous prologue to *The Savage God* he describes the couple as they appeared to him that spring in London: Hughes "a tall, strong-looking man in a black corduroy jacket, black trousers, black shoes," with "dark hair hung untidily forward and a long witty mouth." By contrast, Sylvia "seemed effaced, the poet taking a back seat to the young mother and housewife. She had a long, rather flat body, a longish face, not pretty but alert and full of feeling, with a lively mouth and fine brown eyes. Her brownish hair was scraped severely into a bun. She wore jeans and a neat shirt, briskly American: bright, clean, competent, like a young woman in a cookery advertisement, friendly and yet rather distant." Alvarez met the composed, efficient Mrs. Ted Hughes without realizing she was the poet Sylvia Plath, whose "Night Shift" he had already published in *The Observer.* His impression could have been shared by most people who met the Hugheses for the first time and did not know of her writing: she would have been taken as the keenly intelligent, if somewhat withdrawn, wife of a rising poet.

Ted Hughes always saw Sylvia as a writer and well understood her need for a quiet place to work. He must, however, have been in a dilemma about W. S. Merwin's study, which had been specifically lent to *him*. He was aware that it was always kept locked in Bill's absence and that being given the use of it was a very special favor. But what could he do? The upshot was that in a letter to her mother, after a glowing description of a party at Faber, Sylvia was able to say: "I am at the depressing, painful stage of trying to start writing after a long spell of silence, but the mornings at the study are very peaceful to my soul, and I am infinitely lucky we can work things out so I get a solid hunk of time off, or, rather, time on, a day." Sylvia wrote in Merwin's study every morning (Ted never minded minding Frieda); then after lunch Sylvia took over at Chalcot Square while Ted did his stint in St. George's Terrace. They also had the use of the garden in return for mowing the lawn. A hairdresser friend of the Merwins' looked after the flat while they were away, and fed their Siamese cat. At this time, as at all times, Sylvia and Ted were in perfect sympathy over the rhythm of their working days.

Still, Sylvia, at a loss as to how to use her experience of childbearing, at first found writing difficult. Her poem of June 27 took her straight back to the subject of "Poem for a Birthday." "The Hanging Man," a title taken from a card in the tarot pack, rehearsed in its six stunning lines her old theme of electroconvulsive therapy and suicide:

> By the roots of my hair some god got hold of me.
> I sizzled in his blue volts like a desert prophet.
>
> The nights snapped out of sight like a lizard's eyelid:
> A world of bald white days in a shadeless socket.
>
> A vulturous boredom pinned me in this tree.
> If he were I, he would do what I did.

Back in her private, sleepless nightmare, Sylvia looked to be going on from where she left off at Yaddo. What was new was her style, no longer a pastiche of Roethke but a vivid, hard-edged mode of her own. Other poems she wrote in July were probably "exercises" for which she chose themes from her travels of the previous year: "On Deck," "Sleep in the Mojave Desert," "Two Campers in Cloud Country." Her first poem about childbirth related not to her baby but to her (as she must then have considered them) stillborn poems:

> These poems do not live: it's a sad diagnosis.
> They grew their toes and fingers well enough,
> Their little foreheads bulged with concentration.
> If they missed out on walking about like people
> It wasn't for any lack of mother love.

Here Sylvia found a use for her recurring image of embryo babies in formaldehyde — a leftover from her traumatic visit to the Boston Lying-In Hospital with Dick Norton years before:

> They sit so nicely in the pickling fluid!
> They smile and smile and smile and smile at me.
> And still the lungs won't fill and the heart won't start.

For a light, amusing exercise in self-deprecation, "Stillborn" trails a chill wind.

As she struggled to write, her mind sped ahead with plans for the future. Increasingly she was dissatisfied with their tiny flat. Walking with Frieda along nearby Fitzroy Road one afternoon late in June, she spied a "FREEHOLD FOR SALE" sign in front of one of the houses. "41 Fitzroy Road, *the street where Yeats lived*," she wrote to her mother in great excitement. Immediately she had visions of it furnished and refurbished with a study for Ted, one for herself, a nursery for Frieda, a spare room for "guests (you) now and the next baby (babies)" plus "the dear garden to hang laundry in and put playpens in." It would have been an excellent buy (even in 1960) at £9,250, but in the end they had to let it go, fearful of taking on a mortgage without an assured income.

Moreover, the Somerset Maugham Award had stipulated that Ted spend part of 1961 living abroad. Toward the end of September, still feeling "cowlike" and physically pleased with herself after Frieda's birth, Sylvia wrote to her poet friend Lynne Lawner, who was then in Rome, inquiring if she had heard of any villas to rent furnished, at cheap winter rates. Or were such villas cheaper in small seacoast towns?

With such plans jostling her imagination (and stirring up hopes and fears), Sylvia nursed and wheeled little Frieda through summer and early autumn, writing little. During a two-week holiday in Yorkshire they drove to Whitby with Ted's cousin Vicky. Sylvia found the resort "depressingly mucky," the sand littered with working-class holiday-makers "strewing candy papers, gum and cigarette wrappers" over the beach, so unlike the clean white sands of Nauset on Cape Cod. September saw the publication of "The Manor Garden" in *The Atlantic* and Stanley Kunitz's rave review of *Lupercal* in *Harper's*.

When the Merwins returned from France at the end of the summer, the Hugheses arranged with a Mrs. M., who lived in the flat above them, to let Ted write there during the day while she was away working as a translator for the telephone company. They thought of giving her an occasional bottle of sherry as payment. In fact, Hughes only worked in Mrs. M.'s flat a few times; he felt he was intruding in a private home. In spite of kind words about her neighbor in a letter to Mrs. Plath, Sylvia clearly did not much approve either of her decor or of her occasional gentleman callers (sometimes glimpsed on the stairs). Sylvia's dramatic monologue "Leaving Early" re-creates the attic flat in the words of one of these visitors, who finds himself in a stifling hell of dying flowers. The poem foreshadows later attacks — "Lesbos" and "The Tour," for example — on well-meaning women upon whom Sylvia exercised her gift for malice.

In October, in time for her birthday, Heinemann published *The Colossus and Other Poems*, two copies of which Sylvia sent off by surface mail to her family on October 26. Although upset after spotting two printing errors toward the end, Sylvia was "delighted with the color of the cover — the rich green oblong, white jacket and black-and-white lettering . . . It is a nice fat book which takes up ¾ of an inch on the shelf, and I think they did a handsome job of it." The same letter reports an appointment to record "Leaving Early" and another poem, "Candles," for the BBC's Third Programme. "Candles," together with "Magi," is the first in a series of poems about children Sylvia wrote in her final, fruitful years. "Candles," in particular, evinces a new gentleness that modifies the stark, nerve-peeled surrealism of other poems of this period. Centered on the figures of mother and child, the poem has a Renaissance serenity, like a painting by Raphael or Murillo instead of the usual de Chirico or Dali. Here the candles are "the last romantics," touchingly private, flattering, false but still "sweet as pears." "Kindly with invalids and mawkish women," saintly enough to "mollify the bald moon," like nuns they renounce the insatiable flesh, the hungers. Nevertheless, their ephemeral "globes of light" foreshadow a sorry future; in twenty years the mother will be "retrograde," the baby, adult. The candles weep fruitlessly for the passing of time.

A companion piece, "Magi," directs attention to the poet's baby and her superior bodily innocence as compared to the abstracts of philosophy. The eager student who had opened her mind to Plato with Dorothea Krook at Cambridge now looks with scorn on such "dull angels" as "the Good, the True"; they are "Salutary and pure as boiled water, / Loveless as the multiplication table." For a six-month-old baby "the heavy notion of Evil" is "less than a belly ache," while Love is not a "theory" but "the mother of milk." It was on the slight poem "Magi" that Joyce Carol Oates built a case against Plath's Romanticism in her famous essay "The Death Throes of Romanticism."*

"Magi" and "Candles" are oases in what seems to be a desert of inspiration in 1960. It was not that Sylvia couldn't write, but that the same old images kept cropping up in everything she *did* write. "Love Letter" repeats, with surrealistic embellishments, the imagery of "The Stones"; "A Life," purporting to be a description of a glass paperweight, rehearses the old drowned-father/deserted-daughter story of her "Electra" period. One dream-poem, clearly taken from a nightmare, stands out from among these self-imitations. This is "Waking in Winter," which Ted Hughes says was extracted posthumously by Judith Kroll from "a tangle of heavily corrected manuscript lines, and must be regarded as unfinished":

---

*Joyce Carol Oates accuses Plath of slitting her own throat in this poem, arguing that since language is itself abstract, to reject the achievements of high culture for the sake of the regressive fantasies of Romanticism is tantamount to admitting "to herself and to us that she is inferior to her own infant."

I can taste the tin of the sky — the real tin thing.
Winter dawn is the color of metal,
The trees stiffen into place like burnt nerves.
All night I have dreamed of destruction, annihilations —
An assembly-line of cut throats, and you and I
Inching off in the gray Chevrolet, drinking the green
Poison of stilled lawns, the little clapboard gravestones,
Noiseless, on rubber wheels, on the way to the sea resort.

How the balconies echoed! How the sun lit up
The skulls, the unbuckled bones facing the view!
Space! Space! The bed linen was giving out entirely.
Cot legs melted in terrible attitudes, and the nurses —
Each nurse patched her soul to a wound and disappeared.
The deathly guests had not been satisfied
With the rooms, or the smiles, or the beautiful rubber plants,
Or the sea, hushing their peeled sense like Old Mother Morphia.

"Waking in Winter" indeed rings like "the real tin thing." Even if
only a draft, it is a harbinger of the Ariel poems, its imagery foreshadowing that of "Berck-Plage." It confirms that real inner stability
and calm were still distant. Despite Sylvia's determined outward show
of good humor and achievement, her roots as a poet were proliferating
in the demonic. As Ted Hughes says in his long, penetrating essay on
her journals:

> Though her whole considerable ambition was fixed on becoming
> the normal flowering and fruiting kind of writer, *her work was roots
> only*. Almost as if her entire oeuvre were enclosed within those
> processes and transformations that happen in other poets before
> they can even begin, before the muse can hold out a leaf. Or as if
> all poetry were made up of the feats and shows performed by the
> poetic spirit Ariel. Whereas her poetry is the biology of Ariel, the
> ontology of Ariel — the story of Ariel's imprisonment in the pine,
> before Prospero opened it. [My italics.]

W A R N I N G S

1960-1961

I shall never get out of this! There are two of me now:
This new absolutely white person and the old yellow
    one,
And the white person is certainly the superior one . . .

Without me, she wouldn't exist, so of course she was
    grateful.
I gave her a soul, I bloomed out of her as a rose
Blooms out of a vase of not very valuable porcelain.

— "In Plaster," March 18, 1961

FOR TED HUGHES 1960 was an outstanding year. *The Hawk in the Rain* had been a success; *Lupercal*, published in March 1960, confirmed his growing reputation. As W. S. Merwin had predicted, the BBC was providing him an appreciable income. "Ted's income from the BBC this year has been as good as a salary," Sylvia assured her mother the day before her twenty-eighth birthday. "We've about $1,600 in the bank here from our English writing, and he has an exciting prospect of doing broadcasts for school children, which would go all over England." Ted's stories "The Rain Horse" and "Harvesting" were broadcast before Christmas; his poems, too, were often on the air, and he had contributed to a series of poets' translations of *The Odyssey* commissioned by the Third Programme. All this time Hughes was also writing plays. In Cambridge, Massachusetts, *The House of Aries* had been performed by the Poets' Theatre Company and viewed by a loyal, if somewhat baffled, Aurelia Plath. Meanwhile he was at work on his second play, *The House of Taurus,* an allegory in three acts, as well as the libretto for Chou

Wen-Chung's proposed oratorio based on the Tibetan Book of the Dead.

Although Sylvia purported to share her husband's reaction to publicity ("Both of us are getting more retiring about blazoning biographies and publication-notices everywhere"), she was cast down because *The Colossus* had not had more success. "Since I got no prize or any American publisher," she wrote, "they haven't bothered to advertise it, so I probably won't make a penny on it unless I get some award later to call it to the public's attention."

Still, for Sylvia London continued to be a garden of literary delights. Stephen Spender had got her a press ticket for the last day of the Lady Chatterley trial at the Old Bailey, "very exciting — especially with the surprising verdict of 'not guilty'!" In late October or early November she recorded her first contributions to "The Poet's Voice" on the BBC, broadcast, with readings by nine other poets, on November 20. She went to weekly Italian lessons at the Berlitz School (she and Ted were by now banking on living in Italy for three months in the spring) and began thankfully to write poems again. Chiefly, however, she was at work on stories, determined yet again to break into the popular fiction market. She had found a "fine, lively agent" affiliated with an agency in New York, she told her mother.*

Sylvia's forward-looking, professional mood before leaving London for Yorkshire lasted through Christmas. Helga Huws had given birth to a second daughter in November, making Sylvia "want another *really* small one immediately." She was discovering, she said, that children could be an impetus to her writing, which would certainly proceed apace if she had more space to work in and a woman to babysit or take over the drudgery of housekeeping. "All sorts of queer part-time jobs crop up here," she wrote on the eve of her departure for Yorkshire, begging her mother to send her a speedwriting book. She wrote again from The Beacon on Christmas Eve, expressing approval of Ted's decision not to appear on television as Poet of the Year, "much to his mother's disappointment," and listing her own triumphs — a fine review by A. Alvarez in *The Observer,* another on the radio with *The Colossus* included among new books by Pasternak, Cummings, and Betjeman. Alvarez was particularly perceptive, drawing attention to the technical strength Sylvia brought to her atmosphere of weird threat:

---

*Both agent and agency are unidentified.

There is an admirable no-nonsense air about this; the language is bare but vivid and precise, with a concentration that implies a good deal of disturbance with proportionately little fuss. I think Miss Plath can allow herself this undemonstrativeness because most of her poems rest secure in a mass of experience that is never quite brought out into daylight . . . It is this sense of threat, as though she were continually menaced by something she could see only out of the corner of her eye, that gives her work its distinction.

◄ ◄ ◄

They drove up to Yorkshire for Christmas in their new Morris. Ted's mother had got rid of the piano in the sitting room to make room for Frieda's playpen, and her small, nine-month-old presence, with all the necessities of baby care piled about, made the house seem very full.

Olwyn Hughes, who arrived home from France on Christmas Eve, remembers Sylvia's excitedly describing an exhibition of paintings by Leonor Fini she had seen recently in London. Sylvia had already, in a letter to Olwyn, written about "the fabulous Leonor Fini who divides her time between Corsica and Paris . . . a polyglot . . . given to wearing animal masks about the house and has — among some bad stuff — jewel-like misty otherworldish damsels and cadavers with a weird, terrifying beauty, like necrological mannequins — I'd like to pay a pilgrimage to her Corsican monastery — reachable only by donkey." Olwyn had never seen Sylvia so moved by any artist's work. It was only later, seeing Fini's mastery of the portrayal of doubles, of masks, and of divided beings, that she understood Sylvia's enthusiasm: many of Fini's paintings matched the luminous and eerie world of Sylvia's poems.

With the memory of Sylvia's behavior on the disastrous visit in March to the London flat, Olwyn was, she says, treading carefully around her on this holiday. It may have been the strain of such cautiousness, together with the general exhaustion after the bustle of Christmas, that caused the ensuing unpleasantness. As far as Olwyn can recall, it began with a remark she made in response to some rather "malicious" account of Sylvia's on the behavior of someone Sylvia knew but Olwyn didn't. Olwyn said, " 'I say, you're awfully critical, aren't you?' — ignoring for once the unwritten rule that one just did *not* criticize Sylvia in any way." The reaction was immediate. Sylvia glared accusingly with a half-terrified, half-furious look and drew Ted into the room, having whispered Olwyn's remark to him. Olwyn, losing her temper, asked Sylvia why she didn't behave more normally, why she was so rude, why she so often showed little consideration for others. To these questions Sylvia made no reply but kept up her unnerving glare. Olwyn, who immediately regretted she'd said a word, remembers thinking, "Why doesn't she *say* something?"

Olwyn ended the confrontation with relief by stroking Frieda's silky hair (the baby was sitting on her knee throughout) and saying, "But we shouldn't talk like this over her sweet head." Frieda was ready for bed, and Sylvia silently seized her and went upstairs, not to reappear. Olwyn went to bed later, feeling very contrite. She was wakened at dawn by the departure of her brother and his family (earlier than intended) and only remembers Sylvia's staring up from the doorway at the bottom of the stairs as Olwyn said, still half asleep, "Are you leaving already? Have a good journey." Sylvia made no reply. It was the last time Olwyn saw her.

On the first day of January, in a letter to her mother, Sylvia complained in characteristically extreme language about the scene with Olwyn, which she said had ruined their holiday.* When Mrs. Plath visited Edith Hughes in Yorkshire the following summer and recounted Sylvia's version of the event, Mrs. Hughes was shocked and told Olwyn in a letter that she could only conclude that her daughter-in-law was "very unforgiving." For the sake of family harmony, Olwyn, with her mother's help, had written a suitable apology and posted it on New Year's Day. Sylvia denied ever having received it, and it was some months before the women were again exchanging cordial letters.

From Sylvia's point of view, then, January 1961 began badly (both she and Frieda caught colds), and although she was sporadically cheered by literary prospects — she had been asked to edit an American supplement to *Critical Quarterly* and was to take part, with her husband, in a radio series, "Two of a Kind"† — she slumped with sinusitis, writer's block, and the beginnings of a new pregnancy. In a month of dreary rain and fog she wrote of embarking, "with Ted's help, on a drastic program to pull my health up . . . eating big break-

---

*Later, when she spoke of the episode, she made much of running out into the snow in her nightgown. Olwyn has no memory of this and points out that the confrontation happened around seven in the evening.

†"Poets in Partnership," one of the series "Two of a Kind," was broadcast on January 31, 1961, BBC Home Service. An extended version was repeated on March 19. Sylvia read "Mushrooms."

fasts . . . tender steaks, salads, and drinking the cream from the tops of our bottles, along with iron and vitamin pills." Her appendix was "rumbling," she told her mother in a letter of January 27, and the doctor had advised her to have it out at the end of February. She would keep March free for "resting," she went on, before heading for Italy in April with Ted and Frieda. July would find them back in England preparing for a visit from Mrs. Plath, which Sylvia hoped could be arranged to cover the week of the new baby's birth. It was due on August 17, Ted's birthday.

To combat depression and keep her from brooding over the approaching operation, Sylvia took a temporary job with *The Bookseller,* doing layout for the children's book page of the magazine. On February 2 she reported herself pleased with the work, and her speedy typing "the marvel of the office." Ted was "plow[ing] into his play" during her afternoons away from the flat (looking after Frieda at the same time, apparently), "full of ideas and in wonderful form." The letter went on to describe meeting Theodore Roethke at a party the evening before: "I've always wanted to meet him, as I find he is my influence." Roethke, a "big, blond, Swedish-looking man, much younger-seeming than his 52 years," had told Ted "to give him a nod" any time he wanted a teaching job at the University of Washington in Seattle. Sylvia pronounced herself pleased with the evening, feeling "in much better spirits with the promise of spring and summer and your [Mrs. Plath's] coming."

Between this optimistic letter and a very distressed one of February 6 announcing a miscarriage, much had occurred on the third floor of 3 Chalcot Square that never got mentioned to Aurelia Plath. Sylvia's domestic satisfactions were real enough, but they were often undermined by her oddly unpredictable "jolting jealousies." A clue to the events of early February can be found in one of Sylvia's stories, probably written in 1961. "Day of Success" is about a wife's jealousy over her husband's supposed infidelities, reported to her by a friend, which turn out to be unfounded. The story was written for the popular market, its values geared to the feminine ethos of the day. One imagines that even in 1961 its catch-your-man-and-be-happy philosophy would have sounded naive. But Sylvia's attitude *was* naive; she really *did* imagine that any "real" man would find it a drag to come home to diapers and cod-liver oil instead of the Japanese silks and French perfume of the story. Ted had shown himself to be a loving father and the most domestically centered of writers, but in her heart Sylvia was afraid the editors of *Mademoiselle* and *Seventeen* had got it right, and that, given a glamorous enough rival, she would lose her husband, the chief prop of her precarious happiness.

During the week in which Sylvia met Theodore Roethke, Ted was invited by a BBC producer to come and discuss a series of children's programs he had proposed in outline for the radio. Just as in Sylvia's story, the producer, Moira Doolan, phoned Ted to make the appointment but got Sylvia on the line instead. Although she was in late middle age, Moira Doolan had a lilting Irish voice, which Sylvia instantly associated with flaming red hair and lascivious intentions. Like the heroine of her story, Sylvia was alarmed, anticipating that Moira Doolan, a person she had never met, would make the first, inevitable breach in her perfect marriage. When Ted was not back from the appointment by lunchtime, Sylvia's jealous premonitions escalated into hysteria. After giving Frieda her lunch and putting her down for a nap, her foreboding must have mushroomed into outrage, and she took preemptive revenge.

At the BBC the interview had gone well: Moira Doolan agreed in principle to produce the programs Ted had in mind.* Returning late for lunch to tell Sylvia the good news, Ted entered the flat and encountered a scene of carnage. All his work in progress, his play, poems, notebooks, even his precious edition of Shakespeare, had been torn into small pieces, some "reduced to 'fluff.'" Sylvia had expressed her rage; her husband's punishment for presumed dalliance was the destruction of his work and his most treasured book.†

The incident provides yet another example of Sylvia's irrational and uncontrollable rage. Apart from their children, what linked Ted Hughes and Sylvia Plath throughout their difficult years together was their commitment to a common art. Sylvia's destruction of Ted's work was, as Dido Merwin rightly asserts, "the deliberate, calculated handiwork of a fellow poet who had written — and who believed as fervently as Ted did — that 'writing is a religious act.' Ipso facto she had desecrated what mattered most to both of them." Ted could neither forget nor forgive this desecration; it seems to have marked a turning point in his marriage.

Several days later, early on Monday morning, February 6, Sylvia miscarried. Rage, hysteria, and sorrow (and perhaps an intense dread of her approaching hospitalization for her inflamed appendix) set her

---

*The series of broadcasts, "Listening and Writing," that resulted from this interview was eventually published as Poetry in the Making (London: Faber, 1967) and as Poetry Is (New York: Doubleday, 1970). It is still widely used in schools.

†This account is from Dido Merwin, to whom Hughes confided it in the autumn of 1962, after his breakup with Sylvia.

writing again. In the ensuing fortnight, between February 11 and February 26, when she entered the hospital for her appendectomy, she wrote seven poems. As a group they reflect the characteristic unease of their author. "Parliament Hill Fields"* is an elegy for her lost baby; perhaps, too, for her lost "perfect" marriage: "The old dregs, the old difficulties take me to wife." "Morning Song" and "Barren Woman" speak in curiously similar imagery both of birth and of miscarriage. The tenderness "Morning Song" evinces for the baby acts at a distance:

> I'm no more your mother
> Than the cloud that distills a mirror to reflect its own slow
> Effacement at the wind's hand.

The child is a "new statue" in a "drafty museum" in which "We stand round blankly as walls." "Barren Woman" develops the desolate, de Chiricean museum setting, where

> . . . the dead injure me with attentions, and nothing can happen.
> The moon lays a hand on my forehead,
> Blank-faced and mum as a nurse.

Both these chill, beautiful poems are about sleepless nights ("Barren Woman" was originally titled "Small Hours"), and they surely reflect depression. Images of effacement and the personified moon (later, no longer a nurse but instead the dark lady of death) were to recur at the very end of Sylvia's life in "Contusion" and "Edge."

"Face Lift," exulting in the medical imagery that Sylvia so relished, is livelier, every detail taken from Dido Merwin's life and experience: "When Sylvia asked questions and expressed interest in my incisions and spectacular technicolour bruises . . . she provided me with an opportunity to see a turned-on and intriguing aspect of her that I barely caught sight of again." Yet, as has been often pointed out, the poem also relates to Sylvia's perennial myth of rebirth:

> Mother to myself, I wake swaddled in gauze,
> Pink and smooth as a baby.

(Almost the same line concludes the late poem "Getting There.") Most bizarre among this group is "Zoo Keeper's Wife" with its picture of a woman "digesting" her sisters — a good image for the acid treatment certain disapproved-of women got from Sylvia: "Look, they are melting like coins in the powerful juices." Both "Face Lift" and "Zoo

---

*Part of Hampstead Heath in North London.

Keeper's Wife" find a place for the sock-faces of "The Disquieting Muses." Increasingly, nurses, hills, pigs, even eyes and cries are described as "bald." "Zoo Keeper's Wife" was probably a disguised hit at Ted, as "Face Lift" was at Dido. In "Face Lift," mocking, spiteful, not a little masochistic, Sylvia was already rehearsing the hatred later to find expression in "Medusa," "Lesbos," "The Tour," and "Eavesdropper" — all, curiously, poems about women.

◂ ◂ ◂

On Sunday evening, February 26, Sylvia set off alone on foot for the St. Pancras Hospital and lost her way in the "black Sunday streets of Camden Town." Having asked directions from an elderly couple in a car, she was grateful for their offer of a lift. "I'd rather have a baby; at least you've got something for it," she wailed, breaking down in the back seat. But the next day she was taking eager notes (these have survived). She realized that the operation would constitute another enactment of her resurrection mythology, channeling her once more through "death" to rebirth. In Sylvia's iconography, the hospital was "a religious establishment" where "great cleansings take place." Suddenly everyone was a member of a sect; "everybody has a secret" — the fat girl with a new leg, the noseless old lady a foot in traction, a sour-faced woman in a plaster cast. Flowers were brought in, a ceremony of ritual significance:

> All night they've been breathing in the hall, dropping their pollens, daffodils, pink and red tulips, the hot purple and red-eyed anemones. Potted plants for the veterans. Nobody complains or whines. In the black earphones hung on my silver bedstead a tiny voice nags me to listen. They won't unplug him. Immensely cheerful pink, blue and yellow birds distribute themselves among flowers, primarily pink, and simpering greenery on the white bed-curtains. It is like an arbor when they close me in.

Paradoxically, Sylvia was happy. Quickly accepting that her operation was minor, she shrugged off her old terror of hospitals and began to relish the womblike security of her ward, with its bright furnishings, its pleasant nurses, its entertaining patients, and its scope for her lively interest in all things medical. At McLean she had wanted to die; her agonizing recovery from mental breakdown had taken place in an underworld of glaring cement tunnels leading to places of torture. This time, voluntarily and for purely physical reasons, she had entered a hospital in order to live longer. St. Pancras, with its bright, modern furnishings and youthful nurses, was the ideal setting.

Straight away Sylvia saw that the patients in her ward constituted a society. To be accepted, a new patient had to undergo an initiation — an operation or ritual killing from which she might or might not emerge. On Tuesday, February 28, Sylvia dramatically prepared herself for the ordeal:

> Today is the day. Amid the chatter and breakfasting of all the other patients I alone am quiet and without food. Yet I feel curiously less worried about losing my appendix than being electrocuted . . . I feel slightly sick after all this waiting, but here where everyone is amiable with gracious smiles, it is impossible to indulge in mopes or self-pity, a very good thing . . . Today, after a sleeping pill, I woke when the nurse took my temperature and pulse. Had tea and buttered toast at 6:30. Then they took away my water and my milk . . . As the latest operative case, [I] am of interest. Was I shaved? Will I have an enema? And so on.

Calm, attended to, full of creative urges, Sylvia was at last "at home." Ted, only three weeks after her ravaging his manuscripts, was again her tenderly devoted lover and husband, superior to all other beings: "Ted came last night. Precisely one minute after 7.30 a crowd of shabby, short, sweet peering people was let into the ward — they fluxed in familiar directions, bringing a dark-coated handsome shape twice as tall as all of them. I felt as excited and infinitely happy as in the early days of our courtship."

Ted had brought with him a letter for Sylvia from *The New Yorker* "with a $100 contract for letting them have 'first reading' of all my poems for a year!" The letter was dated February 25, the anniversary of their meeting at the *St. Botolph's* party five years before. It was a consummation, a sign that all would be well. By 10 A.M. she was "prepared for the slaughter — robed loosely in a pink and maroon striped surgical gown, a gauze turban and a strip of adhesive [that] shuts off the sight of my wedding ring . . . Oblivion approaches. Now I'm close enough, I open my arms. I asked to have my flowered curtains left drawn — the privilege of a condemned prisoner." The moment of her "death" was sacred, private as the "bee sting" with which the "handsome lady anesthetist" had branded her arm. Up to the very last minute she waited, pen in hand, until she felt "a bubbly drowsiness take my heart . . . a letter from Ted reached me — my dear dear love."

Sylvia next wrote in her journal on March 3, feeling herself again three days after her operation. Throwing off her "fetters," she got up to wash, array herself in her "frilly pink and white Victorian nightgown," and put her mind to work recording the petty pleasures and annoyances of her neighbors. By March 5 she was "an old soldier." With her stitches still in, she had an interesting wound to discuss with Rose and "Granny" and the entomologist's wife in neighboring beds. She planned to begin a story with the line "Tonight I deserve a blue light, I am one of them"; it would describe a patient's progress through the stages of hospital initiation in the queer, highly rhythmical and ordered society of a large ward. Like a school or a nunnery, the hospital relieved her of responsibility, protected her from outsiders, and limited her scope, enabling her to write without threat. To her mother she wrote on March 6:

> Actually, I feel I've been having an amazing holiday! I haven't been free of the baby one day for a whole year, and I must say I have secretly enjoyed having meals in bed, backrubs, and nothing to do but read (I've discovered Agatha Christie — *just* the thing for hospital reading . . .), gossip, and look at my table of flowers sent by Ted's parents, Ted, Helga Huws, and Charles Monteith, Ted's editor at Faber's.

Ted took charge of Frieda during the day and visited Sylvia in the evening, bringing, with her mail, steak sandwiches, milk, and orange juice. "Poor dear!" Sylvia wrote to her mother. "I'd like to know how many men would take over as willingly and lovingly as he has! Plus bringing me little treats every night."

After an afternoon of reading Pasternak, she began to wonder if she hadn't sacrificed lyricism in her dedication to a "new tough prosiness." In essence the prosiness was a protective pose, a means of distancing herself from her emotions by objectifying and describing rather than by penetrating to confusing depths. When the depth came up unbidden, it came in poetry. So it happened that while Sylvia, in the hospital, was cramming her notebook, the poetic process was already mysteriously at work. The cheerful notes she took at St. Pancras belie the menacing imagery of "Tulips," written (with "In Plaster") ten days after she left the hospital. Ted Hughes says "Tulips" was Sylvia's first spontaneous poem. She wrote it quickly, without recourse to her thesaurus, and it combines exactness of observation with the subjectivity of her hidden, deeper voice.

Now Sylvia was a mistress of her imagery, deploying the colors white and red to convey her imagined death and resurrection. Even halfway through she was siding with the whites of self-elimination and peace against the "too excitable" red flowers:

> I didn't want any flowers, I only wanted
> To lie with my hands turned up and be utterly empty.
> How free it is, you have no idea how free —
> The peacefulness is so big it dazes you,
> And it asks nothing, a name tag, a few trinkets.
> It is what the dead close on, finally; I imagine them
> Shutting their mouths on it, like a Communion tablet.

In such a condition of blissful numbness (her body again "a pebble"), the husband and child "smiling out of the family photo" can only be resented: "Their smiles catch onto my skin, little smiling hooks." This is not quite the same Sylvia as the one who tossed the twenty-first-birthday roses, brought by her mother, into a wastebasket.

The Communion tablet turns up in later poems, where it can represent the "wafer" of her ECT. Here it confirms her death wish, along with the "baggage" the speaker is "sick of," the nurses who pass "the way gulls pass inland in their white caps," and the nunlike purity of hospital whiteness in which the red tulips breathe "like an awful baby." In the end the tulips are seen to be the carriers of that terrible red thing, *life,* slowly complicating the whiteness with which the speaker has effaced herself:

> The tulips should be behind bars like dangerous animals;
> They are opening like the mouth of some great African cat,
> And I am aware of my heart: it opens and closes
> Its bowl of red blooms out of sheer love of me.
> The water I taste is warm and salt, like the sea,
> And comes from a country far away as health.

Resurrection after the "death" of Sylvia's operation came extremely quickly, lifting her spirits and charging her imagination as she set down every detail of the "new" world to which she had "risen." Certain symbolic figures are notable: nurses in her poems are usually ambiguous bearers of love, something between angels of mercy and harbingers of doom, while in her notes they are wholly benevolent, even saccharine: "I am immensely fond of all the nurses in their black and white pin-striped dresses, white aprons and hats and black shoes and stockings. Their youth is the chief beauty about them — youth, absolute starched cleanliness and a comforting tidying-up and brow-smoothing air."

The tulips, of course, were real, sent by Helga Huws. Joan, the entomologist's wife in "Bed 1," was "in a plaster cast from toe to bosom" — a circumstance that inspired "In Plaster," composed on the same day as "Tulips."

"In Plaster," too, develops the vase image, but this time the poet writes out of health — on the life side of her inevitable mirror. At first an "old yellow" person is imprisoned in a "new absolutely white" one. Although this white body is enviably pure, still, and without appetite — "one of the real saints" — she is also, in this poem, disconcertingly "dead." Sickly, hungry Old Yellow at first resents but later warms up to her saintly double, who needs to be loved in order to exist at all. The reconstructed-vase image from "The Stones" recurs here in the third stanza, Sylvia now siding emphatically with Old Yellow and — ferocious — life:

> Without me, she wouldn't exist, so of course she was grateful.
> I gave her a soul, I bloomed out of her as a rose
> Blooms out of a vase of not very valuable porcelain.

Cleverly, "In Plaster" offers a jocular variation of the bell-jar game, which the speaker is winning. In Plath's developing mythology, however, the whited sepulcher of the cast, with its seeming security (and purity), is in reality locked in deadly battle with the living woman within it. The poems can be understood to represent the fierce resentment the inner Sylvia — the real one, the poet — felt in the presence of her artificial exterior. The artifice of "ought," the superego she was readying to smash up (along with all those responsible) in *The Bell Jar,* was one manifestation of this outer construct. The other, more deadly, was the invisible shell of the bell jar itself.

From Chalcot Square on March 17, the day before she wrote "Tulips" and "In Plaster," she got off a healthily robust letter to her mother, who was due to arrive in England in three months. Having her stitches out and a big plaster bandage pulled off had been worse than the operation itself, she said, but she was, as ordered, behaving "like a lady," slowly recovering while Ted did all the baby-lifting and laundry. Frieda was teething. Clearly the glow of Sylvia's hospital days was fading. "I must say that the last six months I have felt slapped down each time I lifted my head up and don't know what I'd have done if Ted hadn't been more than saintly and the baby adorable and charming. I write you about this *now it's over* and not in the midst of it." There had been bad times; would they now be better? With the weather "amazing[ly]" warm for March, Sylvia went out every day with Frieda. On March 18 she began again to use Merwin's study. "Tulips" and "In Plaster" heralded the burst of creativity that produced *The Bell Jar*.

For the next seventy days Sylvia worked "fiendishly," seven mornings a week, on her novel, trying to finish at least a draft before the Merwins returned at the end of May. Nowhere — this is not surprising, considering its subject matter — did she mention to her mother that she was writing it; instead she supplied her with reports of (mainly) Ted's doings: three of his children's poems had been printed in the *Times;* Lord David Cecil had written to announce the 1960 Hawthornden Prize for *Lupercal* — a "very prestigeful" gold medal plus £100; Peter Hall of the Royal Shakespeare Company had commissioned Ted to write a full-length play; and the Hugheses were to do a joint broadcast of poetry and talks about their childhoods for the BBC World Service.

On May Day Sylvia headed her letter "GOOD NEWS GOOD NEWS GOOD NEWS!" Alfred Knopf had agreed with Heinemann to bring out *The Colossus* in New York. Although at Marianne Moore's insistence they wanted certain poems cut (among them "Poem for a Birthday"; Sylvia in turn insisted on retaining two sections of that poem, "Flute Notes from a Reedy Pond" and "The Stones"), she reported herself "delighted." A book of forty instead of fifty poems would be "perfect" to buy as a gift at Hathaway House Bookstore in Wellesley, to see reviewed in the *New York Times,* and in general to get her name into print in the States. "It is like having a second book come out — this one, the Ideal," she wrote.

Ted's Hawthornden Prize was awarded early in June. At the ceremony Sylvia met the previous year's Hawthornden winner, the novelist Alan Sillitoe, and his American-educated wife, Ruth Fainlight, also a writer. Sylvia was instantly drawn to her. The day before, Sylvia had recorded a twenty-five-minute radio program of nine of her poems, reading them with another American, Marvin Kane, for the BBC's "Living Poet" series.*

It was at about this time, too, that Sylvia and Ted attended a dinner party given by a Faber author, Sylvester Stein, and his wife, Jenny, at their Primrose Hill home. Its purpose was to introduce the Hugheses to Helder Macedo, a Portuguese poet who had exiled himself during the Salazar regime, and his wife, Suzette. Ted greatly sympathized

---

*The reading, introduced by Sylvia, was broadcast on the Third Programme on July 8.

with Helder's situation as a foreign poet trying to earn a living by writing in England and over the years attempted to help him get published. Sylvia liked them both, quickly categorizing Suzette as her "chic Latin" friend. She barely discussed her writing with Suzette, but there was lively talk of food and many exchanges of recipes between them.

Suzette Macedo recalls an episode from this period. One afternoon Jenny Stein came around to call on Sylvia during her working hours. Sylvia, who had heard that the Steins' child had measles and was fearful lest it be German measles and thus a threat to her new pregnancy, turned Mrs. Stein away with a brusque "We're working" and shut the door. Mrs. Stein, knowing nothing of Sylvia's pregnancy, was mystified and offended. Sylvia never explained or apologized for her abruptness, yet she wondered later, says Suzette, why Mrs. Stein no longer invited Ted and Sylvia to her parties.

◂　◂　◂

In mid-June Mrs. Plath arrived in London, staying, at the Merwins' invitation, at St. George's Terrace while they were again in France. Sylvia, delighted with her new pregnancy, was at first, no doubt, radiant with pride and happiness, eager to show off Frieda and her pretty flat to her mother. As Mrs. Plath realized, Sylvia was anxious, too, to make the best of her mother's offer to babysit while Sylvia and Ted took a two-week vacation in France. They had booked passage to the Continent on June 30, but well before their holiday began, Sylvia and her mother were, it seems, at loggerheads. By letter Aurelia Plath could be adored and depended upon as a pillar of encouragement and approval. In person, she carried with her the very complex of painful associations Sylvia was daily sitting down to exorcise as she wrote *The Bell Jar*.

Dido Merwin reports that her cat-minder Molly Raybould, who stayed at St. George's Terrace in the Merwins' absence — Sylvia referred to her as "the little Australian hairdresser" — made puzzled inquiries about Sylvia. Mrs. Plath, Molly said, soon began returning to the flat at night in tears, ready to pour out her griefs on Molly's sympathetic shoulder. "Two things that particularly struck Molly," writes Dido Merwin, "were Mrs. Plath's reiterated 'Everything I do is *wrong;* I can't seem to do anything right' and 'I just don't know how Ted stands it.' "

Leaving Frieda with her grandmother at Chalcot Square, the Hugheses set off for France in their Morris Traveller on June 30, planning to drive in a leisurely way through the country before spending a week with the Merwins at Lacan de Loubressac (nowadays spelled Lacam) in the Lot in southern France. On the way they visited Berck-Plage on the Pas de Calais coast with its sanatoria for men wounded in the Algerian war. In the hot sun maimed and wounded men limped their way along the beach among tanned and frolicking holidaymakers. Sylvia, separated for the first time from Frieda and still raw-nerved from reliving her past in *The Bell Jar*, may have been jolted back to those days in her Winthrop childhood when her father, his leg amputated, lay dying. A year later, impressions made on Sylvia here would surface in her long poem "Berck-Plage." Yet Ted Hughes recalls that the visit to Berck-Plage in no way disturbed her outward composure at the time.

Dido Merwin's account of the visit to Lacan records what must have been five acutely uncomfortable days. When they had planned the holiday back in London, Sylvia had said she wanted total *far' niente:* only to rest, get a tan on the terrace, and have lovely food. But almost immediately on arrival she fell prey to one of those strange moods that swept her into irrational behavior. What provoked her was the presence of an unexpected guest. Margot Pitt-Rivers, a close friend of the Merwins', lived in the area, in her chateau at Fons. She was a Spaniard, and had been Duchess of Prima de Rivera, wife of the Spanish ambassador in London, when she eloped with the anthropologist Julian Pitt-Rivers some years before. In her forties she was still darkly attractive. "The idea of anyone's taking exception to somebody as unassuming as Margot had never occurred to us," says Dido. Yet from the moment that Sylvia realized that Mrs. Pitt-Rivers "hadn't just dropped in for a cup of tea," she totally ostracized her.

Merwin and Hughes had long wanted to explore together the *causse,* that strange and empty limestone plateau on the edge of which Lacan stands, and they were eager to start the next day. Over dinner on the Hugheses' first night Sylvia squashed the plan by announcing that she intended to do some sketching then and wanted Ted with her.

When Merwin suggested some records, at the end of dinner, Sylvia said she was going to bed, expecting Ted to go with her. He chose to stay and hear the music. About half an hour later, during "I Know That My Redeemer Liveth," there was "fortissimo stomping on the stairs" and Sylvia, wearing a raincoat over her nightdress, made an entrance, then marched to the front door and out into the night. The ground around the house was rocky and unlit, so Ted immediately followed her. About an hour later they returned and went upstairs without a word. Dido comments, "Sylvia had been in the house for only a few hours but the message was quite clear: it wasn't just a question of when she went sketching. She had to have Ted along or else."

Mrs. Pitt-Rivers, more intrigued than offended by the startling rudeness directed at her, offered to leave. The Merwins felt she should stay at least another day, and the next day did in fact go reasonably smoothly. Dido recalls: "While it was still cool, I took [Sylvia] to pick peaches in a neighbour's orchard . . . and then settled her on the terrace, where she dozed off for an hour or so, which enabled Bill and Ted to take a short clandestine stroll. Margot kept well out of the way until it was given out at lunch that I was taking her home first thing in the morning."

All might have gone well from then on, but on the way to Fons "a front wheel came off our antique Ford van, and Margot and I — lucky to be alive — landed upside down in the ditch. We eventually got ourselves a lift back to Fons, from where I SOS'ed Bill, who had to be chauffeured to the rescue by Ted." Sylvia was left alone for some hours, the axis of Ted's and the Merwins' attention having been wrenched elsewhere. In the interim she somehow managed to consume the entire lunch for three that Dido had left behind that morning. "When the three of us finally arrived back at Lacan, rancour was everywhere, and Sylvia wasn't speaking to Ted or Bill or me." At dinner Dido served some goodies from Margot's larder: "As I watched Sylvia grimly downing the Fons *foie gras* . . . there was little doubt that we were in for a reign of, if not terror, then tiresomeness every bit as effective."

Happily the Merwins discovered that Sylvia liked cards, and they taught her their favorite game, *Ascenseur*. "She took an instant fancy to it, playing with verve and finesse." The combination of an excellent dinner and victory at cards every evening "completely transformed her . . . But next morning . . . that unrelenting, unspoken, omnipresent animosity — which had to be experienced to be believed — was the order of the day once again." This daily pattern was repeated; despite whatever was attempted, indoors or out, Sylvia refused to be humored. Even after Ted had bought her an elegant dress in the nearby town, she sulked at having to wait while Dido shopped for groceries afterward. Merwin's and Ted's plans for exploring the *causse* were abandoned, and while Sylvia sunbathed they "threw themselves into heavy clearing operations [in the orchard] within earshot of the terrace"; Dido clattered about in the tiny kitchen preparing "conciliatory" feasts.

"It was Ted who was finally forced to admit that . . . there was nothing for it but to cut their stay short and take Sylvia away," writes Dido. "It was then that I asked him why he never put his foot down, and he told me that it would only make things worse; that 'she couldn't be helped that way.' " After the Hugheses had gone, the Merwins were embarrassed by the extent of their relief: "Apart from when she was sleeping, eating, sunbathing, or playing cards . . . , their stay at Lacan had been one long scene — a kind of macabre marathon for all concerned." Neither of the Merwins ever saw Sylvia again.

With over twenty-five years' hindsight, Dido Merwin reflects: "In those days one wasn't necessarily on the lookout for psychoses just because somebody was 'difficult' . . . Ironically, it was Sylvia's carefully projected All-Aroundness that provided the camouflage. Because she was brilliant, articulate, overtly ambitious, energetic, efficient, organized, enviably resourceful in practical matters, blessed with a hearty appetite and (as she said herself) 'an athletic physique which I possess and admire,' she seemed infinitely stronger than she actually was." But, Dido goes on, "given that we didn't know, what was it that compelled some of us to act as though we *did* know? Why did we — uncharacteristically and in spite of our disparate and highly intransigent selves — put up with Sylvia's carry-on as if we were the paid attendants of some tiresome and demanding invalid who never said 'please' and 'thank you,' let alone 'sorry'?"

Sylvia sent off a blissful letter from Lacan to her mother, dated July 6: "The Merwins' farm is idyllic, with a superb view, plum trees, country milk, butter and eggs, a billion stars overhead, cowbells tinkling all night softly; and Dido is the world's best cook." The letter is admirably expressed, as always, and, as far as it goes, true enough — or nearly true, the Merwins' small cottage being somewhat upgraded in Sylvia's description. One can only guess at the mortified tears, the swirling terrors and angers, her letter must conceal. The only other record left of the vacation is her poem "Stars Over the Dordogne" with its hint of pervading unease.

Some of the furious anguish that possessed Sylvia at Lacan must have sparked off another poem, "The Rival,"* written, like "Stars Over the Dordogne," later in July 1961. It seems likely that the rival addressed was her own evil "other," a totemic figure that subsumed women she feared or disliked. Essentially this rival was a projection of herself. The poem is a malevolent exorcism by a woman who for

---

*The initial three-part version of this poem can be found in the notes to *Collected Poems.*

some reason not explained in the poem lives under perpetual threat.

By the time the Hugheses returned to London, in mid-July, the strange state that possessed Sylvia at Lacan seems to have dissipated. Almost immediately she and Ted drove Mrs. Plath up to Yorkshire, where Edith Hughes had booked her a room at Sutcliffe's, the best hotel in the area. Ancient and small, set in beautiful surroundings about a mile along the hilltop road from The Beacon, the hotel was an ideal center from which to set off every day sightseeing or to visit relatives of the Hugheses'. On this trip Mrs. Plath became friendly with Edith Hughes and Ted's Aunt Hilda, with whom, after her stay, she exchanged the occasional letter for many years. Mrs. Hughes wrote to Olwyn that it had all gone very well and that Sylvia had been particularly pleasant and helpful. Olwyn remembers her mother's telling her later that one afternoon when she was taking a nap the two visiting women had baked a huge American cream cake: despairing of her tiny kitchen, they had cleared her best mahogany sideboard in the sitting room and done the mixing on that.

The following week Sylvia and Ted, again taking advantage of Mrs. Plath's offer to babysit, drove down to Devon to look for houses. With another child expected in January, the Chalcot Square flat was now much too small. The first part of their long-term plan was to find a house they could afford in the country, big enough to live and work in while they were bringing up their family; later they would try to acquire a second base in London. Confining their search to Devon and Cornwall — two of the loveliest counties in England, where house prices were lower than in regions nearer London — they hoped to escape the heavy expenses of city life, to free themselves from the burden of rent, to grow their own vegetables, to find inexpensive home help nearby, and eventually to cut down on the need to earn money through literary busywork. Only then would they be able to devote their full creative energies to their writing. With these ends in mind, they were willing to tolerate the obvious disadvantages: the distance from good libraries, from the friends and the rich mix of congenial and talented people London offered, and from easy access to films, theaters, exhibitions, and the like. When they did move they greatly missed these things; but they wanted the isolation, too, for its own sake, to block off all other ways out except by writing, and to live on their own terms, in their own place.

They looked at eight houses. Most were impossible, but on the Friday morning they were shown around an old thatched rectory, originally a manor house, with which they both fell in love. "Court Green" was set off from a village near Dartmoor in generous grounds mostly planted with apple trees. With nine or ten rooms, a wide expanse of (nettle-covered) lawn at the front, and at the back a stable-garage, cobblestone court, and small ruined cottage, the house was ideal. It adjoined an ancient church with tottering gravestones and a huge yew tree. At the rear boundary a mound marked a prehistoric moated hill fort. Parts of the house dated from the eleventh century, and the owners were anxious to sell to "people who would have a sense of the historic value of the site," as Mrs. Plath told Warren in a long letter written shortly before she left England.

Almost as soon as they saw it Ted and Sylvia decided to buy Court Green. Importantly for them, the village was at that time only the fourth or fifth stop on the direct train line from London. At first they thought they would need a small mortgage, and before Aurelia Plath flew to Boston she offered to take on the mortgage herself at three percent interest — an offer Ted refused. She then arranged to lend them £500. Edith Hughes provided a gift of £500, which, with their $6,000 savings, made up enough to buy the house outright and cover initial expenses. By August 13 Sylvia was writing to her mother that Ted was thinking of giving up the Maugham travel award: the prospect of combining a trip to Europe with moving "to a house which will need a lot of attention . . . just doesn't seem worth 500 pounds, even though we were hoping to save half of it." Ted wrote to the Maugham trustees but was told to keep the money for future travel.

They advertised the Chalcot Square flat, attracting two offers, one from a "chill, busybody man" who wrote out a check on the spot, the other from a young Canadian poet and his wife, David and Assia Wevill. Immediately taking to the young couple, Sylvia and Ted tore up the first man's check and offered the flat to the Wevills.

By a curious coincidence it was around this time that Helder and Suzette Macedo also first met the Wevills. Almost their first conversation concerned the flat that the Wevills were about to take over from Ted and Sylvia. Over the next few months the Macedos and the Wevills became close friends, and both couples visited the Hugheses once they were established in their new house in Devon.

It was in August, too, while the Hugheses were preoccupied with selling the lease of their flat and arranging to move, that Sylvia completed the first draft of *The Bell Jar*. In the margin of her journal for December 12, 1958, after her entry "Why don't I write a novel?" she was now able to add triumphantly in red: "I have! August 22, 1961: The Bell Jar." The summer also brought news that her poem "Insomniac" had won first prize in the Cheltenham Festival Poetry Competition for that year. Alfred Knopf's poetry editor had written, too, confirming that *The Colossus* would be coming out in New York in the spring of 1962.

For all the joy attendant on their move to Devon, Ted and Sylvia left a congenial ambiance behind them in London. Alan Sillitoe and Ruth Fainlight, the Macedos, and the Wevills were among the couples in an overlapping group of friends they would miss and in the next year visit on trips to the city. Sylvia was growing into what promised to be a rich new chapter of her life. Finishing her novel had cracked right through her writing block. Pregnant with a second child and heady with ambition for her future as a novelist, she must have viewed the prospect of living and writing at Court Green as a dream coming true.

▸ II ◂

T H E   S T I G M A
O F   S E L F H O O D
1961-1962

> Elm
> Jealousy
> Stigma (of selfhood)
> Pheasant
> > — Sylvia Plath's notes on a draft
> > of "Elm"

> When dreams come true, nightmares are also realized.
> > — Peter Davison, private letter

ON THE LAST DAY of August 1961, Sylvia Plath Hughes, with her husband and baby daughter, moved into Court Green, the ancient manor-cum-rectory in North Devon where she was to write the poems that made her famous. The years of frustration and barrenness were over, and with *The Bell Jar* finished — James Michie had received a draft by October 1961 — Sylvia had achieved two of her most coveted goals. Yet within her, more urgently than ever, seethed the powerful ferment of her poetic myth, the anxiously observant novelist-wife-mother containing and in successive poems realizing in her art the old fury and despair she only just repressed in her life. Without the distractions of London, the pressure Old Yellow exerted on the plaster saint began to crack through to the surface, making for the intense, menacing yet undefined threat that infuses every line of "Wuthering Heights," "Blackberrying," "Finisterre," and "The Surgeon at 2 A.M." — poems Sylvia wrote within the first month of moving to Devon.

Outwardly all was ideal. Court Green, with its three acres of lawn,

garden, and orchard, was everything the Hugheses had longed for in
London. On arrival Sylvia chose the largest upstairs bedroom for her
study. Its windows, together with the window of their bedroom,
looked over the lawns to the adjacent church and churchyard atop a
high retaining wall (the "wall of old corpses" in "Letter in November"). At the back of the house, visible from the guest room and
beyond the cobbled courtyard, were two or three wych elms shoul-
dering the mound of the prehistoric fort. Ted set himself up in working
quarters under the high-pitched thatch of the attic, over the bathroom
with its hot-water tank. Sylvia's letter to Helga Huws of October 30
describes the house as they found it:

> It is . . . very very ancient . . . with castle-thick walls in the original
> back part and almost 10 rooms, yet very compact and not at all
> rambling, feeling almost small (except when I look at the floor-
> space . . .) We have a U-shape of out-buildings around a cobbled
> courtyard — a big thatched barn, stables (!), and a thatched cottage
> which someday we would like to make into a guest house for moth-
> ers-in-law and such people. But those are all 10-year plans. The
> house is white, with a black trim and this primeval peaked thatch.
> We have just over two acres of land, mostly stinging nettle, but Ted
> is digging up the big vegetable garden and we'll hope to live on
> them — he's already put in strawberries, and we have about 70
> apple trees, eaters and cookers — though sadly the crop this year
> is very poor everywhere and we are almost through ours. And black-
> berries everywhere in season. I have a tiny front lawn carved out
> of the wilderness — a laburnum tree, lilacs and a few rose bushes.
> We adjoin the town church, Anglican, with its own 8 famous bell-
> ringers.

To her mother Sylvia wrote ecstatically that the house was like a
person, responding to love and attention. She delighted in decorating
it with flowers from the unweeded garden, filling nooks and crannies
with her pewter, china, and copper cooking pots. They were using a
"nice, round dining table" lent to them by the Wevills, who had by
now taken over their flat in Chalcot Square. As autumn progressed,
they acquired carpets with money sent by Mrs. Prouty and Sylvia's
(by now hospitalized) Grampy. One of her notable purchases that
winter was a bright red wall-to-wall Wilton carpet for her study to
keep her "forever optimistic."

Hardly were they established when Sylvia's brother, Warren, arrived, staying from the ninth to the fifteenth of September, happy to
cut wood, mow lawns, look after Frieda, and, with Ted, sand an

enormous elm plank that Ted would make into a writing table for his wife. Besides the apples and blackberries, the garden yielded a hill of potatoes someone had forgotten to dig up in the summer and gaudy "peach-colored gladiolas, hot-red and orange and yellow zinnias." In the spring there would be thousands upon thousands of daffodils and narcissi (famous in the neighborhood), then the flowering cherries, lilacs, and six laburnums. It was, as Sylvia declared, a veritable Garden of Eden. Yet it came complete with a serpent. Sylvia herself identified it the following April, jotting hastily on a draft of her poem "Elm": "the stigma of selfhood."

With Warren, Ted and Sylvia spent leisurely days exploring Exeter, Tintagel — "very commercial" — and the stretch of North Devon coastline where "Blackberrying" had its origin. After Warren had flown back to Boston, Helder and Suzette Macedo arrived for a week-end visit. Suzette found the house lovely, even at this early stage, and remembers Sylvia declaring that London had not been good for her; she was "blissfully happy" in Devon, "superstitiously so." Frieda, who showed the Macedos around the house on their arrival, was blossoming.

By September 27 the writing schedule had resumed control. Sylvia wrote to her mother that day:

> Right after breakfast I go up to my study to work at the marvelous 6-foot natural wood table (which you helped finish, Warren) while Ted carpenters or gardens in the back with Frieda along. He gives her lunch and puts her to bed about noon, and I come down and make *our* lunch and by the time I am through picking up the house and doing dishes, Frieda is up and out front with me . . . and Ted is in his study.

Outside the bastion of Court Green, the village provided a considerable array of characters. Sylvia was delighted with her "cleaning woman," Nancy Axworthy, "a robust blond Devon mother in her 40s" married to a local jack-of-all-trades who combined his profession of joiner with various avocations such as church bellringer, assistant head of the fire brigade, and instructor in woodworking in the evenings. Nancy, who had worked for the previous owner, came in two mornings a week (for two shillings and sixpence an hour) to do the floors, the scrubbing and cleaning, and the ironing. Other neighbors were friendly as well as curious. In one of the cottages in the short lane that led to Court Green from the main road, there was "a nice lively retired couple," pubkeepers from London; in another lived "a great booming wife of a dead tea-plantation owner," while round the corner on the main road itself lived "odd deformities — an ancient hunchbacked lady named Elsie, apparently born without parents of either sex, a wildly blind man and so on — but all very nice."

Yet in moving to Devon Sylvia and Ted must have realized they were taking a risk. The ancient house with its crumbling plaster and "billion birds" living in the thatch provided them with all the necessities: water, electricity, and gas, a doctor's surgery nearby, and a small station a mile away at which to catch trains to London — a three- or four-hour journey. At the same time, the village was embedded in deep country, cut off from the culture as well as from the distractions of the city. They would have to assume responsibility for two tiny children, the second due within five months of their moving in, and for the demanding upkeep of a large property. After the first weeks they had redecorated most of the inside of the house with white gloss on the woodwork and soft pink emulsion on the walls; Ted put up extensive shelving for their library-cum-sitting-room and in the playroom and kitchen. Many of the floors, however, had to be treated for deathwatch beetle or, on the ground floor, replaced with cement; and there were all the other practical worries that come with home-owning: solicitors' fees, taxes, and heating bills. The installation of a new washing machine took plumbers several days, since its pipes had to be bored through four feet of ancient stone wall. Sylvia was undaunted, rejoicing in the spaciousness of the house; "none of the old stowing of manuscripts under the carpet when the cooking pots come out," she wrote to Olwyn, adding that "Frieda loves it and trots around pointing to birds and mimicking sheep and dogs" and that Ted looked "years younger, very vigorous and happy."

Several days after her twenty-ninth birthday Sylvia went up to London to spend two nights with the Sillitoes. At the Guinness Prize ceremony in "the fabulous Goldsmiths hall" on October 31 she received £75 for "Insomniac," reading the poem aloud to a distinguished assembly that included Robert Graves, recipient of much grander honors. Richard Murphy remembers sitting with her before she went up to the rostrum. The next day Sylvia typed up a children's book review for the *New Statesman,* met the fiction editor of *Women's Realm,* to which she hoped to sell a story, dropped off £100 worth of manuscripts with a bookseller who was selling "scrap paper" to Indiana University, and, with a birthday check from her mother, treated herself to attending two new plays by Edward Albee. Returning to Devon, "to clear air and my own acres and two darlings," was a relief, she told her mother, complaining of London's soot, "horrid suburbs," and polluted air. Yet writing to thank Ruth Fainlight —

by now a trusted friend — Sylvia admitted that parts of her badly missed city life. She was "spoiling for company" in the country, "wondering when I will ever see the beloved crapulous face of dear London again."

By this time both Hugheses were enjoying considerable professional success. Ted was writing and broadcasting several of his popular school programs for the BBC, and during September and October he recorded two poetry readings for the Third Programme and four short talks for "Woman's Hour." Douglas Cleverdon was producing his play *The Wound,* first broadcast the following February. Over a dozen poems and three stories by Hughes appeared around this time in American and British magazines, and he was taking on more reviews than before — clearly he was anxious to do as much quick-paying work as he could fit in to meet the expenses of the new house. A shilling anthology of new American poetry that Sylvia had edited for *Critical Quarterly* was selling well, and *The New Yorker* renewed her yearly "first reading" contract, having accepted "Tulips" and "Blackberrying" earlier that year. In November *The Observer* published "Mojave Desert" and accepted "The Rival" to appear in January 1962. *Poetry* (Chicago) would be bringing out five of her "exercises" in March ("Stars Over the Dordogne," "Widow," "Face Lift," "Heavy Women," and "Love Letter"). "Wuthering Heights" went to the *New Statesman* (published on March 16, 1962), and "In Plaster" appeared in the *London Magazine* in February, along with Sylvia's response to a questionnaire, later given the title "Context." Considering that Sylvia accomplished all this while the Hugheses were refurbishing their house before and after the birth of a new baby, it is not surprising that the household was run with machinelike efficiency to a timetable that left few hours for relaxation.

In her first months in Devon Sylvia made a determined effort to fit into village life by attending the Anglican church next door. The view of the church from the house was pretty, its three narrow windows lit up on Sunday evenings gleaming through the silhouettes of the trees. On October 22 she attended Evensong, writing afterward to her mother:

A wild blowy night, with gusts of rain. Went to my first Anglican service with the lively retired London couple down the lane. It's a sweet little church, and I found the service so strange . . . I think I will probably go to Evensong off and on and then send Frieda to Sunday School. I'm sure as she starts thinking for herself, she will drift away from the church, but I know how incredibly powerful

the words of that little Christian prayer, "God is my help in every
need," which you taught us has [*sic*] been at odd moments of my
life.

The church, with its set of bells and Hardyesque bellringers, was
attractive as an idea. But by Christmas Sylvia was writing in horror
of a sermon of the rector's that revealed his reactionary politics. Her
one visit to the church's Mothers' Union sparked off the outraged
disparagement of her short story "Mothers," written at about this
time.

A more congenial entry to village society was through her pregnancy. Dr. Webb's clinic was only a few houses down the road from
Court Green. On her first visit, early in September, Sylvia was somewhat overwhelmed by the doctor's "marvelous midwife-nurse," Mrs.
Winifred Davies — "a short, rotundish but not at all fat, capable gray-
haired woman with a wise, moral face . . . [who] would judge, kindly,
but without great mercy," Sylvia wrote later. For once Sylvia's enthusiastic first impression was justified. As the weeks passed, Nurse
Davies became a "pillar," although she *would* make surprise visits
during morning hours reserved for Sylvia's writing. In notes made the
following spring, Sylvia remarked tartly:

> Nurse D.'s visits invariably came when I most intuitively suspected
> them simply because I had been lax about housework to get to my
> study. Nothing Ted could say could stop her — she would forge up
> the stairs, he preceding desperately to warn me, and I would see her
> smiling white head over his shoulder at the study door. I would be
> in my pink fluffy bathrobe (over my layers of maternity clothes, for
> warmth), and she would say "artist's outfit," go into the bedroom,
> find the bed unmade, and I would have hastily thrown a newspaper
> over the pink plastic pot of violently yellow urine I had not bothered
> to empty, on the principle that all housework should wait till after-
> noon.

One morning early in November, Ted dreamed that Sylvia had won
a prize for her story "Johnny Panic." Sylvia went downstairs to find
a letter from the administrator of the Eugene Saxton Grant — unsuccessfully applied for in America — offering her $2,000 in four
installments, to write prose fiction over the year. She was jubilant.
The Bell Jar had been submitted to Heinemann already, and a contract, signed by the publishers on October 21 and offering her £100
advance royalties, had been sent back, signed by the author, on the
thirtieth. Now it appeared that by delaying publication for a year and
cutting the novel up into four sections as she made final small revi-

sions, she was in a position to earn an extra $500 for each quarterly "parcel" she sent to America.

Significantly, Sylvia said nothing to her mother about the nature of this first novel. Sometime between November 1961 and June 1962, Sylvia must have decided to protect herself, in view of the novel's public portrayal of her mother and of a devastating period in her own personal history, by publishing it under a pseudonym, Victoria Lucas. It was a name drawn from Ted's world: "Victoria" after his favorite Yorkshire cousin, Victoria (Vicky) Farrar, and "Lucas" after his friend Lucas Myers.*

On November 20, 1961, Sylvia wrote cozily to her mother to re-assure her about the grant:

> Don't worry about my taking on anything with the Saxton. Just between the two of us (and don't tell anyone) I figured nothing was so sure to stop my writing as a grant to do a specific project that had to be turned in at the end with quarterly reports — so I finished *a batch of stuff* this last year, tied it up in four parcels and have it ready to report on bit by bit as required. Thus I don't need to write a word if I don't feel like it. [My italics.]

Aurelia Plath knew nothing of the contents of this "stuff" until after Sylvia's death.

"But winter is the real test," Sylvia had written to Olwyn that autumn; "already it is bone cold." As the days grew shorter, she again began to suffer from her cyclical winter depression, triggered this time by two articles she had read in an American periodical, *The Nation*. One had to do with "the terrifying marriage of big business and the military in America," the other with a "repulsive shelter craze" which in the United States had fallen into the hands of unscrupulous ad-vertisers. Both she and her husband were shocked by the jingoistic propaganda coming out of America as Kennedy and Khrushchev tested each other's nerves over Berlin while the armed forces prepared for " 'inevitable' war." "I began to wonder," Sylvia wrote to Mrs. Plath on December 7, "if there was any point in trying to bring up children in such a mad, self-destructive world." It was at about this time that a questionnaire arrived from the *London Magazine* having to do with the moral responsibilities of the writer in a political context. Sylvia coolly assessed her own contribution to world peace by defining

---

*The dedication to her Devon friends the Comptons must have come later, in summer 1962, and may have been dictated in part by her wish not to reveal her authorship of the book to her London circle — though toward the end of her life she abandoned this discretion and spoke of the novel to several London friends.

her poetry as deflective but not escapist: "For me, the real issues of our time are the issues of every time — the hurt and wonder of loving; making in all its forms — children, loaves of bread, paintings, buildings; and the conservation of life of all people in all places, the jeopardizing of which no abstract doubletalk of 'peace' or 'implacable foes' can excuse."

As a defense of art and its meaning in contemporary society, Sylvia's concise manifesto is admirable and moving. But cling as she would to love and the conservation of life, Sylvia's first Devon poems were drenched in death. Even "Blackberrying," at first reading a superb evocation of a windy, clifftop cove, on closer inspection invokes the poet's reluctant hold on life, and how a horror of meaninglessness waits for her around the corner. In a floodlit, surreal landscape, the "I" of the poem proceeds down a "hooked" alley where huge blackberries, "dumb as eyes," squander menstrual juices as they're picked in a "blood sisterhood" she "had not asked for." The berries present an exquisite vision of corruption, one bush "so ripe it is a bush of flies, / Hanging their bluegreen bellies and their wing panes in a Chinese screen." Choughs wheel blackly overhead, "protesting, protesting." The lane's last "hook" reveals nothing but the cliff face,

> . . . and the face is orange rock
> That looks out on nothing, nothing but a great space
> Of white and pewter lights, and a din like silversmiths
> Beating and beating at an intractable metal.

More sinister still is the lordly figure of "The Surgeon at 2 A.M.," defined in "Context" as a poem about "the night thoughts of a tired surgeon." Maybe so, but for this surgeon the hospital ward is a ghastly garden of bodies through which he strolls like God. Tubers and fruits ooze their "jammy substances,"

> A mat of roots. My assistants hook them back.
> Stenches and colors assail me.
> This is the lung-tree.
> These orchids are splendid. They spot and coil like snakes.
> The heart is a red-bell-bloom, in distress.

In the next stanza, blood, "a sunset," is piped beneath the "pale marble" flesh of the "statue" awaiting healing. Museum and hospital imagery fuse. Plastic body parts replace dead tissues swimming in vinegar like "pathological salami." The surgeon is left with teeth and gallstones "To rattle in a bottle and take home"; amputated parts are "entombed in an icebox." When, at the end, the surgeon strides off under "red night lights . . . flat moons . . . dull with blood" (almost identical phrases appear in *Three Women*), he exits in triumph, a hero, a true savior:

> I am the sun, in my white coat,
> Gray faces, shuttered by drugs, follow me like flowers.

At best, these poems, written when Sylvia was burgeoning with life, take place in her world-hospital. To her they must have pointed to health, to whatever lay on the other side of nightmare. Written from the depths again, as at Yaddo, Sylvia's poems began to fill with her unique imagery. She was closing in on her mind's light as she had not before, and her grasp of this unearthly illumination was by now masterly, her armory of poetic techniques impressive, the voice completely her own — her mature voice. The exhilaration of "really writing," as she was to tell A. Alvarez the following spring, was carrying her into a new plane of self-absorption.

The most outstanding of the poems Sylvia wrote in September and October 1961 is "The Moon and the Yew Tree." Speaking of it on the radio in July 1962, Sylvia remarked that the yew tree had taken the poem over completely, as with "astounding egotism" it proceeded to "manage and order the whole affair." But what *was* this yew tree in its churchyard full of graves in the light of a full "mother moon" if not the Man in Black, the dominant dead figure of her psychic landscape? The light of the mind holding Sylvia in thrall was the "cold and planetary" underworld of her fable, from which the moon, with its "O-gape of complete despair," would never set her free. Ted Hughes had set her the subject as an exercise after they observed the full moon setting over the yew in the churchyard early one morning. By midday she had shown him the result. He later wrote of the poem: "It depressed me greatly. It's my suspicion that no poem can be a poem that is not a statement from the powers that control our life, the ultimate suffering and decision in us . . . And I had no doubt this was a poem, and perhaps a great poem. She insisted that it was an exercise on a theme." Inevitably, the churchyard with its father-yew and mother-moon had become yet another reenactment of Sylvia's imprisoning drama.

◀   ◀   ◀

After a spate of poems in October, including the accomplished and rather less austere "Last Words" and "Mirror," Sylvia succumbed to "cowlike" pregnancy and wrote little. Christmas arrived amid household "fixings" and preparations for the new baby. The cold was bitter — it was the coldest winter for many years — but Sylvia splurged on a red patterned carpet and red corduroy curtains that made the sitting room look, as she told her mother, "like the inside of a Valentine." Four "Pifco" electric heaters maintained indoor temperatures at about 50 degrees during the day; in the evenings a wood fire crackled in the grate. It was the first Christmas Sylvia and Ted had spent in their own home without parents, and Sylvia, eight and a half months pregnant, wrote to her mother of "keeping all *our* old traditions alive." She baked from German recipes and decorated the sitting room with red candles and fifty or so Christmas cards. A huge box of presents arrived from Wellesley (together with longed-for copies of the *Ladies' Home Journal* for Sylvia's "lazy," "soppy" moods); they opened it with Frieda under their "fat little tree with its silver birds and tinsel and spice-cake hearts." There were Yorkshire presents, too, among them a wooden garden slide for Frieda from Aunt Hilda. To her mother Sylvia wrote, "Our Christmas was the happiest and fullest I have ever known."

The new baby, due on January 12, 1962, delayed his arrival until the seventeenth, when, at five minutes to midnight, Nicholas Farrar Hughes made his entry into a frozen world after hours of "niggly contractions." All that day Sylvia kept herself busy cooking meals for Ted and Frieda to eat while she was recovering. At eight-thirty the midwife arrived with a cylinder of gas and air, but this time the birth was difficult; for a long time Sylvia's membranes failed to break. Then, as she later wrote to her mother, just as the doctor was on his way to meet the emergency, "this great bluish, glistening boy shot out onto the bed in a tidal wave of water that drenched all four of us to the skin, howling lustily. It was an amazing sight. I immediately sat up and felt wonderful — no tears, nothing."

Nicholas was larger and heavier than Frieda at birth — nine pounds eleven ounces to her seven pounds four ounces. For the birth and for some time afterward Sylvia was temporarily in the guest room, "ideal" for resting, with a view to the back over the wych elms and the ancient mound. "Beautiful clear dawn," she wrote to her mother the day after giving birth; "a full moon tonight in our huge elm." Neighbors called in, curious, kindly, bearing gifts, while the "wonderful" midwife, who came every day, showed Frieda how to hold the diaper pins and help wrap up the baby. Sylvia adored Nicholas from the day his skull-plates shaped up after his long fight to be born. "Very much a Hughes: oddly like photographs of Ted's brother Gerald, dark, quiet, smiley."

Toward the end of January, Sylvia came down with a severe bout of milk fever, which set her back and left all housework and minding of Frieda to Ted. He was being a "saint," but the strain of coping with two tiny children was beginning to tell on them both as January became an even wetter February and eventually the coldest March on record for seventy years.

Before Christmas Sylvia had hit on an idea that she thought might see her back into writing after Nicholas's birth. The village was fascinating, she told Mrs. Plath, "a solid body of inter-related locals . . . then all these odd peripheral people — Londoners, ex-Cockneys, Irish. I look forward to getting to know them slowly." One of the Irish referred to was Marjorie, the wife of the Devonian bank manager whose daughter of fifteen was at a private girls' school in Oxford. The "ex-Cockneys," Percy and Rose, were near neighbors in the lane. Along with getting to know them Sylvia also intended to write about them. By March 4, when she told her mother that she was working "on something amusing which I hope turns into a book (novel), but may be just happy piddling," she was probably using her two or so hours in her study every morning to write working notes on the village and villagers. The notes, separate from her bound journal, survive. She wrote on loose sheets paperclipped into sections, adding pages as she had more to report.

Besides Percy and Rose and the "Smiths," a number of characters offered themselves for inspection: the crippled humpback in a high black boot who kept a stuffed fox in her parlor; blind Mr. "Milford" who lived with his elderly wife in a dark house on the corner: "I could not look into his white eyes"; old, crabbed, half-crazed Mr. "Willis," said to have a piano for sale. Sylvia went with Ted to look at the (hopeless) piano and spy on his "scabrous" kitchen and the placards advertising his grievances in his front windows. So, also, Major and Mrs. "Crump" on the Eggesford Road, Charlie Pollard the beeman (a significant figure), and Nurse Winifred Davies were stored away to be used by Sylvia in future stories and novels, or for training in accurate observation. It may be, too, that this secret writing up of her neighbors gave the somewhat restricted relationships available in Devon a piquancy and interest they otherwise lacked. In her notes she castigates herself frequently for missing some detail of dress or furnishing ("must catalog rugs, upholstery, next time"). It is not surprising that these prose jottings, though vivid, are weighed down by heavy precision. They really leap to life only when Sylvia's own responses become engaged, as in the account of the "Smiths" and

Sylvia's increasing jealousy of their teenage daughter, and in the extended description of Percy's death.* In such passages the writing resembles all Sylvia's successful prose: it says more about Sylvia than about the people she seeks to portray.

It seems that Sylvia never questioned her right to observe and judge her acquaintances; for a writer, she believed, everything was grist. If she became an object of observation herself, of course, she took offense. Even "tall, imposing white-haired" Mrs. Hamilton ("Mrs. Plum" of the *Journals*), with her yappy dachshund, Pixie, and immaculate house, was expected to keep to the invisible rules of Sylvia's regime. One morning late in February Mrs. Hamilton "materialized" outside Sylvia's study. Sylvia recorded feeling "stunned," with a sense of "surprise invasion":

> This is my one symbolic sanctum . . . I asked her in. Ted got a chair, & I & she both realized the awkwardness of it. She had come to say good-bye & see baby before her 2 weeks in Beirut, Rome, etc. I took her to see Nicholas, not before her eyes had taken in the study in such detail as offered . . . The sense that Mrs. P. wanted to see how we lived in the back rooms. She looked at my long unbraided hair as if to take it in, drink the last inch, and make a judgment. I very upset, angry. As if we could be observed, examined at any moment simply because we were too shy or polite to say Nay, or She's working, I'll get her down. Or Please wait here. My anger at Ted for being a mat, not at Mrs. P., really.

In the early spring months one of Sylvia's main achievements was her verse play, *Three Women*. Douglas Cleverdon, who had produced Ted Hughes's *The Wound,* would direct it. *Three Women* is in one sense a recapitulation of what had gone before. All three voices, like the voices of very nearly disembodied wombs, speak for stages in Sylvia's initiation into motherhood, which for her was tantamount to being reborn herself. The play is set in a hospital: that setting recreated her imaginative world and enabled her to group the three voices dramatically. As she told her mother in June, she was initially inspired by an Ingmar Bergman film, though Bergman's influence would seem to be secondary, a matter of tone and presentation.

The play tells of three archetypal "bornings" — or, in the case of Second Voice, of a failure to give birth. All Sylvia's experience of pregnancy, fear of pregnancy (as on Cape Cod in 1957), and mis-

---

*These two pieces can be found in the U.S. edition of *Johnny Panic and the Bible of Dreams;* the notes about other villagers — "Mrs. Plum," the "Milfords," Nancy Axworthy, Mr. "Willis," the "Crumps," Nurse Davies — are included in the *Journals.*

carriage is contained within it, and each voice is recognizably hers. First Voice is that of a fulfilled mother who, "slow as the world" and "very patient," gives birth to the boy child she wants, this "ovulatory triumph" — as Peter Redgrove would say — confirming her creative mission. She returns with her baby to a house very like Court Green in Devon.

Second Voice, also recognizably Plath's, has been heard before, chiefly in "Parliament Hill Fields" and "Barren Woman": deathliness, miscarriage, self-accusation, terrible failure. This voice speaks of blood and loss, menstrual imagery coming into play (as so often in Plath) to emphasize a horror of unproductive womanhood. The unsuccessful mother is bled "flat" as the men she works for. The setting is obviously London:

> I watched the men walk about me in the office. They were so
>   flat!
> There was something about them like cardboard, and now I had
>   caught it,
> That flat, flat, flatness from which ideas, destructions,
> Bulldozers, guillotines, white chambers of shrieks proceed,
> Endlessly proceed — and the cold angels, the abstractions.

Second Voice speaks with the voice of "Magi," mistrusting ideas (all male) and political ideologies of war and destruction. So Second Voice is found wanting, becoming the harbinger of the death Sylvia never escaped:

> This is a disease I carry home, this is a death.
> Again, this is a death. Is it the air,
> The particles of destruction I suck up? Am I a pulse
> That wanes and wanes, facing the cold angel?
> Is this my lover then? This death, this death?
> As a child I loved a lichen-bitten name.
> Is this the one sin then, this old dead love of death?

Although Second Voice is clearly Sylvia-Electra, the beekeeper's incestuous daughter of her Boston period, significantly *Three Women* concludes with her resurrection. An instance of revealing tenderness, the final stanza of this poetic drama suggests a healing through domestic love, as green — for Sylvia usually a poisonous color — becomes emblematic of resurrection:

> I find myself again. I am no shadow
> Though there is a shadow starting from my feet. I am a wife.

> The city waits and aches. The little grasses
> Crack through stone, and they are green with life.

There remains Third Voice, that of Sylvia's neurotic student self, dreading to meet its double in water or mirrors. Third Voice begins by referring to herself as a reflection in a setting that is clearly Cambridge:

> I remember the minute when I knew for sure.
> The willows were chilling,
> The face in the pool was beautiful, but not mine —
> It had a consequential look, like everything else,
> And all I could see was dangers . . .

Third Voice gives birth to a daughter she is unready to bear, leaving her behind in the hospital for adoption after a murderous, deathlike ordeal. For her, the delivery room is "a place of shrieks" where the lights are "flat red moons . . . dull with blood," as previously in "The Surgeon at 2 A.M." Once born, the tiny but malicious girl claims her mother with "hooks"; her little crying face is "carved in wood" (as in "Event"); her cries scratch at sleep "like arrows." It is impossible not to find in this wild rejection something of what Sylvia — like many new mothers — may well have experienced in relation to her newly born babies. *Three Women* developed from personal sources, but it makes an advance on earlier mysteries in Sylvia's work, rising above private iconography to become universal. It is probably the first great poem of childbirth in the language.

◀ ◀ ◀

The winter clung grimly to Devon through March and most of April. Letters home rather desperately urged Aurelia to visit in the summer, though Warren was to be married early in June, after which money would be in short supply for travel. Sylvia's wishes, however, prevailed. The children would be baptized on Sunday, March 25, she wrote, despite her scorn of the rector. She felt she had been "reborn with Frieda . . . as if my real, rich, happy life only started just about then." On March 12 she claimed to be writing chiefly prose — "much easier on me; the concentration spreads out over a large area and doesn't stand or fall on one day's work, like a poem." By March 27, when she must have nearly finished *Three Women*, she was still suffering from the "March megrims." A letter to Helga Huws of about this time complains of feeling cheated of all her summers since coming to England: "And now we are chafing at rain and sleet and a fixed east wind which slices malevolently all round our ancient back door straight through the house." She was morbid with chilblains, demoralized "not so much by the stingy itchy sores themselves but by the idea the cold had secretly got at me when I thought I was winning out."

In April builders arrived to tear up the rough wooden floors in the playroom and hall and lay down a cement foundation for linoleum tiles. Sylvia was still looking for a secondhand piano so that she could play and sing to Frieda, as her mother had to her. Clearly, however much she may subconsciously have rejected her upbringing, she was modeling herself on the ideal as well as the real Aurelia, a creative, caring mother in a chain that had to continue into the future.

While the Hugheses were energetically making a home of Court Green, it happened that death was near at hand in the cottage next to them in the lane. In February, shortly after Nick's birth, Percy was taken to the hospital with "something on the lung." After several weeks of tests — during which Ted, to Sylvia's annoyance, was perforce chauffeur for Rose's hospital visits — he was operated upon for cancer, returning in March, very ill. It was Percy, in his blue peajacket, whom Sylvia lyrically described in the lovely "Among the Narcissi," though throughout the spring the old man's passage to death was anything but lovely. On April 17, two days before Sylvia finished the final draft of "Elm," Percy suffered a monumental series of strokes. Horrified, if fascinated, Sylvia recorded with minute precision each stage of his deterioration:

A terrible thumping on our door about two o'clock. Ted and Frieda and I were eating lunch in the kitchen. Do you suppose that's the mail? I asked, thinking Ted might have won some fabulous prize. My words were cut short by Rose's hysterical voice: "Ted, Ted, come quick, I think Percy's had a stroke." We flung the door open, and there was Rose B, wild-eyed, clutching her open blouse, which showed her slip, and gabbling. "I've called the doctor," she cried, turning to rush back to her cottage, Ted after her. I thought I would stay and wait, and then something in me said, no, you must see this, you have never seen a stroke or a dead person. So I went. Percy was in his chair in front of the television set, twitching in a fearsome way, utterly gone off, mumbling over what I thought must be his false teeth, his eyes twitching askew, and shaking as if pierced by weak electric shocks. Rose clutched Ted. I stared from the doorway. The doctor's car drew immediately up by the hedge at the bottom of the lane. He came very slowly and ceremoniously, head seriously lowered, to the door. Ready to meet death, I suppose. He said thank

you, and we melted back to the house. I have been waiting for this,
I said. And Ted said he had, too. I was seized by dry retching at
the thought of that horrible mumbling over false teeth. A disgust.
Ted and I hugged each other. Frieda looked on peacefully from her
lunch, her big blue eyes untroubled and clear.

With its persistent reminders of Otto Plath's slow death, Percy's
dying, so soon after Sylvia had given birth to Nicholas, must have
affected the inexorable, seemingly subconscious evolution of her poetry. Since there are no journals to take the reader step by step, as at
Yaddo, over the grounds of her development, we must rely upon the
work itself. The only firsthand witness to what was happening to
Sylvia that spring is Ted Hughes, who with brilliant hindsight has
written of the curiously independent process of a gestation he experienced at second hand:

> After *Three Women* (which has to be heard, as naïve speech, rather
> than read as a literary artifact) quite suddenly the ghost of her father
> reappears, for the first time in two and a half years, and meets a
> daunting, point-blank, demythologized assessment. This is followed
> by the most precise description she ever gave of The Other — the
> deathly woman at the heart of everything she now closed in on.
> After this, her poems arrived at a marvelous brief poise. Three of
> them together, titled "Crossing the Water," "Among the Narcissi,"
> and "Pheasant," all written within three or four days of one another
> in early April 1962, are unique in her work. And maybe it was this
> achievement, inwardly, this cool, light, very beautiful moment of
> mastery, that enabled her to take the next step.

Inexorably Sylvia's poetic world was finding its shape. In October
"Blackberrying" had revealed that world's inscape: a mood of dread
and meaninglessness. Now the two April poems to which Hughes
refers — "Little Fugue," with its "point-blank, demythologized assessment" of her father, and "An Appearance," evoking the female
"Other" — give us her chief dramatis personae, those looming archetypal figures that, in these late poems, become the all-powerful
King and Queen of Plath's poetic kingdom. ("Berck-Plage" would
later chart their territory — of sea, hospital, and death.)

The two figures had been glimpsed six months earlier in "The Moon
and the Yew Tree," where the phallic yew with its "Gothic shape"
represents her father. "Little Fugue" begins: "The yew's black fingers
wag; / Cold clouds go over." The vacuous white clouds bring to mind
the eyes of a blind pianist Sylvia had met on the boat to Britain who,
though sightless, could hear deaf Beethoven. The somber yew and the

soaring music of the great German become one: "I envy the big noises, / The yew hedge of the Grosse Fuge." And the combination is identified:

> Such a dark funnel, my father!
> I see your voice
> Black and leafy, as in my childhood,
>
> A yew hedge of orders,
> Gothic and barbarous, pure German.
> Dead men cry from it.

Then she protests (denying responsibility for the sexual element of the clear phallic symbols in the poem): "I am guilty of nothing." In an upsurge of nostalgia she reiterates:

> I was seven, I knew nothing.
> The world occurred.
> You had one leg, and a Prussian mind.

Her father comes into clearer focus:

> I remember a blue eye,
> A briefcase of tangerines.
> This was a man, then!
> Death opened, like a black tree, blackly.

Through a vacuous cloud the yew tree and the soaring music have yielded an apparition undeniable as Hamlet's father's ghost. No longer the mythic Neptune of "Full Fathom Five" or a crumbling stone Colossus, Otto Plath comes back to life, is seen and heard. And the draining effect — the bell-jar effect — of this mighty presence within her is recognized. The cloud is the one she lives in, alienated and unreal:

> I survive the while,
> Arranging my morning.
> These are my fingers, this my baby.
> The clouds are a marriage dress, of that pallor.

"An Appearance" likewise confronts the deathly mother-muse, that part of her psyche which drove Sylvia relentlessly to produce perfection to win chill love. The Other is seen here sardonically as a series of Dali-like machines, efficient and senseless: "The smile of iceboxes," "the steel needle that flies so blindingly," "A Swiss watch, jeweled in the hinges." The poem ends:

O heart, such disorganization!
The stars are flashing like terrible numerals.
ABC, her eyelids say.

Both poems draw substance from what were then daily concerns. Ted Hughes has spoken of Sylvia's growing passion around this time for Beethoven's late quartets, particularly the Grosse Fuge. "The red material" on the sewing machine in "An Appearance" is that of the curtains she has just made.

Hughes says that Sylvia began to write about the giant wych elm on the mound beyond their back courtyard soon after finishing "Pheasant," in which, at the end, the bird "Settles in the elm, and is easy." Sylvia took up the word "easy" and began a variation; the elm was *not* easy.

> She is not easy, she is not peaceful;
> She pulses like a heart on my hill.
> The moon snags in her intricate nervous system.
> I am excited, seeing it there.
>
> The night is a blue pool; she is very still.
> At the center she is still, very still with wisdom.
> The moon is let go, like a dead thing.
> Now she herself is darkening
>
> Into a dark world I cannot see at all.

This first attempt at "Elm" was almost immediately laid aside. Twenty-one draft sheets followed this puzzling inception. In the poem, originally titled "The Elm Speaks," wych elm becomes witch elm, a frightening mother-double of the poet, who offers death as the only possible love substitute. Between the taproot of the tree and the murderous face of the moon, the poet, "incapable of more knowledge," is forced into a terrible acknowledgment of "faults" — suddenly a new word in Sylvia's poetic lexicon. The poem suggests them as somehow built into her nature, bent like a crooked tree by traumatic childhood events: "These are the isolate, slow faults / That kill, that kill, that kill."

Throughout their writing partnership, husband and wife explored a common theme in their poetry: both were interested in anthropology, primitive myth, and religion. But Ted Hughes's work turned outward to the natural world beyond the self as Sylvia Plath's never could. Her entire development as a writer had consisted of steps, in a halting progress that often made it difficult for her to live, toward the revelation of the elusive vision at the core of her being. As Hughes has written: "One can compare what was really going on in her to a process of alchemy. Her apprentice writings were like impurities thrown off from the various stages of the inner transformation, by-products of the internal work." That quite separate entity in her, a true daemon, an independent, energized center of which the moon was the totem and which had gathered into itself all the pain of her early life, was emerging at last. It provided all the illuminations of the poetry. At its heart was impending death, sometimes an image of rebirth through death.

Sylvia had begun to produce a scattering, later to become a host, of her extraordinary Ariel poems. The voice of these new poems, the unique Ariel voice, is enraged and terribly distressed:

> I have suffered the atrocity of sunsets.
> Scorched to the root
> My red filaments burn and stand, a hand of wires.
>
> Now I break up in pieces that fly about like clubs.

As the peculiar nature of her gift took over at last, it inevitably made itself oppressively felt from time to time in her moods; her very essence was imbued with it. For someone isolated in close proximity with her in a country village, the effect could not be other than profoundly disturbing. Ted Hughes must have begun to feel himself trapped under the same doomed bell jar.

◄　◄　◄

Throughout April and May, as if her poems were an irrelevance, Sylvia continued to type out her efficiently organized notes, remarking sourly on Rose's greediness for free daffodils and on her own strong disinclination to visit the cottage "because Percy makes me sick." *Letters Home* during April and May 1962 reports several sets of visitors — too many for Sylvia. A letter of April 16, written while awaiting Ted's return from a day trip to London, complains of a young American and his wife who had come to record an interview with Sylvia on why Americans stay in England. They brought with them "an acquaintance with two of the most ghastly children I've ever seen," she adds, preening herself on her own "firm, loving discipline." Ted, meanwhile, had been recording a BBC program "and seeing Leonard Baskin's show of engravings, for which he has been asked to write the foreword." For his return she had "a nice big Irish stew ready." His broadcasts involved him in day trips of nine or ten hours on the train, leaving Devon at dawn and returning very late, for Sylvia never liked to be alone at night.

Easter weekend, April 21–22, brought summer and a hot sun, together with a short visit from Ted's Aunt Hilda and cousin Vicky from Yorkshire. On April 25 Sylvia expressed surprise to her mother that they had not brought Ted's parents with them: "Evidently the long winter, arthritis, and the prospect of the day's trip put Edith off. I am so glad you aren't a stay-at-home like that!"*

Hilda and Vicky pitched in and helped with the babies and house-work, so they were welcome guests. The day after they left, however, Sylvia "made the mistake of letting a young Swedish journalist [Siv Arb] invite herself" to interview Ted. Although this attractive lady took photographs of Sylvia and her children sitting among the daf-fodils, her visit was hotly resented. "I had found out the time of the last train back to London that day so we would not be stuck with her," Sylvia wrote, mentioning that the bank manager and his wife had called in the nick of time to save Ted and herself from the jour-nalist's unwelcome company. But the "Smiths" themselves were by then "becoming impossible, pushing their very silly snobby 16 year old daughter on us."

Nicola "Smith" remembers why her parents encouraged her to visit Sylvia and Ted. To them, the Hugheses were "intellectuals" who might encourage Nicola to work harder toward a university place. On April 19 Ted had called in for tea with the "Smiths" and had (clearly in deference to their hints) undertaken to explain to Nicola what he thought important about poetry. Nicola, at the time mainly interested in boys and fashions, listened, rapt and flattered, but unable to follow because "it was all above my head." She strolled back to Court Green with him afterward, and as they stood talking outside the house the door opened. There was Sylvia, holding Nick in her arms: "Oh Nicola, are you seeing Ted home?" Her voice was steely. Nicola, who saw Sylvia as a mature and authoritarian figure, fled, chastened and amazed. She was mortified at the time and yet, she says, also euphoric: if Sylvia saw her as a threat, she must also see her as adult and attractive! Sylvia's more detailed account of the incident is recorded in her notes. Ted and Nicola were "standing at opposite sides of the path under the bare laburnum like kids back from the date, she posed & coy." Nicola told her she was returning some records her father had borrowed and asked if she could come over later in the week to listen to Sylvia's German Linguaphone rec-

---

*The unfeeling aside has been cut from the published letter.

ords. "I've a better idea," said Sylvia, and, having gone back into the house for the records, thrust them at her smartly. "This way you can study them to your heart's content." Sylvia, clearly overreacting to the situation, added in her notes: "For some time I seriously considered smashing our old & ridiculous box Victrola with an ax."

The expurgated versions in *Letters Home* hardly suggest the injured petulance that laces Sylvia's letters of that spring. An entry Olwyn remembers from Sylvia's lost journal strikes a poignant note: "We answer the door together. They step over me as though I were a mat, and walk straight into [Ted's] heart."

This was not the case with people Sylvia knew well and liked. Writers, relatives, and happily married couples whose company she craved in her rural isolation were welcomed. When the Sillitoes visited with their month-old son, David, in the first week of May, Sylvia wrote enthusiastically to her mother of their being "marvelous guests — Ruth helps cook, Alan washes up; they take walks on their own, and our life proceeds as usual." Writing to Ruth later, enclosing a dedicatory copy of "Elm," Sylvia exclaimed almost passionately, "It was heavenly having you and Alan and David here — like a vacation for me."

Sometime late in the spring of 1962 a youngish couple with three small children drove from their primitive cottage twenty-five miles away in North Devon to have tea with the Hugheses at Court Green. David Compton, tall and ascetic, was a struggling novelist and playwright. His wife, Elizabeth, blond, statuesque, and in her own way as full of glowing enthusiasms as Sylvia, had written to offer accommodation to Ted and Sylvia after listening to their radio program "Poets in Partnership" in February 1961. On the program the pair had jokingly complained of composing with their writing pads propped against the baby's playpen; they were longing for a place, they said, where they could shout without hearing each other from opposite ends of the house. Amused or intrigued by Mrs. Compton's invitation, Sylvia had kept her letter, and sometime that spring she invited them to visit.

Like Marcia Brown at Smith, Elizabeth Compton (later Sigmund) was touched by Sylvia, overwhelmed by her energy and sense of purpose. Throughout their friendship, which, though based on about a dozen meetings in all, was intense, Sylvia chose to regard Elizabeth Compton as an alter ego or Earth Mother, fulfilling her perennial need for a double. Mrs. Compton's first impression of the "tall, slim, vividly alive young woman, with waist-length brown hair," in a long skirt and dark stockings, brings Sylvia memorably to life:

We sat and had tea in the playroom on deckchairs near a long trestle table, which Sylvia had painted white and decorated with little, enamelled flowers. The room had a black-and-white tiled floor, like a Flemish painting, and looked out onto a lawn with a laburnum tree, and beyond lay the orchard and the village church and its graveyard . . . There was a piano in the room, which Sylvia admitted to "trying to play, but I have no ear. . . ."

Sylvia's approach to me was all questions — children, home interests, and politics. When I admitted to being a member of the Liberal Party, she jumped up and almost shouted, "Thank God, a committed woman!" — which made me smile as it wasn't totally true, but pleasing . . .

Baby Nick was asleep in his pram under the laburnum tree, and Sylvia kept running out to see if he was warm and sleeping well. She told me of the vegetables she was growing and the plans they had for the house . . . All plans, all life.*

Elizabeth noted Ted and Sylvia's "unassailable closeness, a 'keep out sign' " that bound them almost wordlessly together and kept others at a distance. Yet they valued their friendship with the Comptons; in July, on Elizabeth's thirty-fourth birthday, Sylvia and Ted arrived in the evening at the Comptons' cottage bearing a bottle of wine and a "glorious iced cake," baked by Sylvia, with thirty-five candles on it — "One for you to grow on," Sylvia explained.

◂　　◂　　◂

David and Assia Wevill, the couple who had taken over the Hugheses' London flat, arrived on Friday, May 18, for the weekend. After dinner the four of them, the three poets and Assia, sat talking around the table. They talked of Lowell (Ted and David later listened to a recording of his "Quaker Graveyard at Nantucket"), Sexton, Roethke, and people they knew in London and elsewhere. Sylvia went to bed early, and Assia later told Suzette Macedo that Sylvia called down to Ted to come up too, but he said he would be up later and returned to their guests. David, however, found the weekend "cordial, exploratory, gracious. We all seemed to be getting to know one another. Sylvia could be good company — intelligent, witty, interested, good in conversation. How much of an *effort* this cost her I don't know,

---

*Mrs. Sigmund must misremember the occasion of her first visit to Court Green, which she gives as February. The playroom she describes did not then have tiled linoleum, nor was the furniture until April enameled with Sylvia's heart-and-flowers designs. The piano came later still.

and I never knew her well, or over a long time. From time to time one sensed something like terror — a look in her face — breaking through ordinary conversation, as though she were looking inward."

On Saturday morning David and Ted, taking Frieda with them, drove up onto the moor while Assia helped Sylvia weed onions in the vegetable garden. There — as she also did in the evening conversations — Assia spoke of her eventful life, which could not have failed to stir Sylvia's imagination. She had experienced at first hand that European nightmare in which Sylvia could participate only vicariously. After her early years in Germany, Assia had been forced to flee first Germany and then Italy. Her part-Jewish family spent World War II in Palestine and finally settled in Canada. "Brave, resourceful, warm, with many shadows," as David Wevill describes her, Assia, like many other landless, uprooted refugees, had reconstructed her life from a troubled past.

She spoke to Sylvia of her two previous marriages and of the beginnings of her romance with David, on board ship crossing from Canada to England in 1956. At that time Assia was married to her second husband and David was about to enter his final year at Cambridge University. They fell in love and saw much of each other during the next two years. In October 1958 David left for Burma for a two-year teaching stint at the University of Mandalay, and Assia, ending her marriage, joined him in 1959. They married there before returning to London in the summer of 1960. Some remark of Assia's, which it is possible Sylvia misconstrued, suggested to Sylvia that Assia's feelings for David had cooled somewhat since the early days of their relationship.

Assia offered to make a potato salad for Sunday lunch and was peeling potatoes in the kitchen at the back of the house when Sylvia, in the front room with David, heard Ted come in by the back door. She went into the corridor, slipped off her shoes, and went silently to the kitchen. She found Ted and Assia chatting amiably, though it was clear she expected something more compromising.

By Sunday afternoon Sylvia's mood had changed. David interpreted this as Sylvia's inability to sustain too much sociability. After lunch Sylvia silently drove them to the station, and the Wevills departed with a sense that something had gone wrong. Assia confided to Suzette Macedo that Sylvia had picked up "a current of attraction" between Assia and Ted and had reacted badly. Suzette is sure there was nothing of a more romantic nature that weekend than this feeling of attraction; Assia might well have told her if there had been. Assia later gave Olwyn Hughes much the same account she had given Suzette of the

weekend and remarked that she doubted whether the attraction between Ted and herself would ever have developed into an affair, as
it later did, had Sylvia behaved differently.

After the Wevills had gone, Sylvia was evidently left with a good
deal of unresolved fear and anger. Perhaps she sensed, too, that Assia's
quality meant that this "rival" was more likely than other, imagined
rivals to turn into a real one. The next day, May 21, she wrote two
poems: "Event," originally called "Quarrel," and "The Rabbit
Catcher." "Event" is about an alienated couple. The woman records
her sleeplessness —

> Where apple bloom ices the night
> I walk in a ring,
> A groove of old faults, deep and bitter.
>
> Love cannot come here

— and says, in an image of someone turning away, "I cannot see
your eyes." For the first time, in "Event" and "The Rabbit Catcher,"
Sylvia was using her own husband and offspring for material in a
confessional way. Ted Hughes was appalled when he read "Event"
soon after it was written, but Sylvia eventually sent the poem off to
The Observer, where it was published in December. Anne Sexton's
growing success in writing confessional poetry may have prompted
Sylvia's use of private material for her own work. Sexton had sent
her second book, *All My Pretty Ones,* to Sylvia earlier in the year.

"The Rabbit Catcher" — which, unlike "Event," Ted did not see
for some time — is another case of Sylvia's adapting immediate experience to her self-destructive perspective. In her journal entry for
May 14, 1953, three months before her first suicide attempt, she had
written: "I want to love somebody because I want to be loved. In a
rabbit fear I may hurl myself under the wheels of the car because the
lights terrify me, and under the dark blind death of the wheels I will
be safe." In "The Rabbit Catcher," which is partly a cry for help,
partly one of blind terror, and partly an act of emotional blackmail,
the poet almost wills the worst to happen. It originated during a walk
she and Ted had taken some months before. Coming upon a line of
snares along a clifftop, Sylvia had wildly rushed around tearing them
up. As a countryman, Ted Hughes was sympathetic to the simple
economics of village life and saw nothing admirable in Sylvia's harm-
ing the rabbit catcher's livelihood. It was one of the small incidents,
after they came to Devon, that made Ted realize how different their
attitudes toward country life were. To Sylvia the snares were not only

cruel; they were terrifying symbols of an inevitable yet irresistible finality:

> There was only one place to get to.
> Simmering, perfumed,
> The paths narrowed into the hollow.
> And the snares almost effaced themselves —
> Zeros, shutting on nothing.

The last stanza refers directly to her marriage:

> And we, too, had a relationship —
> Tight wires between us,
> Pegs too deep to uproot, and a mind like a ring
> Sliding shut on some quick thing,
> The constriction killing me also.

The relationship is curiously set in the past, and its ending is compared to the noose of a rabbit trap that kills her.

Yet nothing had happened to harm her marriage other than her upsurge of jealousy. The shrill pain of "The Rabbit Catcher" is true only of her own magnified inner terrors and consequent fury. In these two poems, moreover, she avoids mention of her own behavior, unless the "groove of old faults, deep and bitter" includes recognition of this side of things. Her concept of marriage was absolute and all-demanding. It was perfect or it was nothing. As a mother and a "good wife" she was owed total allegiance. And her marriage had to be unlike any other: she seemed unable to conceive even of its "going through a bad patch" to continue with better understanding. And as all self-criticism for the part she played in the rift was absent, what "better understanding" could there ever be?

With "Event" and "The Rabbit Catcher," the scenario for all she wrote of her marriage until her death was set. She was making her self-justifying and unforgiving case in much the same terms as henceforth she would use to sow "the seeds of the myth of her martyrdom"* in presenting her situation to friends and to her mother. In this concept she herself appears guiltless; her children are used to substantiate her role. Her husband is demeaned and blamed, in a total *volte-face* of the godlike image she had earlier, quite as energetically, put forward. He becomes a facet, in her psychodrama, of the huge figure of Otto Plath, who also "deserted" her. This, in essence, was one of the myths she propagated in the marvelously achieved voice of Ariel.

---

*From Richard Murphy's account in Appendix III.

On May 22, the day after Sylvia had written these two poems, Assia Wevill mailed her the makings of a tapestry with a pleasant note warning her not to ruin her eyes working on it. It seems that for another month or so peace, or at least an uneasy truce, returned to the household. On June 7 Sylvia wrote to her mother of doing *gros point* tapestry for cushion and seat covers. "Wonderfully calming," she commented briefly.

Meanwhile, in the nearby cottage, Percy was failing fast. Sylvia's poem "Apprehensions," written on May 28, seemingly had Percy's painful breathing in mind:

> A red fist, opening and closing,
> Two gray, papery bags —
> This is what I am made of, this and a terror
> Of being wheeled off under crosses and a rain of pietàs.

Late May produced "absolutely halcyon" weather. Ted's father, mother, and Uncle Walter arrived for a six-day visit to Court Green — the last in a series of interruptive annoyances for Sylvia. Edith Hughes stayed with them, "sweetly" mending Ted's socks and admiring her grandchildren while the men stayed at the Burton Hall Hotel. Sylvia duly informed her mother that the elder Hugheses had been immensely impressed with Court Green. Mrs. Hughes had clearly noticed nothing amiss and wrote to Mrs. Plath in pleasure: "Sylvia is a lovely wife and mother. You will feel so pleased when you see them all looking so well."

Mrs. Plath was due to arrive in mid-June, and Sylvia wrote to her in keen anticipation of showing off the house ("I wish now you had seen the house in its raw state so you would see how much we have done"). On June 7 all sorts of loving congratulations were sent off to Warren and his bride, Margaret Wetzel, married June 2. Then as one hot summer day succeeded another Sylvia wrote in delight of working in the garden from dawn to dusk and loving it; she and the children were getting brown and fit. She spoke of five-year plans for work still to be done on the house and of a possible lucrative reading tour with Ted two years thence, seemingly having dismissed all thought of serious disruption in her marriage.

Alvarez, who called in on June 8 on his way to Cornwall for a Whitsun break, noticed little amiss. He found the small town unattractive, but Court Green, set among blooming apple trees, lilacs, roses, and laburnums, was an idyll. Sylvia showed him around the house and grounds — "*her* property," writes Alvarez — and delightedly told him she was writing again, "really writing." Yet Alvarez noticed a change in Sylvia, no longer "a housewifely appendage to a powerful husband" but "solid and complete, her own woman again." Ted, meanwhile, seemed content "to sit back and play with little Frieda." Alvarez concluded that "since it appeared to be a strong, close marriage, I suppose he was unconcerned that the balance of power had shifted for the time being to Sylvia." The new independence that Alvarez sensed could have come from pride in her home, or from her new poetic mastery, or from the first stirrings of a will to separate her identity from her husband's and consolidate friendships of her own outside her marriage, or from some combination of all these factors. It could, too, have been simply that Sylvia was beginning to feel at ease with Alvarez.

On June 15 Sylvia wrote a last letter home before her mother's departure from Wellesley. Gleefully Sylvia announced that she and Ted had become beekeepers. At the local bee meeting, "attended by the rector, the midwife, and assorted beekeeping people from neighboring villages," they had watched "a Mr. Pollard make three hives out of one (by transferring his queen cells) under the supervision of the official Government bee-man." Much of this letter has direct bearing on the bee sequence Sylvia would write the following October, again demonstrating how realities at hand — seemingly transient — were seized upon by Sylvia's magnifying imagination and enlarged into archetypal dramas of mysteriously personal significance:

> We all wore masks and it was thrilling. It is expensive to start beekeeping (over $50 outlay), but Mr. Pollard let us have an old hive for nothing, which we painted white and green, and today he brought over the swarm of docile Italian hybrid bees we ordered and installed them. We placed the hive in a sheltered out-of-the-way spot in the orchard — the bees were furious from being in a box. Ted had only put a handkerchief over his head where the hat should go in the bee-mask, and the bees crawled into his hair, and he flew off with half-a-dozen stings. I didn't get stung at all, and when I went back to the hive later, I was delighted to see bees entering with pollen sacs full and leaving with them empty — at least I *think* that's what they were doing.

Mrs. Plath arrived in the third week of June to find an enameled heart in a wreath of flowers painted on the lintel of her bedroom door. "WELCOME, MOTHER, TO COURT GREEN" was inscribed on a homemade greeting card that was placed, along with the gift of a Liberty scarf, on her pillow. All seemed well at first. She was enchanted with the house and garden. Frieda remembered her, and "Baby Nick"

received her with his accustomed smile. A few days after her arrival
Sylvia pointedly took her to have tea nearby with Mrs. Hamilton,
whose house would soon be up for sale. In a letter written long after
the event, Mrs. Plath intimated that Sylvia had entertained some notion of her moving there when she retired — an arrangement that did
not strike Mrs. Plath as at all practicable or desirable. Clearly Sylvia,
with her long-term future as a writer in mind, was angling for a
babysitter as well as for a supportive mother who would live close
at hand.

Apart from such shocks, Mrs. Plath was pleased with everything
she saw. In a letter to Warren she described the first week of her visit
as one of the happiest times in her life. Yet, unknown to her, a number
of threads were drawing the drama to a climax, with Aurelia Plath
herself a not insignificant participant. Next door, Percy was rapidly
failing. By the end of the month this unwitting double of Otto Plath
would be buried. That very month Sylvia had become a beekeeper's
wife as well as a beekeeper's daughter. No question but that Sylvia
herself was the true beekeeper: her beehive, like the furniture in her
children's playroom, was already decorated with her own enameled
flowers. And it was at about this time that Ted first made contact
with Assia Wevill in London.

Meanwhile, a long symphonic poem was forming in Sylvia's mind
even as Percy died, just after midnight on June 25, to be buried on
Friday, June 29, the day before she completed the poem she called
"Berck-Plage." On the afternoon of the twenty-fourth, Sylvia, with
Frieda, had forced herself to visit the cottage to watch "some awful
translation taking place":

> Percy lay back on a heap of white pillows in his striped pajamas,
> his face already passed from humanity, the nose a spiraling, fleshless
> beak in thin air, the chin fallen in a point from it, like an opposite
> pole, and the mouth like an inverted black heart stamped into the
> yellow flesh between, a great raucous breath coming and going there
> with great effort like an awful bird . . . His eyes showed through
> partly open lids like dissolved soaps or a clotted pus. I was very
> sick at this and had a bad migraine over my left eye for the rest of
> the day. The end, even of so marginal a man, a horror.

The next day Sylvia and Ted took advantage of Mrs. Plath's offer
to babysit to get away to London together for two days of broadcasting and seeing friends. Percy was laid out in the cottage parlor
when they returned on the twenty-seventh. Sylvia again forced herself
to observe everything:

When I went down they had just brought the coffin and put him in. The living room where he had lain was in an upheaval — bed rolled from the wall, mattresses on the lawn, sheets and pillows washed and airing. He lay in the sewing room, or parlor, in a long coffin of orangey soap-colored oak . . . the lid propped against the wall at his head with a silver scroll: Percy B, Died June 25, 1962. The raw date a shock. A sheet covered the coffin. Rose lifted it. A pale white, beaked face, as of paper, rose under the veil that covered the hole cut in the glued white cloth cover. The mouth looked glued, the face powdered. She quickly put down the sheet. I hugged her. She kissed me and burst into tears.

On June 29, the day of the funeral, Ted and Sylvia, dressed in black, passed by the church on their way to order groceries. Bowler-hatted undertakers accompanied a "high, spider-wheeled black cart" out of the churchyard. Sylvia noted "the awful feeling of great grins coming onto the face, unstoppable. A relief; this is the hostage for death, we are safe for the time being." Mysteriously assured, she and Ted slipped into the back of the church for the service, afterward following the funeral procession up the hill to the new cemetery. Again, Sylvia noted every particular: the pollarded limes like green balls against the distant red plowed fields (a seam of extra-fertile red earth runs through that part of Devon), the slowly lifted faces of schoolchildren as the procession passed the playground, the "six bowler hats of the bearers left at the first yew bushes in the grass," then the bearers bowing as they lowered the coffin into the "narrow red earth opening" while the women were "led round, in a kind of good-bye circle, Rose rapt and beautiful and frozen . . ." The grave still gaped open as the party left, "an unfinished feeling." Ted and Sylvia walked home, swinging their jackets in the heat, gathering foxgloves.

Percy's death and funeral are re-created in exact detail in "Berck-Plage," finished the next day. But Sylvia weirdly combined the funeral with a completely unrelated experience of the year before: her nightmarish impressions of the sanatoria of Berck-Plage on the Pas de Calais coast. The poem brings together all the recurring symbols indelibly connected with her father's fatal illness and death: the sea, the maimed man, the black boot, the crutches, the dying man and mourning wife, the corpse, the burial. Some of the images were a year old, some a day, but the power of the poem — its emotional turmoil, anguish, and dread — had been locked within Sylvia since Otto Plath's death.

On Berck-Plage something is being concealed from the speaker:

Why is it so quiet, what are they hiding?
I have two legs, and I move smilingly.

Then looms the fearful, recurrent image of amputation: "This black boot has no mercy for anybody. / Why should it, it is the hearse of a dead foot." A priest in a black boot, a black cassock among "Obscene bikinis" draws the onlooker "like a long material / Through a still virulence" into the hospital world where "things, things" glitter on hotel balconies: "Tubular steel wheelchairs, aluminum crutches" — indeed, all that is needed for survival in a hospital dream of "red ribs," "nerves bursting like trees," and a surgeon with "One mirrory eye." As in a nightmare, the scene shifts without warning to Percy's Devon cottage, where "An old man is vanishing. / There is no help in his weeping wife."

Sylvia never saw her father's funeral, and perhaps the real point of this poem was to create one for him, to bury these tenacious images.* The funeral has a sense of the bridal ("the soul is a bride") while "the coffin on its flowery cart [is] like a beautiful woman, / A crest of breasts, eyelids and lips / Storming the hilltop." The coffin, with its dead man and its woman of flowers (an image of Sylvia's father-love), goes down into the hole in the earth, "a naked mouth, red and awkward." But only despair remains: "There is no hope, it is given up."

◀   ◀   ◀

By the time of Percy's funeral Sylvia may have temporarily calmed her anxieties about her marriage. By July 2, however, when she wrote "The Other," her marital troubles were clearly resurfacing in force. On July 9 she and her mother drove to Exeter for a day's shopping. On the way home Sylvia exulted, "I have everything in life I've ever wanted: a wonderful husband, two adorable children, a lovely home, and my writing."

Days later, while Ted was in London, she invaded his attic study, hauled down what papers she could find — mostly letters — and made a bonfire in the vegetable garden. The mother watched, appalled, as her daughter performed whatever rite of witchcraft she thought appropriate. As the fire consumed the letters, Sylvia fanned out the ashes "Between the yellow lettuces and the German cabbage." A "name with black edges" unfurled at her feet: *Assia*. Sylvia now

---

*In *Letters Home* Mrs. Plath tells us Sylvia and Warren were spared their father's funeral. And in sessions with Dr. Beuscher in Boston it was made clear to Sylvia that she had never completed mourning for her father.

had confirmation of the name of her rival, and when Ted returned, she confronted him.*

Soon after the bonfire Assia phoned Ted through a male colleague at her office. Sylvia, who answered the phone, suspected a ruse. After Ted had taken the call, Sylvia yanked the telephone off the wall. Her jealousy, the burning of Ted's letters, and the violence done to the telephone were used, undigested, in three poems Sylvia wrote that summer: "The Other" ("I have your head on my wall"), a poem in which the rival merges seamlessly with the familiar figure of her deathly mother-muse; "Words Heard, by Accident, Over the Phone" (the "bowel-pulse," "tentacle," and "muck-funnel" of the actual phone); and "Burning the Letters" with its relatively straightforward imagery. The only other poem she wrote before late September was "Poppies in July."

After the telephone incident Sylvia insisted that Ted leave Court Green. He bought a suitcase and packed a few things, and Sylvia and her mother saw him off at the station. It was after this, apparently, that Sylvia drove wildly off to the Comptons' with Nick in his carry-cot, arriving distraught and hysterical. Her milk had dried up, she wept; and she could no longer feed her baby. Elizabeth Compton listened to her aghast. Sylvia raved desperately, declaring that she had given her whole heart away and could never get it back. She spent the night on the Comptons' sofa, returning the next day to Court Green. On July 16 Mrs. Plath removed herself to the midwife's house on the hill, explaining to Warren in a letter written the next day that although the babies loved her when she came to look after them, the trouble between Sylvia and Ted had to be settled between them alone.

Somehow in July Sylvia and Ted got enough of their difficulties under control to travel together to Bangor in North Wales, where on

---

*It has been suggested that on this occasion Sylvia also burned an entire novel, written earlier that year, entitled *Falcon Yard,* and based on her love for Ted, which she had intended for him as a birthday present. There is absolutely no documentary evidence that such a novel existed. Ted Hughes knew pretty well what she had been writing and says that he knew nothing about such a work at the time. The only mention Sylvia herself made of *Falcon Yard* was in her journal of 1957–58, when she was planning to write a novel of Cambridge student life. All she kept was the story "Stone Boy with Dolphin," first published in *Johnny Panic and the Bible of Dreams* in 1977 but written in 1958. Sylvia herself makes no mention of the novel either in her letters of 1961–62 or in her poem "Burning the Letters," which, written in August after her mother's departure, refers to the bonfire. A novel of their love and courtship would have been an unlikely birthday present for Ted in any case, since he rarely read her prose; it was her poetry that interested him. Furthermore, there is no trace of a novel of that name in her papers, though it was Sylvia's method to draft new work on the reverse side of other drafts.

July 26 they were engaged to give a joint reading for *Critical Quarterly,* while Mrs. Plath took care of the children. On the way to Bangor the Hugheses stopped for the night with Dan and Helga Huws in Penrhyncoch near Aberystwyth, where Dan Huws was a librarian at the National Library of Wales. Huws "did not gather at the time that the situation was irretrievable." Helga recalls that Sylvia had changed: "Her so characteristic brisk walk was hesitant, heavy. My mother, with us on a visit, remarked how beautiful and distant she looked." Up in Helga's bedroom she and Sylvia had the one "really essential talk" of their friendship. "There she unburdened," Helga writes, "prompted by my mentioning 'The Rival' . . . There was still some of the old fury left, but she was in turmoil and obviously searching for some consolation which only time could bring." Neither Daniel nor Helga Huws believed the problem was anything but temporary.

Nothing between Sylvia and Ted had been settled, however, when Mrs. Plath left for America on August 4. As they waited for her train to pull out of Exeter station, she records in an aside in *Letters Home,* Sylvia and Ted stood stonily watching; "Nick was the only one with a smile." It was the last time Aurelia Plath saw her daughter.

◀ ◀ ◀

By the time of Mrs. Plath's departure Ted and Sylvia were considering a temporary separation in a civilized fashion. They arranged for "fantastically neurotic" friends, a young American writer and his wife, who had been evicted from their flat in London, to stay with them at Court Green in exchange for help with the children and a share of the expenses. This pair was left in charge when Sylvia and Ted, in the middle of August, went together to meet Mrs. Prouty and her sister-in-law, who were visiting London. Mrs. Prouty laid on a splendid dinner, Agatha Christie's play *The Mousetrap,* and a luxurious night at the Connaught Hotel. It must have been difficult for Sylvia to convey the impression to her benefactress that all was well with "the perfect marriage," but apparently she did. The guest-babysitters coped less well. Being left with the children for several days "nearly killed them," Sylvia reported to her mother.

Soon after their return Sylvia ran their Morris station wagon off the road into a deserted airfield in what she later said was an aborted suicide attempt.* On August 25 John Malcolm Brinnin, the poetic

---

*This may have been a hysterical or furious, or even accidental, act, devoid of danger. The airfield, completely flat, lies alongside the Winkleigh road, at this point

entrepreneur and biographer of Dylan Thomas (Sylvia had intensely disliked his book), visited Court Green with his companion, Bill Reid, while on tour of the west country, bound for St. Ives. Brinnin had known the Hugheses in Boston and had wanted to sound Ted out about the possibility of his taking Brinnin's place at the University of Connecticut the following year. In his journal Brinnin recorded only a short visit. He remembers no tension until Ted walked the two Americans to their car and without elaboration rejected the offer on the grounds that there were certain arrangements he had to make in his own life before he could make plans. Brinnin's visit was a small incident in a long, racking summer.

Toward the end of the summer Sylvia badly needed a holiday. A trip to Ireland had been mooted late in July when she wrote to a fellow poet, Richard Murphy, to tell him in advance of official notification that his entry had won first prize in the 1962 Guinness competition at the Cheltenham Literary Festival. (Sylvia had been one of the judges, together with George Hartley and John Press.) In her letter Sylvia congratulated Murphy on his prize, going on to suggest that she and Ted come to Ireland to visit him at the end of August or early in September. Murphy had previously spoken with enthusiasm to them both of an enterprise he had undertaken in remote Cleggan on the Connemara coast, offering sailing and fishing to tourists in a refurbished Galway "hooker." Sylvia made it clear that they were willing to pay for accommodation in the village but that she desperately needed to get away for a week to "a boat and the sea and *no squalling babies* . . . The center of my whole early life was ocean and boats, and because of this . . . you would be a very lovely person for us to visit just now." Murphy, whose cottage was let until the first week in September, replied by telegram: "Do hope you can come after 8 September stay with me and sail."

Sylvia had been ill with a feverish flu for much of August. By the time she and Ted were ready to leave for Ireland in September, the holiday had taken on a practical purpose beyond that of giving them both a much needed rest. It seems that they had agreed to some kind of trial separation for six months or so, during which Ted would go to Spain. Sylvia hoped to winter in Ireland, and Ted was accompanying her to Cleggan chiefly to help her find a cottage. They planned

---

also flat, so it is easy to drive onto it in the dark. Sylvia first told this story to Alvarez, who had confided to her that he sometimes crashed his own car in times of emotional stress, and she may have exaggerated it to emulate him. (Certainly the £1 fine recorded by an earlier biographer in connection with this incident was for a parking ticket.) The car was unharmed.

for the separation to start sometime in November so they could both clear away various work commitments before leaving Devon. It does seem odd that Sylvia wished to exchange the isolation of a Devon village for the even greater seclusion of an Irish one. She may have felt she could face separation only if she could get away from Court Green with its memories, associations, and inevitable village gossip. And she did, as always, intensely crave the sea, and she may have imagined that with Richard Murphy as friend and neighbor she could be happy.

The Hugheses set out on Tuesday, September 11, leaving their children — and car — with a nanny from an agency. They traveled by train and night ferry to Dublin, where they stopped for a few hours for Guinness and oysters with Jack and Maire Sweeney. In Galway they either took a taxi or got a lift north along the lovely Connemara coast to Cleggan, Murphy's village, where they arrived on the evening of Wednesday the twelfth, intending to stay for a week. Murphy welcomed them to his cottage, "The Old Forge," originally the home of the local blacksmith, and put them up in his guest room with its twin beds of native elm, made by an island boatwright. The next day they went sailing in his boat, the *Ave Maria*. "We sailed to Inishbofin," Murphy recalls, "a passage of six miles across open water with a strong current and an ocean swell. Sylvia lay prone on the foredeck, leaning out over the prow like a triumphal figurehead, inhaling the sea air ecstatically." On Friday, Murphy continues, "I drove them to Yeats's Tower at Ballylee and Lady Gregory's Coole Park in my 7 h.p. minivan, used for selling the fish we had caught. Sylvia sat in front, talking to me about marriage and divorce, while in the back, which was too small for seats, Ted talked about poachers and guns and fishing to Seamus [Coyne, the fifteen-year-old boy who helped Richard with his boats]."

At Coole, viewing the huge copper beech in the pleasure grounds, Sylvia urged Ted to climb the spiked iron fence protecting the tree and carve his initials beside those of Yeats; he deserved to be in that company more than some of the writers who had made their marks there, she said. (Ted, remarks Murphy, "was frustrated by the fence.") At that time Yeats's Tower (like Coole Park) was still the deserted ruin Yeats had predicted. After the three poets had climbed the spiral stair to the top, Sylvia tossed three coins into the stream below, with what wishes, in that sacred place, may be imagined. Nearby was an apple tree, heavy with ripe apples, that must have been planted by Yeats. Despite Murphy's protests, Ted and Sylvia persuaded Seamus to climb the tree and shake it while they picked up about a hundredweight of fruit — enough, they told Murphy, to keep him in apple pie all winter.

The day's sightseeing ended with Murphy showing them his birth-place, a decayed eighteenth-century mansion called Milford, set in huge grounds, then owned by a cousin whose mother gave them a somewhat Elizabeth Bowenish tea. It was here that Sylvia noticed the Rangoon prints that appear in her poem "The Courage of Shutting Up."

Murphy's observations are precise and interesting:

> All the arrangements for their holiday had so far been managed by Sylvia, though Ted appeared to approve. That was my impres-sion . . . If I said anything to Ted, Sylvia would be quicker to reply. This did not seem to annoy him. I never heard them quarrel or speak unkindly to each other. In the context of their recent marital difficulties, she told me his lies upset her; he never mentioned any fault of hers in my hearing, either then or subsequently. What he admitted was that after six or seven years that had been marvelously creative for him, the marriage had somehow become destructive: and he thought the best thing to do was to give it a rest by going to Spain for six months. Assia's name was not mentioned, but her role was implied.

To Murphy Sylvia confided that she wanted a legal separation, not a divorce; she could not imagine either of them truly married to anyone else, their union had been so complete on every level. Murphy advised against legal separation, "a cruel alternative to divorce," but "urged her not to divorce Ted on account of an affair that might not last." He told her of his own painful experience of marriage and divorce: his wife had threatened suicide, and after a marital breakup her brother had indeed killed himself, leaving the Murphys with two children to care for and a devastating sense of guilt for not having helped enough. At that time, Murphy affirms, Sylvia "never spoke of suicide as an act she was contemplating herself."

In spite of these painful discussions, Sylvia enjoyed herself. She told Murphy she wanted to spend the winter in Ireland. She intended to write another novel there, she said, a potboiler like *The Bell Jar*. She seemed to have fallen completely in love with Connemara, and her enthusiasm reached a peak when she offered to rent Murphy's cottage with him in it. He was alarmed at this, though Hughes gave no outward sign of minding the suggestion. On Saturday Murphy took them around to see several cottages to rent in the neighborhood, among them one belonging to a local woman, Kitty Marriott, with

whom, to Murphy's amazement, Sylvia entered into a tenancy agreement on the spot, to run from December 1 to the end of February.

That evening the Irish poet Thomas Kinsella arrived by car from
Dublin to spend the weekend. After an excellent dinner cooked by
Seamus's mother, Mrs. Coyne, Murphy's earlier anxiety increased
tenfold when, unnoticed by Hughes or Kinsella, Sylvia rubbed her leg
provocatively against Murphy's under the table. He was particularly
horrified because the collapse of his own marriage had begun in similar
circumstances. "I did not," he states, "want to break up Sylvia's
marriage, or have a secret affair with her, or be used to make Ted
jealous, or to upset Mary Coyne" — who, with her sons, was central
to Murphy's working life in Connemara.

After dinner the conversation turned to Yeats and the occult. Ted
and Sylvia offered to demonstrate the Ouija board, and though Murphy took no part and Sylvia soon went to bed, Hughes and Kinsella
continued to play with it late into the night. The next morning, while
Murphy was out on business, Hughes set out alone to visit the American painter Barrie Cooke in County Clare. When Murphy returned
for lunch, Sylvia told him where Ted had gone, claiming that Ted
had often left her in this way. Richard was nonplused. Ted may have
left a message of thanks or apology with Sylvia, but if he did, she did
not pass it on. Remembering Sylvia's secret sign to him under the
table the night before, Murphy began to suspect she had arranged to
be alone with him. Cleggan was a very Catholic Irish village; to have
a married woman stay with him alone was unthinkable in such a
place. Having explained to Sylvia how his relationship with the local
people, especially the Coynes, would be affected if she stayed, he
asked her to take the opportunity of traveling to Dublin by car with
Tom Kinsella the next day. The effect of this suggestion on Sylvia
was dramatic:

> Instead of accepting this agreeably, Sylvia was enraged. All her
> warmth and enthusiasm, her gushing excitement that colored what-
> ever she noticed with hyperbole, changed into a strangulated hos-
> tility. She scarcely spoke to me, and when she did, she put a strained,
> artificial distance between us. She opened her heart to Mrs. Coyne,
> and sowed in her mind a few seeds of the future myth of her mar-
> tyrdom.

The next day, after stiff good-byes, Sylvia departed with Kinsella,
leaving Murphy to feel that in spite of all his efforts to be a good
host, he had somehow failed.

Thomas Kinsella took Sylvia into his home in Dublin, where she stayed for two nights with him and his wife, Eleanor, a kind, motherly woman to whom, apparently, Sylvia poured out her terrible grief and anger. Now she had yet another grievance to add to Hughes's faithlessness and Murphy's rejection: Ted had "deserted her" in Ireland.

◄   ◄   ◄

Back alone at Court Green, Sylvia's fraught conditions intensified. Her anger hardened to a final decision that Ted must leave for good. This time she would not plead for him to return. At Court Green she found, besides a telegram from Ted in London, letters from her mother, Mrs. Prouty, and her Boston analyst, Ruth Beuscher, responding to Sylvia's distress signals with radical advice. Having survived an enormous upheaval in her own personal life, Dr. Beuscher denounced what she supposed was Ted's weakness and perfidy. Writing again on September 26 as a friend more than as a psychiatrist, she counseled Sylvia to cut her losses — with emphasis on child custody and finance — and sue for divorce while her husband's adultery was still hot. If Ted was going through a crisis of maturity, Sylvia should resist going down in the whirlpool with him. Spare no expense getting a good nanny, run your own life, and, above all, read Erich Fromm's *The Art of Loving,* she advised. Mrs. Plath and Mrs. Prouty also advised her to take effective financial measures against Ted, urging her to dissolve the marriage.

No doubt in her letters to Dr. Beuscher, her mother, and Mrs. Prouty, Sylvia put her case in convincingly self-justifying language and gave the impression that, with adult good sense and resourcefulness, she was fully able to meet and handle the situation. If Ted's adultery had really been the critical issue, their advice would have been sound enough. But neither Aurelia Plath nor Dr. Beuscher expressed awareness of any other side to the story. Both ignored (in their letters at least) the possibility that Sylvia's behavior might have contributed its share to her marital rift. The inflexibility of her self-absorption, coupled with the dark moods that were inseparable from her strange genius, may finally have broken down her husband's defenses at the very time Sylvia's fierce daemon or inner self was emerging.

On the evening of her return Sylvia had an exhaustive three-hour talk with that pillar of good sense, Winifred Davies, who made several helpful suggestions. Among these was the advice — of incalculable value to twentieth-century poetry — to use those early morning hours of black depression for her writing.

Sylvia's letters to her mother, dashed off on September 23, 24, 26, and 29, were full of decisive plans for immediate action: she would go to Ireland, she would see a solicitor, she had withdrawn all the money — about £300 — from her joint bank account with Ted. Her future possibilities proliferate endlessly: living in Rome on a Guggenheim fellowship, doing up the cottage for a proper nanny for summers in Devon and taking a London flat with good schools for the children for the rest of the year ("I would *starve* intellectually here") — these feverish schemes expose the manic pole of her depression.

On September 25 Sylvia went up to London for a "harrowing" session with her solicitor, staying overnight with the Macedos in Hampstead. She wrote to her mother of England's "awful" divorce laws: a wife was allowed only a third of her husband's income, with anything she earned herself deductible. The solicitor had reassured her that as a "deserted" wife, she was within her rights to draw all monies from her joint account. Ted returned at the end of September to find her decision about the separation consolidated by the letters from America, some of which she carried about with her, and she finally ordered him to leave for good. Her frequent recourse to these instructions helped to make negotiations between them difficult from then on. In letters to her mother, to various friends, to Ted's family (deeply upset by news of the separation), and even to slight acquaintances such as Mrs. Coyne in Ireland and Dido Merwin's late mother's housekeeper, Sylvia spoke vindictively about Ted and flaunted her own wronged virtue. To Clarissa Roche, Suzette Macedo, and Jillian Becker, she boasted that she had "thrown Ted out."

Olwyn Hughes, on a brief visit to Yorkshire in November, saw the vituperative letters Sylvia wrote to Mrs. Hughes at the time, and was appalled that Sylvia could have sent them to a woman who had always been kind and generous to her daughter-in-law. Edith Hughes herself, confined to the house with arthritis, was convinced that Sylvia needed help and implored her husband to go down to her in Devon. The crude terms of Sylvia's attack so shocked Mr. Hughes, however, that he refused to become involved. Mrs. Hughes did prevail on her sister Hilda, who promised to go to Court Green as soon as she could free herself from work.*

From London, where he camped at first on Alvarez's spare bed in Fellow's Road and later in a flat in Montagu Square left to Dido Merwin

*Edith Hughes's letters to Aurelia Plath at the time demonstrate how truly upset she was, and how powerless to help.

by her mother, Ted regularly sent money to Sylvia. She attacked or despaired. Ted put distance between them.

The lengths to which Sylvia went to present herself as wholly innocent in a situation in which *both* partners — and their children— were truly victims, arose to a great extent from her gift for wishful exaggeration. This distorting willfulness (which became for her poetic truth), together with her customary flair for dramatic self-projection, can be seen in the curious letter she sent to Richard Murphy after her return to Court Green on September 21. It begins as a thank-you letter, enclosing the unused return half of her train ticket from Galway to Dublin in case he or the Coynes cared to use it. Sylvia then goes on:

> May I say two things? My health depends on leaving England & going to Ireland, & the health of the children. I am very reluctant to think that the help you gave with one hand you would want to take away with the other. I am in great need of a woman like Kitty Marriott & if there is one thing my 30th year has brought it is understanding of what I am, and a sense of strength and independence to face what I have to. It may be difficult to believe, but I have not and never will have a desire to see or speak to you or anyone else. I have wintered in a lighthouse & that sort of life is balm to my soul . . .
>
> Secondly, I was appalled to realize you did not understand we were joking when talking about my writing New Yorker poems about Connemara. I would not do that even if I were able and as you know I have not written a poem for over a year & cannot write poems anyway when I am writing prose. So there is no question of your literary territory being invaded. My novel is set in Devon, and it is this I hope to finish at Glasthule.
>
> I feel very sorry to have to retract my invitation to visit us at Court Green as it would have given me great pleasure to have you see it . . . But Ted will not be here, as I had thought when I asked you, and when he is not here I can see no one. My town is as small & watchful as yours & a little cripple hunchback with a high black boot lives at the bottom of my lane & all day & night watches who comes & goes . . . Please have the kindness, the largeness, to say you will not wish me ill nor keep me from what I clearly and calmly see as the one fate open. I would like to think your understanding could vault the barrier it was stuck at when I left.

This strange letter baffled Murphy. On the one hand she was begging him to be kind; on the other she was almost accusing him of hypocrisy. She seemed to be assuming that he might in some way prevent her taking up her lease because he wanted to defend his literary territory. Her statement about not writing poems was patently false, and he doubted (rightly) that she had ever spent a winter in a light-house. And why was she writing at all if she didn't want to see him? Her seizing on Mrs. Marriott as a person she needed, without having any idea of what Mrs. Marriott was like, was also puzzling. (In the event, Mrs. Marriott's demand for three months' rent when Sylvia eventually canceled her tenancy agreement gave Sylvia an unpleasant shock.) Her reasons for withdrawing her invitation to visit Court Green seemed to be a mockery of his own, for asking her not to stay with him after Ted had left.

So Murphy was at a loss as to how to reply both to this and to a subsequent letter from Sylvia declaring that she was getting a divorce. Finally he didn't reply at all, deciding that "to 'vault the barrier [his] understanding was stuck at' . . . might land us both in deep trouble." He would simply go and see her when she got to Ireland.

Ted had been told late in September to leave Court Green. Early in October he came to collect his things and went back to London. Mrs. Plath was forbidden to return ("I haven't the strength to see you for some time. The horror of what you saw and what I saw you see last summer is between us and I cannot face you again until I have a new life"). Now Richard Murphy, whom she had seen as an indispensable part of her renewal in Ireland, sent her no word. Heartbroken and alone in spite of her brave show, she forged ahead, seeking the new, independent life her divided being dreaded yet desperately craved.

GETTING THERE

1962-1963

Don't talk to me about the world needing cheerful stuff! What the person out of Belsen — physical or psychological — wants is nobody saying the birdies still go tweet-tweet, but the full knowledge that somebody else has been there and knows the *worst,* just what it is like. It is much more help for me, for example, to know that people are divorced and go through hell, than to hear about happy marriages. Let the *Ladies' Home Journal* blither about *those.*

> — *Letters Home,*
> October 21, 1962

> Words dry and riderless,
> The indefatigable hoof-taps.
> While
> From the bottom of the pool, fixed stars
> Govern a life.

> — "Words," February 1, 1963

BETWEEN THE END of September and the first day of December, in the autumnal privacy of her three acres, with little more for distraction than her small children and the nannies who came and went, Sylvia Plath, in an astonishing blaze of creative power, produced forty of her Ariel poems, unique in literature.

In a letter of October 12 she tells her mother: "Every morning, when my sleeping pill wears off, I am up about five, in my study with coffee, writing like mad — have managed a poem a day before breakfast. All book poems. Terrific stuff, as if domesticity had choked me." And to Ruth Fainlight, later in the month, Sylvia reiterated her amazement and delight: "I am living like a Spartan, writing through huge fevers and producing free stuff I had locked in me for years. I feel astounded and very lucky. I kept telling myself I was the sort that could only write when peaceful at heart, but that is not so, the muse has come to live here, now Ted has gone . . ."

Her muse had, in fact, already been with her for about a year — but the strange, internalized world of Ariel had been giving out its secrets intermittently, just a poem or two, here and there. Sylvia, in a turmoil of emotions, was now at a turning point. Alone, in charge of her fate, she was suddenly able to focus the full force of her expert craft, her huge energies, on the unresolved inner predicament that had brought her to this pass. She could now examine every facet of it and definitively conquer the predicament by writing it out. She could then go forth, unencumbered, to a new world full of possibilities. In the long hours she spent alone, the poems came in a spate — ripely, almost effortlessly, with a hugely amplified freedom and felicity.

Letters Home can be seen as one long projection of the "desired image" (the *required* image) of herself as Eve — wife, mother, homemaker, protector of the wholesome, the good, and the holy, an identity that both her upbringing and her own instinctive physical being had fiercely aspired to. Now her submerged and subversive self, utterly true to itself, utterly detached, completely the artist, turned on the Eve scenario and judged it a deception. It had let her down. And what kind of Eve had she been, trapped inside the cruel trauma of the past, in a "black shoe / In which I have lived like a foot / For thirty years, poor and white, / Barely daring to breathe or Achoo"? She eyes herself (in "A Birthday Present") with masochistic scorn:

> Is this the elect one, the one with black eye-pits and a scar?
>
> Measuring the flour, cutting off the surplus,
> Adhering to rules, to rules, to rules.
>
> Is this the one for the annunciation?
> My god, what a laugh!

In merciless, lashing rage she denounces fate for cheating her: "I / Have a self to recover, a queen," is her cry. Her desperate predicament was extreme: to record and master it, the poems too had to be extreme.

As absorbed and intent as a cartographer, Sylvia reported in her poems on the weather of her inner universe and delineated its two poles: "stasis" and rage. At the depressed pole there was a turning in on herself, a longing for nonbeing, "dulling and stilling," as in

"Poppies in July." At the manic extreme were the great storms, projected outward in vituperative exorcism or ferocious tirades. She helped herself to everyday objects and circumstances to hand, transforming them by her vision as surely as van Gogh transformed the sunflowers and the kitchen chair. And her recent furies were transmuted too, becoming indistinguishable from her old buried rages that were now at last fully and freely available to her. It was as though she looked in a glass and a huge mirror image of her traumatized childhood self stared back.

The trajectory of Sylvia's creative quest during September and October 1962 began with the lament "For a Fatherless Son" on September 26, then moved through "A Birthday Present" on the thirtieth and into the charged bitterness of "The Detective" and "The Courage of Shutting Up" on October 1 and 2. The next seven days brought all five of her bee poems, where her practical beekeeping notes yielded poetic gold. The beehive for Sylvia was rich terrain, that of her father, the expert on bees. The very sickness that killed Otto Plath, diabetes, was linked to the cloying sweetness of honey. In "Stings" the enraged, vengeful daughter (later to be given savage speech in "Lady Lazarus" and "Purdah") rises up as Queen Bee:

> . . . I
> Have a self to recover, a queen.
> Is she dead, is she sleeping?
> Where has she been,
> With her lion-red body, her wings of glass?
>
> Now she is flying
> More terrible than she ever was, red
> Scar in the sky, red comet
> Over the engine that killed her —
> The mausoleum, the wax house.

In earlier Ariel poems she had already faced up to the two major figures of her poetic universe — her dead father's black shape and the silver form of her mother-moon-muse. Now at last she encountered the disquieting image of herself: she emerges as weirdly glamorous and "more terrible than she ever was," with "her lion-red body, her wings of glass." But she is wounded — a red scar — and finally dead, or reborn, flying over the "wax house" that "killed her."*

---

*Sylvia greatly prized these bee poems, placing them at the end of her own selection for *Ariel*, where the last line of "Wintering" ended the collection on a note of hope: "The bees are flying. They taste the spring."

Writing to her mother on October 9, the day she finished the bee sequence, Sylvia declared her decision to get a divorce and soberly reported the practicalities of the situation. Ted had agreed to £1,000 a year maintenance. And no, she would never return to the States: "If I start running now, I will never stop."

October 10 brought the cryptic fury of "A Secret." On the eleventh came "The Applicant," with the slick, rapid-fire salestalk of a fairground huckster, jeering at the whole concept of marriage:

> . . . in twenty-five years she'll be silver,
> In fifty, gold.
> A living doll, everywhere you look.
> It can sew, it can cook,
> It can talk, talk, talk.

The Ariel poems emerged from an enclosed world — the crucible of Sylvia's inner being. Sometimes the enclosure is a hospital, sometimes it seems to be a fairground (as with "The Applicant" and "Lady Lazarus") or monstrous Grand Guignol ("Daddy") where fearsome, larger-than-life puppets cavort as they might before a mesmerized child. With "Daddy," written on the twelfth, the nursery-rhyme jingle is incantatory — a deadly spell is being cast. A ferocious rejection of "daddy" is taking place; the most damning charges imaginable are being hurled at him. Yet the wizardry of this amazing poem is that its jubilant fury has a sobbing and impassioned undersong. The voice is finally that of a revengeful, bitterly hurt child storming against a beloved parent. Alvarez rightly declared "Daddy" to be a love poem:

> Daddy, I have had to kill you.
> You died before I had time —
> Marble-heavy, a bag full of God,
> Ghastly statue with one gray toe
> Big as a Frisco seal
>
> And a head in the freakish Atlantic
> Where it pours bean green over blue
> In the waters off beautiful Nauset.
> I used to pray to recover you.
> Ach, du.

In a brilliant essay on Plath, Helen McNeil writes:

> In "Daddy," perhaps Plath's most famous poem, . . . Otto Plath appears coded, first as the patriarchal statue, "Marble-heavy, a bag full of God / Ghastly statue with one gray toe." Then, shockingly, he becomes a Nazi, playing tormentor to Plath's Jew. Although Otto

Plath came from Silesia, in what was then Germany, he was not a Nazi, nor was his daughter Jewish, nor is there evidence that he mistreated her. In a classic transference, "Daddy" transforms the abandoned child's unmediated irrational rage into qualities attributed to its object: if Daddy died and hurt me so, he must be a bastard; I hate him for his cruelty; everyone else hates him too: "the villagers never liked you." . . . Plath knew that she hadn't ever completed the process of mourning for her father, and both she and "Daddy" recognize that in some way she had used Hughes as a double of her lost father.

Helen McNeil goes on to point out that " 'Daddy' operates by *generating a duplicate of Plath's presumed psychic state in the reader,* so that we reexperience her grief, rage, masochism, and revenge, whether or not these fit the 'facts' " (my italics). Anyone who has heard the recording of "Daddy" that Sylvia made for the British Council that October will remember the shock of pure fury in her articulation, the smoldering rage with which she is declaring herself free, both of ghostly father and of husband. The implication is that after this exorcism her life can begin again, that she will be reborn. And indeed on ethical grounds only a desperate bid for life and psychic health can even begin to excuse this and several other of the Ariel poems:

> I was ten when they buried you.
> At twenty I tried to die
> And get back, back, back to you
> I thought even the bones would do.
>
> But they pulled me out of the sack,
> And they stuck me together with glue.
> And then I knew what to do.
> I made a model of you,
> A man in black with a Meinkampf look
>
> And a love of the rack and the screw.
> And I said I do, I do.
> So daddy, I'm finally through.

Jubilant at bringing off such an extraordinary poetic coup, Sylvia was in an exalted state later that same day, October 12, writing to her mother. "It is *over*," she declared. "My life can begin." She went on to tell her mother that she was keeping on the "very expensive" agency nanny until Aunt Hilda arrived, at the end of November, to accompany her to Ireland. From December 1 to the end of February she would be in Glasthule, recovering "on the milk from TT-tested cows (hope to learn to milk them myself), homemade bread, and the sea!" In the same letter she reported that "Nick has two teeth, stands, sits, and is an *angel*. Ted had cut Frieda's hair short and it looks marvellous, no mess, no straggle. She has two kittens . . . : Tiger-Pieker and Skunky-Bunks." Sylvia herself had begun to take riding lessons, loving them. "Blackberrying" was in the September 15 issue of *The New Yorker*, and she marveled to her mother about the "terrific stuff" she was writing. Chafing against Devon's dullness in her old tough prose, she had exciting plans: "I miss *brains*, hate this cow life, am dying to surround myself with intelligent, good people. I'll have a salon in London. I am a famous poetess here — mentioned this week in *The Listener* as one of the half-dozen women who will last — including Marianne Moore and the Brontës!" She wrote in determinedly buoyant spirits, on the same day, to Warren and his wife, Maggie, suggesting a holiday with them in the Tyrol the following summer.

For the next four days Sylvia wrote nothing. Ted had come by to collect his things and then Sylvia had gone down to Cornwall with the children and cats to visit the future victims of "Lesbos."* Mrs. Plath and Warren must have been relieved to receive her optimistic letters of October 12, but by the sixteenth, having demolished her father in "Daddy," Sylvia was busy with "Medusa," a bitter, brutal attack on the Mother of her inner myth, Electra's rival for daddy's love, but at the same time her actual mother:

> Old barnacled umbilicus, Atlantic cable,
> Keeping itself, it seems, in a state of miraculous repair.

With the queer, subversive spite that characterizes these confessional poems, Sylvia gave in the poem's title a clue that Aurelia Plath could not fail to pick up. "Medusa" — in Greek mythology the Gorgon who turned all beholders to stone — is also the name of a species of jellyfish, *aurela*. Mrs. Plath had once joked with Sylvia about her name, which had two meanings, "golden" and "jellyfish." It is possible, of course, that in some strange way Sylvia couldn't imagine the targets of such poems as being harmed or hurt by them or that she thought the confessional mode commanded understanding on a different level from mere real-life human relationships, but if this was her view it was clearly mistaken: such poems have caused enormous pain to the innocent victims of her pen.

---

*The American couple who in August had lodged with the Hugheses at Court Green.

Like "Daddy," "Medusa" secures the speaker of the poem in righteousness by laying blame on the object:

> I didn't call you.
> I didn't call you at all.
> Nevertheless, nevertheless
> You steamed to me over the sea,
> Fat and red, a placenta
>
> Paralyzing the kicking lovers . . .
>
> . . . Who do you think you are?
> A Communion wafer? Blubbery Mary?
> I shall take no bite of your body,
> Bottle in which I live,
>
> Ghastly Vatican.
> I am sick to death of hot salt.
> Green as eunuchs, your wishes
> Hiss at my sins.
> Off, off, eely tentacle!
>
> There is nothing between us.

The poem is hurled out across the Atlantic at Aurelia Plath, but it simultaneously attacks the baby in Sylvia's personality who longs to remain in the "hot salt" of the womb.

The day she wrote "Medusa" (just as after writing "Daddy"), she sent two letters home to her mother. The exorcism "Medusa" should have brought about seems not to have worked. Her letters had a desperate tone. She did know exactly what she had achieved: "I am a genius of a writer; I have it in me. I am writing the best poems of my life; they will make my name." Yet she complained piteously. She was ill again, with high fevers and chills, and helpless without a good nanny. Her problems were all practical: if she could regain her health (she claimed to have lost nearly twenty pounds over the summer), if she had enough money in the bank, she would be able to cope. Ireland beckoned: "the place, a dream; the sea, a blessing." But for the next two months she needed help, fighting as she was "against hard odds and alone." In her second letter of the day she wildly begged that the family chip in to send Warren's wife to the rescue. "Could she come *now* . . . ? I already love her; she would be such *fun* and love the babies. We could go to Ireland together and get me settled in, and she could fly home from Dublin well before Christmas. Do I sound mad? . . . I need someone from *home*. A defender." It was after receiving this letter that Mrs. Plath, ever loyal and generous, cabled the midwife, Winifred Davies: "Please see Sylvia now and get woman for her. Salary paid here. Writing."

Not surprisingly, having dealt with the inner domination of both father and mother figures, Sylvia then attacked her longing for her husband in "The Jailer," written the next day, October 17. In this poem the spooky nursery-rhyme rhythms of "Daddy" are heard again, in a similar extreme attack of frenetic overkill. One can see how any overtures Ted Hughes made toward a reconciliation at this time were doomed to meet a wall of unrelenting rage.

Resourceful as ever, Winifred Davies had come up with a solution to Sylvia's chief practical problem, that of finding reliable help for her children. A young local nurse, daughter of a solid middle-class family in Belstone, on the edge of Dartmoor, said she would "love" to help out. On October 18 Sylvia wrote in some excitement to her mother that Susan O'Neill-Roe would probably come to live in until mid-December for "*half* of the fee for the bastardly nanny who arrived last night." In the event Susan, then twenty-two, slept at home, coming to Court Green from eight-thirty to six daily — just what Sylvia needed. By October 23 "Sue" was one of the family, having in only two days restored Sylvia's seemingly indomitable energy. Although she could stay only to mid-December before returning as a staff nurse to the Great Ormond Street Hospital for Children in London, Susan might well settle Sylvia and her babies in Ireland before she left. In any case the difference she made to Court Green was "a wonder." Now Sylvia could write her "dawn poems in blood" before the children's breakfast, then work uninterrupted on her novel and journals until lunchtime, after which she could nap in the afternoons and chat over a cup of tea before Susan returned home in the evenings. For the first time in her life Sylvia was an independent, prolific, professional writer.

To Ruth Fainlight in Morocco she wrote a long, ecstatic letter, blaming Ted and Ted's family for her predicament in unfair, bitter, accusing language but rejoicing openly in her new power as a writer: "Psychologically, Ruth, I am fascinated by the polarities of muse-poet and mother housewife. When I was 'happy' domestically I felt a gag in my throat. Now that my domestic life, until I get a permanent live-in girl, is chaos, I am living like a Spartan, writing through huge fevers and producing free stuff I had locked in me for years. I feel astounded and very lucky."

Throughout October and November these amazing, disturbing poems continued to flow. She had written the acidly vindictive "Lesbos" on October 18 and an odd, dreamlike evocation of Uncle Walter in "Stopped Dead" on the nineteenth while still feverishly ill with her recurrent flu and while the "old, snobby snoop" of a nanny came and went. There was a poem on the twentieth, two on the twenty-first, and then, sustained by the arrival of Susan, "the prettiest, sweetest local children's nurse," two more poems on the twenty-fourth, one on the twenty-fifth, two more on the twenty-seventh, three on the twenty-ninth, and fourteen more up to December 1!

Three of the October poems, "Fever 103°," "Purdah," and "Lady Lazarus," are merciless self-projections of Sylvia, the central figure of her mythic world. The poems are extraordinary *performances* — not only in their consummate poetic skill, but in that their central figure is giving a performance as though before a single quelled spectator or in a fairground, watched by the "peanut-crunching crowd." This Sylvia figure, as weird in appearance as in the hubris of her vaunted tightrope feats, woos and mocks death and witchily scatters her curses.

"Fever 103°" is the mildest of the trio. The feverish lady, sloughing off sin in her fever, describes herself:

> ... I am a lantern ——
>
> My head a moon
> Of Japanese paper, my gold beaten skin
> Infinitely delicate and infinitely expensive.
>
> Does not my heat astound you. And my light.

She is "too pure for you or anyone." She floats high in the air to become

> ... a pure acetylene
> Virgin
> Attended by roses,
>
> By kisses, by cherubim, ...
>
> Not him, nor him
> (My selves dissolving, old whore petticoats) ——
> To Paradise.

"Lady Lazarus" boasts of even riskier accomplishments:

> I have done it again.
> One year in every ten
> I manage it ——
>
> A sort of walking miracle, my skin
> Bright as a Nazi lampshade ...

Her specialty is unique:

> Dying
> Is an art, like everything else.
> I do it exceptionally well.
>
> I do it so it feels like hell.
> I do it so it feels real.
> I guess you could say I've a call.

And she is very dangerous indeed:

> Out of the ash
> I rise with my red hair
> And I eat men like air.

But the ultimate scourge is the Clytemnestra figure in "Purdah," a high-pitched scream of a poem, in which she threatens to unloose

> The lioness,
> The shriek in the bath,
> The cloak of holes.

These poems, penetrating the furthest reaches of disdain and rage, are bereft of all normal "human" feeling. Hurt has hardened to hate, and death is omnipresent. The Sylvia figure now takes central place in her poetic world, flanked by Otto and the Mother/Other. Other members of the cast simply mirror the attributes of the two parent figures. This mythic Sylvia holds the key to the baffling puzzle of the Ariel poems. She seems to have been presenting the truth of what her mute, traumatized self, "Overexposed, like an X-ray" ("Medusa"), *felt like,* to "generat[e] a duplicate," in Helen McNeil's words, of her "presumed psychic state in the reader," and to reveal the murderous projections of this psychic state onto others. To be her own singer, psychiatrist, and priestess demanded a fund of desperate courage, and that she had: "I am the magician's girl who does not flinch." She had found her subject as a poet — or, rather, it had found her — and she could see nothing beyond without first exploring to the end of it. The result is an unfurling, perhaps unique in poetry, of "unpoetic" negative emotions of an extreme kind.

When Sylvia read "Daddy" and "Lady Lazarus" to Alvarez, calling them "some light verse," he was appalled — they seemed at first hearing to be more "assault and battery" than poetry. It took him some time to appreciate their "weird elegance." The same weird elegance was used to less devastating effect in several versatile poems around this time. "Lyonnesse" and "Amnesiac" — originally written as two parts of the same poem under the title "Amnesiac" on October 21 — chide God, in the first poem, and an errant husband figure in the second, for forgetfulness. "Cut" is a playful poem, written on October 24. It was dedicated to Susan O'Neill-Roe on her third day in the house and commemorates a real event: by accident Sylvia had all but cut off the fleshy tip of her thumb with a kitchen knife. "By Candlelight" and "Nick and the Candlestick," both poems about attending to her baby son at night, strike a different note, musing and melancholy. In "By Candlelight":

> I hold you on my arm.
> It is very late.
> The dull bells tongue the hour,
> The mirror floats us at one candle power.

"Nick and the Candlestick" ends with the beautiful lines:

> Love, love,
> I have hung our cave with roses,
> With soft rugs ——
>
> The last of Victoriana.
> Let the stars
> Plummet to their dark address, . . .
>
> You are the one
> Solid the spaces lean on, envious.
> You are the baby in the barn.

In "The Tour," however, spite returns as Sylvia demolishes, with sharp, surrealistic wit, some "hag" enemy — perhaps the nanny, or some curious visitor or neighbor (as with "Eavesdropper," about another neighbor):

> And you want to be shown about!
> Yes, yes, this is my address.
> Not a patch on *your* place, I guess, with the Javanese
> Geese and the monkey trees.
> It's a bit burnt-out,
> A bit of a wild machine, a bit of a mess!

This gleeful piece was followed on her birthday, October 27, by two perfect lyrics — "Poppies in October" and "Ariel." In the former, a companion to "Poppies in July," the poppies, brighter than sunrise and "the woman in the ambulance / Whose red heart blooms through her coat so astoundingly," are

> A gift, a love gift
> Utterly unasked for
> By a sky

> Palely and flamily
> Igniting its carbon monoxides . . .

The mystical question is, why should the speaker be chosen, why should she be saved? — at the cost, seemingly, of the life of the woman in the ambulance.

There are never, of course, answers to these questions in the electric air of Sylvia's poems, but some sort of resurrection is at least provided in "Ariel." The title "Ariel," like "Medusa," carries multiple meanings; it refers to the ethereal spirit of Shakespeare's *Tempest*, but also significantly, Ariel happened to be the name of the (rather elderly, ponderous) horse on which Sylvia was learning to ride. Most potent of all, Ariel is the spirit of poetry, the romantic embodiment of inspiration or genius.* In the canon of Sylvia's work, "Ariel" is supreme, a quintessential statement of all that had meaning for her. In it she rehearses the whole spectrum of her color imagery, moving from "Stasis in darkness" into the "substanceless blue" of sky and distance as horse and rider, "God's lioness," rush as one through clutching hostilities:

> Nigger-eye
> Berries cast dark
> Hooks ——
>
> Black sweet blood mouthfuls,
> Shadows.

"Something else," too, "Hauls me through air": the speaker, increasingly ethereal, unpeels, like the speaker in "Fever 103°," shedding "Dead hands, dead stringencies" as woman-horse becomes woman-arrow-dew, destroying herself in her unremitting drive toward resurrection. At the end, the "child's cry" that "Melts in the wall" is that of a real child, just as the "the red / Eye, the cauldron of morning" is the real sun rising as she writes. As always — and this is one of the sources of Plath's extraordinary power — every image is grounded in some *thing*, depicted as if with verbal paint.

◄ ◄ ◄

---

*As Judith Kroll has pointed out, Sylvia may have known that Ariel also has a spiritual connotation in Jewish mythology — the sacred flame of Leviticus and Isaiah.

Once Susan O'Neill-Roe was installed in Devon, London became an accessible haven. Sylvia certainly traveled up alone on October 29–30 to record new poems and an interview with Peter Orr for the British Council (and the BBC archives). Amazingly, she completed three of the poems ("Lady Lazarus," "Purdah," and "Nick and the Candlestick") the day before the reading. Her spirits were high when she arrived on Alvarez's doorstep with a sheaf of astounding verse to read aloud to him. While exiled in Devon, she had let her looks go: she was thin after her miserable summer and wore clothes that she had saved from before her pregnancies. Now, mistress of her life and muse, she put up her hair and began to dress smartly. Everything was pointing to success. Alvarez declared she was the first woman poet he had taken seriously since Emily Dickinson. Eric White, literature director of the Arts Council, asked her to organize and introduce the American night of the International Poetry Festival, to be held at the Royal Court Theatre in July 1963. The BBC also recorded her reading "Berck-Plage" (broadcast November 17) and included her among four readers in a program called "The Weird Ones."

Again, on this trip, Sylvia was staying with the Macedos. When Suzette had phoned earlier in October, Sylvia told her that she had thrown Ted out and didn't feel she and Suzette could continue their friendship, as Suzette was Assia's friend. Suzette had protested that she was Sylvia's friend too. The upshot was that Sylvia went on seeing the Macedos but on less open terms than before, maintaining a proud front with them. Her adamant public stance was that her new freedom delighted her and that her decision to divorce was final. She scorned Ted for having left the perfection they shared for "a whiff of Chanel." Suzette was surprised, for she remembered Sylvia's exclaiming enthusiastically about Assia the previous year, "An amazing woman — she has her passport on her face." Suzette was quite aware that David and Assia Wevill were both in a terrible state about the affair. Suzette tried to tell Sylvia that things were not as black and white as she imagined, but Sylvia would not listen. Suzette also realized, unhappily, that Sylvia was giving her the picture she wished her to pass on to Assia, as Assia too was inclined to do in reverse.

Sometime during that October visit Helder Macedo told Sylvia about a Portuguese novel he admired; in it, two men in love with each other conjure up an alluring woman between them. Surprisingly Sylvia said, "I know. I have conjured up Assia." To her Assia was her opposite — the Other. Suzette remembers that Sylvia was very "punishing" about Ted and "didn't have much to say for most people" but that she liked poets and spoke admiringly of W. S. Merwin, Richard Murphy, and Alvarez (none of whom Suzette knew personally). And, too, Sylvia talked excitedly about going to Ireland — the ideal life for her, she said. Suzette was left feeling that Sylvia was making blueprints for life, trying on different lives like dresses.

The Macedos found Sylvia alarmingly "overwrought." Her cut thumb, bound up in a dirty bandage, was clearly septic and in need of attention, but she seemed too distraught to notice. Otherwise she was elegantly dressed in a new outfit, which surprised Suzette, as Sylvia was "obsessive about money." She told them she had not been sleeping properly since Ted left and talked hysterically about the high temperatures she seemed to be running all the time. It was part, she said, of her new creative fever. In the middle of the night Suzette was wakened by deep, heartbroken sobbing from Sylvia's room. She went to comfort her but found to her amazement that Sylvia, now silent, her face wet with tears, was deeply asleep. For Suzette it was Sylvia's only genuine communication since she arrived.

Ted, who had kept in touch with the Merwins since the Lacan visit, wrote informing them that he and Sylvia had separated and that he was staying here and there with friends in London. Dido was due to come to England from France later in October to tidy up the estate of her mother, who had recently died; she would be staying in the large flat in Montagu Square that her mother had leased. Bill's immediate thought was that this would give Ted somewhere to live (and, more important, to work). As soon as Dido arrived in London she rang Ted's mother and got his telephone number. He moved in the same night.

When Ted told Sylvia where he was staying she began to phone him there. She also repeatedly rang up Dido, who was at first very sorry for her, imagining her "wracked with remorse" at driving Ted away. But all Sylvia did, apparently, was to project an image of herself as "martyred model Wife-and-Mother," abuse Ted as solely responsible, and catalogue a series of domestic disasters, in order, Dido suspected, "to harrow me with a view to my harrowing Ted." What surprised Dido was the "sheer momentum of her eloquence" as she reported that her thumb would have to be amputated because of gangrene, that Frieda was down with "a deep regression," and other catastrophes — "seemingly never," Dido noticed, "of sufficient duration to interfere with Sylvia's riding lessons." Finally, says Dido,

I threatened to hang up if she didn't listen. I then delivered a completely fruitless spiel to the effect that almost anyone could be brainwashed into becoming an adulterer and a liar if you went on long enough implying that was what they were. That sooner or later, however much they loved you, they would either get the hell out to avoid your accusations, or console themselves for the sake of their sanity and lie about it for the sake of peace . . . If she wanted Ted back, she would have to stop knocking him for a start. And if she didn't want him back, knocking him to me was a waste of her time and mine.

At this point Sylvia hung up. After that Dido got the housekeeper to "field" the telephone, and the housekeeper then "came in for one or two startling earfuls about Ted."

Sometime around her return to Devon on October 30, Sylvia changed her mind about spending the winter in Ireland and decided to rent a flat in London instead. Alvarez, in his "Sylvia Plath: A Memoir," remembers her mentioning it in one of her visits to his flat earlier than this — and it could well be that the idea first appealed to her as a good one when in his company. Whatever the reason for her change of plan, Sylvia lost no time in putting it into action. On November 4 she was in London again, this time to meet Ted, who approved her new decision to establish a city base and went with her to see several places. Sylvia told her mother, "Ted is behind me in this . . . Now he sees he has nothing to fear from me — no scenes or vengefulness." Sylvia's luck, however, took her alone to Primrose Hill, where she had gone to consult Dr. Horder about her suppurating thumb. Passing a "FLATS TO LET" sign in front of 23 Fitzroy Road with its blue plaque announcing that Yeats had lived there, Sylvia instantly decided it was "*the* street and *the* house" for her. Persuading some builders to let her in, she "flew upstairs" to discover that the top maisonette was, as she wrote to her mother, "*just* right . . . with three bedrooms upstairs, lounge, kitchen and bath downstairs *and* a balcony garden!" Within minutes Sylvia was negotiating with the agents, Morton Smith & Co., for a five-year lease.

Back in Devon, jubilant, full of plans, she consulted Yeats's *Collected Plays,* hoping for a message from the great poet. Sure enough, when she opened the book at random her finger fell on the passage "Get wine and food to give you strength and courage, and I will get the house ready" in *The Unicorn from the Stars.* "I was scared to death," she wrote to Ruth Fainlight on November 20. "I covet it [the flat] beyond belief, with that blue plaque! I would have to furnish it with straw mats and pillows and live on squalid stew, but I actually cried in London, I was so happy to be seeing people . . ."

To Ruth, as to Suzette Macedo — and indeed in bitterly accusing letters to Ted's parents — Sylvia made a great deal of Ted's sticking her away in the country without help, thus preventing her from earning money by writing. By now she believed this, as she believed her own fantasy of extreme deprivation. In fact, with Susan O'Neill-Roe and Nancy Axworthy she had generous help in the house, and she was writing marvelously. Financially, too, she was well off. It is recorded that between October and her death four months later, Hughes gave Sylvia about £900, including an allowance of £20 a week — a fair amount in 1962. In addition, her mother contributed $50 a month (about £20) for emergencies. (Aurelia Plath wished she would bring the children to America but dared not press the matter.) In October Sylvia received a $100 birthday gift from her Aunt Dot and $300 from Mrs. Prouty, with which she bought her new wardrobe. Aunt Dot followed up her initial gift with $700 from her personal savings. All this in addition to Sylvia's freelance earnings. With her prospects of a "salon" in London, together with a new flat, a house in Devon, and a car, Sylvia's spirits soared.

Arrangements for her London flat and other distractions slackened the tempo of Sylvia's poetic output somewhat in November, though she produced fourteen poems that month. Susan's help and her own keen anticipation of what London promised had made her happier and more confident. Though they show her still fingering her wounds, these poems are more reflective than ferocious, and the high-pitched rages of the most extreme October poems are heard no more. The lyric note in "The Couriers," written on November 4, is one of regret for lost happiness. On the sixth came three more poems. "The Night Dances," a haunting poem about her son, and "Gulliver," which sadly sees her husband ensnared by inferior beings, are both fairly serene poems. "Getting There" plunges back into her death/rebirth obsession. Life carries her like an express train toward death. But after the catastrophe she arises:

> . . . stepping from this skin
> Of old bandages, boredoms, old faces
>
> Step to you from the black car of Lethe,
> Pure as a baby.

"Thalidomide," written on November 8, refers to an issue of the early 1960s which revived Sylvia's recurring nightmares about deformed children.

On November 11 she wrote a strange love poem, "Letter in November," possibly with Alvarez in mind, possibly to celebrate her new
independence. Although this was followed by "Death & Co." (November 14) and "The Fearful" (November 16) — both fueled by memories of the summer's upheavals — energy had reasserted its
dominance, and Sylvia, in full throttle, was surging forward:

> O God, I am not like you
> In your vacuous black,
> Stars stuck all over, bright stupid confetti.
> Eternity bores me,
> I never wanted it . . .
>
> The blood berries are themselves, they are very still.
> The hooves will not have it,
> In blue distance the pistons hiss.

It may have been at this time, possibly on November 15, that Sylvia
rearranged the manuscript of *Ariel* for the last time. It contains "Death
& Co.," written the day before, but no poem written later.*

In the third week of November, Susan O'Neill-Roe took a short
holiday while Clarissa Roche came all the way from Kent to Court
Green with a month-old baby. She arrived in the pouring rain to be
met by Sylvia at the deserted local station. "You've saved my life,"
Sylvia told her. At Smith, Paul Roche had absorbed most of Sylvia's
attention; Clarissa had seemed something of an adjunct. Now, however, as a fellow American and a mother, Clarissa was hugely welcome
as a confidante and sympathizer. All the pent-up wrath poured into
poems like "Daddy" and "The Jailer" burst out again in what seems
to have been an unstinted monologue of mockery and aggression.
Sylvia escorted Clarissa with a kind of awe to the threshold of Ted's
study and told her about having gathered papers and bits of hair from
it, preparatory to the witchlike ritual of the bonfire in the summer.
Sylvia also read "Daddy" aloud in a spooky, comical voice that
made both women fall about with laughter. By the time of Clarissa's

---

*The manuscript had already been through earlier revisions; there were former
titles crossed out on the title page, and the order of certain poems changed, with
several of them corrected by hand. Sylvia never typed a final copy of the manuscript.
The poems she wrote later were typed for magazine submission and a copy of each
folded into the manuscript. When one thinks of her manuscript of *The Colossus*,
which went through different forms and titles, each seeming to her at the time to be
the final, ideal one, it is quite possible to imagine that Sylvia would ultimately have
rearranged her *Ariel* to include some of the poems written later than mid-November,
and that she might even have changed the title.

departure Sylvia was in high spirits, writing to her mother on November 19 of having completed a second book of poems in a month, "and the minute I get a mother's helper in London, I will do novel after novel."

She had spent Mrs. Prouty's birthday check in the Jaeger shop in Exeter, buying a camel suit and matching sweater, a black sweater and blue tweed skirt, a green cardigan and red skirt, while in St. Ives she had bought "arty" pewter jewelry and an enameled necklace. With a new hair style and black leather bag, gloves, and shoes, she was going to take London by storm — if only the flat would come through. Thanksgiving found her desperate after the few days without Susan and tense about delays over the lease. Unknown to Sylvia, a prior bid for the maisonette had been made by Professor Trevor Thomas, an art historian with two schoolboy sons who badly needed its three bedrooms. The agents were dithering when Sylvia, with Ted's financial support, agreed to pay a year's rent in advance, giving her mother (*"Professor* A. S. Plath") as a reference. By the end of November all seemed settled. The flat was to go to Mr. and Mrs. Hughes and their children. "When I get safely into this flat, I shall be the happiest person in the world," Sylvia wrote to her mother on November 29. "I shall apply immediately for a live-in mother's help and get cracking on my novel. I hope to finish it by the date of that contest you sent information of; even if I don't win, which I won't, it will be an incentive. This experience, I think, will prove all for the best — I have grown up amazingly."

◀   ◀   ◀

On December 12, after frantic days of packing, braiding onions, seeing to her bees, and arranging for Nancy Axworthy to feed the cats, Sylvia closed Court Green and drove with Susan and the two children to London. It was "a clear, crisp blue day," but they arrived at 23 Fitzroy Road to find the gas stove still not installed and the electricity unconnected. While Susan stayed with the children in the car, Sylvia rushed to the gas board, accidentally leaving the keys in the locked house.

Eventually "the obliging gas boys climbed on the [back] roof and jimmied a window and installed the stove" (so Sylvia told her mother), and the electricity board, under duress, connected them up. Sylvia's first letter to her mother was ecstatic, although two days after the move Susan departed for a "deserved holiday" before returning to the children's hospital, leaving Sylvia alone in an undecorated, hardly furnished flat, at the mercy of her London connections. She had applied for a telephone, but none as yet had been provided — nor would be during the two months of life left to her. The lack of a telephone was one of numerous flukes, simple matters of bad luck, which were to contribute to Sylvia's suicide. Before Christmas, busy painting floors, acquiring an American kitchen, writing articles and programs for the BBC, Sylvia insisted that she had never been so happy in her life.

The Sillitoes were away in Morocco for a year, but Sylvia saw a lot of the Macedos and of new friends, Jillian and Gerry Becker, to whom Suzette had introduced her on one of her London visits earlier that autumn. The Beckers were a South African couple with young children whose large, comfortable house in Mountfort Crescent, Islington, was just around the corner from the Cleverdons' in Barnsbury Square. Gerry Becker, a lecturer at Hendon Polytechnic, and Jillian opened their home to her. Gerry in particular, a big, warm, bearlike man who drove around London in an old taxi, adopted a fatherly/motherly role toward Sylvia. The neighborhood, too, was welcoming, everyone seeming to remember her: the couple at the laundromat, the people who ran the local grocery, the eccentric ironmonger, even the man who collected and delivered Nick's diapers. Nurse Davies's son, Garnett, a young policeman in London, dropped in to see her and help paint the flat. Susan O'Neill-Roe came to see her and the children when she could, and Dr. Horder was again close by — to be constantly in demand in January when Sylvia and both babies contracted flu. Ted Hughes drove to Devon shortly before Christmas to collect the red corduroy curtain material Sylvia thought indispensable for her windows. He came to see Sylvia and the children about three times a week, sometimes more. Sylvia was mostly very bright but kept him firmly in the dark about her doings.

At first, then, Sylvia had every incentive to be her brisk, efficient self. She took Frieda and Nicholas to the zoo, got in touch with Alvarez to show him the completed manuscript of *Ariel,* sat up late writing careful notes on her new poems for a "Living Poet" program on the BBC.

As often happens with brilliant new work, Sylvia's was accorded slow recognition. Howard Moss of *The New Yorker* turned down most of what she sent him on her first-reading contract, accepting only "Lyonnesse" among thirty or more masterpieces; *The Atlantic Monthly,* however, immediately took two of the bee poems ("The Arrival of the Bee Box" and "Wintering"). In England, Alvarez at *The Observer* and Charles Osborne of the *London Magazine* continued to be supportive, but no one — not even Alvarez — understood the intensity of Sylvia's need for reassurance and professional recognition. As it was, her enthusiasm carried her through a superb evocation of her seaside childhood in "Ocean 1212-W," written for the BBC series "Writers on Themselves," while *Punch* commissioned the humorous reminiscence "America! America!" about her schooling in Winthrop and Wellesley.

Sylvia's temporary high apparently excluded the need to write poetry. In her prose pieces she was beginning to try out the sort of journalism-cum-essay she admired in Mavis Gallant and Emily Hahn. Suzette Macedo remembers Sylvia's being very keen to meet Emily Hahn, a friend of the Macedos. Sylvia seemed to have read all Emily Hahn's *New Yorker* pieces and admired her, she said, because she was a "professional," tackling the world arena and earning her living by writing. One of her own dreams, Sylvia said, was to have a contract with *The New Yorker* for prose articles. In late January she wrote "Snow Blitz,"* a charming, amusing piece about London's Dickensian methods of facing up to the dreadful weather, frozen pipes, and electricity cuts she had had to contend with that month. There seems no doubt that Sylvia could have made a success of such occasional journalism. There was also her new novel (Ted Hughes remembers only one or two draft chapters were ever completed) with which she planned to follow up the hoped-for success of *The Bell Jar,* due out late in January.

Letters Home suggests that Sylvia's drive and good spirits lasted through Christmas. Suzette Macedo and Jillian Becker, however, noted with concern her swift changes of mood. Professor Thomas, who lived downstairs, still felt some resentment about the way the Hugheses had preempted the flat he had wanted; in his small encounters with Sylvia as she went in and out, he found her changeable in mood, smartly dressed, and seemingly always busy. Neighbors were no substitute for a literary circle; even fellow mothers such as Katherine Frankfort and Lorna Secker-Walker, with whom she shared baby-sticky teas, were mainly comforting substitutes for the "salon" she had envisaged. It was through Katherine Frankfort that Sylvia discovered a local nursery school for Frieda in the mornings, but her chief concern was to find a suitable au pair girl — a second edition of Susan O'Neill-Roe — who would take over the housekeeping and children in the mornings and evenings. That such a person failed

---

*Not published until 1977, in *Johnny Panic and the Bible of Dreams.*

immediately to materialize again exacerbated Sylvia's depression. She fought it off, spending a Christmas check from Mrs. Prouty on glamorous evening clothes: an Italian blue and white overblouse and velvet skirt, some "fake-fur toreador pants," and a cocktail outfit with a "metallic blue-and-black French top."

Very probably Sylvia was looking for a new man in her life, a relationship that would fulfill her emotionally and intellectually and restore her pride. Richard Murphy having failed her, A. Alvarez may well have been Sylvia's first choice. He was influential, amiable, and attractive; clearly he admired her and fully responded to her new poetry. When she invited him around on Christmas Eve she may have hoped for more than a friendly chat. In his memoir Alvarez implies that his relationship with Sylvia was no more than literary, yet he confesses frankly to a bleak feeling of having let her down. In view of Sylvia's penchant for extremes, it must have been difficult for Alvarez to play a casual role without toppling into the gulf of her terrible need. His description of Sylvia at this time is poignant:

> She seemed different. Her hair, which she usually wore in a tight, school-mistressy bun, was loose. It hung straight to her waist like a tent, giving her pale face and gaunt figure a curiously desolate, rapt air, like a priestess emptied out by the rites of her cult. When she walked in front of me down the hall passage and up the stairs to her apartment . . . her hair gave off a strong smell, sharp as an animal's. The children were already in bed upstairs and the flat was silent. It was newly painted, white and chill . . . rather beautiful in its chaste, stripped-down way, but cold, very cold, and the oddments of flimsy Christmas decoration made it seem doubly forlorn . . . For the unhappy, Christmas is always a bad time.

After Christmas Sylvia ceased to call on Alvarez.

Suzette Macedo remembers Sylvia as being especially distraught just before Christmas: she and the children had nowhere to go. She would break down if she had to cook Christmas dinner alone in her fatherless home. Although Suzette and Helder were to see David and Assia Wevill for Boxing Day, Suzette responded immediately, asking Sylvia and her children to Christmas dinner. Sylvia went and enjoyed herself. To her mother she wrote the next day in her usual rushed, distracted vein:

> We went for Christmas dinner with a very nice Portuguese couple in Hampstead. They cooked a goose which they lit with cognac and gave Frieda a tiny toy piano . . . and Nick a rubber rabbit. I thought

the outfits for Nick and Frieda which Warren and Maggie sent just lovely; do thank them for me. I have been so preoccupied I have barely had time to cook. The little nursery school just round the corner takes children from 9:30 to 12:30, and I shall try Frieda at it next week. She seems to blossom on outside experiences with other children, and I think she needs this . . .

I am hoping the BBC accepts my 20-minute program of new poetry — the producer thinks they are wonderful, but the Board still has to approve. Then I have the commission for a program on my childhood landscape, or in my case, seascape. Did I tell you Mrs. Prouty sent $100? And bless you for your $50. I have double expenses just now — the closing expenses [of Court Green] and the rather large opening ones here, but once I am settled here, it will be five years' blessed security and peace and *no more floor painting*! All of which is much to look forward to and in which time I should have produced a lot of work.

How lucky I am to have two beautiful babies and work! . . .

Through the bravado the reader can sense the anxiety, almost the panic, of a desperate girl who adored her children but needed help if she was to continue to write — as write she must, if she was to support herself. Her predicament was that of all gifted, ambitious mothers with small children, but Sylvia's obsessive drive to accomplish everything at once (including the floor painting), together with the still-raw wound of Ted's departure, made her reject all compromises. Inwardly, her mind raced within its cage. The very day (December 26) that she wrote to her mother of Christmas at the Macedos, she also wrote to thank Daniel and Helga Huws for their gifts to the children, her mood febrile and heavy with grievances. Of Assia Wevill she wrote:

She is part of this set of barren women, which includes Dido Merwin, that I am so glad to get rid of. I guess I am just not like that. I had a terrible experience calling Dido Merwin as Frieda's godmother when I was in London [looking for flats] — she was the only person I thought could advise me about doctors and a flat. She knew I was calling on her as a godmother, but because she was so glad she at last had Ted living at her place, she made it clear she was home but refused to speak to me. Both Ted and I have agreed to write off the Merwins as Frieda's godparents and wonder if you would be her godparents instead. I take this as a very serious thing, & it almost killed me for Frieda's sake, to think of the heartlessness and hypocrisy behind Mrs. Merwin's refusal to answer when she knew I was worried about the babies going into hospital.

It is impossible to read any of Sylvia's letters of this time without realizing they were desperate bids for sympathy and support. Dido Merwin comments that almost every statement about her in this letter is untrue. And the children had suffered from nothing more severe than colds that winter. Ted Hughes had heard of no plan to change Frieda's godparents. In October Sylvia had written to David Wevill, alerting him to Ted's "desertion" — not pausing to consider, it seems, how David would feel about Assia's part in it. To Bill Merwin in New York she implied that Ted was having an affair with Dido, misreading Merwin's character and attitude toward herself enough to suggest that this left her and Bill in a position to explore their own affinities.

One of the most sympathetic witnesses of Sylvia's disturbed, determined behavior in these last months was Daniel Huws, who met her shortly before Christmas at a PEN party in Chelsea. He was surprised to see her smoking, a habit she said she had taken up after being offered a cigarette by her solicitor. They spoke of divorce, Dan, a Roman Catholic, contending that he believed "till death do us part." Sylvia replied with great intensity, "Yes, that's what I believe, too." And indeed though Sylvia had talked widely about getting a divorce in letters and to friends, she never had more than general discussions on her position with her solicitor. It was after this meeting — their last — that Sylvia wrote asking Dan and Helga to be Frieda's godparents, despite the fact that, apart from the Merwins, Frieda already had godparents: Ann Davidow and her husband, Leo Goodman, in America. As Daniel Huws says, he answered Sylvia's letter in the affirmative, "but with a priggish qualification that only the Church could really make godparents."

Sylvia's alleged poverty clearly occupied a salient place in her mythology at this time. In Devon the rector had supplied her with a wooden box marked "POOR BOX" in which to collect small change for use in the parish. This Sylvia had transported to London, displaying it prominently on the shelf over the electric fire in the sitting room. Suzette Macedo says Sylvia made a great fuss when the Beckers' Irish maid gave her a pound note for her and her babies. This was magnified into a huge symbolic event that Sylvia described to Suzette at frequent intervals. She must smell of poverty and abandonment! Suzette herself doubts that the incident ever happened and feels that if it did, Phyllis probably gave Sylvia money to buy sweets for the children for Christmas. Jillian Becker also expresses amazement. Apart from anything else, she notes, Sylvia was always very well dressed; no one could ever think she looked poor. Yet Jillian remem-

bers that when they went out together Sylvia "never had any money
on her." And she explained her new outfits to Jillian by telling her
that "a man" had given her a check to buy clothes. (Jillian assumed
it to be some admirer; Sylvia did not mention Mrs. Prouty's largesse.)

◄　◄　◄

In January, winter settled in with the worst weather England had
known for sixty years, and Sylvia's weak grip on reality began to give
way. Outwardly life became impossible as first the children, then
Sylvia, came down with colds that developed into flu. As she grew
more desperate, the Beckers were alerted to her need for constant
attention. Every week or ten days Gerry would stop off at Fitzroy
Road on his way back from teaching in Hendon. A generous-hearted
man, quick to perceive and respond to other people's needs, he became
in some ways the nurse figure of so many of Sylvia's poems. Jillian
recalls quoting lines by MacNeice to Sylvia as they sat one afternoon
in Jillian's sitting room watching the low winter sun on the garden:
"The sunlight on the garden / Hardens and grows cold," and Sylvia
continuing: "We cannot cage the minute / Within its nets of gold."
After that they often talked together about poetry and writing. Jillian
remembers that she once suggested Sylvia write another novel. Not
mentioning the one she was working on, Sylvia demurred — a novel,
she said, took "acres of time." That month there was a film festival
at the Everyman Cinema in Hampstead to which Jillian invited Sylvia
on several occasions. Sylvia was pleased to be asked but seemed
scarcely to respond to the films. Jillian remembers laughing at a particularly comical incident and then turning to see if Sylvia was also
amused. She was staring at the screen blankly, "lost in her own world
of suffering."

Toward the end of the month the Beckers gave a party to which
Sylvia came. The Cleverdons were also invited and brought Richard
Murphy along. Murphy noted her tenseness (although she seemed to
bear him no grudge) and her feverish face: "She seemed ecstatic."

On another occasion the Beckers were in Soho with Sylvia late at
night, probably after a party or theater and dinner, all too awake to
go home. They went for coffee in an all-night café and stayed en-
grossed in talk until dawn. Jillian remembers Sylvia's telling them that
she had never had much of an ear for music up to the last year or
two, when she had begun to be interested in Beethoven and Bach.
One of the Beckers commented that she must have an ear to write
poetry, and Sylvia vehemently agreed that she had that kind of ear

to an extreme degree, the music behind verse was always with her. She talked too of her plan to write novels and especially about *The Bell Jar,* which was soon to be published in England. Potboilers like that, she said, would come out under a pseudonym because she didn't want them to be judged as the work of a poet. Nothing at all was said of the barely disguised, hurtful portrait of her mother in the novel.

However scornful she was of her potboilers to the Beckers, Sylvia's ambitions received a jolt after Christmas when a letter arrived from Judith Jones, her editor at Knopf in New York, rejecting the novel kindly but with apt criticism:

> I had looked forward greatly to seeing your talents put to use in a novel, if only because it is such a special group that reads poetry . . . But although [your] qualities were indeed apparent in THE BELL JAR, to be honest with you we didn't feel that you had managed to use your materials successfully in a novelistic way. I particularly felt that though the separate happenings made in themselves good stories, you as the author had not succeeded in establishing a viewpoint. Up to the point of her breakdown the attitude of your young girl had seemed a perfectly normal combination of brashness and disgust with the world, but I was not at all prepared as a reader to accept the extent of her illness.

Without realizing it, Judith Jones had put her finger on the dangerous crack in Sylvia's personality. Bravely Sylvia sent the novel off again, this time to Harper & Row. It came back late in January with similarly sympathetic comments from Elizabeth Lawrence: the first part was fresh and arresting, but with the breakdown of the heroine, "the story ceases to be a novel and becomes a case history. It does not enlarge the reader's knowledge of the girl substantially, or have necessary dramatic impact. *The experience remains a private one*" (my italics).

Although Ted Hughes recalls that Sylvia "was in resilient form" for the launching of *The Bell Jar* on January 14, these American rejections must have been disheartening. Reviews of her novel appeared later that month in *The Observer* (Anthony Burgess), the *New Statesman* (Robert Taubman), the *Times Literary Supplement* (anonymous in those days), *The Listener* (Laurence Lerner), *The Spectator* (Simon Raven), and *Time and Tide* (Robert Butler). None was entirely adverse — although Simon Raven advised readers "to stick to home produce" in the field of "unpleasant, competent and funny female novelists" — but neither were they the sort of prominent notices she must have hoped for. What the first reviews promised was that "Victoria Lucas" would be patted on the head for good writing, scolded for weak plotting, and passed over.

Had the weather been easier, Sylvia might not have felt quite so desperate. Snow fell in abundance, then thawed and fell again, coating the unplowed streets with ice, incapacitating the heating systems, and destroying plumbing. Early in January, Paul and Clarissa Roche brought their four children to London from an isolated house they had rented in Kent. Clarissa writes affectingly of arriving with two babies on a doorstep of undented snow, to be admitted by Sylvia in her dressing gown, weak with flu. Unlike Alvarez, Clarissa found the flat warm and inviting, with the large electric fire in the sitting room full on. Sylvia had bought simple rush matting and plain furniture, but her kitchen was full of American-style gadgets. The rooms were tidy, the beds made, and the kitchen so clean that Clarissa suspected Sylvia rarely prepared the meals so carefully planned on her weekly menu. Before Paul joined them with the Roches' older children, Clarissa cooked pork chops and tinned corn for Sylvia and her two. Sylvia ate heartily before returning to bed.

When Paul and the older Roche children arrived in the afternoon, Sylvia rose to the occasion, entertaining them chiefly by abusing the literary "worthies" and "sycophants" who courted herself and Ted. Bullying, she said, was the only way to get on in the literary world. Sylvia was "malicious and dishonest too," Clarissa Roche wrote later. "But, somehow, when [she] talked, she was so animated and amusing there was no sense of the negative, the distortion . . . She laughed and laughed at the toadies, yet I know she was proud to be accepted as a poet by these very people, honored to be published alongside them."

Later in January, at Sylvia's request, Suzette Macedo took her to see Doris Lessing, a friend of Suzette's. Lessing was disturbed by the meeting. Sylvia had joined in the talk animatedly, but to Lessing there was an "incandescent desperation" about her; what came across overwhelmingly was "a total *demand*" directed at herself. Lessing drew back from it. Her hands were more than full at the time, and she had not found Sylvia sympathetic. She remembers saying to Suzette, after their meeting, "I just couldn't cope with her." After Sylvia's death she inevitably regretted not having persevered.

The Roches had made Sylvia promise that if the au pair she was expecting at the end of January failed to turn up she would bring the children down to them in Kent. But Kent, in January 1963, was even more frozen up than London. The Roches were sitting out the cold in a house much less well equipped than Sylvia's, crouching for warmth with their four children in front of the gas oven. The au pair girl evidently did arrive late in January or early in February, for Sylvia wrote on February 4 to her mother, "My German 'au pair' is food-fussy and boy-gaga, but I am doing my best to discipline her. She does give me some peace mornings and a few free evenings." The girl was no substitute for the trained nurse Dr. Horder had provided — expensively, at £10 a day — while Sylvia and her children had been in bed with flu, nor did Sylvia find in her the "sister" she had welcomed in Susan O'Neill-Roe.

It is popularly believed that Sylvia wrote most of *Ariel* in her London flat. In fact, she arrived with most of the poems that would be published in *Ariel* already written. Possibly only her preoccupation with getting her house in order and fulfilling various commissions prevented her from typing them out in final form and sending off the manuscript to her publisher. Or she may have wanted to get publication of *The Bell Jar* over first. Perhaps she hesitated about sending off a collection that contained potentially hurtful poems attacking father, mother, husband, neighbors, and friends — though she seemed to have had no hesitations about sending them to magazines.* In January, when not ill with flu, she concentrated on prose: on January 10 she wrote a Third Programme review of Donald Hall's anthology, *Contemporary American Poetry;* later in the month she worked on a prose piece for *Punch,* "Snow Blitz," and she proceeded with her new novel, a story of a triangle, based on the breakup of her marriage.

The Observer of Sunday, January 27, carried both an approving review of *The Bell Jar* by Anthony Burgess and a poem by Hughes. Apparently this collocation so disturbed Sylvia that she sought out the company of Professor Thomas in the downstairs flat, showing him the newspaper. Thomas did his best to comfort her. It was perhaps this tearful catharsis in his flat, or perhaps the blessed arrival the next day of the au pair girl, that opened up for Sylvia a new vein of inspiration. Nearly all twelve of the poems Sylvia wrote or completed in London dwell on the universal, quasi-religious themes of such poems as "Mary's Song" and "Brasilia," written in Devon in November and December. Although she never quite abandoned her self-preoccupation, toward the end the "self," so prominent as a source of Sylvia's unique rage, all but disappears, as if, with the exorcisms of "Daddy" and "Lady Lazarus," she was able to attain another plane

---

*Few of the Ariel poems were accepted for magazine publication during her lifetime and none of the more ferocious ones for which she is most famous, though she sent off regular batches of all she was writing to literary editors of magazines.

in her mythology. "Mary's Song" addresses not the horrors of self-hood but the "holocaust" of the world in which children helplessly are born to die. The anatomical imagery, still central, is transformed and made universal:

> It is a heart,
> This holocaust I walk in,
> O golden child the world will kill and eat.

The turbulent struggle with her inner demons that had characterized the Ariel outburst in October was succeeded in the poems of the last weeks of Sylvia's life by a strangely elevated and resigned despair. Her mind was still distantly revolving images from her past but in the flat light of a hopeless present that envisaged no future.

"Brasilia," written on December 1, foresees the coming of a de-humanized "super-people," "with torsos of steel / Winged elbows and eyeholes," menacing her child's flesh-and-blood reality. "Childless Woman," composed the same day, speaks scornfully of the barren woman's life-denying narcissism, where

> The womb
> Rattles its pod, the moon
> Discharges itself from the tree with nowhere to go.

In "Sheep in Fog," finished on January 28, death lies in wait:

>   . . . the far
> Fields melt my heart.
>
> They threaten
> To let me through to a heaven
> Starless and fatherless, a dark water.

Sylvia went on, the same day, to write three more poems. "The Munich Mannequins" personifies her hatred of barrenness and its chill perfections in the mannequins, "Naked and bald in their furs, . . . / Intolerable, without mind." "Totem" is a cluster of images on the theme of "Death with its many sticks." Efforts to live are pointless, new departures are in vain:

>   . . . the same self unfolds like a suit
> Bald and shiny, with pockets of wishes,
>
> Notions and tickets, short circuits and folding mirrors.

With superb artistry these poems record a dangerously altered and alienated state of mind. Only her children retain the glow of human warmth and normality. In "Child," her infant's "clear eye is the one absolutely beautiful thing." But she can offer it nothing but "this troublous / Wringing of hands, this dark / Ceiling without a star."

This final, almost disembodied period at the end of Sylvia's writing life continues with "Paralytic" and "Gigolo," written on January 29. "Gigolo" is the male equivalent of "The Munich Mannequins." In a ferociously satirical tour de force, sex without love is shown as a narcissistic vanity, mechanical and dehumanized:

> . . . I
> Glitter like Fontainebleau
>
> Gratified,
> All the fall of water an eye
> Over whose pool I tenderly
> Lean and see me.

"Paralytic" has the old yearning to shrug off life's ties and attain selfless, mystical bliss* — as in passages in "Tulips" and other earlier poems:

> I smile, a buddha, all
> Wants, desire
> Falling from me like rings
> Hugging their lights.
>
> The claw
> Of the magnolia,
> Drunk on its own scents,
> Asks nothing of life.

Three days later, on February 1, came three more remarkable poems. "Mystic" reflects on her predicament. Deathly images of her childhood by the sea come back to her:

> I remember
> The dead smell of sun on wood cabins,
> The stiffness of sails, the long salt winding sheets.

She sees no way out:

> Once one has seen God, what is the remedy?
> Once one has been seized up

---

*On a more prosaic level, the poem may have been suggested by Sylvia's grandfather, immobilized and dying in a home for the aged in Wellesley.

> Without a part left over,
> Not a toe, not a finger, and used,
> Used utterly, in the sun's conflagrations, the stains
> That lengthen from ancient cathedrals
> What is the remedy?

The grand vision has burnt out. What the poet seems to want is a remedy for her inability to accept a form of truth most adult human beings have to learn: that they are not unique nor exempt from partaking in human processes. Her sardonic refusal to accept limitation is evident from the poem's choice of examples of those who do — the rodents of the field, the hunchback content with his cottage, "the ones / Whose hopes are so low they are comfortable." Though titled "Mystic," the poem is that of an uncompromising child — the child who, when told that her father was dead, declared she would "never speak to God again." Meanwhile life, amazingly, still goes on:

> The chimneys of the city breathe, the window sweats,
> The children leap in their cots.
> The sun blooms, it is a geranium.
>
> The heart has not stopped.

Marvelously impressive as these last poems are, they are the work of a poet who, as Joyce Carol Oates pointed out, no longer associates her own life with that of the cosmos. She has accepted a deathly distinction between subject — "I am I" — and object: the fusion between herself and "the things of this world" is refused, if it cannot be on her own terms. It seems that depression was dictating many of these winter poems.

"Kindness," written the same day, is gently ironical about her friends and husband as they bring her the modest comforts of smiles and cups of tea. They have misjudged the situation — "The blood jet is poetry, / There is no stopping it" — and their tiny tokens are ineffectual, indeed irrelevant. She hugs to herself her private knowledge of the grand proximity of death: "My Japanese silks, desperate butterflies, / May be pinned any minute, anesthetized."*

"Words," the third of the poems of February 1, pursues the remorseless logic of her false metaphysic and casts off the last remnants of her faith. The poet's words, she says, ring like the strokes of axes

---

*One of the sources of the poem's imagery was a play by Ted Hughes in which a man runs over a hare, sells it, and buys two roses with the money. "The blue and red jewels of her rings smoke / In the windows" may refer to the window of a room at the Beckers' with blue and red diamond-shaped panes.

that send out into the world "Echoes traveling / Off from the center like horses." But the tree stumps bleed reality:

> The sap
> Wells like tears, like the
> Water striving
> To re-establish its mirror
> Over the rock . . .

With the word "mirror" we are back again in the looking-glass land of Sylvia's hubristic prison; and the pool that at its bottom mirrors the stars is the horror that eats the skull consigned to it. Out on the road the words have become "The indefatigable hoof-taps" of riderless horses. All that will be left of the poet will be disembodied words while "From the bottom of the pool, fixed stars / Govern a life."

"Contusion," written on February 4, utilizes a series of related pictures to complete the disintegration of the will to live in Plath's poetry. A bruise is the "doom mark" that so impressed Sylvia years before when, with Dick Norton, she attended a lecture on sickle cell anemia at the Boston Lying-In Hospital; it is also a "fly," as in "Totem" and "Mystic," that ultimate symbol of meaninglessness and helpless victimization. The "pit of rock" where the "sea sucks obsessively" is the pool of "Words," "Berck-Plage," and many other poems, for her an obsessive symbol of death and here representing also the heart. When the flylike blood clot reaches the heart, the heart shuts, "The sea slides back," and the deceiving mirrors of existence "are sheeted." The consistency of the imagery is preserved right up until the end, when the merest mention of the resonant symbols of Plath's mythology sets the whole construct ringing like the most finely balanced of bells.

In her daily life, however, Sylvia was still fighting the "cold blanks," to which almost all her last poems were pointing. When Sylvia saw Dr. Horder in late January, she told him she was severely depressed and feared she was heading for a breakdown. For the first time he heard something of the history of her attempted suicide. He immediately put her on a course of antidepressants and, as her condition worsened, made attempts to find her a psychiatrist and, if necessary, a hospital bed.

On Monday, February 4, Gerry Becker received an SOS from a call box (Sylvia was still without a telephone): her car had broken down and needed servicing, would Gerry come round and take care of it? Gerry duly arrived and saw the car into a garage, returning it the next day. On Thursday, February 7, Sylvia, hysterical and desperate, phoned Jillian Becker, asking for asylum in Mountfort Crescent that afternoon. Jillian urged her to come, and by teatime Sylvia had arrived with Frieda and Nicholas but no baby supplies of any kind and no suitcase. Suzette Macedo also happened to be there, but on seeing her Sylvia immediately withdrew upstairs to rest, leaving the children with Jillian and her two-year-old daughter, Madeleine. Suzette eventually left, and Jillian went up to Sylvia, who was lying on a spare bed, to ask her to stay for the weekend. Sylvia replied, "I must." The au pair had left her, and she could do nothing alone.

Apprehending that matters were in crisis, Jillian arranged for her two older daughters to stay with their father, her first husband, who lived nearby. Then, realizing that Sylvia lacked clothes, diapers, and bottles for the children, she offered to drive back to Fitzroy Road in Sylvia's car to pick up whatever was needed. Sylvia's list of necessities, apart from baby things, included the metallic-topped cocktail outfit, curlers, cosmetics, and certain papers from her desk. Jillian arrived to find the flat immaculate, which surprised her, considering Sylvia's distraught state. Red corduroy was being sewn into curtains; there were books about — Jennifer Dawson's *The Ha-Ha,* a racking novel of a young girl's breakdown, and Ruth Beuscher's recommendation, *The Art of Loving* by Erich Fromm. But Sylvia had not asked for books. Most of Frieda's clothes must have been in the laundry basket, for Jillian could find very little for her.

Having returned to Mountfort Crescent with what she could find, Jillian bathed Nick and Frieda with her own Madeleine, fed them, lent Frieda some pajamas, and took Nick in to Sylvia for his bottle. Gerry arrived home with incipient flu, worried after failing to find Sylvia at home in Fitzroy Road. At dinner Jillian was surprised to see Sylvia eat her steak with enormous relish, commenting on how wonderful it tasted after her diet of mince. Had she forgotten how often the Beckers themselves had taken her out, Jillian wondered. Throughout Sylvia's stay with the Beckers Jillian was struck by her changes of mood. However distraught Sylvia seemed at other times, she always appeared dressed for meals, was calm at table, ate extremely well, and was warmly appreciative of the food Jillian served.

Dinner over, Sylvia announced that she would have to take her sleeping pills and lie down. Would Jillian come up and talk to her until the pills took effect? Jillian did so, noting with concern that Sylvia swallowed pill after pill — what seemed to her far more than a safe dose — before lying back to rehearse the litany of anguish that was to be repeated day and night throughout the weekend. Finally

Sylvia dozed off, but at three the next morning Jillian woke to hear Nicholas crying. His mother's calling out "Jillian, Jillian, Jillian" had awakened him. Frieda was also awake, so Jillian took both children in to Sylvia, who cuddled them before they went back to bed. Jillian, however, was begged to stay until Sylvia could take her "wake-up" antidepressants, which if swallowed at five-thirty would breathe life into her at about seven. The early morning depression was the worst time; if she could get through that, she would be all right. It was then three-thirty. Jillian listened for two hours to Sylvia's rodomontade, which always trailed round the same course: she hated her mother; she hated Ted for betraying her; "she" (Sylvia would never speak Assia's name) was hateful; the Hughes family had rejected her and Olwyn disliked her.* The happiness she had once enjoyed in a perfect marriage was gone forever, spoiled irretrievably, for what had once been broken, like Henry James's golden bowl, could never be mended. Yet the next minute she would ask, "Why doesn't David [Wevill] *do* something?" Otto Plath had been the first man to desert her, Ted the next — she returned obsessively to this point. And repeatedly she talked of having two children and being deserted, just as her mother had been. Jillian pointed out that her mother hadn't been deserted, but to Sylvia it was all the same. Evasive about the cause of Otto Plath's death, she left Jillian with the belief that it had been sudden and violent, perhaps a suicide. One day, she said, her father was there, then she was sent to the sea, and when she came back he had gone.

Jillian did not know the facts about Otto Plath, so she accepted this, but she did notice the extremely "literary" quality of Sylvia's monologues. Sylvia seemed to be trying out different versions of the various happenings she described, as though writing drafts. Occasionally Jillian would question totally different versions, but mostly Sylvia went on as though she had not spoken. Jillian remembers a small point: Sylvia repeatedly described Assia at Court Green picking her way among the cow pats in high heels. Jillian, who knew David and Assia, remonstrated, reminding Sylvia that even in London Assia habitually wore brogues. "I could practically *see* her penciling a line through the image," Jillian says, "but later it came back again — it was just too good to leave out."

She might just as well have been "a mask hanging on the wall," Jillian says, as Sylvia poured out chaotic memories and obsessions in a feverish delirium. Men she had known in the past — all names

---

*Olwyn Hughes comments that these unjust remarks seemed part of Sylvia's bid for sympathy at the time.

unknown to Jillian — were often flung in: something "Gordon" had said, or "Dick" had done, or "Richard" had written, and how one or another of them had desperately wanted to marry her. At about five o'clock Sylvia dozed off and Jillian returned, exhausted, to bed.

No one in the house had much of a respite the next day. Gerry went to work, blocked and dulled with flu. Sylvia came down, ate a hearty breakfast, and returned to bed. Jillian got the children up and fed them; she was interrupted by a phone call from Dr. Horder, who was extremely worried about Sylvia and had tried to get her a hospital bed for that weekend. Two of the hospitals could not take her, and a third, he felt, was unsuitable. Under no circumstances, he insisted, should Jillian do everything for Sylvia's children; it would be good for her to take care of them herself. Meanwhile he was trying to get Sylvia an appointment with a woman psychiatrist he thought she would trust.

Midmorning, Sylvia made two long telephone calls from the Beckers' bedroom, the first to the au pair girl, whom she tried in vain to persuade to come to work, the second, very long, to Dr. Horder. Later, Jillian says, Sylvia may have driven in to see him. It was evident to them all that Sylvia needed psychiatric treatment, but she dreaded a repetition of electroconvulsive therapy and was exceedingly wary of any doctor she did not know. Most of Friday she spent lying down, talking to Jillian, or taking (three or four) baths. In the evening she packed her cocktail outfit, cosmetics, and hair curlers in a little case Jillian had brought back from Fitzroy Road and set off in her car for a mysterious but "very important" appointment.* Before she left, Jillian remembers her suddenly turning to Frieda, standing bewildered by the door. "I love you!" Sylvia said to her in her most intense tone. Then she was off.

Jillian has no idea where Sylvia went that Friday evening. Had Ted said he was coming to see the children? Had she some business with the au pair girl, whom she had not yet paid? Or was her "very important" appointment some ghoulish rendezvous with Death? Ted remembers seeing her at her flat early Friday evening, not in her evening clothes but about to leave for the weekend. He didn't stay long, as she said she wanted to lock up and go. She returned to Islington by taxi (where was the car?), in street clothes but with her hair curled, very brisk and managerial, as if something had been

---

*Drugged and ill, Sylvia, it seemed, was still anxious to be ready for some possible social occasion. Her cocktail outfit, coming and going in her suitcase from the Beckers', is as poignant in retrospect as Ophelia's flowers.

cleared up once and for all. Then she went to bed, and the whole procedure of the night before was reenacted: pills, ravings, a short sleep, the three o'clock awakening, more pleading for pills, sleep again, and the same hearty breakfast.

Gerry, quite ill, spent Saturday in bed. Sylvia could not have left the Beckers' house without her car, which had been left behind somewhere. On Saturday evening Jillian and Gerry reluctantly dragged themselves to a dinner engagement, leaving Sylvia with the well-meaning Irish maid. A former student of Gerry's who was studying art at the Slade came in expressly to "Sylvia-sit" and spend the night. He and Sylvia listened to records — mainly Beethoven — and drank a little whiskey but exchanged few words. Once only, when Sylvia asked him what he painted and he replied "Abstracts," did she turn to him with a flicker of interest: "What a pity. If I could paint, I would want to paint things. I love the thinginess of things." After the Beckers returned the student retired for the night to the study floor while Jillian and Sylvia again went through the pill-taking, circular-monologue routine, Jillian occasionally interrupting to ask a question. It was usually ignored by Sylvia, who by now appeared to be aware of little that went on outside herself.

On Sunday morning Gerry felt well enough to take the children to the zoo, together with Nest Cleverdon, Douglas's wife. Nest remembers that before they set off, she had to stop at her own house to wrap Nick up properly in something of her son's. Although it was a bitterly cold day, Sylvia had not thought to dress him warmly. Nest remembers this particularly because Sylvia was always so careful with the children. Sunday lunch came and went, with a joint of meat and Sylvia's usual exclamations over its excellence. After eating heartily, Sylvia went up to rest; this time she fell deeply asleep, for the first time in four days, and slept all afternoon. Waking at teatime, she declared she felt better, so much better that she would wrap up the children and take them home. Both Jillian and Gerry anxiously tried to dissuade her. They were delighted she had slept but were happy to give her a home until she fully recovered; at least she should wait until Monday morning to make a decision.

Sylvia was determined to go home. Dr. Horder had found her a nurse, due to arrive at nine the next morning. She had to do the laundry and get Frieda to playschool. Besides, she had a publisher's lunch she couldn't afford to miss. The Beckers still pressed her to stay, but after tea and cake Sylvia hustled Frieda into her coat, packed Nick's paraphernalia in paper bags (she had neglected to bring back the little case with her cocktail dress and cosmetics), and persuaded

296 ▸ BITTER FAME

Gerry, against his will, to get out his old taxi and drive her back to Fitzroy Road. Sylvia took off coatless, with Nick in her arms.

Sylvia left the Beckers' at about six in the evening. Two hours later Gerry returned, extremely distressed. Sylvia had wept all the way home, but though Gerry had repeatedly urged her to return with him, on arrival she had taken the keys from her bag (there was another set back in Islington in the pocket of her coat, which apparently she never missed) and opened the front door, and they all went in. Dr. Horder is sure he saw her that evening at her flat, rather late. Professor Thomas in the downstairs flat was the last person to see her alive. Sylvia went downstairs about midnight and asked to buy stamps from him, which she insisted on paying for there and then, "or I won't be right with my conscience before God." Her real purpose seems to have been to ensure that he would be up before nine the next morning, in time to let in the nurse she expected. She left, but he did not hear her go back upstairs, and after a few minutes he opened the door and found her standing motionless in the freezing hall. He realized she was in a strange state and offered to call a doctor, but Sylvia claimed she was having a wonderful vision. Later Thomas's sleep was disturbed by her walking about on the wooden floors above.

The next morning Miss Myra Norris, the nurse sent by Dr. Horder, arrived at the front door of 23 Fitzroy Road at about nine. The outside door that served both apartments was locked, and no one answered either bell. After the night's sharp frost, there was a long line of householders phoning plumbers from the local call box. The nurse finally reached her agency to check that she had the right address, and then Charles Langridge, a builder who was working on the property, let her into the house. Together they broke into Sylvia's flat one flight up. The smell of gas was unmistakable. Forcing open the door to the kitchen, they found Sylvia sprawled on the floor, her head on a little folded cloth in the oven. All the gas taps were full on. After turning off the gas and opening the windows, they dragged her into the sitting room, where the nurse attempted artificial respiration while Mr. Langridge — or a policeman he had summoned from a call box — went up to the crying children in their upstairs bedroom. Under their door, as under the kitchen door, were towels and cloths Sylvia had pushed in to keep out the gas after she had taped up the cracks. The bedroom window had been thrown wide open, and bread and milk had been left by the high-sided cots. The children were very cold but quite safe.

In the entry hall Mr. Langridge found a note pinned to the perambulator, "Please call Dr. Horder," with his telephone number. Dr. Horder arrived at about ten-thirty and confirmed the death, after which Sylvia's body was driven by ambulance straight to the hospital. Dr. Horder broke the news to Jillian Becker, who in turn phoned Suzette Macedo, who knew Ted's current telephone number in Soho. Suzette herself hurried round and looked after the children until Ted arrived. Sylvia had taken every precaution to keep the gas from her children. But some of the gas, though lighter than air, may have been channeled to the room below the kitchen, Professor Thomas's bedroom, by the flues of the house. He slept on, without his hearing aid, oblivious to all the disturbance. As for Sylvia — it is Dr. Horder's opinion that even if she had been rescued while her body was alive, it is likely that her mind would have been destroyed.

Dr. Horder's testimony is compassionate and clear as to the facts. Sylvia was a model patient, he says, seeming to understand her own struggle against suicidal depression and reporting to him faithfully on the effects of the drugs he prescribed. "She had," writes Dr. Horder, "for several days [before the suicide] received an anti-depressant, in this case, a 'mono-oxidase inhibitor.' Response to any drug of this kind takes from ten to twenty days. There may be a point at which the anti-depressant begins to make a depressed person a little more active, though still desolate, hence capable of carrying out a determined, desperate action." Dr. Horder believed Sylvia had reached the danger point that weekend.

Horder had indeed tried to arrange for a hospital bed for Sylvia after he had seen her condition on the Friday. He had also arranged for an appointment with a psychiatrist for the day after her death. Every day of her last week he had seen her or talked to her on the telephone, and he had visited her at home on the Sunday evening before her death. Aware that she was to be alone that night, he knew he had been taking a risk, but he believed the presence of the children would tide her over until the nurse arrived the next morning. Yet, as he later said, "she slipped through the net."

◄　◄　◄

Did Sylvia Plath really mean to kill herself? Her death was part of the pattern she believed she could not escape, yet somehow she must have imagined living on after death. In Dr. Horder's view, the deliberation with which she set up the suicide was too thorough to interpret as anything but intentional:

The care with which the kitchen was prepared was only too obvious. My judgment has always been that this was a very determined attempt to end her life . . . She "chose" the one period when no one was free to be with her. The act occurred at the time when suicides are most common, at the end of the night. What therefore was to be explained . . . is why she did this when she knew that her two very young children were on the next floor and depended on her absolutely. Was it the irresponsibility of the artist? No, that is so limited an explanation as to be nearly ridiculous. I believe, indeed it was repeatedly obvious to me, that she was deeply depressed, "ill," "out of her mind," and that any explanations of a psychological sort are inadequate . . .

I believe . . . she was liable to large swings of mood, but so excessive that a doctor inevitably thinks in terms of brain chemistry. This does not reduce the concurrent importance of marriage breakup or of exhaustion after a period of unusual artistic activity or from recent infectious illness or from the difficulties of being a responsible, practical mother. The full explanation has to take all these factors into account and more. But the irrational compulsion to end it makes me think that the body was governing the mind.

A week earlier, when Sylvia wrote "Edge," she was not concerning herself with "irrational compulsions." She was, as Elizabeth Hardwick perceived, at the end of her life both the dramatist and the tragic heroine of her "murderous art," "frighteningly there all the time. Orestes rages, but Aeschylus lives to be almost seventy. Sylvia Plath, however, is both heroine and author; when the curtain goes down, it is her own dead body there on the stage, sacrificed to her own plot."

EDGE

The woman is perfected.
Her dead

Body wears the smile of accomplishment,
The illusion of a Greek necessity

Flows in the scrolls of her toga,
Her bare

Feet seem to be saying:
We have come so far, it is over.

Each dead child coiled, a white serpent,
One at each little

Pitcher of milk, now empty.
She has folded

Them back into her body as petals
Of a rose close when the garden

Stiffens and odors bleed
From the sweet, deep throats of the night flower.

The moon has nothing to be sad about,
Staring from her hood of bone.

She is used to this sort of thing.
Her blacks crackle and drag.

► E P I L O G U E ◄

Tragedy is not a woman, however gifted, dragging her shadow around in a circle, or analyzing with dazzling scrupulosity the stale, boring inertia of the circle; tragedy is cultural, mysteriously enlarging the individual so that what he has experienced is both what we have experienced and what we need not experience — because of his, or her, private agony. It is proper to say that Sylvia Plath represents for us a tragic figure involved in a tragic action, and that her tragedy is offered to us as a near-perfect work of art, in her books.

> — Joyce Carol Oates, "The Death
> Throes of Romanticism"

A poet is a combination of an instrument and a human being in one person, with the former gradually taking over the latter. The sensation of this takeover is responsible for timbre; the realization of it, for destiny.

> — Joseph Brodsky,
> *Less Than One*

"EDGE" WAS POSSIBLY the last poem Sylvia Plath wrote — beautiful yet terrible in its pitiless foreshadowing of what was to come. For a time it seemed that her valiant attempt to come to terms with her daemon, in that astonishing outpouring of poems in the autumn, might save her. But her final set of winter poems, with their cold metaphysic of inevitable engulfment by the world's indifference, were somber ones. In a less vulnerable poet such poems could have marked a melancholy stage toward a wider, more mature spirit. As it was, their chilly dissociation from the world held the risk of what came to pass. In the end, the heroine of "Edge," wearing a "smile of accomplishment," has freely chosen the perfection of death, and the deathly moon, "used to this sort of thing," does not interfere.

Only a few days before she died, Sylvia had been picturing a return to Devon in the spring. On February 7, before leaving for the Beckers', Sylvia had written confident letters to the Comptons and Nancy Axworthy. The letters arrived after her death, the unbelievable death of this lively young woman full of schemes and enterprise. She was eager to take up horseback riding and beekeeping again, to finish her novel, and to welcome friends. Marcia and Mike Plumer were to visit Court Green. Ruth Fainlight Sillitoe was to join her there with her son while Alan toured the Soviet Union. And Ruth planned to arrive with a maid brought back from Morocco so that she and Sylvia would be free to write together in Devon. But even as Sylvia hopefully formed such dreams, they had already been dismissed by her implacable deeper self. Her poem "Totem" sees such "pockets of wishes, / Notions and tickets" as no more than "short circuits and folding mirrors."

The Sillitoes, still in Morocco, read of Sylvia's death in *The Observer*. Like many others on both sides of the Atlantic, family and friends, acquaintances and fellow poets, they were shocked and incredulous. In America, many at first knew nothing of her suicide, since word went out that she had died of pneumonia, a fiction Mrs. Plath understandably wanted believed. She had heard of her daughter's death from her sister, who received a telegram from Ted on February 12: "Sylvia died yesterday." It explained nothing, only giving details of the funeral, to be held in Heptonstall that Saturday. In the event, only Warren and Maggie were able to attend.

On the day before the funeral the inquest was held at the St. Pancras County Court. Ted Hughes identified the body of the deceased as that of his wife, Sylvia Plath Hughes, age thirty years, an authoress, of 23 Fitzroy Road, St. Pancras, NW1. Miss Myra Norris and Constable John Jones were present to give evidence. The coroner also heard from Dr. John Horder. There remained Dr. Peter Sutton's report on the postmortem. In his opinion the cause of death was carbon monoxide poisoning, a verdict the coroner duly recorded before concluding the inquest: "Did kill herself." The official history of Sylvia Plath was over.

Sylvia had once casually expressed to Jillian Becker the belief that she would one day lie in the churchyard adjoining her Devon house. But in Devon the Hugheses were newcomers; in Yorkshire the family was established. Since there seemed to be no question of transporting Sylvia's body back to the States, Heptonstall was a logical resting place. After the inquest Ted accompanied Sylvia's body to his family home, and in the early afternoon of Saturday, February 16, the service took place in the weathered nineteenth-century church that adjoins the ruins of the medieval parish church of Heptonstall. The Beckers came up by train for the service and the "breakfast" afterward in the village. All around the church, Jillian Becker recalls, fields and distant moors were covered by pure, untroubled snow, against which the fresh grave, dug deep into a vein of yellow clay, yawned ocher. Its color repeated the color the stained-glass windows threw into the church when, during the service, the sun faintly penetrated the February clouds.

The Hughes children did not come to the funeral but remained in London with Aunt Hilda, who had gone down on the day of Sylvia's death to take care of them. As for Aurelia Plath, the pain of Sylvia's loss was multiplied by the sad confusion of their relationship. The unrelieved venom of "Medusa" and parts of The Bell Jar were blows she received before she had begun to recover from the brutal fact of death itself. Soon she was in close communication with Ted Hughes, who eventually returned to Devon with the children. In the following years both children flew to America on visits to their grandmother in Wellesley; she herself came to Devon as often as she could.

Letters Home, a book published in 1975 to show the world the positive side of Sylvia's double nature, gives the impression that Aurelia Plath was unaware of the voids of negation and blackness that pulled Sylvia in a contrary direction. The truth is that Mrs. Plath knew better than anyone how difficult it was to view Sylvia from any perspective simple enough to comprehend her interior contradictions. After Judith Kroll had completed her analysis of Sylvia's poetry in Chapters in a Mythology, Mrs. Plath wrote to her in December 1978. The letter runs to two closely typed pages, acknowledging hurt as well as love. One paragraph describes Sylvia's terrible legacy:

> [Sylvia] made use of everything and often transmuted gold into lead . . . These emotions in another person would dissipate with time, but with Sylvia they were written at the moment of intensity to become ineradicable as an epitaph engraved on a tombstone . . . She has posthumous fame — at what price to her children, to those of us who loved her so dearly and whom she has trapped into her past. The love remains — and the hurt. There is no escape for us.

Over the years Ted Hughes has had to arrange for the publication of Sylvia's work, with a view to its effect both on the public and on the family that has had to live "trapped into her past." In 1963–64

Hughes decided to include some of the fine late poems in *Ariel*, arranging the collection in such a way as to represent the full range of Plath's work and, as far as he could judge at that time, to make her extreme gift acceptable to readers. Since then, the rest of the poems written in the Ariel voice over the last two years of her life have become available in *Crossing the Water, Winter Trees,* and finally her *Collected Poems*.

Sylvia Plath described herself, in her poem "Medusa," as "Overexposed, like an X-ray." Her raw-edged response to personal sorrows and joys, her apprehension of the world's horrors and injustices, as well as its beauty, were excessive to an unusual degree. To counter this great vulnerability she devised complex defense systems in both her life and her art. The jaunty, cynical protective coloring of Esther in *The Bell Jar* is one vivid example. At a higher register, we hear the clamorous self-assertion of the Ariel voice, plangent with griefs and beauties. With long years of patient, disciplined effort at her craft, Sylvia Plath was able to forge a universal art and transform crippling disability into exalted achievement.

Plath's fame in our time is greater than she could ever have imagined. She died at thirty, an age when most of us who are her contemporaries were only beginning to find our voices as writers. There is almost no one writing poetry today who has not been affected by the power and passion of Plath's poetry. Although I never met her, I am only two months her junior. I remember clearly the shock of reading of her death in *The Observer* in February 1963. "The loss to literature is inestimable," Alvarez wrote at the time. How inestimable was made doubly evident in 1965 with the publication of *Ariel*. Her writings — particularly the poems and the journals — conspire to give her early death "the illusion of a Greek necessity." Yet how tragic it is that some lucky accident did not enable her to move on into a world with which perhaps she could have come to terms.

Twenty-five years later, my admiration for Plath's astonishing literary genius is in no way diminished, but my sense of the tragedy of her death is heightened by a heartbreaking recognition of just how little time she allowed herself in which to mature. Her work seems to me now a set of intricate, obsessive variations on a few themes, ever more insistently pressing into crescendo in an immense passacaglia, only to die away just when they should have developed new motifs.

The peculiarities of her work have spawned countless theories and controversies; many revere her for reasons that have little to do with her reality. I can only hope that this book will go some way to unravel the mystery and make her great qualities recognizable for what they really are. As Olwyn Hughes has written, "Sylvia may be a *poète maudit,* but she is an achieved mature one: her work is hermetic, even, on ethical grounds, questionable. But as art it is unassailable." She herself has become a victim of her myth's huge aggrandization, her body not even suffered to lie in peace under its yellow rose in the Heptonstall churchyard. When I had all but finished this book, I went with a friend to visit her grave. All we encountered was a pathetic patch of garden, a wind-beaten rose, and a chip of flat rock with "SYLVIA PLATH" inscribed on it in black paint. The vandals who made the temporary removal of her tombstone necessary were women for whom the legacy of Sylvia Plath was no more than a simplified feminist ideology.

The inscription from the *Bhagavad Gita* on her vanished stone is still appropriate: "EVEN AMIDST FIERCE FLAMES THE GOLDEN LOTUS CAN BE PLANTED."

Appendices
Sources and Notes
Acknowledgments
Index

Ah, Youth . . .
Ted Hughes and Sylvia Plath
at Cambridge and After

BY LUCAS MYERS

I DECIDED TO TRY to get into Cambridge University one day in February 1954, but applying for a place wasn't easy. I was a merchant mariner on a decommissioned ship under tow by a seagoing tug, headed for an anchorage up the Houston channel near Beaumont and rounding Cape Hatteras at four knots an hour. I wrote a letter to my parents asking them to make a start on applications to several of the Cambridge colleges, stuffed it into a bottle which I stopped with a cork, and waited for a boat to pass near enough to hail.

There were nine of us aboard, five other able-bodied seamen, the captain, an engineer, and a cook, with little to do but check the line to the seagoing tug and play cards in a wooden bunkhouse that had been erected topside because all the hatches were sealed. The captain, a Dane, didn't play cards. He spent his time making a tent out of canvas for his son and lamps out of bottles and line he wove around them for his wife.

We passed six miles off Miami where the sea was full of fishing boats, and I signaled one. It came alongside and netted the stoppered bottle when I threw it into the sea. We glided on, past the Florida keys, into the Gulf of Mexico. The Gulf was placid and warm and blue; flying fish skittered over its surface. The captain had finished his tent and lamps; he put out fishing lines from the fantail and the fish bit. We hauled up a number of dolphins — the fish, not the porpoises — and as they gasped and slapped the deck, their color changed from burnished green to gold green to blue and finally to an iridescent, mortal white. We hauled up a barracuda which, with its scattered, sawblade teeth and ninety-degree gape, arched across the deck ready to take somebody's foot off at the ankle until the captain darted in and knocked it cold with a marlinspike. I sought out a private place in a lifeboat and wrote a poem called "Dolphin Catch."

At Cambridge that autumn, I submitted this and another shipboard poem to *Chequer,* an undergraduate literary magazine. The co-editors came around to my room in Downing College and found a transatlantic innocent whom they were prepared to take in hand. When *Chequer* came out, my poems appeared with work by poets named Ted Hughes and Daniel Huws. Here were two soul mates, I decided, who would certainly dispel the loneliness I was beginning to feel if I could get to know them.

One afternoon I was in the tea line at the university library and Daniel came up and introduced himself. I was grateful to him for doing so because he was known to be unusually reticent. Just over six feet tall and Celt dark, he walked the university with wire in his brogans, hands clasped in front of a rusty black jacket, and lips slightly pursed in a physiognomy of marked sensitivity.

In January, one of the *Chequer* editors brought Ted Hughes around to my room. Ted had been at Pembroke and graduated with a degree in social anthropology (which I was also "reading," English for "majoring in") that June. He worked from time to time in a rose garden, then returned to Cambridge for as long as his money would last to study in the library, write, and talk about poetry with friends who gathered at a pub by the Cam called the Anchor. He was an inch or so taller than Daniel and wore, as I recall, the brown leather greatcoat that had been issued to an uncle in World War I. His brown hair fell across the right side of his forehead and his voice modulated curiously at certain significant points in his speech. His eyes and his mouth were powerfully expressive.

The next time Ted came up, he stayed with me. I had grown weary of life in college and, failing to rent a disused water tower, put a classified advertisement in the undergraduate newspaper, *Varsity,* for a "shack or shed." My advertisement was answered by a courtly note on blue letter paper from a Mrs. Helen R. Hitchcock of St. Botolph's Rectory. She was the widow of the former rector whose successor, a bachelor don in one of the colleges, allowed her to stay on in the Rectory and let rooms to students, which apparently accounted for much of her income. A more fitting destiny would have had her in a large country house with someone else to do the accounts. She had blue eyelids and a nervous disorder which made her bat them continually; obviously she had once been beautiful.

I was to stoke the fire in the morning and the evening in exchange for lodging in a hut in the garden. The church was in the middle of town, but the Rectory was over the Cam, some distance away. It had enough rooms for six lodgers if Mrs. Hitchcock holed up in the sewing room and took her meals in the kitchen. The garden was large, surrounded by a wall higher than a man, and full of fruit trees. My tutor, a kindly historian who was always marching about town in antique processions carrying a mace, agreed resignedly when I asked to move out of college. He'd given up on me some time before when he'd invited me to a rugby match, and my face, always registering my feelings before I could control it, flashed out my valuation of rugger.

The hut had served as a chicken coop a few years before. I washed it out and painted it. When the bed was in and the desk and chair arranged at the large window looking out on a tangle of green and over to apple and pear and peach trees, you could open the door seventy degrees, shoulder in, sit down, and close the door. When I woke at dawn with the orchard full of birds singing and light streaming through the green branches over my window, I could as well have been in the Garden of Eden.

The first night Ted stayed there, I thought he should sleep in the bed and I under it because he was the guest, but he refused out of hand. Years later, in the course of giving me some hints on a story in which I had the hero falling in some droppings in a zoo, he claimed that his green pullover still smelled of chicken soil, but he didn't admit to discomfort at the time. In any case he soon bought a tent and pitched it near the hut.

Most evenings, we met a crowd of Scots, Welshmen, Irishmen, Northcountrymen, and jazz musicians at the Anchor. Daniel sang obscure and haunting melodies in Welsh, Ted sang "Sir Patrick Spens" and "Waltzing Matilda," Terrence McCaughey, later chaplain of Trinity College, Dublin, or Ted told astonishing tales. Another American, Hal Bloom, the critic, often came in to hold a genial mug over his round stomach and recite verbatim any poem we could name.

Through Daniel Huws we were introduced to a second, younger and smaller group including his suitemate, David Ross, who became known for his children's stories, Danny Weissbort, poet and later translator and editor, and Than Minton, now a psychiatrist. Towards the end of May, X, of Peterhouse and a peripheral member of this group, invited Miss Y, whose canvases now hang in leading galleries, up to Cambridge for a few days and, out of thrift, omitted to arrange for a place for her to stay.

Cambridge colleges were comfortable, with wine cellars, old wood, old glass, beams, and doors, and porters at the gate, mostly retired veterans of the colonial occupations who had to use "Sir" not only with proper gentlemen but with students from outposts of the Empire whom they must secretly have thought of as "wogs," and had to close the gate at ten and bar it at midnight, after which hour the wog or gentleman was obliged to climb his college wall at some invariably well-established and well-trafficked point and float illicitly to earth with his black academic gown — always worn out in town unless you wanted to risk the penalties of the proctors and their "bulldogs," swift, porterlike types — flapping behind him as he alighted in his college compound. X one night had insinuated Miss Y into Peterhouse and, for some still obscure reason, had directed her to Daniel's bed, perhaps merely because it was empty, perhaps thinking that Daniel was away.

As it happened, Daniel, Ted, and I were abroad well past midnight that night. A Peterhouse porter, passing Daniel's room in the exercise of his duties, noticed a head of long, wheaten hair on Daniel's pillow and threw the covers back to expose the naked Miss Y. She could not be and was not allowed to stay in college. She was sent away at once. When eventually Daniel climbed the wall, the porters intercepted him and told him they would have no choice but to inform his tutor the next morning.

Meanwhile Ted and I made our way back to St. Botolph's garden, and I shoved my door open the seventy degrees. In the filtered moonlight, I saw a head of long, wheaten hair on my pillow. Miss Y awoke, and we set about disposing ourselves for the night as reputably as the circumstances would permit.

The Peterhouse tutors held preliminary interviews with Daniel and David the next day. At Downing, I too was called because X had implicated me and Ted and St. Botolph's garden in the scandal. Time passed, the authorities deliberated, and we waited nervously for our various sentences. On a bright afternoon, Daniel and David and I, with Danny and Than, opened two bottles of red wine in the gloom of the ancient rooms where the trouble had begun. Ted had returned to London; by this time, he was working as a night watchman in a warehouse. With a glass in hand, David remarked that he had always wanted to edit a magazine, and, if we hadn't all been sent down (in American, kicked out) by then, he would found one the next academic year. Who would the contributors be? Look about you, they were all there except Ted and Danny's brother George, a London painter. What would the publication be called? *St. Botolph's Review,* everyone agreed, the garden was our spiritual home.

These plans unfolded over many hours and, from time to time, I withdrew to jot down verses of a rhyme, "Knaves Dispatched," which was writing itself in my head. This became the first contribution to the *St. Botolph's Review*. The knaves of the verse were obtuse creatures not unlike our college tutors, but the knaves in danger of being dispatched were the undergraduates then gathered in the oldest rooms of the oldest college in Cambridge.

Dispatch came to Daniel, a favorite of the dons, who were sure he would in due time put on better clothes and join them at the high table as a member of the faculty of Celtic studies, in the form of being sent down for the rest of the term, four days. David, a diabetic who had in any case to go to London for treatment, received the same sentence. But X was sent down for good.

At Downing, my tutor devised a more unkind sentence than Daniel or David had received. I remember hearing it very well because my left eye had been blackened in a scrape, and I was sitting with my right profile to him, trying to hide the left side of my face in the shadows. He told me I would have to move out of the hut in St. Botolph's garden. When Mrs. Hitchcock said I could move into her dining room the next autumn, he reluctantly agreed. And the university authorities forbade Ted, for a period, I think, of one year, to come within three miles of Great St. Mary's, a circle over which the university had legal jurisdiction. Ted ignored the prohibition.

In September, I discovered that Mrs. Hitchcock had installed an au pair girl in a room on the ground floor, a dark and intense girl from Bonn named Helga Kobuszewski, and we at once found ourselves in alliance against three types who appropriated the kitchen at breakfast time, three aspiring la-dee-das from not quite la-dee-da colleges. They quarreled every morning over the consistency of eggs, with dominant A somehow enforcing the cooking on B and the dishwashing on C. I introduced Helga to Daniel, and it led later on to another alliance, one that is still flourishing in Wales. All that autumn, the first and only issue of *St. Botolph's* was being forged.

Towards the end of the term, my tutor announced that he thought it would be best if I moved out of St. Botolph's altogether, and in January, I sadly gave up the dining room to Bertram Wyatt-Brown, a childhood friend who had come over that September to King's and is now an innovative though sound historian. Mrs. Hitchcock also found a cubbyhole upstairs for Daniel.

We planned a party to signalize the appearance of the *Review* and hired a good-sized hall on the second floor of the Cambridge Women's Union. The Anchor crowd of itself contained a jazz band, and its trombonist, Michael Boddy, at twenty stone, took the butt of a piano up the stairs, with several others hauling on legs and sharps and flats.

It was a Saturday in late February 1956. All afternoon, teams of contributors and friends fanned out among the colleges to sell the magazine. I went along with David, and I seem to remember he got most of his money back from sales. In the early evening, Bert and Ted and I and a number of others gathered in the St. Botolph's dining room for a drink before going on to the party.

The hour came, I went to pick up my girlfriend, and Ted, who was alone, went by Queens to apply grog to Danny, down with the flu, and persuade him to come along. The music was loud and the hall nearly full when my girlfriend and I arrived.

After a time, a well-dressed American girl with red shoes named Sylvia Plath came up the stairs. Ted was at the back of the hall, and Daniel and Helga at the front with me and my girlfriend, Valerie, and, between renditions by the jazz band, Danny was at the piano. None of the *St. Botolph's* contributors knew Sylvia, but we knew who she was because she had been publishing well-made poems in Cambridge magazines. We disapproved of the poems in spite of their being well made, or rather partly because of it. Her ambition shined through them, or so we thought, and we thought it was not legitimate to write poetry, which should come down on the poet from somewhere, out of sheer will. Only Ted hadn't commented. Much later, I learned that Bert had sold Sylvia a copy of the *Review* that afternoon, that she had read it, seen him again, and asked how one might get an invitation to the party, and that he had told her it would be very informal and she could just drop by.

The music was fast. Sylvia introduced herself to me and we began to dance the twist. Valerie, a sweet flower of London's bohemia and a good painter, was sitting in an armchair against the wall with one leg tucked up beneath her and a soulful expression. Sylvia began to recite "Fools Encountered," a companion piece to "Knaves Dispatched" in the *Review*. She recited it entire as we danced the twist. Valerie, I soon learned, was thinking, "Is he going to leave me all alone for this flashy American girl?" Sylvia, it seems, was thinking, "This person has had far too much to drink, he doesn't seem to hear his poetry which I am reciting, and his twist is impossible to follow." I looked over at Valerie and wondered, "Does she think I am ignoring her because I have found a compatriot?" The twist ended, and Sylvia passed up the hall. I didn't see her meet Ted, I didn't see her kiss him and bite him on the face, but the next day I saw that he had been bitten.

A couple of weeks later, when Ted had gone back to London, working by that time as a reader at Pinewood Studios, I invited Sylvia over to my new digs in Barton Road for supper. She sat on a cushion on the floor and I sat in a chair preparing food on a gas ring. She was at Newnham College, tall and pretty, and, unless my memory tricks me, wearing bobby sox. Her skin was smooth, like cellophane I thought at the time. She was effusive and a little like one of my sisters; there was something in her I liked. There was also something in her that met with my puritanical disapproval, and the disapproval registered on my face in spite of my effort to disguise it. We talked about Wallace Stevens, and I approved of this, but she told me about working for or publishing in magazines like *Mademoiselle* and *Seventeen*, and I disapproved of that. The average circulation of magazines I thought it was proper to write for would have been around two thousand. What surprised me most about Sylvia was that she didn't seem to notice my disapproval. She chatted on, with energy.

I told Sylvia that, at the beginning of the spring vacation, which was coming soon, I would be joining Ted for a couple of days in a flat Daniel's father kept in Rugby Street in London. His father was a graphic designer who tolerated incursions of Daniel's friends when he wasn't there; the Lamb was nearby, the British Museum not far away. If she would give me the number of her hotel in London, Ted and I could meet her for a drink. Ted had let me know he would like to see her. He did see her in the few days before she went off to the Continent. I went down to Surrey, where another of my sisters, who had married an English civil servant, now Lady Thornton and Sir Peter, lived.

That spring, I moved again, to digs in Tenison Road. An overling at Pinewood had called for Ted and said, "You don't seem to be settling in here very well, do you?" Ted kept an Oxford rice-paper Shakespeare in his drawer at the studio and would read a scene between the books he had to review and report on as possible sources of films. "No, I don't," Ted had replied. He emptied his desk and came up to Cambridge with a folding cot he put out in my room. He would wake before me, sit on the cot, and, taking care not to make a sound, write in a red eight-by-five-and-a-half-inch triplicate book. At night, he would come round and whistle a few bars of "The Wearing of the Green" under my window, and I would go down and let him in.

Ted spent almost all his time that spring with Sylvia. He was falling in love but resisting it. To our circle, poetry was the single claim and any kind of ongoing commitment to flesh and blood an unfaithfulness, an abandonment. Sylvia was in love, eager to marry Ted, eager to have children, to engage any experience which might come her way or she might seek out. They both were writing a lot; Ted was a little embarrassed by the flattering poems she wrote about him. At the end of the term, I took my degree. Sylvia had another year. They were married in June, secretly, because Newnham girls reportedly weren't allowed to be married till they got their degrees and possibly for other reasons of Sylvia's as well. I met them by chance a week or two later in Paris. They looked very happy, happier than I had ever seen them.

Ted and Sylvia were in Spain that summer and Cambridge that autumn. I was in Rome with David; Daniel and Helga joined us in the winter. "I find myself rebelling against writing midnight supervision papers . . ." Sylvia wrote in March 1957 from Eltisley Road in Cambridge. "I am rather oppressed by my colossal ignorance of traditional lit. — I ignored everything except poets & novelists who were of use to my writing & now it looks as if I have to swallow all of English lit. before the end of May —." Ted was teaching lads destined for the trades in a secondary modern school. In the remaining years of Sylvia's life, I saw them rarely, but I had a full account of them from Ted's letters, which were frequent.

Ted and Sylvia were a united couple, and they complemented each other. Without Sylvia, Ted might have had to work in rose gardens and warehouses for quite a few more years. Competent and organized in the American, specifically the Eastern seaboard, manner and to an extraordinary degree, Sylvia always had Ted's poems, like her own, meticulously typed and out at English and American magazines. A number, both of his and of hers, were being published, and those that weren't accepted the first time went right out again. It was Sylvia who got Ted's first book, *The Hawk in the Rain,* to the Harper contest, which it won, establishing him. I don't think Ted would have heard of the Harper prize on his own. Over the next year or two, while studying, teaching, jointly keeping house, and typing her own work and Ted's, she sent out a bunch of my poems and offered to type up a long fiction.

What Ted and Sylvia shared was an unsurpassed single-mindedness about their art. They were quite determined to put into words the best that was in them, but, I thought, in somewhat different ways. Sylvia was determined that it should be read. Ted was determined that it should exist. In fact they were different in a good many ways, so many that I had not expected them to marry even though, in the spring of 1956, they were visibly in love and Sylvia was urging marriage. I had expected Ted to preserve his freedom from everything but poetry and, if he were eventually to get married, to marry someone much like his present wife, highly intelligent but close to nature, a daughter of the English countryside. I was afraid Sylvia would pull him into a struggle for income, shoes, tableware, functioning appliances, perhaps into the American English Literature Establishment, a shallow sea hostile to his happiness, or else that he would make a stand against all this and the marriage would explode. When I saw how strongly rooted the marriage was, I put those thoughts behind me, at least on the conscious level, at least for a long while.

Ted responded to Sylvia's vitality and her appetite for life; he needed this in his wife and friends. He was not put off by the unselfconscious expression of qualities which made her well-disposed English friends uncomfortable and gave the ill-disposed an opportunity to condescend. At that time, in the 1950s, Americans hadn't yet been exposed much to television or acquired its secondhand cosmopolitanism. Americans were rich; the products of Europe's long traditions and ruined wealth had to watch crowds of untutored but confident Yanks eat in the best restaurants and tramp through their museums making ludicrous observations. Most American universities, in the English Departments at least, were nursery schools compared to Cambridge. Sylvia's effusiveness, which disguised her intelligence, and her seemingly commercial approach to literature, which had brought out my puritanical reaction the night we had discussed Wallace Stevens and *Mademoiselle,* exposed her to mockery at Cambridge. While I was still there, she had published some enthusiasms about a vacation visit to Paris in the same student newspaper where I had placed the appeal for a shack or shed that eventuated in the St. Botolph's garden, and I was convinced that the editor had mousetrapped her into giving him an article that would allow his readers to condescend to Americans. Ted shared this view, and his touching defensiveness on her behalf was the first sure index I had to the depth of his feelings for her. As it happened, the editor later gave her some good assignments on the paper, so my suspicions may have been unjust.

It would have been unlike Ted to have said to her, "Look, they're making a fool of you." He always let his friends, and doubtlessly Sylvia too, come at their own epiphanies. Ted had a unique way of helping, stimulating, encouraging writer friends and even casual acquaintances; after spending an afternoon with him, they could come out with a batch of new poems from parts of themselves that had been dormant. He tended to overestimate the work and the writer, or, more precisely, to see the writer's possibilities, like an aura, and charge him with energy or insight which sometimes brought them out.

Ted himself practiced certain disciplines like concentrating on the base of the spine and several points along it for ten minutes before beginning to write, but, rather than give specific prescriptions to others, he transmitted ideas and resolution. From the time I first met him, he had a maturity and understanding that came from some quarter other than mere experience. He and Sylvia reinforced each other's energies and determination and she was preeminently suited to receiving his additional transmissions. He knew a great deal about animals, trees, astrology, the motions of the psyche, other literatures, other arts. Her powers and judgment evolved rapidly.

After Cambridge, Ted and Sylvia spent two and a half years in the United States. I moved to Paris and met his sister, Olwyn, a striking woman two years older than Ted and very close to him. She made her living at first in the NATO typing pool, the confessor of a cadre of gentle parsons' and schoolmasters' daughters seeking life and somewhat lost in Paris who were her colleagues there, and, later on and more satisfactorily, with Martonplay, an international theatrical and film agency run by Hungarians. We saw each other often and exchanged news from America. She lived with a Hungarian journalist in a huge and elegant top-floor room on the boulevard Garibaldi and introduced me to a Left Bank circle that included a concert violinist and 1956 refugee from Budapest named Agnes Vadas, whom I married a number of years later in America.

Ted had been to the Continent several times, once on a wine tour with his Uncle Walt, a small manufacturer, and most recently on his honeymoon, but he had never lived abroad. Sylvia had returned to her American college, Smith, to teach, and she was carrying a heavy load. They set up in Northampton, and that winter Ted took a position teaching English at the University of Massachusetts at Amherst. His observations of American life made interesting reading; they formulated reasons I was expatriating myself. He would not use a word that failed precisely to convey his intention. He would never send a letter that had gone wrong in the writing. He would never pronounce a social formula that did not express his sentiment with sincerity. Given this last disqualification, he found himself in an awkward position in America, particularly at the parties Sylvia's friends, overflowing with enthusiasm and American openness, arranged when they first arrived. He felt uncomfortable receiving their generosities and professions of friendship and being incapable of replying in kind.

"I have never known it so hard to write," he said in a letter later on. ". . . Every bit of ground you try to put your root into is composed of the very latest from every state in the Union. This gets into the words, the expressions on people's faces, the general mental atmosphere . . . But it's a dangerous society that drives you to think your individuality is the only meaningful possession possible." In a subsequent letter he wrote, "I'll not soon again be caught in a small American town."

I'm sure Ted didn't say any of this to Sylvia, at least not explicitly. She had been eager to get home and probably had not understood or even considered what a difficult adjustment America would be for Ted. As an undergraduate at Smith, in spite of or perhaps not in spite of her suicide attempt, she had been a heroine, a published poet, a quintessential American "success." Americans of her time and place seemed to assume all human qualities were measurable, like seconds in the 100-yard dash; colleges gave prizes not only for excellence in mathematics but in character, and, since this was a competitive society, everyone could be ranked in an order as accurate as a poultry yard's, whether they were quarterbacks, members of the Chamber of Commerce, or young poets. But Sylvia came back to Smith as an instructor, at the bottom of the English Department, a toiler over high stacks of "eye-socket searing" term papers, and by the end of the year she was, Ted wrote, "brutally disenchanted" but freed of the "easy delusions" of her sophomores' utopia.

They were in a better setting in Boston the next year. I saw them in September 1958 on the way back to Paris from a visit to my family in Tennessee. We walked on the Boston Common and Ted knew all the birds and trees; we watched fishing boats unloading crabs at the docks and Ted and Sylvia cheered as a few of them escaped into the water. Sylvia was different, very sober at times, hanging back in conversations, standing back, looking different, not like the pretty American girl of the *St. Botolph's* party, but more interesting and more thoughtful. I was surprised by the sober-sidedness and doubt that it was her inevitable manner that whole year. It probably had something to do with me, for, though I thought of them abstractly at that time almost as an amalgam, the fact was that Ted was my close friend and I wasn't as close to her, and the fact must have asserted itself.

The summer of 1959, they drove across the country and in Yellowstone Park played a Teddish game of counting bears: who sighted the most won the game. The theme turned up in a story Sylvia wrote and published in the *London Magazine* the next year. She had the couple counting bears and the last bear, the fifty-ninth, killing the husband. I found the story unsettling. Though a bear had in fact snuffled dangerously around their camp, though the thought was a natural enough product of the subconscious, I was surprised she made a story of the killing of a husband for her husband and their friends to see.

Ted responded to the variety and magnificence of the continent and, among the people, to parts of the American character which had attracted him in friends and in his wife. They stopped by my family home in Tennessee (I was in Paris; in Cambridge days, I had visited Ted's family in Yorkshire in his absence) on their way back to Massachusetts and to Yaddo, the writers' colony in upstate New York. A few months later, Ted wrote that Sylvia had suddenly produced twelve remarkable poems, in a manner altogether new.

They returned to London in December. Ted thought of it as the end of exile but didn't say so, I'm sure, to Sylvia. Originally they had planned to go down to Italy, and Ted had asked me to look for a house for them in Corsica, where I was living at the time, but Sylvia was expecting a child and instead they took a flat in Chalcot Square, where Frieda was born on April 1. I spent the first half of March in England, on the way to the United States. My first night in London, I went by Chalcot Square for supper. The flat was so small that Ted did his writing in a little hallway by the entrance door, while Sylvia wrote in the living room or the bedroom, I can't recall which. Sylvia was preparing the meal when I arrived, and Ted and I went to a pub to get some beer. I suggested we have a drink there, and we left Sylvia, cooking supper and eight months pregnant, alone for forty minutes. The figure forty sticks with me, although such precision seems suspect at this distance.

Ted told me it was hard to write in the flat. Sylvia tended to call out to him and that morning he had decided to count — she had done it 104 times. Since he never said anything critical of Sylvia to me, it was odd he had mentioned it. I doubt if he ever told her, "Look, I can't work like this." I don't think that is the way the marriage functioned; otherwise it probably would have ended early on. All this may have been the effects of pregnancy, the return to England, the search for and move into a flat, but instinctively I disbelieve this explanation. At the time, my assessment was even more unkind. I was thinking something about the demanding style of some American women of the period.

When we returned to the flat, Sylvia would scarcely speak to us. I remember her standing in the dining space, which was on a sort of rise, and staring down at us seated on the couch. What I remember is not the tall, gravid figure, but the eyes, boring down at us. When we went to the table we found three bowls of clam chowder somewhat less than half full. Full stop for supper. Ted and I washed and cleaned every crumb and corner, ostentatiously trying to make amends, but it was no good.

A few days later, Olwyn, over from Paris, joined Ted and Sylvia and me at the flat for lunch. She was staying with a friend and former colleague from the NATO typing pool and brought her along. Sylvia didn't speak to or acknowledge the friend. It was the only time I ever saw Olwyn disconcerted. The next day Olwyn was ready to go back to Paris, but Ted rang and asked her to come by so the air could clear. She went by, expecting, she said, an apology, to be followed by her own quick "Oh, what the hell," but Sylvia behaved as though nothing had happened. I recall that I said to Olwyn or she said to me about this time, "Sylvia's trying to swallow him whole." There were moments during the marriage when it looked as though Sylvia didn't want Ted talking to anyone but herself.

A week later, Daniel, Helga, and Ted saw me off on a ship bound for New Orleans. Sylvia, now two weeks away from giving birth, didn't join that farewell. Ted was disappointed that I was giving up my "beachhead in Europe" just as they got back. I had for a while been planning to settle in London rather than the United States when I left Corsica.

Ted and Sylvia were happy in parenthood. Nicholas was born in January 1962. They had by then bought Court Green, an old, eleven-room thatched house in an orchard by an ancient church in Devon. Ted was always better off in the country, and I think the move to Devon restored him. When I saw Court Green later on with evidences of Sylvia all about it, I thought she must have been well off there, too. Together they took the house in hand and Sylvia painted the children's furniture white with red roses and hearts and strawberries. She had already finished her novel, *The Bell Jar*. When it came out under the pseudonym Victoria Lucas, I narcissistically thought she had chosen the names of Ted's first cousin Vicky and of his friend as a code for Ted himself and as an expression of the juncture between the partners in that marriage, a powerful unity which lasted most of its seven years.

I didn't realize there was trouble between Ted and Sylvia until the summer of 1962 — there probably wasn't an excessive amount until a little before then. Daniel wrote me in Cyprus, where I was living by that time, describing a visit he and Helga had had from Ted and Sylvia. Ted's letters didn't give much indication of tensions, and I had assumed that after the birth of Frieda Sylvia had been happier and easier to live with. But Ted strayed and they separated. Sylvia's rival had been misrepresented. She was a touch too elegant for her own well-being, fundamentally very vulnerable, needed a lot of affection, and could remember SS boots outside the railway carriage compartment as her family, half Jewish, approached the Swiss border.

On February 13, 1963, if I recall the date correctly, I arrived in London on the way from Cyprus to the United States. I took a cab to Cleveland Street, where Ted had been staying, but the landlady told me that something had happened to his wife and he had gone to the country. Picking up Daniel Huws's sister, Catherine, who gave me some idea of what had happened, I went to Fitzroy Road, where Sylvia and the children had been living, and Ted came down to the door. Sylvia had killed herself by putting her head in the gas oven on February 11.

My first thoughts when we got upstairs were, what if the gas had got to Frieda and Nick, who were sleeping in a room on the floor above the kitchen, or to someone else in the building; what if a spark had blown the whole place up? Ted's Aunt Hilda from Yorkshire was there to help him with the children and preparations for the funeral and burial at Heptonstall, Ted's village in Yorkshire. Ted was sure that Sylvia thought she would be rescued. Obviously she didn't want the gas to get to the children, whom she had left in their cribs with milk and bread by them; in her state of mind, the idea that it could do so must not have come to her. Ted also believed they would have been together again within two weeks. He had spoken to Sylvia a few days before the suicide and they were to have met two or three days after it occurred.

In December of that year I went to Court Green and spent four months with Ted, Olwyn, Frieda, and Nicholas. Olwyn had come back from Paris some time before and was devoting herself to the care of the children. Things had stabilized, but the time was still black. Ted set me up in the only room on the top floor, with starlings in the thatch, windows out of it, and a sense of removal, put two superb seven-foot-long rough-cut elm boards on barrels and a chair in front of them, and told me to write, to write a play, which I had never done before. I wrote one. It had Large Intestine, Small Intestine, Lung, Bladder, Backbone, and all the rest of them except Heart reborn and coming down from the theater's flies into a murky afterworld, where they were so miserable they decided to assemble themselves as one and return to the world of typewriters and freeways from which they had come.

Ted and I shared a preoccupation with the shamanic dismemberment and reconstitution of the body, with *The Bacchae* and the Orphic myths. Two years before, he had reviewed Mircea Eliade's *Shamanism* and written me about it; I had read it and reviewed it too. Four years earlier, he had written me that every work, mine or his, must thence-forth include an episode of "the tearing of the cat."

The tearing experience must have visited Ted not only in the form of some shamanistic apperceptions he may have laid hold of but in the banal, day-to-day jealousies of the various connections who were making claims on him. He drew people to him, and in Cambridge days, that presented him with no difficulties: he engaged them all. When he got out into the world, though, friends, colleagues, ambitious writers and academics, and, more naturally, his native and marital families came upon him with more claims than any one person could manage. The rub was that he had no talent for fending anyone off and did not gauge, or gauged but couldn't deal very well with, the egotism of his familiar quotidians.

Already, a year after her death, a lot of people were preparing to board the Sylvia train, some of them with small baggage of scruple. Ted's responsibility while the children were growing up was, as much as possible, to restrain its velocity and protect them from a destructive legend. In 1963, England was still somewhat enclosed in a gray pen-uriousness which succeeded the glories of the Second World War, and the first contingent of legendmakers, who saw Sylvia's suicide as a meaningful act in a gray world, were already busy. Sylvia's unpub-lished literary legacy was standing on a table in the living room at Court Green when I was there; in the succeeding years, Ted let it out bit by bit. He kept the children away from London, and they, for-tunately, came to adulthood without unwholesome distortions. He had the decisive help of his present wife, Carol, in this.

It occurred to me and I may have said to Olwyn that Sylvia should have had the support of a close but removed woman friend in 1962 and 1963 who would have told her, "Give him some air to breathe and everything will be all right." But that thought was idle. Sylvia, by then, had acquired the technical mastery to write lasting poems, but the fuel at her disposal to propel the poems into being was the same substance that provoked her suicide. At cost to herself and her survivors, she doubtlessly attained what she wanted most from life, a permanent place in the history of twentieth-century poetry in En-glish.

Vessel of Wrath:
A Memoir of Sylvia Plath

BY DIDO MERWIN

> . . . haunted all your life by the best of you
> Hiding in your death
>
> — W. S. Merwin

> Poetry is the language of organic fact, that is, fact which has live
> consequences.
>
> — Pasternak

OUR FIRST MEETING with Ted Hughes and Sylvia Plath was in Boston at the end of '57 or the start of '58 at the apartment of Jack and Maire Sweeney. John L. Sweeney ran the Lamont Poetry Library in Cambridge at the time. He liked nothing better than to bring poets together. A meeting between Ted Hughes and W. S. Merwin was an obvious must, since Bill had hailed Ted's first book *The Hawk in the Rain* with a rave in the *New York Times Book Review*. The meeting took the form of a dinner party for the six of us. Ted's foot was in plaster. He didn't say much and appeared to be watching attentively from the touch line. Sylvia, on the other hand, was all outgoing sociability.

The next time we saw them was at our fifth-floor walk-up on West Cedar Street. "The Merwins' high Boston apartment opens its wide-viewed windows like the deck of a ship," Sylvia wrote in her journal at the time. Ted had a job getting up the stairs, but the moment he hobbled in the door he opened up. There was talk about lots of things, but the all-absorbing topic was the sixty-four-thousand-dollar question of how to survive without having to teach. Bill had proved it was possible. He was just then, to all intents and purposes, the only

One That Got Away, and, as such, an authentic and experienced refusenik — not only on account of what he had managed to avoid so far (including the plummy position of Poetry Consultant to the Library of Congress) but also because he had actually done what Sylvia and Ted claimed they wanted to do: travelled, light and foot-loose with a ruthless disregard for inessentials, picking up whatever was to be had by way of a living, in no less than three European countries (France, Portugal, and Spain) besides England, over a period of several years.

Sylvia's feelings about what she saw as "the neat grey, secondary air" of academe were expressed in various letters, mostly to Warren Plath, around the time of our first meeting:

> Ted and I have been hashing this over and over . . . I don't like meeting only students and teachers . . . We need the stimulation of people, people from various jobs and backgrounds . . . The sacrifice of energy and lifeblood . . . Trying to be articulate in front of a rough class of spoiled bitches . . . When I'm describing Henry James' use of metaphor to make emotional states vivid and concrete, I'm dying to be making up my own metaphors . . . I don't like talking *about* D. H. Lawrence and about critics' views of him. I like reading him selfishly for an influence on my own life and my own writing . . . Vacations, as I'm finding out, are an illusion, and you must spend summers preparing new courses, etc. . . . I see too well the security and prestige of academic life, but it is Death to writing.

In her journal she refers to teaching as "a public-service Vampire that drinks blood and brain without a thank you."

She and Ted were hoping that when they got to England they would be able to count on the BBC for at least part of their daily bread, and Bill was full of encouragement. The Beeb, in his view just about the only institution in the world that was not a booby trap, had, after all, kept him from the moment he set foot in London. The Third Programme had led off with a commission for a new translation of the medieval Spanish epic *El Poema del Cid* (still in print) and followed it up with another of *La Chanson de Roland*.

At that time, the BBC Third Programme had the galaxy of talent that worked virtually freehand to make it unique. The rich, quirky mix of poets (MacNeice, Rodgers, and Tiller), novelists (Heppenstall and Sykes), journalists, historians, communists, avant-garde maver-icks, drama producers of the calibre of McWhinney, and above all the incomparable Douglas Cleverdon had a track record that has never been equalled in the history of broadcasting. Douglas was Bill's good angel right from the start, as he had been Dylan Thomas's and would be Ted and Sylvia's. In her last letter to her mother, a week before she died, in 1963, she wrote: "London is the one city of the world I'd like to live in . . . There is nothing like the BBC in America."

Douglas Cleverdon, writing of those two golden decades of radio, describes the overlapping and "very fluid production techniques" that he and his colleagues were able to evolve, and the resulting "communal social relaxation of producers, writers, composers, technicians, actors, secretaries, et al" centered on the George and Stag pubs, as "the nearest parallel to conditions in Elizabethan theatres and the Mermaid."

Our meeting with Ted and Sylvia in Boston generated a solidarity and determination to do everything we could for them, and we picked up exactly where we had left off when they turned up in London two years later. Bill took care of the literary string-pullings and introductions to all the people who had helped him: Douglas Cleverdon, Eric White (Literary Directory of the Arts Council), and the late Siriol Hugh-Jones (of the Sunday *Times* and *Vogue*), etc., while I got on with the logistical and above all medical bits. Fixing up the very pregnant Sylvia with the right National Health Service doctor was the first priority. The best ones, like my own GP and friend, John Horder, tended to be oversubscribed; but he took her on all the same and handed her over to his obstetrician partner.

They were hunting for somewhere to live. As luck would have it, I had noticed that there was a flat to let in Chalcot Square, near Regent's Park and just around the corner from our flat in St. George's Terrace. Once they had made their minds up about it, we were able to dig out most of the furniture and "fittings" they needed from our attic.

When you set out to do what you can for someone, to the extent of finding them a place to live virtually next door, you tend to assume that it's not merely a case of being on their side but also that you like them. Up to that point I would have been prepared to swear that Sylvia's and my relationship was unlikely to pose any problems for either of us, which was probably why I had given it little or no serious thought. On the basis of her protestations with regard to cutting corners the better to buy time in which to write, I naturally assumed that we saw eye to eye in the matter. I therefore assured her that whatever Bill and I had been unable to provide could be bought secondhand for a song down the Chalk Farm Road.

Her summary and unexpectedly graceless rejection of this well-meaning suggestion was like a warning shot across the bows: things, it seemed, were not going to be such congenial plain sailing as I had supposed. But if the Hugheses elected to go splurging on a posh cooker, refrigerator, and bed, what the hell? Never mind if it made no sense to a couple of flea-marketeers like Bill and me. It would have made complete sense, of course, had we had any inkling of the besetting insecurity that was the root cause of Sylvia's need for morale-boosting toys.

As it was, what with Ted's protective "management" (in the medical sense) plus the dodgy, deep-seated complexities of her impregnable defence system, one regularly found oneself totally baffled and frequently on the wrong foot. Which doesn't mean that one didn't keep on trying — at least to maintain some sort of neutrality. But it wasn't always easy.

Within a few days of their moving into Chalcot Square, Ted asked me if he could borrow a beat-up old card table he'd spotted in our attic. It was rickety and moth-eaten, but he assured me it was exactly what he needed. It turned out that he was setting up a work place in the single square meter (give or take) of dark, unventilated vestibule where the coats were hung. Into this space it was just possible to squeeze the card table and a chair — provided nobody tried to open the front door.

Sylvia, at her own admission and quite understandably, was making no attempt to work during the remaining two months of her "time in waiting." All she felt like writing, she said, apart from letters to her mother, was "in my diary." She liked to "lie down in the afternoons, which rests me enough to sleep at night," and she also enjoyed reading (mostly books borrowed from Bill), pottering in the kitchen, and walking when she felt like taking the air on Primrose Hill.

That she had the entire flat in which to rest, while Ted had only what we privately called the Black Hole of Calcutta to work in, struck us as an unfair dispensation. When he cheerfully declared that he found hermetic, womblike quarters conducive to concentration, we took it — with a literal pinch of salt — for another of his protective spiels with which we were gradually becoming familiar. In point of fact it was nothing of the sort. Sylvia had come honestly by her lion's share, and by all accounts Ted digs Little Eases and *oubliettes* to this day.

On the face of it, however, the setup looked pretty lopsided. So much so that Bill was moved to do something he had never even considered before: he offered Ted the use of his study whenever he was away from London. For someone so psychically alert and wary of Bad Medicine, this was an ultimate mark of respect, concern, and trust, implying a strictly one-to-one arrangement.

We left for our house at Lacan in France at the beginning of May, and Ted duly took over the study as planned. Within four weeks Sylvia was also installed: "The mornings at the study are very peaceful to my soul," she wrote to her mother. Not that we knew anything about it until quite some time later. The truth eventually filtered through by way of a passing reference in one of Ted's letters.

As time went on, one reluctantly came to see that Sylvia was a natural-born appropriator, whose innate self-righteousness (the hall-mark of *Letters Home*) apparently rendered anything in the nature of a By- or With-Your-Leave entirely superfluous. Had she not been the high priestess of semantic nuance, one would have said that she didn't seem to know the meaning of the word "compunction" or "please" and "thank you" either, if it came to that. For us, that first half of 1960 was a time of surprises and — *a fortiori* — of second thoughts.

In March 1960, a few weeks before Frieda was born, Bill and I were given a couple of seats for Middleton's *The Changeling* at the Royal Court. When something cropped up, on the morning of the performance, that prevented him from going, Bill gave his ticket to Ted, who had dropped in to see him. Ted was delighted: *The Changeling* — like most of the minor Elizabethans — is rarely done and there-fore something of a collector's piece. When I came home for lunch Bill told me that they had fixed up for Ted to call for me so that we could go down to the theatre together.

Later in the afternoon Ted reappeared and announced that "on the whole" he thought it would be "better" if Sylvia used Bill's ticket. No doubt as a result of the Black Hole misunderstanding, I asked rather owlishly if it wasn't perhaps Sylvia who thought on the whole it would be better. He said either way it wasn't worth making a fuss. One concluded that "fuss" was a euphemism for any eventuality arising out of her not getting her own way. That she didn't want Ted to go out and enjoy himself was their business; but the ticket was ours. The reasonable course of action would have been to have given us a chance to dispose of it elsewhere. As no ticket was forthcoming, I had either to ask for it back or give Ted mine and buy another for myself — which is what I did.

The incident would not be worth mentioning but for the fact that it was my first experience of Sylvia's talent for putting people in a spot — a very minor spot, on this occasion, but it worked. As I wasn't prepared to be made to feel shabby there wasn't a thing I could do. I couldn't have asked for the ticket back any more than Bill could have said anything about the study once Sylvia got her foot in the door.

Her way of generating a climate of guilt where none whatsoever was justified was a ploy that brought to mind a character out of Strindberg, as did her predilection for carrying the war into the enemy's camp — which was how some of us discovered that we *were* the enemy. Typically Strindbergian too was her apparent disregard for cause and effect whenever it conflicted with her rigorously schematic view of people and situations. Whichever way the cookie crumbled, she was never in the wrong, and as long as I knew her, I never heard her say she was sorry for or about anything.

I know of only one admission on her part regarding any kind of foible or fallibility — and even that was more or less inadvertent. It slipped out (ironically late in the day) in one of her letters to her mother in the autumn of '62, by way of an explanation as to how Ted came to be taking her flat-hunting in London after their separation: *"Now he sees he has nothing to fear from me — no scenes or vengefulness."* Hell-bent, in spite of everything, on hammering home the image of "the happiest of women" full of the "joy, fun, ideas and love" that could and should have been the cornerstones of the marriage that she had demolished, Sylvia blew her own cover by the use of that telltale adverb "now" — signifying "not as formerly."

Elsewhere in *Letters Home* there is not the faintest hint of her running Hot and Cold Eumenidean wrath. Nor did Ted ever make the least mention of it as such when he was making excuses for her. Apart from just once, obliquely, and even later in the day — twenty years, in fact — in a parenthesis at the end of his foreword to the *Journals:* "(in those days I regarded forgetfulness as an essential part of survival)."

There had been, of course, no visible evidence of a "scene" and certainly no call for "vengefulness" in the *Changeling* incident, merely a somewhat embarrassed go-between in the person of Ted. Nevertheless, in that the cause of the trouble had been a well-intentioned arrangement cooked up by him and Bill, it turned out to be the harbinger of my first brush with the full treatment.

On the final day of the 1960 CND Ban the Bomb demonstration during the Easter weekend, Bill's and my goddaughter, Frieda Hughes, was sixteen days old. Bill as usual had gone on the three-day march.

Ted was keen to see it come into London, and I had agreed — when the two of them suggested it — to go along with him, despite my dislike of being buffeted and elbowed around.

During the previous two weeks, a radiant Sylvia had been blissfully preoccupied getting to know her beautiful first-born. At no time, so far as anyone knew, had there been the slightest indication that she was interested in the march, let alone wanted to see it. If there had been the remotest suggestion of taking Frieda, they could have counted me out. Toting a two-week-old infant around in those huge crowds would have been something I didn't want to know about.

Ted and I went to the Albert Memorial. We didn't stay long. I had soon had enough of the crowds, and he was anxious to get home, which seemed altogether natural and normal — although at that stage I didn't know the half of what was natural and normal in the Hughes menage. For instance, that even the suggestion of Ted's going anywhere with anyone automatically triggered abreactions great or small, which went double if the "anyone" was a woman.

There was no sign of Sylvia and Frieda when we got back to Chalcot Square, except for a note saying that they had "gone to the march." If it hadn't been for the acute anxiety about Frieda, this display of *lex talionis* would have been laughable. In any other context, Sylvia herself would have been the first to ridicule the invocation of a silent-movie Mother-Heroine, newborn babe in arms, alone and fraily tottering amid the madding multitudes . . . What she had actually done, once Ted had gone, was to ring up his friend, Peter Redgrove (who happened to own a carry-cot), and invite him to "come along with *us*" (family outing implied) to Trafalgar Square. It had the desired effect, as did the note she left for Ted. There was no knowing where she had gone, and therefore no way that he could go looking for her. Sylvia's account of the march as an "immensely moving experience" that was "the baby's first real adventure" (*Letters Home*) is a typical example of what she herself described as "verbalizing the desired image" (*Journals*) — in other words, the process of "ordering" and "shaping" *un*desirable reality.

By the time Bill and I left for France, towards the end of May, my illusions concerning a normal, easygoing friendship with Sylvia had evaporated. It was becoming hard to differentiate between raised eyebrows and hackles, and harder still to ignore the problem of how to accommodate her morbidly prickly ego with one's own sense of outrage.

The answer — if there was one — seemed to lie in her penchant for categories and stereotypes, plus the fact that, manifestly from her point of view, an amenable stooge was a better bet than an unmanageable *soi-disant* friend. "Unmanageable," after all, implied unpredictable, and anything in that line was suspect. Otherness made her uneasy. What she needed was the reassurance of docile doppelgängers and supportive soul mates and yes-persons. It wasn't her fault that she and I happened to be polar opposites. We had been dealt our respective confidence quotients willy-nilly, and were stuck with them for better or worse.

In the introductory paragraph that precedes her all-A Wunderkind's first letter home from Smith, Aurelia Plath accords the reader a proud mother's-eye-view of an eighteen-year-old achievement addict already irrevocably hooked:

> Sylvia's letters from Smith show the effort of a conscientious student striving for high grades, partly to satisfy herself and build up her own image and partly to prove herself worthy of the generous financial aid she was receiving from various sources . . . Added to this effort was her need to project the image of the "all-around" person; i.e., the student who not only did well scholastically but was socially acceptable by both sexes, and the service-oriented person who made a contribution to her peer group and the community. To all this, Sylvia added her own burning desire: to develop creatively in her chosen field — writing — and to win recognition there. The pressure that developed from her involvement in all these areas was periodically overwhelming, both physically and psychically.

Programmed for "immediate and long range objectives" (*Journals*), as driven as a flagellant by the "old need of giving Mother accomplishments" with "reward of love . . ." (*Journals*), what made "your bright-eyed Sivvy" tick was the good old Work Ethic: What you conscientiously strove for, you got. What you didn't, you didn't. And the devil took the hindermost. And the hindermost consisted of the shameless and unmotivated ones (like me). For a supercharged Strindbergian ant, there was plenty to disapprove of in a laid-back Chekhovian cicada — even without my three marriages, voluntary childlessness, and lifted face.

Several husbands and no children was reprehensible but old hat. Cosmetic surgery, on the other hand, was worth looking into. Like most of us, Sylvia was only a moralist when it suited; but she was nothing if not a poet at all times. Added to which, medical imagery was her Thing. Nothing if not shameless, I never understood (and still don't) why procedures like massage and having your hair dyed or your teeth capped should be admissible, while face lifting was (and still is) coyly taboo. I had been saving up for mine quite openly for donkey's years, so when Sylvia asked questions and expressed interest in my incisions and spectacular technicolour bruises it seemed perfectly natural. Nor did it ever occur to me that she wouldn't — let alone shouldn't — make use of her findings. It wasn't remotely confidential, for the simple reason that to my mind she was far too erratic for one to risk telling her anything in confidence.

The scooping of my face lift was a unique interlude in our rather ambivalent relationship, in that this time our exchanges appeared to be entirely free of constraint. Whether it was because, bruised and swaddled in bandages, I gave the impression of being at a disadvantage, or merely that for once she forgot or couldn't be bothered, Sylvia temporarily dropped her guard — or seemed to, at least. Either way she provided me with an opportunity to see a turned-on and intriguing aspect of her that I barely caught sight of again.

In the poem that resulted from her researches, the hostility and contempt that went into that marvelously observed, spot-on caricature was by and large what you'd expect. One swallow doesn't make a summer; and it must be remembered that when she actually wrote "Face Lift," three months or so later, Sylvia was already back and holed up as usual, sniping from behind the barricades.

It was essential to possess all three keys to her labyrinth before one could make head or tail of a number of things that, at the time, were totally incomprehensible. In all, it took about twenty years: in '65 the *Ariel* poems disclosed the consuming hatred and fury, the implications of which none of her self-styled biographers, so far as I know, have ever had the objectivity and guts to face up to. In '75, the gospel according to the Desired Image — *Letters Home* — appeared, introducing us to a highly organized mythologising that turned everything to favour and to prettiness. Finally, in '82, the *Journals* revealed Sylvia's personal Armageddon: the struggles between what Ted in his foreword called "her warring selves." It also confirmed that the name of her Dybbuk was Fear.

Bumbling around then and there, trying to work out a nonflammable *modus vivendi*, one was faced with such a welter of contradictions that there was nothing to be done but play it by ear from day to day — or give up. Not that how it was played made much difference, because everything depended on Sylvia's mood of the moment.

It is now clear that her attitude to the people she knew was more complicated than it appeared to be. It seemed, on the face of it, that we were divided more or less arbitrarily into two categories consisting of the sheep and the goats. The sheep — that included Bill — were a small, admired elite, for whom it was worth minding her p's and q's and putting her best — impressively sparkling — foot forward, and with whom she tended, at times, to go over the top with the soft soap. And then the rest of us: the goats, who had their ups and downs. My most notable up (apart from that glimpse of what might have been possible owing to the face lift) only came to light years later, when I discovered myself richly and strangely transmogrified into a sort of Dame Kindness figure in *Letters Home*.

The advantage of being a goat was that nothing much was expected of us. The disadvantage was the ever-present possibility of finding ourselves in the wrong place at the wrong time (as I was on the day of the march) inexplicably transformed into nonpersons and/or accessories after the nonexistent fact — because Sylvia happened to be feeling vengeful. But whoever the culprit turned out to be, Ted's presence was essential to the scene. Without him it would have collapsed, because someone would simply have told Sylvia to come off it. With him there she had everyone over a barrel and wanting Out.

Her public and/or chronic scenes, as witnessed by various people in London, Yorkshire, and France, followed a characteristic pattern which is not easy to describe, in that from the point of view of dramatic action virtually nothing happened. To call them sulks because they were conducted in silence — apart from the occasional monosyllabic shrug — would be to suggest a switched-off, withdrawn dissociation on Sylvia's part that was exactly the opposite of the inescapable blast of active hostility that she directed at each individual who happened to be involved. This nonstop dispensation of condemnatory *Schadenfreude* made for a climate of sickened bewilderment that was (and still is) unforgettable and, I suspect, not believable for anyone who never came into contact with the anger of which Sylvia wrote: "I have a violence in me that is hot as death-blood."

The private and acute scenes in which her vituperative powers were brought into play, were, presumably, reserved for the two pillars of her mythological world, on whose loyalty she knew she could count: her mother and her husband. At this distance it is possible to see that although she looked down on the former and up to the latter, what Sylvia increasingly demanded of Ted was the all-indulgent, all-forgiving, devotion (unadulterated by any element of choice) that she had always had from Aurelia; in other words, one-hundred-percent nonbiodegradable mother love.

Not that Ted ever volunteered the least hint about what went on in private. Mrs. Plath, on the other hand, proved rather less reticent, at least during her visit to London in June '61 while she was sleeping at our flat in our absence. She would return in the evening and pour out her heart to our resident Australian cat-minder, Molly Raybould. Two things that particularly struck Molly were Aurelia's reiterated "Everything I do is *wrong;* I can't seem to do anything right" and "I just don't know how Ted stands it."

As Sylvia's "need to project the image" of an "all-around," "socially acceptable," "service-oriented" person did not extend to passing the time of day with a "little Australian hairdresser," Mrs. Plath's lamentations found a sympathetic ear — which no doubt accounts for her having opened up to the extent that she did. That, and the fact that Molly was a complete outsider who had only the vaguest idea of what Mr. and Mrs. Hughes severally got up to every day in Bill's study. Diffident, naive, and spinsterish, with a vermillion rinse that only enhanced her mousiness, she made no bones about being "scared stiff of that Mrs. Hughes," and would have been astounded had she been told (what none of us knew then except Ted) that "that Mrs. Hughes" was probably a lot more scared than she was.

Not of Molly herself, but of lots of other things . . . Notably, Ted's attitude to people: his completely unselfconscious benevolence and availability — where no doubt the children's books and the schools broadcasts came from. How could Sylvia, who felt excluded unless she had Ted all to herself, all the time, not have resented it? Even to the point of actually saying so in the sanitized *Letters Home:* "Ted is, if anything, too nice to his relatives and friends." And somewhere in one of the two lost journals there was an unforgettable *cri du coeur* that I once heard quoted: "We answer the door together. They step over me as though I were a mat, and walk straight into his heart."

That anything on her side might have been the cause of such a distressing effect apparently never occurred to her. Her manner of "answering the door," for instance, to the Mollys and goats of this world, or the slamming of it in their faces . . . "Only connect," said E. M. Forster. But this was something that Sylvia couldn't seem to see her way to. By her lights she wasn't wrong — ever. And *ipso facto* "they" were. She was like a car with no reverse gear and increasingly faulty brakes, a disastrous combination that was the nexus of her obsessive self-regard, her lack of conscience, her unwisdom, and, of course, her jealousy problem.

That one had existed right from the start was obvious. The climate of the *Changeling* and march "fusses" — which had prompted me to lower my profile — had been unmistakable. If "they" could "walk straight into [Ted's] heart," then any man, woman, or child could be a potential threat. Which seems to indicate that the real *casus belli* was any experience — however harmless — that he might happen to share with someone other than her. That way intimacy lay and the stuff of reminiscence (a malady most incident to in-laws and old acquaintances). And beyond that, just out of sight, was Hieronymous Bosch-ville with its Garden of (nameless) Delights.

An ironic and typically Strindbergian twist was the fact that of all Sylvia's bedevilling hang-ups and bugbears, the question of Shared Experience was the most nonsensical of the lot. Nobody could have come anywhere near a relationship with Ted that compared with what was between the two of them. Their working symbiosis was a genuine "marriage of true minds," a one-off confluence that he prized above everything apart from his own writing.

He proved it over and over again, not only by his forbearance in the teeth of that "day to day struggle" between Sylvia's "warring selves," but also by his tolerance when she behaved badly to people he was fond of. He respected, rejoiced in, and cherished her talent, and manifested a constant protectiveness towards her as an artist, as his wife, and as the mother of his child. As long as I knew them as a couple, he was invariably "if anything, too nice" to Sylvia. It might even have been better for them both if he had been less consistently gentle and loyal.

His single-minded, wholehearted, visceral identification with their common objectives was "an ever fixèd mark" that she need never have doubted for an instant. Her putting it at risk by mounting an embattled defence of what needed no defending was the ultimate example of her self-destructive unwisdom. What the two of them shared, because of what they were capable of doing together, was unassailable from the outside. Their joint mystery was their private myth. Only one or the other could have desecrated it. Any Hosts of Midian prowling and prowling around were figments. The Holy Ground was safe as houses. *Except* from betrayal by what was "false within" — which one would have sworn was unthinkable. Until it happened.

At the start of '61, although Sylvia was delighted to be pregnant again, she had begun to be bothered by a grumbling appendix. This, and the fear of going into hospital, caused, or at least contributed to, one of her periodic writer's blocks. As a remedial distraction, there-fore, she took on some "very pleasant" copy editing on a temporary basis. Ted, meanwhile, was on the lookout for another source of income to provide for the second child. During the first week of February an interview at the BBC resulted in a contract for a regular series of schools broadcasts, which meant they were in the clear financially.

In October '62 (over eighteen months later) Ted wrote to tell us that he had left Sylvia, which came as no surprise at all. In fact, we found it amazing that he had stuck it out as long as he did. He gave no details beyond that he was now kipping here and there with friends in London. Bill's immediate reaction was concern about Ted's having nowhere to hole up and work undisturbed. But I had to go to London on my way back to New York to settle the estate of my mother, who had recently died. It meant that Ted could have a room at her flat in Montagu Square until I disposed of it. I duly rang his mother for his telephone number the day I got to London and he moved in that same evening and stayed on after I left in November until the last of the furniture went to the saleroom just before Christmas.

Having conscientiously condoned and paid lip-service to his loyal excuses and camouflages in the past, I asked him as the first question on that first evening — partly to mark and partly to test out a new, and presumably uncensored, dispensation of things — what had been hardest to take during the time he and Sylvia were together. His answer was simply to recount the beginnings of what had by then become his highly successful broadcast series.

The head of the Schools Broadcasting Department, Moira Doolan — a lady of a certain age — had telephoned to arrange a meeting. Sylvia had answered and decided that the timbre and lilt of the voice on the line boded Shared Experience beyond the call of duty. Ted returned half an hour late for lunch (having secured the job he was after) to find that she had torn up all his work in hand: manuscripts, drafts, notebooks, the lot. As a final, gratuitous act of pure spite, she had also gralloched his complete Shakespeare. Only the hard spine and the end boards had stood up to the onslaught. The text had been more or less reduced to "fluff." There were just a few scraps of Ted's work that he managed to salvage and stick back together with Scotch tape.

Tearing a sizable amount of paper into small pieces is a fiddly and laborious undertaking. So Sylvia had ample time to reflect on the fact that to desecrate what mattered more than anything to both of them was inviting poetic justice with a vengeance. Yet rather than admit to being at fault, she resorted to red-herring recriminations about having been made late for her afternoon job. So far as I know, that marked the first time that she failed to shift the blame for whatever she had done — which is why, rightly or wrongly, I tend to see that episode as some sort of watershed whether either of them was aware of it or not.

Wherever the truth lies, if Sylvia had been capable of making even a moderate effort to learn from experience, the marriage might have survived. It was quite clear, six months later, that Ted was still hoping — vainly, as it turned out — that a move to the country, a house of their own, a new baby, and ideal working conditions would settle her down into some sort of serenity. Enough, at least, to subdue that dangerous predisposition to drive him further away by obsessively tightening the marital *cordon sanitaire*.

As it was, Nemesis came up with a truly Strindbergian *deus ex machina*. In the course of the following weekend the baby due to be born in August miscarried, and "the most blessed kind person in the world" was fully occupied looking after Sylvia for quite some time thereafter. Her instant amnesia, needless to say, made short work of what she had done — there is not the faintest hint of it in her letters to her mother. But then, had the need arisen, Sylvia could have "ordered" and "shaped" *The Dance of Death* into *Smiles of a Summer Night*.

The establishing of *Letters Home* as Holy Writ, the part it played in the promotion of the Plath Bonanza, and, for that matter, how and why it came to be published at all, really needs a study to itself. I am inclined to think that the Letters Homogenization process probably had its origins in Sylvia's besetting need to fend off self-doubt. What clearly started as girlish attitudinizing before an enraptured Magic Mother on the Wall apparently became an addictive *modus operandi* for keeping reality at bay. Approximately seven hundred transfusions of Desired Imagery (on average one per week over a period of twelve years) seems like an awful lot of reassurance to lavish on someone who, outside the letters, usually got the kind of short shrift that Mrs. Plath did, which raises the question as to whether those relentlessly complacent outpourings were not infinitely more necessary to Sylvia herself. Or, rather, to *one* of her selves. In this case one by Horatio Alger out of Emily Post, endlessly ambushed and traduced by those manifold "devils" that haunted the journals, where at least Sylvia could come out of the closet and admit she was "a hell of a person." Apart from an iconoclastic urge to do what little I can to straighten a record deliberately falsified for political, commercial, and possibly chauvinistic ends, I am concerned with the Plath Bonanza for only one reason: namely, the belief that — regardless of the cost to Sylvia herself and to others who are still paying — the worst-of-both-worlds intermixture of enraged self-exaltation and petit-bourgeois pretension was the richest and strangest element in the magma out of which her later poetry was conjured, when at last what Proust calls the sub-merged self was finally able to recognize and handle it.

How the conflicting drives and priorities of Medea and Emily Post affected Sylvia's social-surface self and those close to her appears so far to have been tacitly sidestepped. There aren't, of course, all that many people in possession of the facts; and among those of us who are, there must be one or two who can't afford to fall foul of feminist apartheid or risk a boycott by the Lib Lobby. Moreover, nobody I know was prepared to say a word as long as Sylvia's children were growing up, with the result that her hagiographers got a head start of two decades plus in which to shape their apotheosis, which snow-balled onward and upward virtually unchallenged.

To give an objective, firsthand account of the effects arising out of the conflict between Sylvia's B-movie beatitude and her implacable Graeco-tragic fury is a sure way, I imagine, to invite accusations of bias and exaggeration if not downright malice. In fact, there are no more hard feelings in anything I have to say about her than there were in my description of my dear friend Robert Lowell, at his bal-loon-faced, manic worst, that appeared in Ian Hamilton's biography. As an unstoppably irrational cat among unhappily rational pigeons, creating and dominating surreal, tragicomic situations from which we all wanted Out, Lowell had more than a little in common with Sylvia. The pattern of their public scenes was remarkably similar except that he used words like a Tommy gun whereas she used silence like nerve gas. In some ways, her method was the more disconcerting, especially if you happened to be under the same roof, as we were when she and Ted came to Lacan.

That was a very instructive visit in several respects; and later one came to see that her behaviour throughout was more or less a mi-crocosm of the negative aspects of the marriage that would drive Ted away within twelve months. What has made their stay even more revealing in retrospect is that it received double (i.e., submerged and surface) coverage by way of the poem "Stars Over the Dordogne" and a letter to her mother dated 6 July '61; each of them is a textbook example of Sylvia's ability to distil on the one hand and disguise on the other. Or, to put it in her own words, "The blood jet is poetry" against "Sugar is a necessary fluid."

The idea of their coming to France had been mooted, and a standing invitation issued right from the start in Boston. It was out of the question during their first summer in London because of Frieda, but it was taken for granted by all four of us that they would come as and when it suited them. They eventually turned up in their natty new car (paid for by the Third Programme) in the first week of July 1961.

Both were in need of rest and change. Before leaving London, Sylvia — three months pregnant again — had declared categorically that she wanted no excursions, no sightseeing, no walks even, and above all not to lift a domestic finger. What she craved was total *far' niente*, lots of unfamiliar food and to lie all day in the sun and get herself a real dark tan: the requirements, in short, of an ideal guest, as far as I was concerned. Ted was all set to explore the *causse*: the great, empty limestone plateau (on the edge of which the hamlet of Lacan is built), catacombed with underground rivers and crisscrossed by immemorial sheep paths and dry stone walls. He already knew quite a bit about this arid landscape from Bill, who wrote of it: "The secret becomes no less itself for our presence in the midst of it . . ." Ted was looking forward to catching sight of a wild boar, and perhaps even an eagle, and to the tree toads in the junipers and truffle oaks, the dew ponds, potholes, ruins, caves, menhirs, and dolmens that Bill had been wanting to show him ever since *The Hawk in the Rain.* On the face of it, all that was needed to ensure that the Hugheses enjoyed themselves was good weather. And it was, in fact, quite perfect during the whole of their stay.

Sylvia's letter from Lacan, with its cosmetic excisions and ambiguous punctuation, is palpably *du côté de chez Post.* "If you call a dog Hervey I will love him," said Dr. Johnson. If you call a former smallholder's modest farmhouse a "farm" and intimate that it produces its own milk, butter, and eggs, it can be assumed that the owner of this desirable property has a pretty lovable lifestyle. It was in such upwardly mobile surroundings that Sylvia claimed that she was getting tanned, that Ted was already "so rested" that it did her heart good, and that a service-oriented Dame Kindness endlessly toiled over a hot stove confecting gastronomic goodies for the houseparty. Of such was the kingdom of heaven at Trianon-Sunnybrook . . . Meanwhile, at Lacan de Loubressac things were not only rougher but a whole lot ruder.

The innocent catalyst and Spanish fly in the ointment was — of all unlikely people — our friend the late Margot Pitt-Rivers (to whom Bill had dedicated *The Saint of the Uplands* and his translation of *El Poema del Cid*). Although she had twice faced a firing squad in the Spanish Civil War, Margot was scared of sleeping alone when both her husband, Julian, and the cook happened to be away from their château at Fons. On these rare occasions, either Bill or I or both of us would go over and keep her company for a couple of nights or she would come over to us — quite often at very short notice. Which was how she came to be in the wrong place at the wrong time. The idea of anyone's taking exception to somebody as unassuming as Margot had never occurred to us; and had she been an equally charming man, probably everything would have been all right. As it was, she came in for the full ostracism-of-nonpersons treatment from the moment that Sylvia discovered that she hadn't just dropped in for a cup of tea.

At the beginning, such blatant rudeness rather intrigued Margot. Eloping with an anthropologist had made her an enthusiastic fieldworker; and as former Spanish ambassadress in London, adapting to dodgy contingencies was diplomatic second nature. But, inevitably, she began to worry about making things awkward for us, and we felt guilty on her account, and, hey presto, there we were: in a spot and over a barrel . . .

The Catch-22 about wanting Out at Lacan was that there was nowhere to go. That made for an element of farce: one Spanish Duchess, one irrational poetess, a brace of rational bards, and an aging soubrette — all stuck in the French sticks — is a hundred percent Feydeau even before you add the Shared Experience motif. It was as if the familiar unpalatable Strindberger was being served up à la française in a sauce piquante.

By the end of dinner on the first evening, Sylvia had successfully kiboshed Bill's and Ted's plans to expore the *causse* next day. She had decided to do some sketching, it seemed, and for this she had to have Ted along — presumably as a precautionary measure against Margot's getting in on the *causse* jaunt. Coming on top of the heavy ostracism ops, that virtually put paid to further conversation; so Bill suggested some music, which was Sylvia's cue for retiring to bed. Ted, despite a peremptory summons to go too, said he wanted to listen and stayed put. Half an hour later, in the middle of "I Know That My Redeemer Liveth," there was fortissimo stomping on the stairs, and Sylvia, with a raincoat over her nightdress, made an entrance. She paused accusingly, just long enough to insure that we were looking rather than listening, then turned and silently swept to the front door and exited dramatically into the night. Which of course effectively dislodged Ted, who had to dash after her to stop her breaking her neck in the rugged French outback. They returned some time later and went up to bed without a look or a word. Sylvia had been in the house for only a few hours, but the message was quite clear: it wasn't just a question of when she went sketching. She had to have Ted along or else.

We got through the next day reasonably well. While it was still cool, I took her to pick peaches in a neighbour's orchard (which she later immortalized) and then settled her on the terrace, where she dozed off for an hour or so, which enabled Bill and Ted to take a short clandestine stroll. Margot kept well out of the way until it was given out at lunch that I was taking her home first thing in the morning. We were counting on her departure to clear the air. From then on, it was hoped, so long as we watched our steps, there was no foreseeable reason why there should be any more trouble.

A little over halfway back to Fons, a front wheel came off our antique Ford van, and Margot and I — lucky to be alive — landed upside-down in the ditch. We eventually got ourselves a lift back to Fons, from where I SOS'd Bill, who had to be chauffeured to the rescue by Ted. When the three of us finally arrived back at Lacan, rancour was everywhere, and Sylvia wasn't speaking to Ted or Bill or me.

Had one known what one came to know later, it would have appeared entirely in keeping with her Darby-and-Joan syndrome and the Liaisons Dangereuses phobia that had transformed Mrs. Doolan into a concupiscent colleen on the basis of a fleeting aural contact. What is more, one would have been down on one's knees giving thanks that no vengeance had been wreaked in our absence.

The more one thinks about it, the more one wonders if Sylvia ever really wanted to be alone except when she was working. Whether perhaps abstractions like Peace, Quiet, and Privacy, in her book, implied "with Ted along," working, or otherwise grappled by some occupation, and located in some place that she could account for.

Nothing could have been less accountable than his being whipped off to a Spanish enchantress' castle. Could it have been a put-up job? Why hadn't they at least suggested that Sylvia go along? All manner of alarming reasons for being excluded may well have occurred to her, except the real one — that nobody would have had the face to take her to Fons after what had gone on at Lacan. But with her instant amnesia and total inability to see herself as others saw her, how could she *not* have felt hard done by?

What still remains a mystery is how she managed to put away the entire midday meal that I had left for her, Ted, and Bill. And that this Pantagruelian triple lunch in no way diminished the gusto with which she silently tucked into her dinner, doing more than justice to sundry delectable coals of fire contributed by Margot.

As I watched Sylvia grimly downing the Fons *foie gras* for all the world as though it were "Aunt Dot's meat loaf," there was little doubt that we were in for a reign of, if not terror, then tiresomeness every bit as effective. As Out was not logistically practicable, there was no alternative but to work towards détente.

Bill and Ted threw themselves into heavy clearing operations within earshot of the terrace among the blackberries, eglantines, elders, and ivy rioting in the orchard. In her "geranium-lined" solarium, on a level with the tops of the old Saint Antoine plum trees, Sylvia was lulled by the sounds of billhook, sickle, saw, and scythe wafting up from below. Thankful to be "cumbered about with much serving" — like the reprehended Martha of Bethany — I too contributed reassuring noises, clattering about in our small, curtained-off kitchen, preparing concilatory blow-outs — any one of which would have sustained Bill and me for several days.

Sylvia's baleful silence was eventually broken with an announcement that she wished to see a cow milked. A state visit to the neighbour's barn, with Ted in waiting, was laid on forthwith. While the Ford was out of action, I had to be taken shopping. She couldn't overtly object, since that way the victuals lay. She did the next best thing though, by coming along and demanding to be taken round the shops, including that of some friends who made attractive, rather expensive, one-off dresses. Having leisurely tried on the entire stock, grumbling that nothing fitted her interesting condition, the patronne agreed to alter the model she liked best, and Ted bought it for her — after which she sulked at having to "hang about" while I shopped for the food. And so it went . . .

I remember being force-fed at school with Evelyn Underhill's "Immanence," the first line of which was "I come in the little things saith the Lord." The wear and tear to which Sylvia subjected one's good will had a way of manifesting itself "in the little things," most of them so insignificant, at this distance, as to be barely worth recalling. But laid end to end, when they didn't actually overlap, they made for the sort of exasperated frustration that brings one out in a rash. Not that one hadn't had guests whose jumbo-sized solecisms were far more radical than anything she got up to: arriving with unspeakable, uninvited hangers-on, losing the house keys, and (ultimate nightmare) blocking up the septic tank. But those people, however disruptive, were appreciative and well-disposed. And Sylvia wasn't. So it was probably, more than anything, the highhanded way in which she used up all the hot water, repeatedly helped herself from the fridge (breakfasting on what one had planned to serve for lunch, etc.) and rearranged the furniture in their bedroom that wore one and tore one.

Perhaps the most baroque feature of that visit was the discovery that she had a liking for cards and was always keen to master an unfamiliar game. Introduced to our favourite *Ascenseur,* she took an instant fancy to it, playing with verve and finesse. Winning was obviously instant Desired Image, so naturally we had to play every night, which suited us fine. The combination of eating herself to a standstill and then grand-slamming her way to the title of *Maîtresse du Jeu* completely transformed her; and on the first too-good-to-be-true evening it really looked as if the rancour in the air had turned to *glasnost.* But the next morning the "ice eye" (*Journals*) was on the lookout again for "the weak," "the false," and "the sickly in soul." In other words, Sylvia was back on the warpath, and that unrelenting, unspoken, omnipresent animosity — which had to be experienced to be believed — was the order of the day once again.

This arbitrary shuttling between a diurnal and a nocturnal regime was the ultimate absurdity. It was Ted who was finally forced to admit that Out was the only solution for all of us. There was nothing for it but to cut their stay short and take Sylvia away. It was then that I asked him why he never put his foot down, and he told me that it would only make things worse, that "she couldn't be helped that way." I thought he was just fobbing me off with the usual excuses. What I didn't realize then was that he was also telling me the truth. How can you dissuade or even warn someone who is incapable of accepting that they might be wrong? Not that that was the moment to ask him to explain what he meant. Nor would he have, so long as they were together, as they would be for another twelve months.

It was in her *Maîtresse du Jeu* persona that Sylvia departed from the field of yet another Pyrrhic victory that would bring her even closer to losing the war: sunburned, smiling, "renewed," and waving triumphantly as they drove away. For some time afterwards, the customary quota of Strindbergian guilt remained hanging around — this time, in the form of embarrassment at the extent of our relief. Apart from when she was sleeping, eating, sunbathing, or playing cards, to a greater or lesser degree their stay at Lacan had been one long scene — a kind of macabre marathon for all concerned.

The picture that emerges from Sylvia's "Stars Over the Dordogne" leaves little doubt that virtually nothing could have been done to prevent their visit from being a fiasco, quite simply because what was on offer at Lacan would never really have found favour with her. In the poem her morbid mistrust of the unaccountable is the subject of a meditation as poignant and as sumptuous as a Chopin nocturne.

The night sky at Lacan, raining midsummer meteorites, images perfectly an *embarras de richesse* that Bill and I had hoped to be able to share with the two of them but from which Sylvia could only recoil: "There is too much ease here; these stars treat me too well." Still knocking ourselves out to placate her, we had ceased to be friends writ in syrup and became foes writ in blood.

Neither of us ever saw her again. By the time we got back to London in the autumn, she and Ted had moved to Devon. At the beginning of '62, St. George's Terrace was let until we decided to sell it a year or two later. From then on, apart from the six weeks that I spent in London disposing of my mother's flat and effects, both of us were mostly either in New York or in France. Ted wrote fairly regularly, keeping us posted about the finding of Court Green, the removal from London, the birth of Nicholas, and, of course, about the end of the marriage — rural amenities notwithstanding.

Just before they left London, Sylvia had written to her mother: "I have never seen [Ted] so happy. Both of us feel a wonderful deep-breathing sense of joy at the peaceful, secluded life opening up for us." "Secluded" is the buzz word there, and "opening up" Desired Imagespeak for "closing in." The Darby-and-Joan syndrome was entering its terminal phase — about which, of course, I know nothing at first hand.

When, in October '62, I arrived at my mother's flat and Ted moved in as Bill had suggested, as soon as he let Sylvia know where he was she began to bombard me with telephone calls. It goes without saying that I was terribly sorry for her, as one had to be for anyone who had thrown a pearl away and pulled off a do-it-yourself demolition job. I had been picturing her wracked with remorse, though I should have known better by that time.

Her unique preoccupation throughout our exchanges was to project the Desired (and expedient) Image of herself as martyred model Wife-and-Mother, and Ted as solely responsible from the start for every aspect of the ordeal to which she was now being subjected. Her calls took the form of monologues, opening with holier-than-thou set piece variations on the theme of the All-Around Monster. This would be followed by a constantly updated catalogue of misfortunes that sometimes changed in the course of a single day. Having announced in the morning, for instance, that her thumb would have to be amputated owing to the onset of gangrene, when she cornered me again in the evening there was no mention of this but Frieda would be down with "a deep regression." The following day something equally catastrophic would have befallen them, but seemingly never of sufficient duration to interfere with Sylvia's riding lessons.

The instant amnesia with regard to anything she or anyone else might have said or done only a few hours previously was nothing new; but what ruled out the possibility of any kind of rational discussion was the sheer momentum of her eloquence. It was then that I got some idea of what Ted and her mother must have been exposed to. Not that Sylvia really wanted to *discuss* anything. The idea, apparently — and it wouldn't have been such a bad one, had she tempered the Player Queen make-believe a bit — was to harrow me with a view to my harrowing Ted. In the circumstances, the fact that I was a Barren Woman made me a pretty obvious choice for a go-between.

Women in her Barren category were candidates for the Bottomless Pit. Not only because of what we couldn't or wouldn't do, but for what we were likely to get up to. To be sexually active and nonreproductive was tantamount to being morally serio-positive. Barren Women were unaccountability made flesh. As such, we were the polar opposites of Earth Mothers, whose teeming (as against the BW's "rattling") wombs immunized them against temptation, kept them on the rails and out of harm's way.

This docketing of individuals as types did away with Sylvia's having to bother about how they ticked. It also compounded her belief in her own rightness, rationalized her disregard for cause and effect, and virtually guaranteed that any attempt to manipulate people was liable to blow up in her face; also that when this occurred she would be genuinely outraged. To suggest that what had gone wrong had something to do with her, was asking to be recycled to the scapegoat pool, along with "the weak," "the false," and "the sickly in soul."

I was there anyway on account of Ted's having come to Montagu Square. In for a penny, in for a pound, and despite his categoric "she can't be helped that way" at Lacan, after about a week of Sylvia's tirades, I threatened to hang up if she didn't listen. I then delivered a completely fruitless spiel to the effect that amost anyone could be brainwashed into becoming an adulterer and a liar if you went on long enough implying that that was what they were. That sooner or later, however much they loved you, they would either get the hell out to avoid your accusations, or console themselves for the sake of their sanity and lie about it for the sake of peace. I also reminded her that KGB-like restrictions, censorship, interrogations, and surveillance would make a refugee of anybody. If she wanted Ted back, she would have to stop knocking him for a start. And if she didn't want him back, knocking him to me was a waste of her time and mine. That was as far as I got before she hung up. After that I had the housekeeper field the telephone, which was how she too came in for one or two startling earfuls before Sylvia turned her attention elsewhere.

I arrived back in New York to find that she had been attempting to mount a double-barrelled comeuppance, the linchpin of which was Bill — undoubtedly the most unsuitable cat's-paw that anyone with half a mind could possibly have picked on. Except Sylvia, of course — because she couldn't see herself as others saw her, because she couldn't call to mind what they had seen. She had written to him at considerable length, tipping him the wink that Ted and I were living together and saying that as they (Sylvia and Bill) had *always* been soul mates, hadn't they, could she now please dedicate a poem to him as she'd always longed to, etc., etc.

Bill's lethally polite brush-off, declining the honour, would have shamed most women into dropping the come-hither like a hot potato, but back had come an even longer and more fulsome overture that he had, of course, quite simply ignored. That Sylvia's bash at making a pass had not solely been prompted by spite, perhaps, was the one aspect of the undertaking that one could understand and genuinely sympathize with: she was not the first and would not be the last, as Leporello pointed out to Donna Elvira. But to have banked on the sneak-as-twin-soul as an effective approach (to Bill of all people) goes a long way to explaining why, during her lifetime at least, for all her vengeful propensities, she never really managed to harm anyone except herself.

Faced with bosh shots, boomerangs, and damp squibs of her own impulsive devising, constitutionally incapable of knowing where to stop and how to cut her losses, what Sylvia couldn't cover up she had to justify. As Bill had not replied to her second advance, an admonitory Parthian swipe was called for. But we were on the wrong side of the Atlantic, and there wasn't a lot that she could do about having the last word at that distance — beyond proclaiming how awful we were. Or rather, how awful I was. Hell might know no fury, but, again like Donna Elvira, Sylvia was not above hedging her bets.

It was twenty-five years or so before that second denunciation surfaced — in a letter dated 26 December 1962 to Daniel and Helga Huws. It is worth quoting because it provides an example of the Letters Home process, used in reverse, as an outlet for the rage that was fuelling the poems and apparently becoming more and more unmanageable and destructive on the surface:

She [Assia Wevill, who along with Ted and myself was also a target in this letter] is part of this set of barren women which includes Dido Merwin, that I am so glad to be rid of. I guess I am just not like that. I had a terrible experience calling Dido Merwin as Frieda's godmother when I was in London — she was the only person I thought could advise me about doctors and a flat. She knew I was calling on her as a godmother, but because she was so glad she at last had Ted living at her place, she made it clear that she was home but refused to speak to me. Both Ted and I have agreed to write off the Merwins as Frieda's godparents and wonder if you would be her godparents instead. I take this as a very serious thing, & it almost killed me for Frieda's sake, to think of the heartlessness and hypocrisy behind Mrs. Merwin's refusal to answer when she knew I was worried about the babies going into hospital. But then, she has always disliked children & devoted her life to herself. I find now that this breakup has occurred I am free of many such people who courted Ted for his fame, and of course it has hurt me deeply that he has more or less sold out to them.*

Since truth was always relative, to say the least, for Sylvia the born fiction writer, it is the wild incoherence even more than the whirling unreality of this irruption of overkill that shows how close to the edge she was by then. One wonders if the letter of the same date to her mother was written later in the day to steady herself before "dropping over to the Frankforts . . . for a 'Boxing Day' supper with them." It seems quite possible.

What I have written about her will no doubt be interpreted as speaking ill, not to say flippantly, of the dead — the inevitable price of attempting to give a truthful account of what I witnessed. That it sometimes gave rise to ludicrous situations made it no less tragic, as

---

*This excerpt quoted from the letter to the Huwses contains various fictions: (1) The Barren Woman category has become a "set." Assia Wevill and I didn't know each other until we met in early November, and, so far as I know, had no friends in common. (2) If Sylvia had telephoned when she was up in London, the housekeeper would certainly have mentioned the godmother bit, which is pure fiction. (3) Why would I be "the one person" who could "advise" about pediatricians? Sylvia had only to ask her nanny (Susan O'Neill-Roe), who was a staff nurse at a London children's hospital, or the doctor at the Horder practice who attended to her cut thumb. (4) I was certainly not the only person who could advise her about flats. As she wrote to her mother, *Ted* "took me round looking at places." She had only to ask him to ask me if I knew of any flats — which I didn't, as I was no longer living in London. (5) There was never any mention — let alone "agreement" with Ted — of writing off Bill and me as Frieda's godparents. (6) "The babies" never suffered from anything worse than colds in the autumn of '62 and were never hospitalized. Had there been the remotest suggestion of such a thing, I would have heard about it from Ted.

did the fact that none of us had any idea she was in that sort of trouble. Except Ted, of course, who was always aware of the casualty, whereas we only knew the aggressor.

Things might have been different if it had all happened today. But in those days one wasn't necessarily on the lookout for psychoses just because somebody was "difficult" or whatever the euphemism happened to be. Ironically, it was Sylvia's carefully projected All-Around-ness that provided the camouflage. Because she was brilliant, articulate, overtly ambitious, energetic, efficient, organized, enviably resourceful in practical matters, blessed with a hearty appetite and (as she said herself) "an athletic physique which I possess and admire," she seemed infinitely stronger than she actually was. This impression was reinforced by Ted, whose efforts to keep her on her feet at all costs tended sometimes to give him the appearance of a henpecked husband. That those of us on the touch line — as long as I was there — were unaware of the true situation, is not, therefore, surprising.

What has always puzzled and intrigued me, though, is: given that we didn't know, what was it that compelled some of us to act as though we *did* know? Why did we — uncharacteristically and in spite of our disparate and highly intransigent selves — put up with Sylvia's carry-on as if we were the paid attendants of some tiresome and demanding invalid who never said "please" and "thank you," let alone "sorry"? My own semi-tongue-in-cheek dogsbodying, which had started off on a basis of free-range good intentions and deteriorated into a pretty joyless arrangement the like of which I have never had with anybody else, can't altogether be accounted for by our affection and respect for Ted or (as far as I was concerned) by good manners.

An empirical explanation might be that Sylvia's case made cases of us all in one way or another. Were we subconsciously troubled by a genuine subliminal SOS? Or were we — Ted most of all — manipulated to a greater or lesser degree by the deep, instinctive cunning of someone driven to get her own way? Who knows? Certainly not me. Which isn't a reason for not setting down what it felt like. Any firsthand evidence of the effect Sylvia had on people must reveal something about that flawed psyche that made her not so much her own worst, as her only, enemy — a vessel of wrath "fitted to destruction."

De mortuis nil nisi bonum . . . To have introduced the harsh daylight of personal experience, where only the roseate glow of speculative theory and expediency has been authorized, is to invite dyspeptic reactions. This profanation of a Desired, painstakingly graven, Image might well be construed as a malicious retaliation. But there was absolutely nothing to be retaliatory about. For a start, Sylvia's malice was pathological and therefore doesn't count — any more than the reflexes of the threatened animal, about whom some immortal goon allegedly exclaimed: "Cet animal est très méchant: Quand on l'attaque, il se defend!" (This is a very bad animal: When one attacks it, it defends itself.)

In point of fact, any tendency to judge her after the fashion in which her hagiographers have judged Ted was taken care of by a turn of events that occurred shortly before I began to write about Sylvia. Diagnosed as having cancer with a poor prognosis, I found myself in the situation summed up by Dr. Johnson when he said, "Depend upon it, Sir, when a man knows he is to be hanged in a fortnight, it concentrates his mind wonderfully."

Another wonderful aid to concentration is a reprieve, however temporary. Mine has provided an opportunity to consider what Sylvia was up against in a way that perhaps might not have been possible in other circumstances. The more one thinks about her, the more one finds oneself coming back to Forster's deceptively simple "Only connect," something that her social self was never, seemingly, able to do, while the submerged self zoomed on to recognition and immortality — divining and pinpointing affinities, analogies, assonances, linking, fusing, conjugating, juxtaposing, nuancing, and illuminating with high-definition virtuosity and ever-increasing mastery. It was as if she was quite at home with differential calculus but couldn't put two and two together to save her life or even escape from her own shadow.

To have ignored the difference between moral and material give-and-take in her marriage, to have had no other recourse than force-nine rages and manic bravado when faced with doubt and unhappiness, and — saddest of all — for as long as I knew her to have seen help (apart from palliatives) as a threat to be wary of and to be resisted, added up to a state of defenselessness that put Sylvia permanently at risk and that made what happened almost inevitable, sooner or later.

This memoir is dedicated to Dr. Peter Blake of the Royal Marsden Hospital, London, and to everyone there who has helped him to help me.

A Memoir of Sylvia Plath and Ted Hughes
on a Visit to the West of Ireland in 1962

BY RICHARD MURPHY

MY FIRST MEETING with Ted and Sylvia was at the Mermaid Theatre in London on Monday 17 July 1961. We were taking part in a festival called "Poetry at the Mermaid," promoted by the Poetry Book Society, with John Wain as director. Twelve poets had been commissioned by Arthur Guinness Son & Company to write poems of 50 to 200 lines on subjects of their own choice. Eight of these twelve had been invited to read at the festival that evening. We rehearsed in the morning; there was a reading by Ted with Clifford Dyment and Geoffrey Hill at one o'clock; Ted and Sylvia joined me for a meal in the restaurant that afternoon.

Our talk was more about living in the country, fishing and the sea, than about poetry. Ted made a strong, silent impression, speaking much less than Sylvia. But they both seemed interested in my struggle to make a living with a boat on the west coast of Ireland. I had refurbished an old Galway hooker called the *Ave Maria*, which I was operating in the summer, taking tourists out sailing and fishing. Cleggan was a tiny, remote, impoverished village. Most of its fishermen had been drowned in 1927; and the place had never recovered. In 1961 I bought the blacksmith's cottage, and began living there with a boy who helped me sail the hooker.

I met Sylvia once again on 31 October 1961, when she received a Guinness Award at a reception in the Goldsmith's Hall in London. We sat together before she went up to the rostrum. Neither of us knew many of the people there except by name.

Sometime in the spring of 1962, after the manuscript of *Sailing to an Island* had been accepted by Charles Monteith and T. S. Eliot for publication by Faber, I entered my poem "The Cleggan Disaster" for the Guinness Awards at the Cheltenham Festival. The judges that year were George Hartley, Sylvia Plath, and John Press; and the pseudonym

I used was "Fisherman." The poem celebrates a fisherman who survived by holding on to his nets instead of giving up the struggle. Before the official verdict came from the chairman of the festival, I received Sylvia's letter dated July 21 (1962), telling me that the lyrical epilogue had got the prize. By this time I was running two boats under sail with tourists every fine day, while my cottage, "The Old Forge," was let to families who chartered one of the boats. I replied to her letter with a telegram saying: "Do hope you can come after 8 September stay with me and sail."

They arrived on Wednesday 12 September, by train to Galway, and by car for the 57 miles to Cleggan. They were intending to stay for a week as my guests. I gave them a room, with twin beds made of native elm by an island boatwright. The day after they arrived, I took them out on the *Ave Maria*. We sailed to Inishbofin, a passage of six miles across open water with a strong current and an ocean swell. Sylvia lay prone on the foredeck, leaning out over the prow like a triumphant figurehead, inhaling the sea air ecstatically.

On Friday 14 September I drove them to Yeats's Tower at Ballylee and Lady Gregory's Coole Park in my 7 h.p. minivan, used for selling the fish we had caught. Sylvia sat in front, talking to me about marriage and divorce, while in the back, which was too small for seats, Ted talked about poachers and guns and fishing to Seamus, who was fifteen years old. We went first to Coole, where I showed them the copper beech tree in the pleasure ground. Sylvia urged Ted to climb the spiked iron fence that had been erected to protect the tree, and to carve his initials beside those of Yeats. She said he deserved to be in that company more than some of the Irish writers who had made their now almost illegible mark. He was frustrated by the fence.

The tower at that time was the ruin predicted by Yeats in the poem carved on a stone at Ballylee. Everything that could be moved had been stolen by people in the neighborhood. The Tourist Board had not begun to take an interest in its restoration. The road was still untarred. Jackdaws exploded as we climbed the spiral stairs. From the top, Sylvia threw coins into the stream. Then they noticed a large apple tree that must have been planted by Yeats, with a heavy crop of bright red apples. Ted and Sylvia both insisted that we should steal them. I protested. Ted said they would make good apple pie, enough to keep me through the winter. They made Seamus climb the tree to shake the branches, and they went to work among the nettles picking up the apples, gathering more than a hundredweight. I was reluctant to take them in the van, but my objections were brushed aside by Ted very firmly, as if these were not mere cookers but

The silver apples of the moon.
The golden apples of the sun.

From Ballylee we went to Milford, my birthplace, where I showed them the Rangoon prints which appear in Sylvia's poem "The Courage of Shutting Up." Milford was an early eighteenth-century house at the end of a lime tree avenue three quarters of a mile long, aloof and decayed, belonging to a first cousin of mine. My aunt took Ted and Sylvia into the drawing room but sent Seamus off down a dark corridor, saying, "This way to the kitchen, Seamus: I'm sure you'd be much happier there."

All the arrangements for their holiday had so far been managed by Sylvia, though Ted appeared to approve. That was my impression, confirmed by her letters. If I said anything to Ted, Sylvia would be quicker to reply. This did not seem to annoy him. I never heard them quarrel or speak unkindly to each other. In the context of their recent marital difficulties, she told me his lies upset her; he never mentioned any fault of hers in my hearing, either then or subsequently. What he admitted was that after six or seven years that had been marvelously creative for him, the marriage had somehow become destructive, and he thought the best thing to do was to give it a rest by going to Spain for six months. Assia's name was not mentioned, but her role was implied.

To counter this move of Ted's, Sylvia told me she wanted a legal separation, not a divorce. She could not, she said, imagine either Ted or herself truly married to anyone else. Their union had been so complete, on every level, that she felt nothing could really destroy this. She never spoke of suicide as an act she was contemplating herself. I argued with her that a legal separation was a cruel alternative to divorce; but I also urged her not to divorce Ted on account of an affair that might not last. I told her about my experience of marriage and divorce. My wife had threatened suicide, and her brother had indeed killed himself after his wife had died suddenly in her sleep, leaving us with his two children and a devastating sense of guilt, of not having done enough to help.

One way in which my help was apparently needed by Sylvia was in finding her a house which she could rent for the period of Ted's visit to Spain. She said she would be writing another novel, a potboiler, which is what she also called *The Bell Jar*. She seemed to have fallen in love with Connemara at first sight; and when her enthusiasm reached its peak, she even offered to rent my cottage and let me stay in it. This proposal alarmed me. I took them to see two or three houses in our neighborhood and introduced Sylvia to Kitty Marriott, with whom she made a tenancy agreement beginning on 1 November. Sylvia eulogized Mrs. Marriott, and made her plans with astonishing decisiveness. I think we looked at houses, and she decided, on Saturday 15 September.

My alarm increased at dinner that night in my cottage, a feast which was cooked for us by Seamus's mother, Mrs. Mary Coyne. (There is a letter to her from Sylvia dated 15 December 1962.) Mrs. Coyne's husband had died of cancer just after the birth of her third child; and she had reared her children by knitting, gardening, and farming five acres of very poor land. Her small thatched cottage, where I had often stayed, was the oldest in the village, and the most hospitable. My life in Cleggan, including the sailing of two Galway hookers, entirely depended upon her and her two sons. They provided a home for me in the village; and through the boats I was able to provide them, and myself, with summer jobs. Mrs. Coyne was most generous in helping me to entertain visitors, such as Ted and Sylvia. But there was a limit, dictated by strong village opinion at that time and place, and inviting a married woman to stay with me on her own was beyond that limit. Sylvia was not aware of this until it was too late.

At dinner that night we were joined by Thomas Kinsella, who had driven down from Dublin, where he worked in the Department of Finance, to stay with us for the weekend. To my relief, they greatly enjoyed each other's company. But sometime during the meal, in the presence of Ted and Tom, though not noticed by them, Sylvia rubbed her leg against mine under the table, provocatively. It made me inwardly recoil. My own marriage had begun to break up after a literary guest had seduced my wife on a weekend visit in 1957. I did not want to break up Sylvia's marriage, or have a secret affair with her, or be used to make Ted jealous, or upset Mary Coyne.

After dinner, the conversation came around, perhaps through Yeats, to the Ouija board, which Ted and Sylvia were willing to demonstrate. So after cutting out letters, and choosing a suitable wineglass, they began a séance, in which I took no part. Sylvia gave up soon and went to bed, but Ted and Tom continued late into the night; as I discovered next morning, when I found on the table some pages of poetry in Kinsella's hand, but in one of the manners of Hughes, on a mythical theme. Tom was the first guest to appear, and when I expressed surprise about what the spirits had produced, Tom confessed to having helped by pushing.

That Sunday (16 September), I went out in the morning on some business connected with the two Galway hookers, and when I returned to my cottage, Sylvia was there on her own. She explained that Ted had gone to stay with Barrie Cooke, the painter, in County Clare, where he was hoping to do some trout or salmon fishing. I had been expecting them both to stay until the following Wednesday. Sylvia said she had her return ticket from Galway to Dublin and planned to meet Ted on the train on Wednesday.

It was strange of him to leave like this; but her secret sign to me under the dinner table the previous night made me suspect that she might have encouraged him to go. Though she complained that he had walked out on her like this before, I feared she had arranged to be alone with me after he and Tom had gone. So I reacted by asking her to take the opportunity of getting to Dublin by car with Tom the next day. I did try to explain the problems I might have in the village if she were to stay on.

Instead of accepting this agreeably, Sylvia was enraged. All her warmth and enthusiasm, her gushing excitement that colored whatever she noticed with hyperbole, changed into a strangulated hostility. She scarcely spoke to me, and when she did, she put a strained, artificial distance between us. She opened her heart to Mrs. Coyne, and sowed in her mind a few seeds of the future myth of her martyrdom. Though she thanked me and said good-bye, under duress of her upbringing and mine, Sylvia left me feeling that, after all the effort I had made to entertain them both, I had been mean.

Sylvia wrote to me from Devon on 21 September. I never answered her letter because I did not know what to say. As I had asked her to leave my house, to avoid problems I might have had in Cleggan, she withdrew her invitation to me to stay with her at North Tawton, giving a hilarious excuse that was a mockery of mine. I felt that if I were to "vault the barrier my understanding was stuck at" when she left, as she urged me to do in her last paragraph, it might land us both in deep trouble; and she confused me by saying, "I have not and never will have a desire to see or speak to you or anyone else." After all she had said of her visit, I found this hard to believe. She had picked Mrs. Marriott as a person she needed, without any true perception of Mrs. Marriott, who was to give her an unpleasant shock by demanding three months' rent when Sylvia cancelled her tenancy agreement.

On the one hand, Sylvia was imploring me to be kind to her; on the other, she was unkindly accusing me of hypocrisy, and saying, "You shall see neither hide nor hair of anybody." I would have loved to continue the long conversation we enjoyed in the first flush of her visit to Connemara. Both she and Ted had encouraged me to write dramatic monologues, rather than straight narrative, in "The Battle of Aughrim." Their company was much more of an inspiration than a threat. But I did not want to be devoured, or to become as deeply responsible for keeping another person alive as I had been during my marriage. Sylvia may have felt I had this capacity but was withholding it from her.

I was aware that she had been joking when she spoke of writing *New Yorker* poems about Connemara, but the paragraph in which she tried to reassure me that she had not written a poem for over a year, and would only be writing prose, struck a false note. I disliked the implicit accusation that I was trying to defend my "literary territory"; nor did I like her thinking in those terms. Had I not invited them to stay? It's now known that she had written one or two of her best poems in that previous year.

So I puzzled over what to say in a reply which never got written, and then I got another letter (October 7, 1962), in which she said kind things about a review I had written for *The Observer,* with some references to Yeats's Tower. She also mentioned she was "getting a divorce, and you are right, it is freeing." I had recommended divorce, rather than a legal separation, because it freed both parties to marry again; but I do not remember recommending divorce in itself as liberating. I had found it hurtful. I thought that the best answer to this letter would be to go and see her as soon as she arrived at Mrs. Marriott's house, 1½ miles from Cleggan. But she changed her plans suddenly and moved to London instead.

I went to London for the publication by Faber of *Sailing to an Island* at the end of January (1963), and met Sylvia, for the last time, at the Beckers' house in Islington, where I was taken by Douglas Cleverdon. He had produced "The Cleggan Disaster" and commissioned "The Battle of Aughrim" for the BBC Third Programme. I had been told by the Cleverdons that Sylvia was in a very tense state. Her face looked feverish, and she seemed ecstatic. She said she was happy now, and glad to have got the flat in a house where Yeats had lived, with a plaque on the front wall. She thought this was the best thing to have done, instead of coming to Ireland. There was no trace of ill feeling towards me; and in view of her need for medical help for herself and the children, I felt she had made a wise decision.

On the same visit to London, I had just been asked by Leonie Cohen to take part in a series of BBC talks called "Writers on Themselves" in which Ted and Sylvia had already been included, Sylvia having contributed "Ocean 1212-W." To write my talk, I went back to Cleggan for about a fortnight. When I returned to London on 14

February, I heard about Sylvia's death, and Ted asked me to meet him at her flat, where I also met his Aunt Hilda, who was looking after the children. That was just before he went to Heptonstall for the funeral. I was tormented for a long time with a terrible feeling of guilt for not having given her the haven she needed in Connemara. But at the same time I was appalled by the cruel suffering her suicide inflicted remorselessly on Ted and their families and their friends.

Kandy, Sri Lanka, 10 February 1988

LETTERS FROM SYLVIA PLATH TO RICHARD MURPHY *

Court Green
Devonshire, England
Saturday: July 21 [1962]

Dear Richard,

I don't know how fast the cogs of officialdom work, but I could not deny myself the pleasure of letting you know right away that "Years Later," the Epilogue of the "Cleggan Disaster" has won first prize in the Cheltenham contest. I suppose you have already heard, or will soon hear this from Mr. Wilkinson, the chairman of the festival. The epilogue, because we felt that touched heights perhaps *greater than in the earlier part.*

I now have a question to ask you. Is there any chance of Ted & me coming to Bofin around the last week in August or first week in September? I don't know how long you run your boat, or what your terms are, but for me at least, I desperately need a boat and the sea and *no squalling babies.* We are now trying to negotiate a family to come & mind Frieda (2 years) and Nicholas (6 months), and I should know Monday if and exactly when they can come. If they won't, then I shall have simply to hire someone. But if you could let me know right away if any week in late August or early (first week) September would connect us with you & and your blessed boat, it would be so nice.

It would also be lovely to see you again. The center of my whole

---

*Printed by courtesy of the Estate of Sylvia Plath.

early life was ocean and boats, and because of this, your poems have been of especial interest to me, and I think you would be a very lovely person for us to visit just now. Is there any kind old soul on the island who would feed & bed us & would it be possible to bring the car there, or would we have to leave it on the mainland? I hope, while in Ireland, we may also collide with Jack & Maire Sweeney, of whom we are very fond. And maybe Dublin. I have never been before.

Do tell me I am not being an awful bother. And please do say we may come on your boat. I have always desired, above many things, a friend with a boat. Ted sends his best, and hopes you will take us on.

Again congratulations, & warmest good wishes,

Sylvia Plath

P.S. Eric White said something.
About Fabers & Eliot having accepted your poems.
I am so very glad. It is so deserved.

Court Green
Devon.
Friday: August 17 [1962]

Dear Richard,

Your latest telegram arrived yesterday when we were away for the day in London and we have no phone, so I am writing. As things now stand, I am reasonably sure we can leave Devon on Monday, September 10. I don't know how long it will take to get to you, but when we do we could stay about a week. Do you have life preservers! I don't want you writing another prize-winning poem about our eyeballs boiling in the sea!

Could you drop us a note with some advice about the best way to get to your place from wherever the boat to Ireland lands? We will be without a car & travel by train or bus or mule or whatever is most expeditious. Do let us know what to do about getting to your island! I don't know when I've looked so forward to anything. I am sick of the bloody British sea with its toffee wrappers & trippers in pink plastic macs bobbing in the shallows, and caravans piled one on top of the other like enamel coffins.

Fond regards,

Sylvia

Court Green
Devonshire, England
September 8 [1962]

Dear Richard,

Thank you so much for your good letter. We have got a nanny for the babies so can leave here with easy heart. We plan to take the train to Holyhead Tuesday night, cross to Dublin by night, say hello to Jack Sweeney & come by rail to Galway Wednesday eveningish. Shall call as soon as we arrive. We would love to stay in your cottage. I don't know when I have looked so forward to anything.

Warmest good wishes,

Sylvia

Court Green
Devonshire, England
September 21 [1962]

Dear Richard,

I am enclosing my unused ticket from Galway to Dublin, good for three months, in hopes that you or Seamus or Owen may find it of use. I cannot thank you enough for your hospitality & the wonderful food of Mrs. Coyne. The boats & the sea were like a great cure for me.

May I say two things? My health depends on leaving England & going to Ireland, & the health of the children. I am very reluctant to think that the help you gave with one hand you would want to take away with the other. I am in great need of a woman like Kitty Marriott & if there is one thing my 30th year has brought it is understanding of what I am, and a sense of strength and independence to face what I have to. It may be difficult to believe, but I have not and never will have a desire to see or speak to you or anyone else. I have wintered in a lighthouse & that sort of life is balm to my soul. I do not expect you to understand this, or anything else, how could you, you know nothing of me. I do not want to think you were hypocritical when showing me the cottages, but it is difficult to think otherwise. Please let me think better of you than this.

Secondly, I was appalled to realize you did not understand we were joking when talking about my writing New Yorker poems about

Connemara. I would not do that even if I were able, and as you know I have not written a poem in over a year & cannot write poems anyway when I am writing prose. So there is no question of your literary territory being invaded. My novel is set in Devon, and it is this I hope to finish at Glasthule.

I feel very sorry to have to retract my invitation to visit us at Court Green as it would have given me great pleasure to have you see it —— I think you have a feeling for land, and this is very beautiful land & I imagine I feel about it the way you do about your hookers —— proud of it, and of what I have made of it and hope to make of it, and eager to feel it is appreciated, not hated. But Ted will not be here, as I had thought when I asked you, and when he is not here I can see no one. My town is as small & watchful as yours & a little cripple hunchback with a high black boot lives at the bottom of my lane & all day & night watches who comes & goes. This is really very funny. There is nothing for the poor woman to see. So I am very sensible to your concerns. I shall try to bring a nanny with me in December & then maybe get someone to live in & help with the children, & you shall see neither hide nor hair of anybody. Other people only get in the way of my babies & and my work & I am dedicated to both as a nurse-nun. Please have the kindness, the largeness, to say you will not wish me ill nor keep me from what I clearly and calmly see as the one fate open. I would like to think your understanding could vault the barrier it was stuck at when I left. Sincerely, Sylvia

Court Green
Devonshire, England
Sunday: October 7 [1962]

Dear Richard,

The review was lovely, it was fine to see it there in the middle of everything, and so spacious. Only Ted says they were jackdaws. As far as I'm concerned every black bird is a rook. It was like a brilliant enamel, your account of the place, & made me homesick for it, the first pure clear place I have been for some time.

Please let me know you got my note & if the ticket was any use. I shall be coming to Moyard with Ted's aunt as a companion & hope to get an Irish girl to live in & accompany me back, if I have the luck of the Irish. I shall try for a good Catholic, and maybe she can convert me, only I suppose I am damned already. Do they never forgive divorcees? I am getting a divorce, and you were right, it is freeing. I am writing for the first time in years, my real self, long smothered. I get up at 4 a.m. when I wake, & it is black, & write till the babes wake. It is like writing in a train tunnel, or God's intestine. Please make me happy & say you do not grudge me Moyard. I shall be well & eternally chaperoned & only the cows shall see me. It would hurt me terribly to think of you with clenched teeth in Cleggan.

And tell me about Cheltenham. Regards, Sylvia

23 Fitzroy Road
London N.W. 1

December 15, 1962

Dear Mrs. Coyne,

I have had to move to London for the winter to have my little boy's eye seen to by a specialist & operated on,* so I would be very grateful if you would send on my sweater & the little girl's sweater suit to me at the above London address, if you have not already sent them to Court Green. If you have already sent them there, they will be forwarded to me.

Do tell Mr. Murphy I am living in Yeats' house in London — with the blue plaque and all. It will amuse him, as Yeats was a famous Irish poet & I am very lucky to be living in his house, it is a real inspiration to my writing.

Best wishes for the Christmas season,

Sincerely,

Sylvia Hughes

---

*This was an invention.

▸ S O U R C E S A N D N O T E S ◂

SOURCES

For a complete list of works by and about Plath, see Stephen Tabor, *Sylvia Plath: An Analytic Bibliography* (London and New York: Mansell Publishing, 1986).

The works listed below were especially helpful for this biography. An abbreviation in brackets after a title indicates the form of the title that is used in the Notes.

Works by Sylvia Plath

The Colossus. London: Heinemann, 1960; New York: Knopf, 1962.*

The Bell Jar [BJ]. London: Heinemann, 1963 (published under the pseudonym Victoria Lucas); republished Faber, 1966; New York: Harper & Row, 1971. The U.S. edition contains drawings by Plath and a Biographical Note by Lois Ames; text references are to this edition.

Ariel. London: Faber, 1965; New York: Harper & Row, 1966.*

Crossing the Water. London: Faber, 1971; New York: Harper & Row, 1971.*

Winter Trees. London: Faber, 1971; New York: Harper & Row, 1972.*

Letters Home: Correspondence, 1950–1963 [LH]. Ed. with commentary by Aurelia Schober Plath. London: Faber, 1975; New York: Harper & Row, 1975.

The Bed Book. London: Faber, 1976; New York: Harper & Row, 1976.

Johnny Panic and the Bible of Dreams: Short Stories, Prose, and Diary Excerpts [JP]. London: Faber, 1977; New York: Harper & Row,

---

*The American editions of these volumes differ from the British in the order and number of poems. The American collections are slightly longer, except in the case of *The Colossus,* for which U.S. editors requested that some of the poems be omitted.

1980. Again, the contents of the two editions vary. The U.S. edition, which is slightly larger, has been used for text references.

The Collected Poems [CP]. Ed. Ted Hughes. London: Faber, 1981; New York: Harper & Row, 1981. The two editions, which are identical, contain all known poems by Sylvia Plath from 1956 on, and a selection of 50 early poems from the 220 known juvenilia listed (manuscripts of which are in the Lilly Library at Indiana University and at Smith College).

The Journals of Sylvia Plath [*Journals*]. Ed. Frances McCullough; consulting ed. Ted Hughes. New York: Dial Press, 1982.

Collections of Essays

Alexander, Paul, ed. *Ariel Ascending: Writings About Sylvia Plath*. New York: Harper & Row, 1985.

Butscher, Edward, ed. *Sylvia Plath: The Woman and the Work*. New York: Dodd, Mead, 1977; London: Peter Owen, 1979.

Newman, Charles, ed. *The Art of Sylvia Plath: A Symposium* (reprinted from *Tri-Quarterly*). Bloomington: Indiana University Press, 1970.

Individual Books and Essays

Alvarez, A. "Prologue: Sylvia Plath." In *The Savage God*. London: Weidenfeld & Nicolson, 1971. Reprinted (revised) as "Sylvia Plath: A Memoir," in Alexander, ed., *Ariel Ascending*. (Text references are to page numbers in Alexander's collection.)

Brink, Andrew. *Loss and Symbolic Repair: A Psychological Study of Some English Poets*. Hamilton, Ont.: Cromlech Press, 1977.

Bundtzen, Linda K. *Plath's Incarnations: Woman and the Creative Process*. Ann Arbor: University of Michigan Press, 1983.

Campbell, Wendy Christie. "Remembering Sylvia." In Charles Newman, ed., *The Art of Sylvia Plath*.

Davison, Jane. *The Fall of a Doll's House*. New York: Holt, Rinehart and Winston, 1980.

Davison, Peter. *Half Remembered: A Personal History*. New York: Harper & Row, 1973; London: Heinemann, 1974.

Hamilton, Ian. *Robert Lowell: A Biography*. New York: Random House, 1982; London: Faber, 1983.

Hardwick, Elizabeth. "On Sylvia Plath." In Alexander, ed., *Ariel Ascending*.

Heaney, Seamus. "The Indefatigable Hoof-taps." *Times Literary Supplement*, 5 Feb. 1988, p. 134ff. Reprinted in *The Government of the Tongue.* London: Faber, 1988; New York: Farrar, Straus & Giroux, 1989.

Holbrook, David. *Sylvia Plath: Poetry and Existence.* London: Athlone Press, 1976.

Hughes, Ted. Foreword, *The Journals of Sylvia Plath.*

———. Introduction, *The Collected Poems of Sylvia Plath.*

———. Introduction, *Johnny Panic and the Bible of Dreams.*

———. Note Introducing Ten Poems by Sylvia Plath. *Encounter,* 21 (Oct. 1963).

———. "Notes on the Chronological Order of Sylvia Plath's Poems." In Newman, ed., *The Art of Sylvia Plath.*

———. "Sylvia Plath and Her Journals." In Alexander, ed., *Ariel Ascending.*

Kopp, Jane Baltzell. " 'Gone, Very Gone Youth': Sylvia Plath at Cambridge." In Butscher, ed., *Sylvia Plath: The Woman and the Work.*

Kroll, Judith. *Chapters in a Mythology: The Poetry of Sylvia Plath.* New York: Harper & Row, 1976.

Krook, Dorothea. "Recollections of Sylvia Plath." In Butscher, ed., *Sylvia Plath: The Woman and the Work.*

Lameyer, Gordon. "Sylvia at Smith." In Butscher, ed., *Sylvia Plath: The Woman and the Work.*

———. "Who Was Sylvia? A Memoir of Sylvia Plath." Unpublished.

McNeil, Helen. "Sylvia Plath." In Helen Vendler, ed., *Voices and Visions: The Poet in America.* New York: Random House, 1987.

Morris, Irene V. "Sylvia Plath at Newnham — a Tutorial Recollection." Letter to *Newnham College Roll,* 1975.

Oates, Joyce Carol. "The Death Throes of Romanticism: The Poetry of Sylvia Plath." In Butscher, ed., *Sylvia Plath: The Woman and the Work,* and Alexander, ed., *Ariel Ascending.* (Text references are to the page numbers in Alexander's collection.)

Perloff, Marjorie. "Sylvia Plath's 'Sivvy' Poems: A Portrait of the Poet as Daughter." In Gary Lane, ed., *Sylvia Plath: New Views on the Poetry.* Baltimore: Johns Hopkins University Press, 1979.

———. "The Two Ariels: The (Re)Making of the Sylvia Plath Canon." *American Poetry Review,* 13 (Nov.-Dec. 1984).

Plath, Aurelia S. "Letter Written in the Actuality of Spring." In Alexander, ed., *Ariel Ascending.*

Redgrove, Peter. *The Black Goddess and the Sixth Sense.* London: Bloomsbury, 1987.

Redgrove, Peter, with Penelope Shuttle. *The Wise Wound.* London: Victor Gollancz, 1978; Paladin, 1986.

Roche, Clarissa. "Sylvia Plath: Vignettes from England." In Butscher, ed., *Sylvia Plath: The Woman and the Work.*

Rosenblatt, Jon. *Sylvia Plath: The Poetry of Initiation.* Chapel Hill: University of North Carolina Press, 1979.

Schulman, Grace. "Sylvia Plath and Yaddo." In Alexander, ed., *Ariel Ascending.*

Sexton, Anne. "The Barfly Ought to Sing." In Newman, ed., *The Art of Sylvia Plath.*

Sigmund, Elizabeth. "Sylvia in Devon: 1962." In Butscher, ed., *Sylvia Plath: The Woman and the Work.*

Steiner, Nancy Hunter. *A Closer Look at Ariel: A Memory of Sylvia Plath,* with an introduction by George Stade. New York: Harper's Magazine Press, 1974; London: Faber, 1974.

Van Dyne, Susan R. " 'More Terrible Than She Ever Was': The Manuscripts of Sylvia Plath's Bee Poems." In Linda W. Wagner, *Critical Essays on Sylvia Plath.* Boston: G. K. Hall, 1984.

Wagner-Martin, Linda. *Sylvia Plath: A Biography.* New York: Simon and Schuster, 1987; London: Chatto & Windus, 1988.

Manuscripts

The great bulk of Sylvia Plath's manuscripts and papers is divided between the Lilly Library and the Smith College Library. The papers in the Lilly are largely from the early part of Plath's life in the United States. Smith College houses the material she took with her to England and the manuscripts of her mature years.

The Lilly Library, Indiana University (*Lilly*), obtained its collection from Aurelia Plath in 1977. It includes Plath's typescripts of early work: poems, short stories, and other prose pieces. Nearly all surviving letters from Sylvia Plath to her family are here, plus childhood and adolescent ephemera, photographs, and so on. It contains, too, her childhood journals and correspondence mainly up to the time of her departure for England in September 1955.

The Neilson Library, Rare Book Room, Smith College (*Smith*), acquired its Sylvia Plath archive from Ted Hughes in 1981. This collection includes manuscripts and worksheets from all periods of Plath's adult life, with, importantly, her working drafts of the so-called "Ariel" late poems. It also contains the typescripts of poems, her novel *The Bell Jar,* stories, and other prose writings. Her journals covering her college years at Smith and Newnham College and her return to America (1950–59), with unbound fragments through 1962, are also here, as are notes on submissions of work to journals and publishers, correspondence, financial records, photographs, diaries, and so on.

NOTES

i   "If you can't give": Anna Akhmatova, trans. Amanda Haight, in *Anna Akhmatova: A Poetic Pilgrimage* (London: Oxford University Press, 1976)

v   "There was a tremendous": Dostoevsky, trans. David Magarshack, *The Devils* (London: Penguin Classics, 1953)

v   "Oh, only left": *Journals*, p. 223

Preface

xi   "Dying / Is an art": "Lady Lazarus," *CP*, pp. 244–247

xi   "The blood jet": "Kindness," *CP*, pp. 269–270

xii   "harsh wit": A. Alvarez, "Sylvia Plath: A Memoir," p. 212

xii   " — nurtured in great part": W. S. Merwin to Olwyn Hughes, 1987

xiii   "A baby": "Ocean 1212–W," *JP*, p. 23

xiv   her mother wrote: Aurelia Plath to Judith Kroll, December 1, 1978, *Smith*

xv   "The last thing": Carolyn Kizer, *The Nearness of You: Poems* (Port Townsend, Wash.: Copper Canyon Press, 1986), p. 65

xv   "The world is blood-hot": "Totem," *CP*, p. 264

1. The Girl Who Wanted to Be God, 1932–1949

1   "As soon as my": *LH*, p. 31

1   "When mother": Unpublished, *Lilly*

1   "Today I brought": *LH*, p. 34

1   "incredible that": *LH*, p. 34

2   "I thought that I": *LH*, p. 34

2   "I was overjoyed": *LH*, p. 34

2   "How frail": *LH*, p. 34

2   "The girls' guidance": "America! America!," *JP*, p. 54

3   "just too weird": "America! America!," *JP*, p. 55

3   "zero," "hollow nothing": Sylvia used these words repeatedly in her journal.

6   "lifelong adventure": *LH*, p. 6

6   "a healthy": *LH*, p. 12

6   " a son, two and a half": *LH*, p. 12

7n Mrs. Plath describes: *LH*, p. 16

8   "It just hurts": *Lilly*

9   "upstairs-downstairs": *LH*, p. 18

9   " 'The Adventures' ": *LH*, p. 19

9   "a new way": "Ocean 1212–W," *JP*, p. 21; cited by Aurelia Plath in *LH*, pp. 31–32

10   "How could such": *LH*, p. 23
10   "I'll never speak": *LH*, p. 25
11   "I PROMISE NEVER": *LH*, p. 25. My description of this incident, and of others from Sylvia's childhood, closely follows Aurelia Plath's account.
12   "rowdy seaside town": "America! America!," *JP*, p. 52
12   "beautiful, inaccessible": "Ocean 1212–W," *JP*, p. 26
13   "complicated guilt system": Unpublished journal, *Smith*
13   "pale skin": "Superman and Paula Brown's New Snowsuit," *JP*, p. 271
13   "When I was learning": "Ocean 1212–W," *JP*, p. 21
14   "a sign of election": "Ocean 1212–W," *JP*, p. 24
14   "not forever": "Ocean 1212–W," *JP*, p. 24
15   "The high school years": *LH*, p. 38
15   "I feel infinitely sad": *LH*, pp. 39–40
16   "never, never": *LH*, p. 40
16   "I want, I think": *LH*, p. 40

2. A Smith Girl, 1950–1952

17   "We had our": *LH*, p. 46
17   "God, who am I?": *Journals*, p. 17
18   according to Mrs. Plath: *LH*, p. 37
19   "unreasoning, bestial purity": *Journals*, p. 12
19   "I stood there": *Journals*, p. 6
19   "When you see me": *LH*, p. 39
20   "rather more subtly": Eddie Cohen to SP, *Lilly*
20   "I'm sarcastic": SP to Eddie Cohen, *Lilly*
21   "had it pretty easy": Eddie Cohen to SP, *Lilly*
21   "I can't deceive": *Journals*, p. 18
22   "But with your father": *Journals*, p. 26
22   "After supper": *LH*, p. 48
23   "Now I know": *Journals*, pp. 17–19
23   "Tonight I wanted": *Journals*, p. 12
24   "to furnish": *Smith College Handbook, 1986–1987* (Smith publication)
24   "Our unanimous vocation": Steiner, *A Closer Look at Ariel*, pp. 80–81
25   "Never have I felt": *LH*, p. 48
25   "There is so much": *LH*, p. 61
26   "Dissect your sentences": Unpublished journal, *Smith*
28   "Stretching out": *Journals*, pp. 27–28
28   "Picture me then": *LH*, p. 75
29   "I stood open-mouthed": *LH*, p. 76

29 "I do not love": *Journals*, p. 34
30 "Imagine saying": *LH*, p. 85
30 "The first thing": *LH*, p. 86
30 "really wise": *LH*, p. 87
31 "the magnetic whirlpool": *Journals*, p. 51
31 "working, living": *Journals*, p. 51
31 "It is like lifting": *Journals*, p. 51
31 " 'shack,' red half-house": *Journals*, p. 54
32 "old jalopy": *Journals*, p. 55
32 "From the tip": *BJ*, pp. 90–91
32 "So I press": Unpublished journal, *Smith*

3. The City of Spare Parts, 1952–1955

34 "The storerooms are full": "The Stones," *CP*, p. 136
34 "dear stern lovable": Unpublished letter, *Lilly*
35 "as in a God": SP to Dick Norton, *Lilly*
35 "God, if ever": *Journals*, pp. 59–60
36 "Guess what": *LH*, p. 100
37n "was driven, periodically": Steiner, *A Closer Look at Ariel*, p. 75
37 "I aimed straight down": *BJ*, pp. 114–115
38 "BREAK BREAK BREAK": *LH*, pp. 101–102
38 "All in all": *LH*, p. 102
38 "the hairy yellow": *LH*, p. 103
38 "somewhat taken aback": Lameyer, "Who Was Sylvia?"
39 "Gordon is utterly lush": SP to Aurelia Plath, *Lilly*
39 "heart and soul": *LH*, p. 102
39 "unclimbed Annapurnas": *LH*, p. 109
39 "the major man": Lameyer, "Sylvia at Smith," p. 32
40 "Dick is barely": SP to Aurelia Plath, *Lilly*
40 "revolts me physically": Unpublished journal, *Smith*
40 "intense unrest": Dick Norton to SP, *Lilly*
40 "lovely, immoral": SP to Eddie Cohen, *Lilly*
41 "plushy air-conditioned": SP to Eddie Cohen, *LH*, p. 129
41 "Thursday night": SP to Aurelia Plath, *Lilly*
41 "valuable": SP to Aurelia Plath, *Lilly*
41 "I have learned": *LH*, p. 117
42 "wealthy, unscrupulous": *LH*, p. 120
42 "deformed men": *LH*, p. 120
42 polite behavior: As reported by Edward Butscher in his unreliable biography, *Sylvia Plath: Method and Madness* (New York: Seabury Press, 1976), p. 104
42 "terrible things": *BJ*, p. 37
43 "We're stargazers": *Mademoiselle*, August 1953

43   "I must make choices": *Journals,* p. 84
44   "a great change": *LH,* p. 123
44   "those senseless curlicues": SP to Eddie Cohen, *Lilly*
44   " 'I just wanted to see' ": *LH,* p. 124
45   "Pretty soon": *LH,* p. 130
45   "God on la mer": Lameyer, "Who Was Sylvia?," p. 14
45   "Cobwebs touched my face": *BJ,* p. 179
46   "Have gone for": *LH,* p. 125
46   "BEAUTIFUL SMITH GIRL": *Western Daily Globe,* August 25, 1953
46   " 'Oh, no!' ": *LH,* p. 125
46   "Do we still own": Lameyer, "Who Was Sylvia?," p. 16
47   "You are by far": Elizabeth Drew to SP, *Lilly*
47   "We are very proud": Evelyn Page to SP, *Lilly*
48n "I brought her": Aurelia Plath to Judith Kroll, December 1, 1978, *Smith*
49   "Siamese twins": Steiner, *A Closer Look at Ariel,* p. 55
50   "under a plethora": SP to Aurelia Plath, *Lilly*
50   "I am God": Richard Sassoon to SP, *Lilly*
50   absinthe addict: SP to Aurelia Plath, *Smith*
51   "It is Art!": Richard Sassoon to SP, *Smith*
51   "Has it ever occurred": Eddie Cohen to SP, *Lilly*
52   "when reality intrudes": Eddie Cohen to SP, *Lilly*
52   "the blond bitch": Steiner, *A Closer Look at Ariel,* p. 71
53   "The exclusiveness": Steiner, *A Closer Look at Ariel,* p. 54
53   "dreadful": Steiner, *A Closer Look at Ariel,* p. 73
54   "like a third person": Steiner, *A Closer Look at Ariel,* p. 63
55n "the importance": *LH,* p. 153
55   "a very strict man": *LH,* p. 149
55   "handsome middle-aged": SP to Aurelia Plath, *Lilly*
56   she had sold her clothes: *LH,* p. 161
56   "The burning at the stake": *LH,* p. 135. Mrs. Plath says in *LH* that this letter is undated, but the letter, in *Lilly,* is dated February 25, 1955.
56   "for what we call forever": Gordon Lameyer to SP, November 29, 1954, *Lilly*
56   "a weird little chap": Gordon Lameyer to SP, November 29, 1954, *Lilly*
57   "I teach girls": Richard Sassoon to SP, *Lilly*
57   "a respite": *LH,* p. 165
57   "Tell my mother": *LH,* p. 175. (Mrs. Plath uses an indirect quotation.)
58   "$30 Dylan Thomas": *LH,* p. 176
58   "My cup runneth over": *LH,* p. 176

4. Pursuit, 1955–1956

59 "in my head": *Journals*, p. 96
59 "There is a panther": "Pursuit," *CP*, p. 22
59 "I'm rather sure": Lameyer, "Who Was Sylvia?," p. 79
60 "one or two small prizes": Richard Sassoon to SP, *Lilly*
60 "Mother revised": SP to Warren Plath, *Lilly*
60 "laughing faithlessness": SP to Richard Sassoon, *Lilly*
60 "What can I say": Richard Sassoon to SP, *Lilly*
61 "in a white dress": Davison, *Half Remembered*, pp. 170–171
62 "a very conservative": SP to Warren Plath, *Lilly*
62 "wonderful": SP to Aurelia Plath, *Lilly*
62 "a genial versatile": SP to Aurelia Plath, *Lilly*
62 "the most enchanting": *LH*, p. 182
63 "I only met": *LH*, p. 182
63 "which should slowly": *LH*, p. 186
63 "miraculous smorgasbord": *LH*, p. 185
63 "a magnificent, acid": *LH*, p. 186
64 "a conspicuously tall": Krook, "Recollections of Sylvia Plath," p. 49
64 "somewhere really": Kopp, " 'Gone, Very Gone Youth,' " p. 62
65 "knowing I could not": *Journals*, p. 102
65 "fair-skinned": *LH*, p. 188
65 "tall, rather handsome": *LH*, p. 188
65 "Yesterday was most": *LH*, p. 197
66 "dulled with a cold": SP to Aurelia Plath, *Lilly*
66 "caricature series": SP to Olive Higgins Prouty, *Lilly*
66 "My favorite man": SP to Olive Higgins Prouty, *Lilly*
66 "in the beginning": *Journals*, p. 92
67 "shady": Kopp, " 'Gone, Very Gone Youth,' " p. 69
67 "despite the fact": Kopp, " 'Gone, Very Gone Youth,' " p. 69
67*n* "two very vivacious": SP to Aurelia Plath, Lilly
67 "having a whirl": SP to Aurelia Plath, *Lilly*
67 "painted whores": Unpublished journal, *Smith*
68 "On the train": *Journals*, p. 94
68 "The train is dragging": "Getting There," *CP*, pp. 247–249
68 "Red earth": *Journals*, p. 95
69 "about the most lovely": *LH*, pp. 203–204
69 "My New Year mood": *LH*, p. 205
69 "stillborn children": Unpublished journal, *Lilly*
69 "excruciating pains": Unpublished journal, *Lilly*
70 "Meanwhile you are": *Journals*, p. 98
70 "Will Richard ever": *Journals*, p. 102

70 "Actually, as you probably": *LH*, p. 211, and *Lilly*
70 "To whom it may concern": *Journals*, p. 97
70 "smiling that smile": *Journals*, p. 97
71 "all the edges": *Journals*, p. 99
71 "just to meet him": *Journals*, p. 99
71 "so much easier": *Journals*, p. 100
71 "The vampire is there": *Journals*, p. 100
71 "I fight all women": *Journals*, p. 100, and *Smith*
71 "A Life Is Passing": *Journals*, p. 101
71 "someone to bring me": *LH*, p. 217
72 "a lousy sinus cold": *Journals*, p. 107
72n "Then, too, a boy": *Journals*, p. 108
72 "cleansed, and once again": Unpublished journal, *Smith*
73 "His brown hair": Myers, Appendix I. All quotations from Myers in this section are from Appendix I unless otherwise noted.
74 "I long so for someone": *Journals*, p. 109
74 "some ugly gat-toothed": *Journals*, p. 110
74 "great verve": Daniel Huws notes, February 1986, supplied by DH to author
75 "slobbing around": *Journals*, p. 111
75 "Then the worst thing": *Journals*, pp. 111–112, and unpublished journal, *Smith*
76 "And I screamed": *Journals*, p. 112
76 "Now let me tell you": Luke Myers to author, 1987
78 "What Ted and Sylvia": Myers, Appendix I
78 "Somehow these sluttish": *Journals*, p. 113
78 "I do want to tell you": *LH*, p. 220
79 "I got a letter": *Journals*, pp. 117–118
79 "I am inclined": *Journals*, p. 122
80 "physically beautiful": *LH*, p. 208
80 "*March 6*": *Journals*, p. 127, and unpublished journal, *Smith*
80n "the neat, almost mechanical": Steiner, *A Closer Look at Ariel*, pp. 54–55
81 "A huge joy": *Journals*, pp. 130–81
81 "hell": *Journals*, p. 132
81 "sweet, if pedantic": *LH*, p. 229
81 "emotional, irresponsible gushing": Unpublished journal, *Smith*
81n "my absurd overflowing": Unpublished journal, *Smith*
81 "listening to screams": *LH*, p. 229
82 "steak tartar[e]": *Journals*, p. 134
82 "I had been ready": *Journals*, p. 135
83 "a good-looking chap": Unpublished journal, *Smith*
83 "increasingly attentive": *Journals*, p. 136

83   "he can come": *Journals,* p. 137
83   *"Don't drink much": Journals,*, pp. 137–138
84   "small dark sleazy": *Journals,* p. 140
84   "orange-juice-and": *Journals,* p. 141
84   "like brother and sister": Unpublished journal, *Smith*
84   "Can I be good": *Journals,* p. 139
84   "in a fatal dance": *Journals,* p. 142

5. Fire and Flower, 1956–1957

85   "Dear Sylvia": Olive Higgins Prouty to SP, *Smith*
85   "I took a plane": *Journals,* p. 214
85   "the door closed": Nathaniel LaMar to author, 1987
85n "with a rapt": Nathaniel LaMar to author, 1987
85   "the strongest man": *LH,* p. 233
86   "Richard went off": *LH,* p. 233
86   "Something very terrifying": *Journals,* p. 143
86   "spent too, brutally": *Journals,* p. 144
86   "Your letter": Richard Sassoon to SP, *Lilly*
86   "It is this man": *LH,* p. 234
87   "To our circle": Myers, Appendix I
87   "The reason why you must": *LH,* p. 244
88   "both of them making": *LH,* p. 252
88   " 'Plato and Mrs. Krook' ": Krook, "Recollections of Sylvia Plath," p. 60
88   "If we got married": *LH,* p. 252
88   "crying for him": *LH,* p. 253
89   "Ted and Sylvia were": Myers, Appendix I
90   "When Ted and I see": *LH,* p. 258
91   "Why two weddings?": *LH,* p. 258
92   "happy, happier": Myers, Appendix I
92   "a necessity": *LH,* p. 259
92   "You saw right down": Ted Hughes, "You Hated Spain," *Poetry Book Society,* Winter Supplement, December 1984, and (U.S.) *Ploughshares,* 1984
92   "I'd imagined": *LH,* p. 263
92   "Arena dust rusted": "The Goring," *CP,* p. 47
93   "bad dirty bathroom": *Journals,* p. 144
93   "as though she had": Olwyn Hughes, interview with author
93   "Alone, deepening": *Journals,* pp. 146–147
94   "We wake about seven": *LH,* p. 265, and *Lilly*
95   "an incredible, wild": *LH,* p. 268
95   "dear, simple Yorkshire": *LH,* p. 269

96   "a fine and handsome thing": *LH*, p. 269

96   "sick, sick, sick": SP to Peter Davison

97   "hectic suffocating": *LH*, p. 277

97   "ghastly yellow": *LH*, p. 283

97   "the passionate *rage*": Krook, "Recollections of Sylvia Plath," p. 55

97   "the dearest": Quoted in Kopp, " 'Gone, Very Gone Youth,' " pp. 75–76

98   "Victorian virgins": *LH*, p. 257

98   "stunned and sick": *LH*, p. 284

98   "the crass materialistic": *LH*, p. 282

98   "some island or other": *LH*, p. 284

99   "her clothes were American": Olwyn Hughes to author

99   "the somewhat stygian kitchen": Olwyn Hughes to author

99   "I imagine I shared": Olwyn Hughes to author

99   "She selected the heavy": Olwyn Hughes to author

100 Danny Weissbort remarks: Danny Weissbort to Olwyn Hughes, 1987

100 "Olwyn, Ted's sister": *LH*, p. 288

101 ". . . Let idiots": "Spinster," *CP*, pp. 49–50

101 "What would happen": Krook, "Recollections of Sylvia Plath," pp. 55–56

102 "the most rich": *LH*, p. 287

102 "Sylvia spoke about it": Olwyn Hughes, interview with author, 1987

103 "We have such lovely": *LH*, p. 289

104 "The bronze boy": *LH*, pp. 79–80

104 "I thought that": *Journals*, p. 117

104 "break your image": *Journals*, p. 117

105 "It will make it": *LH*, p. 297

105n "In her diary": *LH*, p. 297 footnote

105 "sanguine effigy": "The Lady and the Earthenware Head," *CP*, p. 69

106 "the sky a seethe": *LH*, p. 293

106 "living at the University": *LH*, p. 308

106 "rather oppressed": SP to Lucas Myers

106 "enjoying my work": *LH*, p. 308

107 "I am taking time": *LH*, p. 314

107 "that black terror": *LH*, p. 314

107 "a mean, vague": *LH*, p. 315

107n "Ran to catch Krook": *Journals*, p. 128

108 "I . . . got a note": *LH*, p. 315

6. Disquieting Muses, 1957–1958

109 "Mother, mother": "The Disquieting Muses," *CP*, pp. 74–76
109 "All my life": *Journals*, p. 188
109 "I myself am the vessel": *Journals*, p. 195
110 "John and Nance": Olwyn Hughes to author
110 "After her exams": Ted Hughes to Olwyn Hughes
111 "customs man": SP to Lynne Lawner, July 1, 1957 (*Antaeus* no. 28 Winter 1978, p. 35)
111 "immensely sparkling": SP to Lynne Lawner, July 1, 1957
112n "a flashy light one": *Journals*, pp. 172–173
112 "black lethal two weeks": *Journals*, p. 171
112 "I will write": *Journals*, p. 165
112 "glittering and coming": *Journals*, p. 171
113 "for life itself": *Journals*, p. 165
113 "with the beach": *Journals*, p. 173
113 "write every story": *Journals*, p. 173
113 "the weird spectacle": *Journals*, p. 174
113 "The crab-face": "Mussel Hunter at Rock Harbor," *CP*, pp. 95–97
114 "Last night I felt": *Journals*, p. 175
114 "I cannot ignore": *Journals*, pp. 176–177
116n "cracking under the strain": Ted Hughes to Olwyn Hughes, 1957
116 "I can't be really frank": *LH*, p. 327
116 "My ideal of being": *LH*, p. 329
117 "He didn't say much": Dido Merwin, Appendix II
117 "composed": Ted Hughes to Olwyn Hughes, 1957 (undated)
117 "high Boston apartment": *Journals*, p. 191; quoted in Appendix II
117 "Ted had a job": Merwin, Appendix II
118 "Every time you make": *LH*, p. 330
118 "Although it is": *LH*, p. 332
119 "pretty good relation[s]": *LH*, p. 334
119 "Air lifts, clears": *Journals*, pp. 179–180
119 "And my lectures": *Journals*, p. 183
119 "blue and squinch-toothed": *Journals*, p. 183
119 "A call from Mr. Fisher": *Journals*, p. 183
120 "fumings of humiliation": *Journals*, p. 184
120 "grit into pearl": *Journals*, p. 184
121 "Blundering, booted": *Journals*, p. 184
121 "kernel chapter": *Journals*, p. 185
121 "A girl wedded to": *Journals*, p. 185
122 "green-eyed, spite-seething": *Journals*, p. 185
122n "Hospitals and mad women": *Journals*, p. 187

122   "commercially . . . curled": *Journals*, p. 208

122   "blond witchy": *Journals*, p. 193

122   "pale with a mouth": *Journals*, p. 194

123   "How I love": *Journals*, p. 305

123   "the right title": *Journals*, p. 193

123   "I've discovered": *LH*, p. 336

123   "I was taken": *Journals*, p. 210

123   "I longed for": *Journals*, p. 210

124   "have unique power": *Journals*, p. 211

124   "1) Inside a ruined temple": *Journals*, p. 211

124   "All through the poem": "The Living Poet," BBC broadcast, July 8, 1961

125   "With heads like darning-eggs": "The Disquieting Muses," *CP*, pp. 74–76

125   "violation[s] of actual": Richard Wilbur, quoted by Aurelia Plath, "Letter Written in the Actuality of Spring," p. 214

125   from her mother's: Aurelia Plath, "Letter Written in the Actuality of Spring," p. 215

125   "When on tiptoe": "The Disquieting Muses," *CP*, pp. 74–76

126   "[Sylvia] sits and writes": Ted Hughes to Olwyn Hughes, 1958 (undated)

126   "old need of giving": *Journals*, p. 278

126   "I felt I couldn't": *Journals*, p. 281

126   "Arrogant, I think": *Journals*, pp. 211–212

127   "in loud, clear tones": *LH*, p. 339

127   "Little, round and stumpy": *Journals*, p. 217

127   "feverish in lavender": *Journals*, p. 218

127   "tuberculosis, deep": *Journals*, p. 218

128   "Another title": *Journals*, p. 223

128   Hughes has written: Notes in *CP*, p. 287

128   " 'And it's old and old' ": *Journals*, p. 223

128   "Old man, you surface": "Full Fathom Five," *CP*, pp. 92–93

129   "a transparent lid": *Journals*, p. 227

129   "Joan of Arc's": *Journals*, p. 227

129   "Superstitious about separations": *Journals*, p. 222

129   "was ashamed of something": *Journals*, p. 230

129   Ted was unaware: Factual correction by Ted Hughes to author

130   "armed with various": *Journals*, p. 230

130   "about the joy": *Journals*, p. 231

130   "striding out": *Journals*, p. 232

130   "intuitive visions": *Journals*, pp. 232–233

131   "Air cleared": *Journals*, p. 235

131   "I identify him": *Journals*, p. 279

7. Electra on Azalea Path, 1958–1959

133 "I am the ghost": "Electra on Azalea Path," *CP*, pp. 116–117

133 "Coming down in the subway": *LH*, p. 340

133 "On the whole": *LH*, p. 341

134 "a queerly ambiguous": *Journals*, p. 251

134 "It is as if my life": *Journals*, p. 240

134 "Seated at the typewriter": *Journals*, p. 242

135 "You see what happens": *LH*, p. 345

135 "prodigal scent": *Journals*, p. 236

136 "I have a violence": *Journals*, pp. 237–238

136 "She would describe": Hughes, "Sylvia Plath and Her Journals," p. 155

136 "Even if our own": *Journals*, p. 245

137 "Among other penetrating": *Journals*, p. 245

137 "I only brush away": *Journals*, p. 251

137 "Berries redden": "Moonrise," *CP*, p. 98

138 "venomous blowup": *Journals*, p. 256

138 "Fury jams the gullet": *Journals*, p. 256

138 "very small": Ted Hughes to Olwyn Hughes, 1958

138 "very sober": Myers, Appendix I

140 "raucous, shrill tones": Unpublished journal, *Smith*

140 "How odd": *Journals*, p. 295

140 "snotty": *Journals*, p. 261

140 "sitting firm": *Journals*, p. 259

140 "anything — only": *Journals*, p. 262

140 "I am going to work": *Journals*, p. 262

141 "vicious circle": *Journals*, p. 261

141 "I got the man talking": *Journals*, p. 262

141 "answering phones": *Journals*, p. 263

142 "It was the opinion": Quoted in *Journals*, p. 263

142 "I've a dream": "Johnny Panic and the Bible of Dreams," *JP*, p. 154

142 "pursuing a vocation": "Johnny Panic and the Bible of Dreams," *JP*, p. 153

142 "queer and quite slangy": *Journals*, p. 276

143 "They extend me": "Johnny Panic and the Bible of Dreams," *JP*, p. 166

143 "At the moment": "Johnny Panic and the Bible of Dreams," *JP*, p. 166

144 "pay money for her time": *Journals*, p. 266

144 "like a shot": *Journals*, p. 266

145 "hag": "All the Dead Dears," *CP*, pp. 70–71

145 "a religious act": *Journals*, p. 272

145 "*Mother*: What to do": *Journals*, p. 271
145 "*Writing*: My chain": *Journals*, p. 271
145 "what I have not": *Journals*, p. 272
145 "So many women": *Journals*, p. 267
146 "steady through life": *Journals*, p. 267
146 "tears . . . in her eyes": *Journals*, p. 267
146 "Her daughter was": *Journals*, pp. 268–269
146 "Main Questions": *Journals*, p. 273
147 "a charming warm": *Journals*, p. 275
147n "two acrid fights": *Journals*, p. 278
147 "Read Freud's": *Journals*, p. 280
147 "Went to library": *Journals*, p. 284
148 "a kind of relief": *Journals*, p. 284
148 "pure soul": *Journals*, p. 285
148 "watching or participating": *Journals*, p. 286
148 "great, stark, bloody": *Journals*, pp. 286–287
148 "the dark, cruel": *Journals*, p. 287
149 "primitive: all at penis-fetish": *Journals*, p. 288
149 "I need to have written": *Journals*, p. 288
149 "Very bad dreams": *Journals*, pp. 288–289
149 "a corridor": *Journals*, p. 289
149 "I feel, am mad": *Journals*, p. 289
150 "I said a few": *Journals*, p. 298
150 "suicides sometimes meet": Sexton, "The Barfly Ought to Sing," p. 178
151 "criticism of rhetoric": *Journals*, pp. 300–301
151 "the whole point": Sexton, "The Barfly Ought to Sing," p. 181
151 "Ted's thinking idea": *Journals*, p. 298
152 "Three graveyards": *Journals*, pp. 299–300
152 "I had a great yearning": *BJ*, pp. 196–197
153 "that casual, gay verve": *Journals*, p. 301
153 "The day I woke": "Electra on Azalea Path," *CP*, pp. 116–117 (December 31, 1958)
153 "the stilts": "Electra on Azalea Path," *CP*, pp. 116–117
153 "maestro of the bees": "The Beekeeper's Daughter," *CP*, p. 118
153 "[What can I] do": *Journals*, p. 294
154 "What inner decision": *Journals*, p. 297
154 "What good does talking": *Journals*, p. 300
154 "And a story": Unpublished journal, *Smith*, June 13, 1959
154 "On Monday": Peter Davison to author, 1987
155 "Ted labored": *Journals*, p. 285
155 "Robert Lowell": *Journals*, p. 294
155 "a Grantchester poem": *Journals*, p. 296
155 "playful, adventurous": *Journals*, p. 292

155 "Big head": *Journals*, p. 276
155 "joyous news": *Journals*, p. 301
155 "Financial worries": Ted Hughes to Olwyn Hughes, 1959
156 "40 unattackable poems": *Journals*, p. 302
156 "I wrote a book": *Journals*, p. 303
156 "Most Beds are Beds": *The Bed Book*
156 "My main flaw": *Journals*, p. 306
157 "green-eyed fury": *Journals*, p. 304
157 "But A[nne] S[exton] is there": *Journals*, p. 302
157 "hostile silences": *Journals*, p. 302
157 "What to do with anger": *Journals*, p. 305
157 "I feel that this month": *Journals*, p. 307
158 "gone barren": *Journals*, p. 311
158 "How can I keep Ted": *Journals*, p. 312

8. Poem for a Birthday, 1959

159 "I shall perish": *Journals*, p. 327
159 "The IDEAS kill": *Journals*, p. 333
160 ". . . a cloud": "Two Campers in Cloud Country," *CP*, pp. 144–145
161 "a stiff artificial piece": *Journals*, p. 314
161 ". . . It is dry": "Sleep in the Mojave Desert," *CP*, pp. 143–144
162 "high and sunny": May Swenson to Peter Davison, 1987
162 "air clear enough": *Journals*, p. 313
163 "novel on a daughter-mother": *Journals*, p. 323
163 "fine originality": *Journals*, p. 321
163 according to Grace Schulman: Schulman, "Sylvia Plath and Yaddo," pp. 165–177
164 "never-satisfied gods": *Journals*, p. 314
165 "sweetbreads, sausages": *Journals*, p. 314
165 "with one large cramp": *Journals*, p. 315
165 "making an iron statue": *Journals*, p. 316
165 "diatribe against": *Journals*, p. 318
165 "the monologue": *Journals*, p. 319
166 "The child who dreamt": *Journals*, p. 319
166 "syllabic exercise": *Journals*, p. 320
166 "Is it because": *Journals*, p. 320
166 "*October 3*": *Journals*, p. 319
166 "Writing is my health": *Journals*, p. 327
166 "get rid of": *Journals*, p. 314
166 "commercial American": *Journals*, p. 325
166 "jealous, queen-bitch": *Journals*, p. 324
166 "cold self-consciousness": *Journals*, p. 328

167   "for their own sake": *Journals*, p. 328
167   "the idea of a Novel": *Journals*, p. 322
167   "pure intrigue": Unpublished journal, *Smith*
167   "a horror that I": *Journals*, p. 326
167   "a few psychological": *Journals*, p. 326
167   "traces of passive": *Journals*, p. 327
167   "unencumbered by any": *Journals*, p. 333
167   "so rare, so special": *Journals*, p. 322
167   "How many couples": *Journals*, p. 329
167   "I would bear": *Journals*, p. 312
167   "Children might humanize": *Journals*, p. 324
167   "a vehicle, a pure": *Journals*, p. 317
167   "outcast on a cold star": *Journals*, p. 321
168   "the old father-worship": *Journals*, p. 323
168   "I shall never get": "The Colossus," *CP*, p. 129
168   "The sheer color": *Journals*, p. 324
168   "Ambitious seeds": *Journals*, p. 324
168   "a surgical picture": *Journals*, p. 325
168   "That greenhouse": *Journals*, p. 325
169   "an exercise begun": *Journals*, p. 325
169   "having a five-months": *Journals*, p. 325
169   "The month of flowering's": "Who," in "Poem for a Birthday,"
      CP, pp. 131–137
170   "Fear was my father": Theodore Roethke, "The Lost Son," in *The
      Collected Poems of Theodore Roethke* (New York: Doubleday,
      1966), p. 56
172   "There ought, I thought": *BJ*, p. 290
173   "a terrific blocking": *Journals*, p. 326
173   "One or two unpleasant": *Journals*, p. 327
173   "no life separate": *Journals*, p. 328
173   "I will hate a child": *Journals*, p. 329
173   "My old admiration": *Journals*, p. 329
173   "She was not up": May Swenson to Peter Davison, 1987
173   "a bad, impossible": Unpublished journal, *Smith*
174   "When I think of living": *Journals*, p. 356
174   "This was really": *LH*, p. 356

9. Ariel in the Tree, 1959–1960

175   "A woman is dragging": "A Life," *CP*, pp. 149–150
175   "How shall I tell": "Candles," *CP*, pp. 148–149
175   "litany of dreams": Quoted in Editor's Note to *Journals*, p. IX
176   "a brilliant tense presence": Robert Lowell, Introduction to U.S.
      edition of *Ariel*

176   "Ted and Sylvia": Olwyn Hughes to author, 1987
177   "I had asked my mother": Olwyn Hughes to author, 1987
178   "ask Dr. B[euscher]": *Journals,* p. 294
178   "which proceeded": Olwyn Hughes to author, 1987
178   "I get along with her": *LH,* p. 360
178   "I had wanted": Olwyn Hughes to author, 1987
179   "a cold, cheerless": *LH,* p. 361
179   "The landlord": Daniel Huws notes, February 1986, supplied by DH to author
179   "But as time wore on": Helga Huws to Linda Wagner-Martin, February 16, 1986; copy supplied by HH to author
180   "unbelievably big": *LH,* p. 363
181   "After finding": Helga Huws to Linda Wagner-Martin, February 16, 1986; copy supplied by HH to author
181   "very homesick and blue": *LH,* p. 363
182   "I haven't even": SP to Lynne Lawner, February 18, 1960 (*Antaeus* no. 28, p. 48)
182   "blue & black": SP to Lynne Lawner, February 18, 1960 (*Antaeus* no. 28, p. 49)
182   "galaxy of talent": Merwin, Appendix II
182   "along with the baby": SP to Aurelia Plath, *Lilly*
183   "resplendent in black": *LH,* pp. 365–366
184   "She appeared carefully": James Michie, interview with Peter Davison
184   "They do very few": *LH,* p. 366
184   "Sylvia was relaxed": Michael Horovitz, letter to author
184   "living and writing": *LH,* p. 368
185   "The flat was so small": Myers, Appendix I
185   "I really put": *LH,* p. 368
186   "studiously sieving applesauce": Olwyn Hughes to author, 1987
186   "Had Sylvia said": Olwyn Hughes to author, 1987
186   "As Olwyn had spoken": Letter from Janet Crosbie-Hill to *New Review,* June 1976
187   "What I had just witnessed": Olwyn Hughes to author, 1987
187   "Amusing to see": *LH,* p. 369
187   "Whether she was blind": Olwyn Hughes to author, 1987
188   "Wednesday evening": *LH,* p. 369
188   "I'm sorry I was": Olwyn Hughes to Lucas Myers, March 8, 1961
188   "There was, as far": Lucas Myers to Olwyn Hughes, March 12, 1961
189   "Within a few days": Merwin, Appendix II
189   "one of the best places": Ted Hughes to author, September 1986
189   "one of those foreign": *LH,* p. 371
190   "since the baby": *LH,* p. 371

190   "capable little Indian": *LH*, p. 373
190   *"Ein Wunderkind"*: *LH*, p. 373
190   "The whole experience": SP to Lynne Lawner, September 30, 1960 (*Antaeus* no. 28, p. 50)
191   "Ted's people": *LH*, p. 376
191   "An immensely moving": *LH*, p. 378
192   "On the final day": Merwin, Appendix II
193   "Her public and/or chronic": Merwin, Appendix II
194   "Peter is worse": *LH*, p. 380
194   "we stayed long enough": Peter Davison to author, 1987
195   "The Eliots live": *LH*, pp. 380–381
195   "that unique combination": *LH*, p. 383
195   "voluminous mail": *LH*, p. 384
195   "several projects going": *LH*, p. 383
195   "a marvelous vermillion": *LH*, p. 385
196   "a tall, strong-looking": Alvarez, "Sylvia Plath: A Memoir," p. 187
196   "I am at the depressing": *LH*, p. 386
197   "By the roots": "The Hanging Man," *CP*, pp. 141–142
197   "These poems do not live": "Stillborn," *CP*, p. 142
197   "41 Fitzroy Road": *LH*, p. 387
198   "guests (you) now": *LH*, p. 388
198   her poet friend Lynne Lawner: *Antaeus* no. 28
198   "strewing candy papers": *LH*, p. 391
198   "delighted with the color": *LH*, p. 397
199   "the last romantics": "Candles," *CP*, p. 148
199   "dull angels": "Magi," *CP*, p. 148
199n "to herself and to us": Oates, "The Death Throes of Romanticism," p. 32
200   "a tangle of heavily": Ted Hughes, Notes in *CP*, p. 290
200   "I can taste": "Waking in Winter," *CP*, p. 151
200   "Though her whole": Hughes, "Sylvia Plath and Her Journals," p. 153

10. Warnings, 1960–1961

201   "I shall never get": "In Plaster," *CP*, pp. 158–160
201   "Ted's income": *LH*, p. 398
202   "Both of us": *LH*, p. 400
202   "Since I got": *LH*, p. 399
202   "very exciting": *LH*, p. 399
202   "fine, lively agent": *LH*, p. 401
202   "want another *really*": *LH*, p. 400
202   "All sorts of queer": *LH*, p. 402

202 "much to his mother's": *LH*, p. 403
203 "There is an admirable": Alvarez, *The Observer*, December 18, 1960, p. 21
203 "the fabulous Leonor Fini": SP to Olwyn Hughes, November-December 1960 (undated)
203 "I say, you're awfully": Olwyn Hughes to author, 1987
204 characteristically extreme language: SP to Aurelia Plath, *Lilly*
204 "with Ted's help": *LH*, p. 405
205 "I've always wanted": *LH*, p. 407
205 "to give him a nod": *LH*, p. 407
205 "jolting jealousies": *Journals*, p. 294
205 "Day of Success": The manuscript for this story is in *Smith*, bearing the address 3 Chalcot Square, London, NW 1. Date unknown, 1960-61
206 "reduced to 'fluff' ": Merwin, Appendix II
206 "the deliberate, calculated": Dido Merwin to author, 1987
206 "writing is a religious": *Journals*, p. 272
207 "The old dregs": "Parliament Hill Fields," *CP*, p. 153
207 "I'm no more": "Morning Song," *CP*, p. 157
207 ". . . the dead": "Barren Woman," *CP*, p. 157
207 "When Sylvia asked": Merwin, Appendix II
207 "Mother to myself": "Face Lift," *CP*, pp. 155-156
207 "Look, they are": "Zoo Keeper's Wife," *CP*, pp. 154-155
208 "black Sunday streets": *Journals*, p. 334
208 "a religious establishment": *Journals*, p. 333
208 "everybody has a secret": *Journals*, p. 333
208 "All night they've been": *Journals*, p. 334
209 "Today is the day": *Journals*, pp. 335-336
209 "Ted came last night": *Journals*, p. 336
209 "with a $100 contract": *Journals*, p. 336
209 "prepared for the slaughter": *Journals*, p. 336
209 "bee sting": *Journals*, p. 336
209 "a bubbly drowsiness": *Journals*, p. 337
210 "fetters": *Journals*, p. 337
210 "an old soldier": *Journals*, p. 338
210 "Tonight I deserve": *Journals*, p. 338
210 "Actually, I feel": *LH*, p. 412
210 "Poor dear!": *LH*, p. 413
210 "new tough prosiness": *Journals*, p. 341
211 "I didn't want": "Tulips," *CP*, pp. 160-162
211 "I am immensely fond": *Journals*, p. 340
212 "in a plaster cast": *Journals*, p. 342
212 "Without me": "In Plaster," *CP*, p. 159
212 "like a lady": *LH*, p. 413

212 "I must say": *LH*, p. 414
212 "fiendishly": *LH*, p. 416
213 "very prestigeful": *LH*, p. 415
213 "GOOD NEWS": *LH*, p. 417
213 "It is like having": *LH*, p. 418
214 "chic Latin": Suzette Macedo, interview
214 "the little Australian": *LH*, p. 418
214 "Two things that": Merwin, Appendix II
216 Dido Merwin's account: See Appendix II
217 "The Merwins' farm": *LH*, p. 420
219 "people who would have": Aurelia Plath to Warren Plath, *Lilly*
219 "to a house": *LH*, p. 422
219 "chill, busybody man": *LH*, p. 423
219 "Why don't I write": *Journals*, p. 273

11. The Stigma of Selfhood, 1961–1962

221 "Elm / Jealousy": Manuscript, *Smith* (see illustrations)
221 "When dreams come true": Peter Davison to author, June 1987
222 "It is . . . very very": SP to Helga Huws, October 30, 1961
222 "nice, round dining table": *LH*, p. 427
222 "forever optimistic": *LH*, p. 435
223 "peach-colored gladiolas": *LH*, p. 428
223 "very commercial": *LH*, p. 429
223 "blissfully happy": Suzette Macedo to author, 1987
223 "Right after breakfast": *LH*, pp. 429–430
223 "a robust blond": SP to Helga Huws, October 30, 1961
223 "a nice lively retired": SP to Helga Huws, October 30, 1961
223 "a great booming wife": SP to Helga Huws, October 30, 1961
224 "odd deformities": SP to Olwyn Hughes, October 1961
224 "none of the old": SP to Olwyn Hughes, October 1961
224 "the fabulous Goldsmiths hall": *LH*, p. 435
224 "scrap paper": *LH*, p. 437
224 "to clear air": *LH*, p. 435
225 "spoiling for company": SP to Ruth Fainlight, October 6, 1961
225 "A wild blowy": *LH*, p. 433
226 "Mothers": Published in *McCall's*, October 1972, as "The Mother's Union," and reprinted in *JP*, pp. 10–19
226 "marvelous midwife-nurse": *LH*, p. 429
226 "a short, rotundish": *Journals*, p. 354
226 "pillar": *Journals*, p. 354
226 "Nurse D.'s visits": *Journals*, p. 354
227 "Don't worry about": *LH*, p. 437
227 "But winter is": SP to Olwyn Hughes, November-December 1961

227 "the terrifying marriage": *LH*, p. 437

228 "For me, the real": "Context," *JP*, pp. 64–65

228 ". . . and the face": "Blackberrying," *CP*, pp. 168–169

228 "the night thoughts": "Context," *JP*, pp. 64–65

228 "A mat of roots": "The Surgeon at 2 A.M.," in *CP*, pp. 170–171

229 "astounding egotism": "A Comparison," *JP*, pp. 61–63

229 "It depressed me": Hughes, "Notes on the Chronological Order of Sylvia Plath's Poems"

229 "cowlike": *LH*, p. 441

230 "like the inside": *LH*, p. 440

230 "keeping all *our*": *LH*, p. 440

230 "lazy," "soppy": *LH*, p. 439

230 "fat little tree": *LH*, p. 440

230 "Our Christmas": *LH*, p. 440

230 "niggly contractions": *LH*, p. 452

230 "this great bluish": *LH*, p. 443

230 "Beautiful clear dawn": *LH*, p. 443

230 "Very much a Hughes": SP to Helga Huws, March-April 1962 (undated)

231 "saint": *LH*, p. 444

231 "a solid body": *LH*, p. 439

231 "on something amusing": *LH*, p. 448

231 "I could not look": *Journals*, p. 347

231 "scabrous": *Journals*, p. 350

231 "must catalog rugs": "The Smiths," *Johnny Panic and the Bible of Dreams*, p. 39

232 "tall, imposing": *Journals*, p. 344

232 "materialized": *Journals*, p. 346

232 "This is my one": *Journals*, p. 346

233 "slow as the world": *Three Women, CP*, pp. 176–187

233 "ovulatory triumph": Redgrove, *The Wise Wound*

234 "reborn with Frieda": *LH*, p. 450

234 "much easier on me": *LH*, p. 450

234 "March megrims": *LH*, p. 450

234 "And now we are chafing": SP to Helga Huws, March-April 1962 (undated)

235 "something on the lung": "Rose and Percy B.," *JP*, p. 74

235 "A terrible thumping": "Rose and Percy B.," *JP*, p. 71

236 "After *Three Women*": Hughes, "Sylvia Plath and Her Journals," pp. 161–162

236 "The yew's black": "Little Fugue," *CP*, 187–189

237 "The smile of iceboxes": "An Appearance," *CP*, p. 187

238 "She is not easy": First draft of "Elm," *Smith*

239 "One can compare": Hughes, Foreword to *Journals*, p. xi

239   "I have suffered": "Elm," *CP*, p. 192
239   "because Percy": "Rose and Percy B," *JP*, p. 73
239   "an acquaintance": *LH*, p. 452
240   "Evidently the long winter": *LH*, p. 453, and *Lilly*
240   "made the mistake": SP to Aurelia Plath, *Lilly*
240   "becoming impossible": SP to Aurelia Plath, *Lilly*
240   Nicola "Smith" remembers: Nicola "Smith" to author, 1987
240   "standing at opposite": "The Smiths," *JP*, pp. 48–49
241   "We answer the door": Olwyn Hughes to author, 1987
241   "marvelous guests": *LH*, p. 454
241   "It was heavenly": SP to Ruth Fainlight, May 12, 1962
241   "tall, slim": Sigmund, "Sylvia in Devon: 1962," p. 100
242   "We sat and had tea": Sigmund, "Sylvia in Devon: 1962," p. 100
242   "cordial, exploratory, gracious": David Wevill to author, 1989
243   "Brave, resourceful, warm": David Wevill to author, 1989
243   Assia offered: Suzette Macedo and Olwyn Hughes, interviews
243   "a current of attraction": Suzette Macedo, interview
244   "Where apple bloom": "Event," *CP*, pp. 194–195
244   "I want to love": *Journals*, p. 80
245   "There was only one": "The Rabbit Catcher," *CP*, pp. 193–194
245   "groove of old faults": "Event," *CP*, pp. 194–195
246   "Wonderfully calming": *LH*, p. 456
246   "A red fist": "Apprehensions," *CP*, pp. 195–196
246   "absolutely halcyon": *LH*, p. 455
246   "Sylvia is a lovely": Edith Hughes to Aurelia Plath, June 5, 1962, *Lilly*
246   "I wish now": *LH*, p. 457
246   "*her* property": Alvarez, "Sylvia Plath: A Memoir," p. 192
247   "attended by the rector": *LH*, p. 457
247   "We all wore masks": *LH*, p. 457; see also *JP*, pp. 55–56
247   "WELCOME MOTHER": *Smith*
248   Ted first made contact: Factual correction from Ted Hughes to author
248   "some awful translation": "Rose and Percy B," *JP*, pp. 75–76
249   "When I went": "Rose and Percy B," *JP*, p. 76
249   "high, spider-wheeled": "Rose and Percy B," *JP*, p. 76
250   "Why is it so quiet": "Berck-Plage," *CP*, pp. 196–201
250*n*   In *Letters Home*: *LH*, p. 25
250   "I have everything": *LH*, p. 458
250   "Between the yellow": "Burning the Letters," *CP*, p. 205
251   Elizabeth Compton listened: Sigmund, "Sylvia in Devon: 1962," p. 104
251   explaining to Warren: Aurelia Plath to Warren Plath, July 17, 1962, *Lilly*

252 "did not gather": Daniel Huws notes, February 1986, supplied by DH to author
252 "Her so characteristic": Helga Huws to Linda Wagner-Martin, February 16, 1986; copy supplied by HH to author
252 "Nick was the only": *LH*, p. 458
252 "fantastically neurotic": *LH*, p. 459
252 "nearly killed them": *LH*, p. 459
253 Brinnin recorded: Personal information via Peter Davison
253 "a boat and the sea": SP to Richard Murphy; see Appendix III
254 "We sailed to Inishbofin": Murphy, Appendix III
258 "I would *starve*": *LH*, p. 462
258 "harrowing": *LH*, p. 463
258 "thrown Ted out": Jillian Becker and Suzette Macedo, interviews; and Clarissa Roche to Olwyn Hughes, 1987
259 "May I say": See letters from SP in Appendix III
260 "I haven't the strength": *LH*, p. 465

12. Getting There, 1962–1963

261 "Don't talk to me": *LH*, p. 473
261 "Words dry and riderless": "Words," *CP*, p. 270
261 "Every morning": *LH*, p. 466
262 "I am living": SP to Ruth Fainlight, October 22, 1962
262 "black shoe": "Daddy," *CP*, p. 222
262 "Is this the elect": "A Birthday Present," *CP*, p. 206
262 "I / Have a self": "Stings," *CP*, p. 215
262 "dulling and stilling": "Poppies in July," *CP*, p. 203
264 "If I start running": *LH*, p. 465
264 ". . . in twenty-five years": "The Applicant," *CP*, p. 221
264 "Daddy, I have had": "Daddy," *CP*, pp. 222–224
264 "In 'Daddy' ": McNeil, "Sylvia Plath," pp. 486–487
265 "It is *over*": *LH*, p. 466
266 "Old barnacled umbilicus": "Medusa," *CP*, pp. 224–226
267 "I am a genius": *LH*, p. 468
268 "Please see Sylvia": *LH*, p. 470
268 "*half* of the fee": *LH*, p. 471
268 "dawn poems in blood": Sigmund, "Sylvia in Devon: 1962," p. 105
268 "Psychologically, Ruth": SP to Ruth Fainlight, October 18, 1962
269 "old, snobby snoop": *LH*, p. 471
269 "the prettiest, sweetest": *LH*, p. 474
269 "peanut-crunching crowd": "Lady Lazarus," *CP*, p. 245
269 ". . . I am a lantern": "Fever 103°," *CP*, p. 231
269 "I have done it": "Lady Lazarus," *CP*, p. 244

270 "The lioness": "Purdah," *CP*, p. 242

270 "I am the magician's": "The Bee Meeting," *CP*, pp. 211–212

270 "assault and battery": Alvarez, "Sylvia Plath: A Memoir," p. 195

271 "I hold you": "By Candlelight," *CP*, p. 236

271 "Love, love": "Nick and the Candlestick," *CP*, p. 241

271 "And you want": "The Tour," *CP*, p. 237

271 "the woman in the ambulance": "Poppies in October," *CP*, p. 240

272 "Nigger-eye / Berries": "Ariel," *CP*, p. 239

273 Again, on this trip: All details attributed to Suzette Macedo were given in an interview.

274 Ted, who had kept in touch: See Merwin, Appendix II

275 "Ted is behind me": *LH*, p. 478

275 "*the* street and *the* house": *LH*, p. 477

275 she consulted Yeats's: *LH*, p. 480

275 "I was scared to death": SP to Ruth Fainlight, November 20, 1962

276 ". . . stepping from": "Getting There," *CP*, p. 249

277 "O God, I": "Years," *CP*, p. 255

277 "You've saved my life": Roche, "Sylvia Plath: Vignettes from England," and in an interview

278 "and the minute": *LH*, p. 480

278 "*Professor* A. S. Plath": *LH*, p. 481

278 "When I get safely": *LH*, p. 482

278 "a clear, crisp": *LH*, p. 488

278 "the obliging gas boys": *LH*, p. 488

279 He came to see: Confirmed by Ted Hughes to Peter Davison, March 1989

280 Professor Thomas: Wagner-Martin, *Sylvia Plath*, p. 232

281 "fake-fur toreador": *LH*, p. 491

281 "She seemed different": Alvarez, "Sylvia Plath: A Memoir," p. 205

281 "We went for Christmas": *LH*, pp. 492–493

282 "She is part": SP to Daniel and Helga Huws, December 26, 1962

283 "till death do us": Daniel Huws notes, February 1986, supplied by DH to author. Two poems by Daniel Huws about Sylvia — "O Mountain" and "The Voice of a Child" — are included in his collection *Noth*, 1972

283 She must smell of poverty: Suzette Macedo, interview; Jillian Becker, interview

284 "never had any money": Jillian Becker, interview

284 "The sunlight": From Louis MacNeice, "The Sunlight on the Garden," in *The Earth Compels* (London: Faber, 1938)

284 "She seemed ecstatic": Murphy, Appendix III

285 "I had looked forward": Judith Jones to SP, January 16, 1963, *Smith*

285 "the story ceases": Elizabeth Lawrence to SP, January 1963, *Smith*

285 "was in resilient form": Hughes, "Sylvia Plath and Her Journals," p. 163
286 "malicious and dishonest": Roche, "Sylvia Plath: Vignettes from England," p. 93
286 "incandescent desperation": Doris Lessing, interview with Olwyn Hughes
287 "My German 'au pair' ": *LH*, p. 498
287 she sought out: Wagner-Martin, *Sylvia Plath*, p. 237
288 "It is a heart": "Mary's Song," *CP*, p. 257
288 "with torsos of steel": "Brasilia," *CP*, p. 258
288 "The womb / Rattles": "Childless Woman," *CP*, p. 259
288 ". . . the far / Fields": "Sheep in Fog," *CP*, p. 262
288 "Naked and bald": "The Munich Mannequins," *CP*, p. 262
288 "Death with its many": "Totem," *CP*, p. 264
289 "clear eye is the one": "Child," *CP*, p. 265
289 "I / Glitter": "Gigolo," *CP*, p. 267
289 "I smile, a buddha": "Paralytic," *CP*, p. 266
289 "I remember / The dead": "Mystic," *CP*, p. 268
290 as Joyce Carol Oates pointed out: In "The Death Throes of Romanticism"
290 "The blood jet": "Kindness," *CP*, p. 269
291 "The sap": "Words," *CP*, p. 270
291 "doom mark": "Contusion," *CP*, p. 271
291 "cold blanks": "Apprehensions," *CP*, p. 196
291 On Monday, February 4: Details of Sylvia Plath's last weekend come from interviews with Jillian Becker.
294 she had not yet paid: Wagner-Martin, *Sylvia Plath*, p. 242
296 Professor Thomas: Wagner-Martin, *Sylvia Plath*, pp. 242–243
296 Her real purpose: Alvarez, "Sylvia Plath: A Memoir," p. 208
297 But some of the gas: Alvarez, "Sylvia Plath: A Memoir," p. 210
297 "She had for several days": Dr. John Horder to Linda Wagner-Martin; copy sent to author
297 "she slipped through": Dr. John Horder, interview
297 "The care with which": Dr. John Horder to Linda Wagner-Martin; copy sent to author
298 "frighteningly there": Hardwick, "On Sylvia Plath," p. 102
298 "The woman is perfected": "Edge," *CP*, pp. 272–273

Epilogue

300 "Tragedy is not": Oates, "The Death Throes of Romanticism," p. 26
300 "The poet is": Joseph Brodsky, "A Poet and Prose," in *Less Than One* (New York: Farrar, Straus & Giroux, 1984)

301 "pockets of wishes": "Totem," *CP*, p. 264

302 "[Sylvia] made use": Aurelia Plath to Judith Kroll, December 1, 1978, *Smith*

303 "The loss to literature": *The Observer*, February 17, 1963; quoted in Alvarez, "Sylvia Plath: A Memoir," p. 213

304 "Sylvia may be": Olwyn Hughes to author, 1987

ACKNOWLEDGMENTS

Grateful acknowledgment for permission to quote from published and unpublished sources is made to the following:

To Oxford University Press for a quotation from Anna Akhmatova, *Anna Akhmatova: A Poetic Pilgrimage,* trans. Amanda Haight. Copyright © 1978 by Oxford University Press.

To Peter Owen, Ltd., and Dodd, Mead & Co. for quotations from Edward Butscher, *Sylvia Plath: The Woman and the Work.* Copyright © 1977 by Edward Butscher.

To Janet Crosbie-Hill for passages from her letter to *The New Review.*

To Peter Davison for quotations from his *Half Remembered: A Personal History.* Copyright © 1973 by Peter Davison.

To Ted Hughes, Executor of the Estate of Sylvia Plath, for all previously unpublished passages from the journals, letters, and poems of Sylvia Plath, and for published passages from the letters, journals, and poetry of Sylvia Plath; and to Ted Hughes for his own reminiscences, letters, writings, poems, etc.

To Judith Jones and Alfred A. Knopf, Inc., for a quotation from Judith Jones's letter dated January 16, 1963, to Sylvia Plath.

To the Society of Authors as the literary representative of the Estate of James Joyce for a quotation from *Finnegans Wake.*

To Blanche C. Gregory, Inc., for quotations from Joyce Carol Oates, *The Death Throes of Romanticism: The Poetry of Sylvia Plath.* Copyright © 1973 by Joyce Carol Oates.

To Faber & Faber, Ltd., for a quotation from Louis MacNeice, *The Collected Poems.* Copyright © 1966 by Louis MacNeice.

To Alfred A. Knopf, Inc., and Faber & Faber, Ltd., for quotations from Sylvia Plath, *The Colossus and Other Poems.* Copyright © 1962 by Sylvia Plath.

To Harper & Row, Publishers, Inc., and Olwyn Hughes for a quotation from Sylvia Plath, *The Bed Book*. Copyright © 1976 by Ted Hughes as Executor of the Estate of Sylvia Plath.

To Harper & Row, Publishers, Inc., and Faber & Faber, Ltd., for quotations from Sylvia Plath, *The Bell Jar*. Copyright © 1963 by Sylvia Plath.

To Harper & Row, Publishers, Inc., and Olwyn Hughes for quotations from Sylvia Plath, *The Collected Poems of Sylvia Plath*, ed. Ted Hughes. Copyright © 1960, 1965, 1971, 1981 by the Estate of Sylvia Plath; editorial material copyright © 1981 by Ted Hughes.

To Harper & Row, Publishers, Inc., and Faber & Faber, Ltd., for quotations from Sylvia Plath, *Johnny Panic and the Bible of Dreams: Short Stories, Prose and Diary Excerpts*. Copyright © 1952, 1953, 1954, 1955, 1956, 1957, 1960, 1961, 1962 by Sylvia Plath.

To Doubleday, a division of Bantam, Doubleday, Dell Publishing Group, Inc., and Olwyn Hughes for quotations from Sylvia Plath, *The Journals of Sylvia Plath*. Copyright © 1982 by Ted Hughes as Executor of the Estate of Sylvia Plath.

To Harper & Row, Publishers, Inc., and Faber & Faber, Ltd., for quotations from Sylvia Plath, *Letters Home: Correspondence 1950–1963*, edited with commentary by Aurelia Plath. Copyright © 1975 by Aurelia Schober Plath.

To Olwyn Hughes for all drawings by Sylvia Plath and for all letters, quotations, and other statements by herself and from members of the Hughes family no longer alive.

To Faber & Faber, Ltd., and Doubleday, a division of Bantam, Doubleday, Dell Publishing Group, Inc., for quotations from Theodore Roethke, *The Collected Poems of Theodore Roethke*. Copyright 1947 by Theodore Roethke.

INDEX

Abels, Cyrilly, 41, 42
Abercrombie, Lascelles, 193
"Above the Oxbow" (Plath), 157
Academy of American Poets Prize, SP wins, 58
African Folktales (Radin), SP impressed by, 163
Albee, Edward, SP at plays of, 224
Aldermaston antinuclear march, SP and TH at, 191–192, 327–328
Alfred, William, 139
All My Pretty Ones (Sexton), 224
"All the Dead Dears" (Plath), 105, 108, 170
Alpha Phi Kappa Psi, 29
Alvarez, A.: translations brought by, 183; *Lupercal* review by, 190; TH interviewed by, 196; *Colossus* reviewed by, 202–203; SP on "really writing" to, 229, 246–247; on SP and TH, 246–247; TH stays with, 258; on "Daddy," 264; SP reads to, 270, 273; SP's admiration of, 274; and "Letter in November," 277; support from, 279–

280; SP may have looked for relationship with, 281; on SP's death, 303
"America! America!" (Plath), 8, 280
Ames, Elizabeth, 162
"Amnesiac" (Plath), 270–271
"Among the Bumblebees" (Plath), 13
"Among the Narcissi" (Plath), 235, 236
Anderson, Jane, 26
"And Summer Will Not Come Again" (Plath), 18, 20
Anthropology, as theme for SP and TH, 238
Antinuclear march, SP and TH at, 191–192, 327–328
"Appearance, An" (Plath), 236, 237–238
"Applicant, The" (Plath), 264
"Apprehensions" (Plath), 246
Arb, Siv, 240
"Ariel" (Plath), 137, 271, 272; and "Whiteness I Remember," 66n
Ariel (Plath), xi; sun images in, 68; and Smith coffee-shop scene, 120; manuscript of, 277, 277n; Alvarez sees, 279; writ-

House of Taurus, The (Hughes),
201–202
How the Whale Became
(Hughes), 94
Hughes, Carol (second wife of
TH), 321
Hughes, Edith (mother of TH),
95; and SP, 102; visits from,
195, 246; SP's mother visits,
204, 217, 218; flowers from,
210; gift from, 219; SP sees as
stay-at-home, 240; and SP-TH
breakup, 258, 258n
Hughes, Frieda Rebecca (daughter
of SP): Ouija board prediction
of, 136; name derivation of,
161, birth of, 190–191, 230; at
ban-the-bomb demonstration,
191–192, 327–328; on Yorkshire visit, 203; at SP–Olwyn
Hughes confrontation, 204;
mentioned with parents, 223,
230, 246, 247–248, 248, 266,
279, 354; SP on Sunday School
for, 225–226; baptism of, 234;
nursery school for, 280; at
Christmas, 281; at Beckers',
292, 293, 294, 295
Hughes, Gerald (brother of TH),
77
Hughes, Nicholas Farrar (son of
SP): birth of, 230–231, 319;
baptism of, 234; mentioned
with parents, 242, 246, 247–
248, 251, 266, 279, 354; at
Christmas, 281; at Beckers',
292, 293, 295
Hughes, Olwyn (sister of TH),
77, 98–99, 100, 102, 316, 320;
on SP, 93, 176–177, 293,
304, 319; on SP and TH, 110;
SP's luncheon animosity toward, 185–186, 187, 188, 319;

and Yorkshire visit scene, 203–
204; Mrs. Hughes's letter to,
218; SP's letter to, 227; recollection of journal by, 241; Assia
Wevill account to, 243–244; and
SP's letters to TH's mother, 258
Hughes, Ted, xii, 76–77; Plath
reads poems of, 72; in Myers
memoir, 73–74, 308, 309, 311,
313, 316–317, 320–321; and
SP, 75–76, 77–78, 85–86, 86–
88, 89, 90–92 (*see also* Plath,
Sylvia, AND TED HUGHES); with
BBC, 96–97, 195, 201, 206,
225, 239, 323, 333–334;
schoolteaching job of, 103; U.
Mass.-Amherst teaching job of,
119; and Baskin, 122; on SP's
feverish creativity, 126; reading
at Harvard by, 127; Guggenheim to, 155; and *Modern Poetry in Translation*, 183; on
"Waking in Winter," 199; 1960
successes of, 201–202; on SP
after separation, 283, 285
Hughes, Walter (uncle of TH),
95, 246, 316
Hughes, William Henry (father of
TH), 77, 95, 102, 210, 258
Hugh-Jones, Siriol, 324
Hungarian revolution, SP's reaction to, 98
Hunter, Nancy (later Nancy
Hunter Steiner), 24–25, 37n,
49, 52–54, 64, 164
Huws, Catherine, 320
Huws, Daniel, 73; SP reviewed
by, 69; on SP at party, 74–75;
in Rome, 106; on Rugby St.,
179; daughter of, 187;
Hugheses stay with, 252; gifts
from, 282; godparent request
of, 283; in Myers memoir, 308,